CONSCIOUSNESS
Towards **ABUNDANCE**

DR SIN MONG WONG

Consciousness Towards Abundance

Copyright © 2021 by Dr Sin Mong Wong.

Paperback ISBN: 978-1-63812-099-5
Ebook ISBN: 978-1-63812-100-8

All rights reserved. No part in this book may be produced and transmitted in any form or by any means, electronic, or mechanical, including photocopying, recording, or by any information storage and retrieval system, without permission in writing from the copyright owner.

The views expressed in this work are solely those of the author and do not necessarily reflect the views of the publisher hereby disclaims any responsibility for them.

Published by Pen Culture Solutions   08/27/2021

Pen Culture Solutions
1-888-727-7204 (USA)
1-800-950-458 (Australia)
support@penculturesolutions.com

CONTENTS

Acknowledge And Preface xiii

Chapter 1　The Language Of Abundance: Thinking, Speaking And
　　　　　　Writing 1
　　　　　　Introduction.. 1
　　　　　　Vision of a Rich Life 4
　　　　　　The Power of Consciousness 5
　　　　　　The Analogy between Mastering the
　　　　　　Language of the Basics and Games 6
　　　　　　The Four Elements of the Mastery Strategy 7
　　　　　　Mission and Destiny 12
　　　　　　Mastering the Language of the Three Basics 16
　　　　　　Thinking Well 17
　　　　　　Speaking Well 23
　　　　　　Writing Well 25
　　　　　　Assertiveness and Aggressiveness 26
　　　　　　Discovery of How to Make a Difference 28
　　　　　　Overcoming Limiting Beliefs 31
　　　　　　Summary 36

Chapter 2　Developing The Mindset For Abundance 39
　　　　　　Introduction to Financial Freedom 39
　　　　　　The Difference between Financial Security
　　　　　　and Financial Freedom... 41
　　　　　　My First Attempt to Create Residual Income 42
　　　　　　Create Cash Flow Using Business...................................... 45
　　　　　　Strategies of Business Mind-Set and Creating Wealth 47

	Follow Your Passion and Do What You Love 49
	An Example of Success in Both Sport and Learning 51
	The Mind-Set of Innovative People 54
	Summary 57
Chapter 3	The Language Of Money 60
	The First Lesson of Money... 60
	Truth Path to Wealth 61
	Dependent Mentality and Attitude 63
	A Paradigm Shift towards Financial Education 65
	Creating Residual Income Requires a Paradigm Shift 72
	More than One Possible Solutions in the Real World 74
	Understand the Language of Money 76
	Types of Debts 79
	Income.. 79
	Expenses 80
	Simple Interest and Compound Interest......................... 81
	Assets 81
	Paper Assets or Stocks 82
	Commodities 83
	Businesses 83
	Liabilities 84
	The Two Faces of Debt 84
	Cash Flow 85
	The Choice of Money Language 86
	Expand Your Means.. 87
	Entrepreneur and Technological Inventions 88
	Summary 90
Chapter 4	The Language Spoken By Healthy And Happy People ... 92
	The Language of Healthy People 92
	Good Diet... 95
	Cholesterol Does Not Cause Heart Disease 96
	Habits, Lifestyle and Aging... 98
	The Danger of Dietary Supplements.............................101
	An Example of Liver Damage due to Ignorance 102
	The Most Dangerous Disease in Developed Countries 102
	Natural and Nutritional Foods-A Better Choice 104

Overcome Joint Pain 105
The Importance of Adequate Sleep 107
Regular Exercise Helps Prevent Cancer 109
Other Benefits of Regular Exercise through
Simple Movements 111
Take the Supplement Coffee Three Times a Day 112
The Language of Happiness 113
The Beliefs and Habits of Happy People 115
General Habits of Happy People 118
Turn Failure into Success 121
Lessons on Habits of Happy People 124
Accept What Cannot Be Changed 125
Let Go of Grudges 126
Treat Everyone with Kindness 126
Express Gratitude for What We Have 127
Don't Sweat over the Small Stuff 128
Speak Well of Others 129
Regard Problems as Challenges 129
Dream Big 130
Avoid Making Excuses 131
Live in the Present 131
Don't Compare Yourself with Others 132
Wake Up at the Same Time Every Morning 132
Surround Yourself with Positive People 134
Take Time to Listen 134
Nurture Social Relationship 135
We Do Not Need Other's Approval 136
Be Honest 136
Establish Personal Control 137
Exercise Regularly to Keep Fit 138
Eating Well Increases Happiness 139
Living A Simple and Orderly Life 140
Increase Your Spirituality 140
Imitate Some Good Habits of Happy people 142
Overcome Past Unhappiness 144
The Marriage Effect on Health and Longevity 145

	Summary	146
Chapter 5	The Language Of The Mind	148
	Introduction	148
	The Evolution of Consciousness	149
	The Language of the Mind to Achieve Abundance	151
	The Conscious Gap towards Abundance	155
	Meditation to Activate Your Subconscious Mind	156
	The Power of Intuition	159
	Optimisation in Reprogramming the Mind	160
	An Extraordinary Example	161
	Overcoming Rejection	164
	Overcoming Conscious and Unconscious Fear	167
	Overcoming the Fear of Public Speaking	168
	Overcoming Fear of Asking Questions	170
	Overcoming the Fear of Height	171
	Natural Healing Using Our Subconscious Mind	172
	Consciousness and Financial Freedom	178
	Applying Visualisation to Basketball Game	183
	Stay in the State of Flow	187
	Never Too Late to Dream another Dream	191
	Happiness Drives Productivity	201
	Three Fuels Helping You in Achieving Your Dreams	205
	The Winning Attitude and the Losing Attitude	209
	Consciousness of Social Standards	216
	Financial Knowledge	218
	The Wisdom of Residual Income	219
	Leverage, Cash Flow and Residual Income	221
	Strategies of Creating Residual Income	223
	Summary	229
Chapter 6	Assets To Create Residual Income And Cash Flow	230
	Introduction	230
	The Difference between Spenders and Savers	231
	Consciousness Approach	232
	Some Money Mistakes to Avoid When You Are Young	235
	Save Money by Shopping Alternative Sources	237
	The Power Leverage in Properties Investment	238

	The Danger in Commercial Property Investment	239
	Real Estate Investment Trust (REIT)	242
	Summary	243
Chapter 7	Stock To Create Residual Income And Growth	244
	Introduction	244
	Follow Investment Leaders	247
	Simple Guiding Principles	249
	Gold, Silver and Platinum Investments	257
	Performance of Stocks in 2015 and 2016	259
	CAPE Introduced by Benjamin Graham	261
	A Glimpse of Light at the End of the Tunnel for the Oil Sector	262
	Shifting of Energy Landscape	266
	Biotech Companies for the Future	267
	Dividend as Residual Income	269
	Overcome the Belief that Investing in Stocks is Unfair	271
	Human Behaviours in Stock Investments	273
	Investment Golden Rules	280
	A Glimpse of Light for Mining Stocks	285
	The General Market Situation from 2016 Onwards	285
	An Alternative View of the Market after 2016	287
	Alternative Investments during Uncertainties of Stocks After 2016	289
	Understand the Subconscious Mind	290
	The Language of Stock	292
	Understand another Term: The Trend	294
	The Emotional Stock Market	297
	Don't Follow the Language of the Herd	299
	An Analogy of Herd Mentality	300
	A Bigger Picture of Investing in Stocks	301
	Invest in Tiny Growth Stocks	303
	Speak the Language of Investment Confidently	306
	Balance Sheet	309
	Income Statement	311
	Cash Flow Statement	311
	Statement of Shareholders' Equity	312

	Statement of Shareholders' Equity	313
	Advantages of Investing in Tiny Value Stocks	314
	Mistakes Can Be Your Blessing	315
	Strategy for Change	317
	Make a Fortune in Stock Market If You Are Right 60 Per cent of the Time	319
	Investments for the Future	320
	Understanding Inside Trading	324
	Ways of Investing Your Money	324
	A Simple Strategy for Option Trading	325
	Make Money When the Market Goes Up or Down	326
	Using Credit - Spread Strategy	327
	An Interesting Story	328
	How Warren Buffett Use Option to Make Millions	329
	Earning Steady Income Selling Option	330
	The 2016 - 2017 Bear Market Survival Program	332
	Dividends versus Interest in Australia	333
	Harry Dent Prediction	334
	S& P SOO Index	336
	The S&P 500 Index from 1996 to the Beginning of 2016	337
	Relationship between the Price of Gold and US Dollars	337
	Stock Investment for Long Term	338
	Summary and Generalisation	340
Chapter 8	Direct Selling To Produce Residual Income	344
	Introduction	344
	Network Marketing and Franchising	345
	Financial Security and Financial Freedom	348
	People's Fear	349
	Direct Marketing through Established Network Companies	350
	Ways to Become Rich	351
	Successful People in Network Marketing Business	354
	Adopt a Visionary Approach	355
	Some Successful Stories	357
	Further Examples of 4Life Network Marketing Success	359

	Inter Personal Skills for Success in Network Marketing....	362
Chapter 9	Internet Marketing And Digital Publishing	367
	Introduction	367
	The Advantage of Online Publishing	369
	Online Business	370
	Digital Publishing	372
	Dedication and Perseverance	374
	Why the World Needs Digital Information	375
	Another Strategy to Create Passive Income	376
Chapter 10	The Language Of Abundance	379
	Introduction	379
	Experience, Growth and Contribution	380
	The Language of Affluent Consciousness	383
	Some Changing Lessons towards Abundance	386
	Empowering Beliefs	387
	Simple Steps towards Abundance	390
Chapter 11	The Language Of Spirituality	392
	Introduction	392
	Spirituality	393
	Strategies to Enhance Spirituality	395
	The Benefits of Being Spiritual	396
	Spirituality through Meditation	397
Chapter 12	Reflections And Summary	403
	The Necessity of Thinking Big through Thinking Well	406
	The Advantage of Speaking Well	406
	The Reward of Writing Well	407
	The Strategies to Help You Achieve Wealth	407
	The Necessary Steps towards Fulfilment	408
	A True Abundance Mind-Set	411
	Habits and Practices of Successful People	411
	Some Secrets of Abundance	413
	Words of Reflections	413
	New Resolutions	415

ACKNOWLEDGE AND PREFACE

Ninety seven percent of the time, our life is ordinary. Only three percent of the time life is extraordinary. These extraordinary times are rare. They only occur a few times in our life. The ability to recognise and act on these extraordinary moments will make your life rewarding and great. I share my experiences of these great moments in my life in this book. These three percent moments can happen in learning, sport, business, stocks, property investments and writing. Seizing the challenges and opportunities that come your way rarely is the only chance to achieve a life of abundance. Many people see the opportunities but do not follow through on the big challenges they set for themselves. They stop short of the finisihing line. This explains partly the reason that many people don't succeed. This consciousness is explored in this book and hopefully after reading it, you will act on the three percent extraordinary moments which will give you a life of abundance. This awareness is critical. A life of abundance is never about your resources; it's about your resourcefulness during these extraordinary moments. You need to open up your mind to seize the moments when opportunities strike. A successful adventure starts with your mindset. Being used to condition to have negative thoughts, beliefs and behaviours cause us to procrastinate and these rare opportunities are missed. Retraing your brain and shifting your thinking to set new goals and take immediate actions when opportunity emerges. It's your thoughts and what you choose to believe in yourself that will determine the success in the venture or business you do. Your thoughts have controlled over the cells of your body and are responsible for your well-being and happiness. Make an effort to embrace a new life that gives you joy, purpose and meaning. Priming your life for success should be your first step. Follow some of the strategies and models adopted in this book will give you a headstart towards your success and a comfortable retirement. Concentrate and focus on what you want to create and achieve instead of your lack. Do not allow what you don't know stop you from learning how. Many examples are found in this book to help you learn what you do not know. These are the examples you want to emulate to give you a headstart and help you to reach another level of life. You need a performance plan to bring you to your next level of financial freedom. This analogy is sound. Do not get into a car without an idea of your destination, just hoping that you will end up in a right place. Your financial life is no different. If you do not have any idea where you want to be, you will end up in poverty when you retire. With new knowledge and cutting edge information, you can become more flexible and more action oriented. Plan your financial freedom as early as possible. Working life can be short. Make full use of the three percent of extraordinary moments of your life will eventually make the difference to your financial freedom and retirement. Recognise and act on these three percent moments happening in stocks, properties and business ventures will make all the difference. Consciousness and awareness of these extraordinary moments require training and great intuition. Do not blindly aim for a magic number in retirement saving and take it as your financial security. Financial freedom comes from a diversity of sources and various streams of residual income and cash flow. Follow the natural laws of attraction for your wealth creation. Make a habit to give more than you expect to receive. Providing service and value for others first and you will have value for yourself. Care more on what you are going to share than what you intend to get. All the consciousness strategies will help you to choose love over hatred, and help you to live a more fulfilled life. You will not easily be fooled by others rules that do not serve you. This book serves to awaken your unconscious mind, helping you to move towards abundance. This attitude will ensure your success and financial freedom in whatever you try to do. The strategies towards abundance unveiled in this book are just the beginning. Adopt the four elements of the Mastery Strategy to any skill or project of your dreams. Many others possible approaches are available in Google. Make a commitment to enrich your subconscious mind which will ultimately help you achieving a life of abundance.

First I need to acknowledge my wife for her home management and other supports to enable me to develop my full potential as a teacher, administrator, investor and writer. My children are my inspiration to strive for a healthy, happy and abundant life. Their academic achievements add an extra feather to my own. From a humble beginning, we try our best to take advantage of the few rare moments of opportunities to help achieving a life of abundance. I appreciate the help of many of relatives and friends. Without their help I may not be where I am now. Many thanks to my students, their parents and friends who supported me in various projects initiated by me when I was serving as principal of La Salle High School in Malaysia. I was able to carry out various school improvement projects both physical and academic successfully during my term of service because of their helps. I still cherish those memories with me.

Each season of my life brings excitements, experiences and growth. The first part of my childhood was tough. I enjoyed three stages of learning through secondary school, college and university. My working life was short and exciting. I've just experienced the best stage of my life. The retiring stage of my life turns out to be the best period of my life. After spending almost thirty years of my life in the learning stage, I believe I was well prepared for my working life. I went to University at the age of twenty six and started working as a graduate teacher at the age of twenty Nine and retired at the age of fifty one. Serving last eight years of my teaching career as high school principal was most rewarding. Creating value for others through my administration and writing, I have indirectly created value for myself. My working life lasted only about twenty three years. I achieved what I set out to do and I had to move on to a new season of life. Many of my students are now established professionals. Some of them are serving as CEOs of big corporations. I have great friends, a wonderful family, enjoying financial freedom and a busy retirement. My basic principles for life based on experience, growth and contribution continue.

When I was a student, I took up sport seriously and played my favourite game basketball well. Consciousness of drill strategy helped me to become an outstanding player. I represented my school, my home town team, my club team, college, university and the states Kedah and Penang. As a student and a veteran I also played for Malaya in many international tournaments. Now in my retirement I play tennis and golf. I am in my seventies and I still enjoy my tennis. I am always healthy and fit because of my involvement in active sports. I live on a simple and balanced diet to keep me lean and healthy. I am always happy and enjoy my life. This book gives me an opportunity to shares some of my experiences of living a healthy, fit and happy life. I am still enjoying my abundant life.

As a student, I became conscious of my subconscious mind and its role for my life of abundance later on. Abundance in this context embraces financial freedom, well being, influence, happy, fit and healthy. My conscious mind helps me to set my goals and it is the unconscious mind that determines my success. The greatest adventure for me is the ability to turn my dreams into reality. When I was a student, mastering the three basics: thinking, speaking and writing became my immediate goals. I applied the same elements of the Mastery Strategy for both my games and the learning of the three basics. Writing this book allows the analogy for success in both sports and learning to be revealed and shared. Hopefully you may be interested to give the mastery strategy a trial. When I was working as a teacher, I learned the language of money, the language of happiness, the language of investments, the language of business and the language of spirituality. My full commitment to be fit and healthy throughtout my life ensures my well-being. If you start a business which requires all your attention and work alone, you just find yourself a job. To be successful in business as an entrepreneur, you need to learn many languages of various fields and you also need to train your star players so that you can easily duplicate your business every where without your involvement in its daily routine. In stock investmests, the first thing to learn is not to be narrow minded. It's rarely a good thing to help you making money. The more knowledge you have the more flexible you are, the more profit will accumulate in your account. Network marketing and digital publishing can also make you rich. Follow your passion and pick the field that you love doing. You will learn from many sources instead of relying on one source only. This book provides various views of the current market situations; you are the one to decide which one will suit your investment strategy. This awareness motivates me to learn various languages from stocks to properties and business. Speaking these languages fluently and committing to take actions enable me to have financial freedom. First thing I avoided when I started to invest in stocks is to ignore all the noises of the market and not to follow the crowd. Depending on the noises of the market and the analysis of any individual is a recipe for disaster. I always remember the quotation of Sir Issac Newtom after he lost his fortune during the South Sea Bubble in 1720. He said:

> "I can calculate the motion of the heavenly bodies but not the madness of the crowd."

What is stated by Newton is still applicable to our market today. I learn to do my own research and due diligence before I buy a stock. Learn the language of stocks well and speak it fluently. This enables me to grow my networth year after year without a single year of loss. My new focus is not based on past earnings but a company's future earnings. The past is a guide and the future is what I look for. Earning growth of a company is what I look for in any investment. Knowing the true value of a stock is most important. Buying under-valued stocks during a big correction is my investment practices. The quality called patience is my winning habit. As an investor, you always must have spare money while waiting for opportunity whenever the market corrects. Lessons from my golden rules teach and guide me to avoid mistakes average investors make. Buying companies which I know best become my guiding principle. Great growth companies are my choice. My stock investment adventure is less exciting but more profitable. It allows the combination of dividends and strong fundamentals of my stocks to enhance my investment capital. Using the principle of leverage and good debts help me to acquire two investment properties. These add value to my financial freedom when I retire. Allowing the wonder of compounding in my investments to take its natural course helps to build and accelerate my networth. I am able to retire at the age of fifty one with financial freedom. These are examples and stories I share in this book. You too can make use of these rare opportunities to secure your financial freedom.

I was equally successful as a career teacher. Speaking well made me a natural born teacher. The ability to communicate in simple language made most of the mathematics concepts simple. One thing I learn during my career as a teacher is that I teach best when I neeed to learn it. Especially when I needed a new way of associating mathematics concepts with students' daily life experiences. And that drove me to use all my mental resources available. My thinking faculty is fully stretched. Thinking well helped me to the discovery of humanising the teaching of mathematics concepts. These combinations allowed me to become an excellent teacher. I began to see miracles others missed. Knocking at the door of curriculum materials that can help others learn mathematics came naturally. Unexpectedly textbooks and guidebooks publications started to open their doors to me. The reward of writing well enables me to become an established writer. The creativity helped me to get where I wanted to be. My passion paved the way for my PhD in mathematics curriculum innovation and renewal. My mission is to help students learn mathematice and indirectly I have created value for my financial freedom. These unexpected streams of residual income in the form of royalties gave me the financial muscles and leverages, enabling me to invest in properties, stocks and businesses joint-ventures. I worked hard and took repetitive actions in order to attain my goals. The rewards exceeded my expectations. And I am grateful for all my efforts and energies involved. My financial freedom is given the blessing. This is the greatest adventure I experienced making my dreams of financial freedom a reality. It is also my contribution to education.

My purpose in life is simple. I am here to experience, grow and contribute. I follow the seasons of my life allowing new experiences to guide me. Learning becomes my life-long hobby. The adventure for knowledge motivates my growth. Various experiences of my life add colours and flavours to my journey through four seasons of my life. All these experiences are recorded in my first motivation book, "The Journey through Four Seasons of Life".

Growth is an important component for happiness and a new purpose of life. When you are not growing you are standing still. The worst is that you are going backwards in your business. All of us meet the same struggles, the same roadblocks and the same mistakes over and over again. This book provides some simple strategies to help you overcome all these out-dated beliefs. I use meditation and creative visualization to help me to face these challenges. I only visualize once or twice a day. Each visualization takes only a few minutes. When visualizing, I see, hear and feel. I take action and share my imagination with others. Enjoying the feeling of each visualization is important. I use to put myself in the final picture of the visualization. I go straight to the end as if I am already living the dreams. I will teach others what I want to achieve and I become my number one student. I imagine and share my new reality. Keep growing becomes my mission in all three stages of my life. The secret trait of successful people is easily recognised. When they get advice from others or create an idea of their own, they immediately get to work. They keep working over and over again to perfect the system to become prosperous and lead a more fulfilled life. At the age of fifty two, I went back to University of Queensland to pursue the last piece of the jigsaw puzzle of my life. I was rewarded with the highest degree I can ever get. This is the climax of my contribution to education. In addition, I have written more than two dozens of mathematics books before and during my retirement. I have just completed two motivation books. The third, "Live an Abundant and Productive Life for Eighty Five Years and More" is on the way. Whenever I visualise a thing, I immediately put myself in the picture and start acting. This sharpens my focus and creativity in whatever I do. My purpose is to contribute to human advancement and help others to have an abundant life. I always believe busy people are usually productive and fulfilled. This book is written specially for parents who are their children first significant teachers. They are the best persons to help their children to plan and take actions so that they too can live an abundant and fulfilled life. The intention of this book is to show the ways. Life is a process of learning, improving and growing. And our growth is a result of adding new concepts and finding new meaning in the things we experience. The earlier the children subconscious minds are reprogrammed with the characteristcs of successful people, the better chance for them to act on them and become successful themselves. Starting with thinking, speaking and writing, they will find it easier for them to master the following languages: money, stocks, technology, investment, the mind, spirituality and language of abundance. This book explores some common strategies to help you and your children to achieve financial freedom. Many interesting stories of successful people in various fields are included to provide examples to emulate and follow. Providing alternative choices of businesses and careers are the main purpose of this book. All the experiences will shape your thinking. Lessons of abundance learned the hard way will usually rob us years or even decades of our precious time. They set us back prevent us from reaching our full potential. Helping your children to reprogram their subconscious minds as early as possible is a flexible alternative to avoid any delay and waste of their precious time. Do not allow your ignorance of the role of the subconscious mind and about change to lengthen their suffering from mental blocks. Allowing their outdated beliefs and fear for the unknown to hold them back is sheer waste of talents. Beliefs and habits of successful people of various fields can easily be learned and repricated. Help them to choose the field they are passionate about. Learn the characteristics of the business and digest them well. The field of preference must suit your qualification and temperament. Once you have decided to embrace a certain field, surround yourself with a circle of influence. This book will serve as your first influence. Go into Goggle and read more about your field of interest. A better way is to get support and mentor from people who are successful in the field. The commitment to practise these characteristics until they become autopilot will ensure your success in your chosen field. Anyone with exposure and knowledge, and is committed to practise these beliefs and habits consistently, persistently and playfully will achieve their goals. The greatest adventure for most of us is the ability to turn our dreams into reality. The ultimate goal of this book is to help parents and their children to do just that and live a rich, healthy, happy and balanced life. The inspirations found in this book will empower you to get in touch with your creative spirit. Turn your creative dreams, visions or ideas into your purpose. Your creative side projects can be more than just a hobby. You can build a creative, sustening career out of what you love to do. Infusing creativity into your whole life can bring more joy and fulfilment into your career. A life of abundance is waiting for you as soon as you take the first step towards your dreams. As the saying goes, 'the journey of a thousand miles begins with the first contemplated step.' As soon as you finish reading this book, make a commitment to take your first step of your greatest adventure to make your dreams a reality. Start living the life of abundance you deserve!

CHAPTER ONE

THE LANGUAGE OF ABUNDANCE: THINKING, SPEAKING AND WRITING

Introduction

I am one of the lucky people who are aware of the power of the subconscious mind very early in my life. I began to recognise the important role plays by the subconscious mind when I was a secondary school student in Penang. This awareness has led to some life-altering truths, practising mental exercises, forming good habits and developing focus on the basics, helping to take me to the next level of life. This awareness together with consistent practice to master the language of the basics helps me to live a life of abundance later on. What is abundance? Abundance embraces financial freedom, well-being, happiness and fulfilment, good relationship, fitness and good health. Living a life of abundance and making meaningful contribution to my community become my dreams. What is contribution? Contribution can come in many forms. It can be materials, ideas, systems, publications, financial helps and others, helping humanity to move forward. I dream and hope to leave a significant mark behind, no matter how small it is. Hope and dreams are not strategies. Having a big goal is an aspiration. Having an ambitious goal followed by actions allows my full potential to be developed. Enjoying the journey of my life all the way is a good habit.

The purpose of my life is simple. I am here to experience, grow and contribute. The development of my full potential is one of my goals. A better prepared 'me' will lead to a better world for my family and my community. When I was a secondary school student, my conscious mind helped me to set my immediate goals to master the language of the basics: thinking, speaking and writing. The act of setting my goals activates the 'genius' part of my brain, that is, the centre of the brain or the subconscious mind. I want to speak the language of the basics well as early as possible. Visualising my goals brings excitement and anticipation which motivated me to be proactive. These new beliefs became engrained in my subconscious mind replacing the outdated ones wired during my childhood. However the little negative voice in the mind was still there telling me not to act. It had to be overcome. Eliminating the negative habits and beliefs that stood between me and my mastery of the basics is my top priority. The first thing I learned is not to give excuses for not taking action in both the sport I loved and the education I needed. The thinking is crystal clear and the goals are set leading to an abundant life later on. My first educational goal is to have at least a Form Five education with a Senior Cambridge Certificate of Education. That minimum qualification would enable me to apply for a job as a teacher. Initially turning the tiny ray of hope into a rainbow of possibility was a big challenge. There was no secondary school in my village town. When I started secondary school in Penang, I was already 16 years old. The opportunity was provided by my eldest sister. I was an overaged student with no foundation in English. I had just six years of Chinese primary education. The medium of instruction in Malaya was English at the time. No government school would enrol me as a student. Attending private missionary school catering for weak and overaged students was the only alternative. There were plenty of excuses the little voice in the mind was telling me. Excuse like my English was too poor for me to even try to learn other subjects. Education was not for me. Coming from an uneducated family became my immediate obstacle. I felt that I was too old to start learning. I did not know where to begin.

When I started my secondary school in Penang, I realised that my life was affected by my childhood behaviours, beliefs and habits. These beliefs are telling me all the negative things, discouraging and sabotaging my immediate goal of getting my formal education. I did not give in to these negative beliefs. Being motivated by my immediate goal triggered my awareness that I had to recondition and reprogram my mind. What does it mean? It simply means that these mental blocks had to be cleared before I took massive action to improve my life. At that point of time, I realised that there was a big gap between the life I was living and the dream life of abundance I envisioned for the future. The root cause of my mediocre life is clear. The beliefs, habits and practices were already unconsciously programmed in my mind and I lived exactly as being wired that way, no more, no less. The subconscious mind played an important role in my daily life and it affected my perceptions of abundance, learning and the game, basketball, I played.

To bridge the gap immediately, I had to start thinking well. Thinking well helps me to speak well and eventually write well. Directly or indirectly the subconscious mind is influencing my conscious mind. The subconscious mind is a few thousand times more powerful than my conscious mind. My poor environment and my family background seemed to reinforce the life I had and my beliefs about learning, money and success. A life of abundance for every one of my future family was my immediate dream. How to live a rich, happy and healthy life? I started thinking. Developing positive habits is my first step. Positive habits are necessary for me to gain peace of mind, sound health and a positive mental attitude. I am prepared to do the unusual so that I do not have to settle for the ordinary. All of us want to be rich and fulfilled. Fulfilment is more important than happiness, though both go hand in hand. This was the success mindset I wanted to have. The changes must come from within me. How do I go about doing it?

First I learned to be observant. Successful people behave and believe differently. They seem to be happier, they think differently and they speak different language from me. What are the success secrets shared by most wealthy and successful people? I read about their stories and their transformations of their mind-sets towards money and abundance. They create their own definite plan to carry out their desires and do them at once, whether they are ready or not, to put their plans into action. Being proactive, they seldom procrastinate. They live a rich, happy, fulfilled and healthy life. They think before they speak. Simple, they think well. They make sure that whatever they say benefit them and do not injure others. In other words, they speak well. They live an abundant life. Cultivating this healthy mindset and the habits of thinking and speaking was just the beginning. Consistently practising them daily helped me in the process of thinking and speaking, helping to bring abundance to my life later on.

Vision of a Rich Life

Everyone dreams of a rich and healthy life. But what is a rich life? To some people it means the ability to take frequent holidays to wherever they want to go. For others, it means the ability to have many homes, cars and luxurious things they want. For some others, it means being a philanthropist and making contributions to society. For me, it simply means that I can spend a lot of time with my family, play my favourite game, pay for their education and enjoy our healthy lifestyle together. I can have the freedom to do the things that I am passionate about. Most importantly, I can help to create values in the lives of those I love. Dreaming of living a rich, happy and fulfilled life motivated me to take action. I also keep dreaming how to give back and contribute to society what I have benefited. Regardless of our definition of a rich life, financial freedom is an important component. I do not want to be just rich but also fulfilled and healthy. What is fulfilment? Fulfilment is the happy feeling I want to have every day. I believe that I am more likely to achieve success if I follow my wealth purpose anyway. Money in itself will not be enough to motivate me in the long run. It's a good start and it's not everything. Success is the natural end result of finding my wealth and health calling first. I must be ready to share with others. I will need many wealth strategies to magnetise my calling. I also need to work on my health to be fit and healthy. Knowing various strategies is just one of my possible paths towards a life of wealth, success and fulfilment. To facilitate and shorten my journey to financial freedom, I need to master the three basic things needed to help me achieve my goals and dreams. When I was studying, I focused on the three fundamental things: thinking, speaking, and writing. I realise very early that I have to do these three fundamental things well as early as possible if I want to succeed in my life. Enjoying financial freedom, an important component of abundance, is my first goal. Doing these three fundamental things well will help me function effectively in my study, work and eventually they will help me to achieve my life of abundance. I needed to activate my subconscious mind by setting my goals and dreams through my conscious mind. Visualising them generated excitement and anticipation, which motivated me to take immediate action. Discipline, persistency, consistency and most importantly, playfulness are the necessary ingredients to help me succeed. I must keep repeating and enjoying the process to think well, speak well and write well daily. Since my new context 'think, speak and write well' was clear, action was required to achieve them. I need to find out what are these three fundamental things in detail. What are the strategies I need to learn? Once I find out, I must start downloading them into my subconscious mind so that I can keep practising them to ensure success. The next context to embrace is to live an abundant life. Knowing that changing my context, I will change my life. But what is a context? Simple, anything we believe or any intention to do something is a context. You can think of other contexts such as religions or philosophies. Why is the belief of religions a context? Different religions have different contexts. Muslims accept Jesus as a prophet but to the Christians, Jesus is the Son of God. It clearly shows that Christians have a different context from Muslims. Their beliefs and contents are different. Our home is another physical context which reveals a poor, middle class or rich family. A church and a gym are physical contexts. We go there for different purposes. The former helps spiritual revival and the latter is for physical revival. My new context 'I need to think, speak and write well' activated the spirit of adventure and I eventually acted on it. The result is that I started to learn the language of the basics well very early. Acting on this context laid the foundation for a life of abundance later on.

The Power of Consciousness

The power of consciousness is directing the course of my life. It helps me to set my goals and dreams. But most of us tell ourselves that dreams are just dreams. They are out of reach. I do not have to entertain such a belief. It does not have to be true if I do not want it. There is a deeper passion in me to move forward and act on a new calling according to my new context. There are many skills I need to develop to live a successful life. I agree with Dr David Eifrig Jr and Mark that the three most critical basic skills are thinking, speaking, and writing. I believe that a better prepared 'me' in the three basics will lead to a better future for me. The secret of my success in life is the awareness of the importance of mastering the three basics helping me to live a life of abundance later on. Why do I need to think well, speak well, and write well during my school days? Why are they important to me? How do I master them? I must find my answers to these questions. I started to embrace the habit of thinking well every day. Every issue I encountered, I always examined it and started thinking of alternative possibilities. Whenever I was involved in conversation, I began to focus on worthy things to say. I was aware that I needed to say what I actually meant. I also started the habit to write down things which were important to me. Mastery of these three essential things required me to practise them again and again until I reached the stage of automation. They became my immediate habits in life. I discovered the secret of repetition for mastery when I trained my basketball skills and tennis strokes. This was the quantum leap to my consciousness evolution. The strategy of mastering the three basics is analogous to master the basic skills of basketball. I moved from reactive to proactive. I disciplined myself to do it consistently, persistently and playfully. Enjoying what I am doing repeatedly for mastery is the secret of my success. This had helped me to avoid burn-out and other fatigue symptoms. Unconsciously, I learned that happiness increases productivity and you will do more. By doing more, the repetition brings mastery and you become an expert.

The Analogy between Mastering the Language of the Basics and Games

A lack of clear planning and consistent actions towards the goal of mastering the basics: thinking, speaking and writing, causes many people from living a life of full potential. Not thinking and speaking well become their stumbling blocks. Remember you can't write the next chapter of your life if you keep only reading your last sad chapter. You may not be aware that last chapter of your life may be lacking in the three basics. There is another comparison. To me, there is another crystal clear analogy between mastering tennis strokes and mastering the three basic things in life. The same analogy is also applicable to other important strategies of creating a life of abundance. Everyone knows that playing tennis involves only five main types of strokes: serving, forehand, backhand, overhead and volley. Any player needs plenty of repetitions and practices of these strokes to become a good tennis player. Similar to be successful in life, we just have to master the three fundamental things: thinking, speaking and writing as early as possible. How to do it? Simple, we have to keep learning and repeating to master those skills. For me, instead of just dreaming, I make a commitment to learn and practise these three basic things repeatedly until I can do them well as soon as possible. I also make up my mind that I am going to enjoy doing them every day. Being happy and enjoying the process of learning provides the acceleration in productivity. This sentiment helps to accelerate the mastery of the three fundamental skills. These beliefs and habits are going to be ingrained deeply in my subconscious mind replacing whatever thoughts which were already there. All the negative thoughts or beliefs have to be eliminated to provide space for more positive ones. Doing the three basic things well helped me in my study, career and eventually gave me a life of abundance.

The Four Elements of the Mastery Strategy

Most of us believe that knowledge is power. It appears true superficially. That's why all of us value higher education or specialist training. We think that the more qualified we are, the more value we have. But in today's world it is not necessarily true. Something is missing in our life's equation. To be successful in any project, the lack of knowledge is not the problem. According to T. Harv Eker, a motivational writer, knowledge is only one of the four elements of the 'Mastery Formula'. He stated the following necessary elements towards mastery:

First, mastery needs high-impact learning. The best way to cement new knowledge or skill is via accelerated learning... specific techniques of gaining new knowledge or skills that deliver the best results in the shortest possible time.

Second, it requires high-frequency practice and exposure. Repetition engrains information and skills into your mind at a deeper level.

Third, it needs ongoing support - to keep you focused and help you overcome any obstacle that crops up when you start apply the knowledge.

Fourth, it requires the right mindset (a.k.a. the inner game). Habits are tied to the subconscious mind. So even if you consciously think you want to be wealthy, if you don't have that mindset, you will end up with habits of poor people. Success starts in the mind. If you don't believe in your very roots of your being that you can achieve the success you want, you'll never achieve your goals.

I concur with him absolutely. My experience reveals that focusing sometime can be a pain. It takes courage and determination to focus at one task at a time. Clarity of what you want is power. What do you want to master? If the goal is to master the language of the basics, you are the designer and owner of your own path. The four steps mastery formula will be your action plan.

Here are some analogies I experienced leading to mastery. was a basketball player during my school days. When I was boarding in my eldest sister's home, I was 16 years old. I was passionate about the game. I wanted to represent the state and the country. That was my goal and dream at that point of time. How do I achieve my dream? I read about the achievements of some NBA players in USA and their training schedules. Many of them came from poor families. They became great players through sheer perspiration and hard work. This is equivalent to high-impact learning. Repetition is the secret of mastering any skill whether sports or learning habits. This principle was downloaded into my mind replacing the outdated belief that great players are born. I was committed. I followed this basic drill strategy every morning.

There was a basketball court behind my sister's house. The more I repeated those skills-dribbling, shooting and various types of lay ups-the more I enjoyed them because I could perform such skills without thinking during a match. I was patient with my focus stamina in developing these skills. Regular breaks of training with application of these skills during actual games gave me further encouragement. These skills became my weapons when I played competitive games and I enjoyed it more. Within a few months of intensive and consistent practices of various basketball skills every day, I became an extraordinary player with skills in dribbling, ball control, shooting, and various lay ups. I started to perform well for my team and soon I was drafted into the state team. With high frequency practice and repetition, most of the skills became engrained into my physical system. I do not have physical advantage in terms of height but my skill in ball handling, lay ups and shooting accuracy helped me to become an outstanding player.

Another factor is that I started to get extra support to help me overcoming obstacles I encountered while playing. My teammates and coach were there to guide me. Playing together with other state players in competitions helped to cement extra skills required to be a good player.

One more factor that helped me in the game is my mindset. Confidence began to take root when I began to believe in my skillset. I went into every game believing that I had all the weapons to win the game. Most of the games I played, my team won. The results gave further encouragement for me to train harder. I was motivated further and I practised more. My team was the champion team in Penang state senior basketball league for many years while I was a student.

Another experience seems to reinforce the same principle of mastery stated above. I am a tennis player and I play reasonably well to enjoy the game. My experiences to excel in tennis reveal that the four mastery elements mentioned above are necessary for me to play the game well. Knowing the five fundamental strokes well and be able to execute them in practice will not make you a good tennis player. To excel in tennis or to be a professional player, you need more than just be able to hit forehand, backhand,

overhead, serving and volley well. My experience tells me that I have to practise these strokes for hours each week. I need constant repetitions under playing condition before I can execute these strokes automatically. I also need coaches and supports as I move up the skill levels. I also need to make a commitment to play well. The journey to become a good player requires plenty of perspiration and hard work. It takes determination, persistence, consistency and investment of time. More importantly, I need a right mindset to become a good player. This is the absolute truth for professional players. Many aspiring players quite when the training becomes tough and they face failures. To be successful as a tennis player, you need not only playing skills but also mental strength and a winning mindset.

This mastery principle is also applicable to learning skills. I used the mastery principle successfully to speak the language of the three basics fluently. Making a commitment to think well, speak well and write well is just the beginning. Awareness of strategies and daily practices are the necessary approach to succeed. Parental help and teachers' guidance are also important factors. Another factor which is equally important is the influence of peers. Mixing with friends who speak the language of the basics well is already a head start. All these extra supports will help to cement the mastery of the three basics. Willingness and the attitude of learning and practising are equally important. The mindset must be there. The subconscious mind has to be programmed with the necessary steps required to speak the language of the basics well. Consciousness of the important of mastering the basics and their implications for living a life of abundance are the motivating factors for consistent practices.

Another experience I had, using my self-study strategy, seems to concur with the above four necessary elements of the 'Mastery Formula' to achieve academic success. Self-study strategy has been my study habit all my life. Even in my retirement such a habit is still kicking. It involves preparing lessons in advance before attending class. I even wrote down questions to ask my teachers to clarify mathematics and science concepts I did not grasp while doing self-study. Repeating this strategy every day, the strategy became my habit towards learning. This accelerated mode of learning helps to cement mathematics and science concepts into my mind quickly. Repetition of understanding is critical. Two of my classmates took tuition from me and when I repeated the lessons to them, teaching them applications of concepts and formulae, I seemed to understand and remember better. Learning becomes easy. Formulae and concepts seemed to stay in my mind. Applications of formulae and concepts came naturally with practice. And my results tell all the stories. This is the secret of the natural law of academic success. If you help others to understand, you understand better. Just like you create values for others, you actually create values for yourself. To commit to use the strategy every day requires a determined mindset. It boils down to repetition, consistency and controlled habit. Doing and enjoying such learning habit helped to shatter my excuses, my limiting beliefs and my unproductive habits. I managed to identify what was really holding me back. I wanted to eliminate my feelings of uncertainty and doubt that had caused me to procrastinate from implementing my self-study strategy. I made a serious commitment. So I decided to take action to stick to my self-study strategy for me to move forward and succeed. I decided to take control of my own learning. After a few months sticking to my self study strategy, I started to perform at a higher level of productivity. My results after one term gave me further motivation to accelerate and intensify my strategy. This self-study strategy is my valuable weapon and it becomes my study habit throughout my life. I set my ambitious goals. Now I look back, I feel the satisfaction of sticking to my self-study strategy to achieve my goals, one at a time.

Our journey towards success in life is no difference. If we want to achieve abundance or mastering the language of the basics, we need to follow all the four elements of the 'Mastery Formula'. There is no instantaneous success for any one. So do not get frustrated after a few attempts blaming that the strategies do not work for you. Just remember, to be successful, you need to be great in what you do. The ability to speak the language of the three basics well is necessary. Master of your chosen field of speciality requires the elements of the mastery principle. Parents are advised to be aware of these four components of the 'Mastery Formula' to help your children to succeed in life. To begin with, your children need to do the three elementary things well first before trying any other strategies to become successful in their chosen fields. Recognise the importance of these three basics and encourage your children to master them as early as possible.

Thinking well is the first step towards living well. So brain health is central to all health and success in whatever you do. When your brain works right, you think right and work right. When your brain is in trouble, you do not think right and most likely you will be in trouble. If you cultivate a healthy brain, you think better and you will have a better life leading to success and abundance. To begin with, teach your children to live an active and healthy lifestyle. Encourage them to think and speak well. Writing well will be the product of thinking well and speaking well. Many parents are facing the same problem. If you yourself do not think well and speak well, how are you going to teach your children what you are lacking? I hope this book will help to bridge the gap of many parents who are not equipped with these three basics. It's never too late to master the three basics for anyone. You must know how to master them with the necessary knowledge, practices and strategies. The intention of this book is to help and facilitate, making the mastery of the three basics permanent in your life. A life of abundance is waiting for anyone who is willing. The intention of writing this book is mainly targeting parents who are interested to help their children to gain abundance. If you are a parent, you will be in better position to help your children if you have master the three basics well.

Mission and Destiny

Why do you need to think well, speak well and write well? These are the fundamental things essential for us to live well. Just like asking a state basketball player why he needs to do the basic skills well. It's simple. If you cannot do the fundamentals well, you'll never be a good player. Similarly if I cannot speak the language of the three basics well, I will not succeed in my life. Making an impact as well as creating abundance for my family starts with the mastery of the three basics. I also wanted to create facilities and values for others. Living and using my full potential is the way to go. This provides the inspirational ability to defy convention and dogma for me to live an extraordinary life. I take responsibility of my own life and it offers immense rewards and challenges. How do I go about achieving my goal? The three steps principle: identify, eliminate and act, following the command of my subconscious mind, is strongly adhered to. The first step is to start thinking well. Identify what I want in life is the next step. The identification of the things that are holding me back is critical. I have to eliminate these mental blocks as soon as possible. Aware of what I speak is the beginning. The words I speak have the power to bring either prosperity to my life or more struggle. Speaking negative words will help to shape my thoughts and actions, which will bring poverty instead of prosperity. I have to eliminate negativity from my life. I am always happy to be alive. So I need to speak words of affirmation wherever and whenever possible. Speaking words of encouragement will also benefit others. This helps to cultivate a positive attitude towards life. All the steps and actions I take have to be in alignment with my goals.

Before this realisation, I had made some mistakes and had used words carelessly. I managed to eliminate this habit of negativity. I remember when I accepted Jesus into my life, I started to utter prayers for various issues to live a better life. This act becomes a habit and I learn to say positive and encouraging words for others. Now I realise that I can change anything that is detrimental to my life. What do I want to change? Knowing how to identify problems and making sound decisions are important to me. This consciousness tells me that there are three fundamental things I must do well. This awakening came from inspiration when I was a secondary school student in Penang. I shifted my perspective to one that serves me and started to cultivate self-love. I started to remove the mask to allow my own truth and brilliance to shine. I realise that the universe is willing to give it to anyone who aspires to achieve abundance. If I did not put my hand up to receive it, the universe would have chosen someone else. I would have missed the opportunity of a lifetime. The three essential fundamental things: thinking, speaking and writing, I must do well as soon as possible. My thoughts and my words will define my life. I began to think positively and affirmed positive words to enrich my life and others. I am still doing it. Doing these three fundamental things well is the prerequisite for me to succeed in achieving abundance including financial freedom. I have found the secret to achieve a life of abundance that is more amazing than I probably think possible. I have found an amazing gift to create and to enhance most of the areas of the life I really deserve. The areas include financial freedom, loving, relationship and appreciating myself, attracting friendship, inner peace and good health.

Having a good social life motivates me to dream bigger dreams, solve bigger problems and hack happiness to achieve a state of flow most of my time. How do I go about achieving all these? Since I have identified the role of the subconscious mind I have to work on. I have to eliminate my outdated beliefs and habits first before I unload new ones practised by successful people. Once unloaded, I must follow the habits and practices of successful people diligently, consistently, persistently and playfully. The last is most important because when you enjoy doing and it increases productivity. There are three fundamental things: thinking, speaking and writing that most successful people do well. Doing these three fundamental things well as early as possible will serve as a highway to every aspect of my life including confidence, happiness, relationship, self-esteem, balance and a vision of a better world. I discovered early that realising my destiny is my only obligation. What is my destiny? I did not know initially. I had only a vague idea as I responded to my calling as an educator. I wanted to make a difference in the world of mathematics education. Perhaps my destiny is my mission to contribute and provide materials in the form of ideas to help students learn meaningfully. A new mission was born and I worked towards the direction of becoming a curriculum developer. There are two very important days in my life: the day I was born and the day I found out my purpose in this world. I started breathing the day I was born. I became part of the universe. The universe lives in me. Finding my purpose in life was triggered when I responded to my calling, making teaching my career. My relatives discouraged me because teaching does not pay well. They wanted me in business, especially my mother. They wanted me to be rich. I ignored their expectations. My conscious and unconscious mind signals to me that abundance can come from any profession. There is no limit to abundance when your subconscious mind is loaded with beliefs and habits of successful people. Anyone can become a limitless person. Anyone can enjoy abundance. I am determined to be one of them.

I have identified my mission. To make a difference to learning became my calling. Turning my mind into an idea machine was ignited. I wanted to make my contribution in the field of mathematics education. So I have to exercise my idea muscles every day. To accomplish this mission, the natural path for me to take was to become a teacher of mathematics, the subject I am passionate about. Teaching the subject created a platform for me to experiment my new idea of humanising the teaching of mathematics. What does it mean? Humanising the teaching of mathematics is simply a process connecting mathematics concepts with human experiences. It enhances meaningful learning of mathematics. It makes mathematics learning interesting and meaningful to the students. Hoping to influence students to like and enjoy mathematics was my main objective. To be a person of influence in mathematics education, I need to create something of importance. Mathematics textbooks for students become my contribution. I knew very early that habits and unique etiquette of people of influence can be replicated. What are the unique characteristics of great writers? Their ability to use simple language, their clarity of thoughts, their presentations and explanation are noted. In our computer age, it is analogous to downloading these habits and practices of these people into my subconscious mind. I did that during my secondary school days when I was highly motivated to help underprivileged students learn. Just downloading these habits and practices into our minds is not enough. Just like playing basketball or tennis, knowing the rules and the skills required will not make you a great player. We have to put these practices into our daily life and use them to become what we want to be. Repetition is the secret formula for my success. We have to be passionate about what we are doing. Just like my passion in playing basketball game, I not only practised all the essential skills each day, I also surrounded myself with established players or state players to help me excel in the game. Similarly, if you want to be rich, successful and influential, you have to do the same thing. Other than practising the required skills, surround yourself with respected and authentic people who are successful. A simple observation applies: 'birds of the same feather flock together.' My experiences reveal that if you want to succeed or to influence others, you need not be an entrepreneur or a business man; it can be something simple you want to create to serve others. This triggers the concept of thinking. How to think well? Everyone has dreams. Never give up your dreams. Everything in our life is created from within us. When we change our attitude, the outer world changes to accommodate us. Loving yourself is the most important way to improve yourself and as you improve yourself, you improve your chance of achieving abundance. And you probably know that our life is created within us. The central of the mind, the subconscious plays the important role. So learn to love yourself and accept yourself better today than yesterday. Take initiative for your own transformation. Start to invest in yourself. It will be the greatest investment you ever make. What you intend to do and to achieve is your own responsibility.

To begin with, make inner changes for these three important basic things in life. The personal power is within all of us. For many of us, this consciousness is not activated. Perhaps after reading this book, you are ready to unload these characteristics into your mind and start practising them to achieve the abundance you always dream off. Spend a little money buying this book so that you will begin to identify your problem in your mind, eliminate those that are not useful to you and replace them with habits and beliefs of successful and wealthy people. Start immediately to implement them consistently, persistently, with discipline and playfully until they become yours. Playfully will ensure that you do them happily and enjoy them. Soon you will be on the way towards financial freedom and abundance.

Mastering the Language of the Three Basics

Before you embark on your journey to create abundance, you need to pay attention to the three basics: thinking, speaking and writing. As a parent, you are the first teacher to your children. The responsibility is on your shoulders. Doing these three basic things well as early as possible will ensure that your children are on the bullet train towards their destination called abundance. Many people fail to create a wealthy and fulfilled life partly because of their unawareness of the importance of the three basics. They are not exposed to the importance of the basics because they are struggling in their lives. They do not know because they are not thinking well themselves. They also do not know what it means to speak well. They are not aware of the advantages of thinking well and speaking well. People are attracted to you when you think well and speak well. People want to do business with you. They enjoy talking to you. They tend to like you and want to engage you. When you think well and speak well, you are just like an electromagnet attracting all the good things in life. These are all the necessary ingredients to help you achieving abundance. The important thing for you is to spend a little bit of time to understand these three basics

Thinking Well

It is true that everybody can think. But there are some people who think better than others. What is thinking well? Thinking well, to most people, is having the capacity to reason. To me it means able to analyse, assess and solve problems. This includes the ability to create, follow logic and follow a trend of thought. It also includes the ability to recognise good ideas from bad ones. Thinking well is the first sign of awareness of other possibilities. An abundant thinker has different ways of thinking. He or she celebrates little bit of thinking well first and keep improving the power of thinking. They think well before making decision based on information and not emotion. Abundant thinkers are aware of their thinking based on their own inner transformation than on others' influence. They think differently from other thinkers. If they want relationship, financial freedom, well-being and happiness, they start thinking of ways of getting them and work on them to achieve what they want. They think well because they are aware of illogical thinking or faulty thoughts and they learn to avoid them. What is so important of thinking in our life? Many philosophers know that we do not see life as it is, but we see a version distorted by our hopes, fears and other attachments. The Buddha said, 'Our life is the creation of the mind.'

> Marcus Aurelius commented,"Life itself is but what you deem it."

The quest for wisdom in most communities begins with this insight. They introduce practices for reducing attachments, thinking more clearly and finding solutions to every day emotional torments of normal mental life. The focus here is how to think well as part of our mental health. The misconception of what we think is causing us pain and stress. When we face a problem, it's easy to get trapped in a spiral of negative emotions - frustration, anxiety, stress... and many more. Where to find answer to your problem? It all begins with thinking! A simple mind shift will help to eliminate any negative emotion weighing you down. You need to clear your mind, gain clarity and tap into your thinking power. Advices from others are just opinions providing alternative thinking. You can show respect to their opinions but you do not have to follow their thoughts. The whisper from your conscience and reasoning will help you to think logically. Always be aware of alternative opinions and it is your logical thinking to decide which course to follow. So the earlier we train our children to think, it will give them a head start.

What are the advantages of thinking well? This ability gives us a great competitive advantage. We are able to solve problems and accomplish our objectives efficiently. The ability to think always makes life easier and it enhances our relationship with others. People recognise us as smart and consider us as capable persons. Thinking well will lay the foundation for our social skills. What is the difference between thinking well and intelligence? The former is a skill and the latter is a natural capacity. Having a sizable intellect is always a great asset. It facilitates the process to think well, but it does not guarantee that. The advantage of thinking well is that people think that we are intelligent. As parents, it's important that we teach our children how to think instead of what to think. The idea goes back as far as Socrates. The Socratic way is fostering critical thinking. This encourages our children to question their own unexamined beliefs as well as receiving wisdom from the elders and those around them. It may cause some discomforts initially, but the process will lead to better understanding. The journey of thinking well begins at home. First, parents have to think well themselves if they expect their children to follow. We do not expect the blind to lead the blind. My observation reveals that there are many intelligent people who do not think well. Perhaps they are not taught how to think. They do not pick up the skill at home. They do not have the home advantage. They lack exposure and role model. They become emotional and sometimes illogical. They cannot argue in a cool and calm manner. They lose their temper easily and live with anger. They become depressed because they do not get things the way they want. They want to be right all the time. When they are wrong, they blame others. They do not take responsibility of their misjudgements. They become less tolerant and are disconnected with others. Some of them grow up to be adults who are not capable to fend for themselves. They live out their lives dependent on the kindness of others. I don't want any of my kids to be such a person. The idea of cultivating thinking well is also a strategy to discourage distorted thinking in our children. As parents, it is important that we understand distorted thinking and are able to lead by examples. Download these distorted thinking into your mind so that you are in better position to advise your children. Here are some cognitive distortions listed by Robert L. Leahy, Stephen J. F. Holland and Lata K. McGinn. Most of these distorted thinking have become our daily habits and they are deeply engrained in our subconscious mind. Hopefully after reading them, you become aware of them. Helping your children to avoid such thinking is just the beginning for them to start thinking well.

(a) Do not practise mind reading. Many of us assume what people think without having sufficient evidence of their thoughts. For example, we hear children saying : "He thinks I'm a loser. My parents do not love me because they do not help me financially."

(b) Do not embrace fortune telling. Many of us predict the future negatively such as things will get worst, or there is danger ahead. Other examples we hear people saying: "I will not get the job or I will fail my exam. His future is not going to be good. People will take legal action against your mistakes! You are going to be a failure in your life."

(c) Do not catastrophize. Many of us believe what has happened or will-happen; will be so awful and unbearable that we won't be able to stand it. For example: "It would be terrible if I failed. It will cost me a lot of money if I join him in the project. Following your big dream will lead you into bankruptcy."

(d) Avoid labelling. We assign negative global traits to ourselves and others. For example: "I am unbearable. He is a rotten person. He is an ass hole. He is good for nothing."

(e) Discounting positives. We claim that positive things we or others do are trivial. For example: "That's what wives are supposed to do-it does not count when she is nice to me. Those successes are easy and they don't matter."

(f) Do not practise negative filtering. We tend to focus exclusive on the negatives and seldom notice the positives. For example: "Look at all of the people who don't like me. He is useless and always depend on others"

(g) Do not overgeneralise. We have the tendency to perceive a global pattern of negatives on the basis of a single incident. For example: "This generally happens to me. I seem to fail in a lot of things. He has mistaken a name, and he is going to be unreliable."

(h) Do not practise dichotomous thinking. We have the habit to view events or people in all-or-nothing terms. For example: "I get rejected by everyone. It is a complete waste of time."

(i) Do not practise blaming. We focus on the other person as a source of our negative feelings and we refuse to take responsibility for changing yourselves. For example: "She is to blame for the way I feel now. My parents caused all my problems."

(j) Do not practise emotional reasoning. We tend to let our feelings guide the interpretation of reality. For example: "I feel depressed; therefore my marriage is not working out."

(k) Inability to disconfirm. We tend to reject any evidence or arguments that might contradict our negative thoughts. For example if a person feels that he is unlovable; he rejects any evidence as irrelevant that people like him. His thought cannot be refuted. He fails to examine other issues and other deep rooted problems.

(l) What if? Some of us keep asking a series of questions 'what if' something happens, and they fail to be satisfied with any of the answers. All 'what if' questions are not healthy for your growth. We use to receive 'yes or no' answer. The person who has the habit of such response usually thinks he is smart. But it is not always so. Be careful of uttering such response unless your reasoning is fantastic.

So it's important that we realise that thinking well is a skill that can be learned. Thinking well can also be taught. Parents are the significant persons to sensitise this consciousness and awareness to their children. A lot of thinking habits of our children are caught at home. If we, as parents, are not aware of faulty thinking and practising them regularly, our children will pick them up. They use them because they think that these faulty thoughts are normal and acceptable. So it's important that we let your children know the fundamental faults most people are suffering with regard to thinking. Some of the faults pointed out above can slowly be downloaded into your children's mind. Teach them with examples, one at a time, of how to avoid such faulty thinking. This awareness is important especially when your children are growing up. By avoiding faulty thoughts in their daily interaction with peers and family members, they are better prepared to start thinking well. With regular practise, they are sure to be ahead of their peers in terms of thinking. Do not leave the task of teaching children thinking well to others or school. In addition, these three simple strategies can easily be downloaded into our or our children's subconscious minds. When they become parents, they will be better equipped. What are these three ways?

First, have regular thoughtful conversation with our children. Parents need to master the simple art of communication. Speak to our children like a friend. Taking our time to discuss problems with them is a good start. Sharing some common faulty thinking and discussing how to avoid them can help them to be aware of such thinking. Asking questions and questioning their answers trigger their thinking capacity. Encourage them to form their own ideas. Always allow your children to form alternative opinions. Society and religions want to make us think alike. Under the prevailing situation, children will not develop the ability to think well. Parental intervention and encouragement to think outside the box are critical to give our children an advantage. Teach them the common faults of thinking like blaming, labelling, speculating, overgeneralising, and others listed above. This book encourages parents to think well first before they can teach their children how to think.

Second, another important thing parents can do is to give them a good formal education. This includes literature, liberal arts, language, history, debate and art. A little bit of critical thinking can be included in their formal education. Encourage your children to join discussion group or debating team. Getting children to discuss school lessons or current issues in small group will help to activate their thinking power. Once your children start to reason, time is right to discuss the common faults of thinking with them. Discussion of common issues and common faults in thinking not only helps children but also parents to think well. The more discussion and repetition of avoiding faulty thinking will enhance children's thinking. Relationship will improve not only with your children but also with friends and working colleagues. Parents and children will stand tall and handsome together.

Third, parental role is important especially when children are too involved in TV, iPhone or hand phone, computer games and the Internet. Their influence in terms of thinking and speaking is significant. Some of the attitude and language usages in those media are atrocious. A right start is important. Parental control is the key. Do not allow your children all the freedom to do what they want. Only encourage and allow programs that are educational. There are plenty of programs available, including fundamental thinking games about discrimination, recognition, sorting and pairing. Most of these games encourage analysis and logical thinking. Parental effort initially will provide the path leading children to think well. Remember, a parent is your child first most important teacher.

Since all of us want to be rich and fulfilled, then we must cultivate the habits to think like a successful man or woman. We want to follow and imitate the thoughts and habits of wealthy and healthy people. The universe is generous and there is nothing wrong to be rich. You will be in better position to serve and create values for others. By doing so, you are actually creating values for yourself. The first thing we need is to have faith in ourselves. We want to overcome illogical fears. We begin to see risks as opportunities. This book provides various strategies necessary for people like you to become rich, happy, fit and healthy. You can easily be one of them if you pick any of the approaches used by millionaires to achieve what they have. Learn their strategies. Get rid of your outdated thinking and implant the beliefs and habits of the rich into your subconscious mind. Make full commitment to use the new strategy and keep repeating it until you become successful and fulfilled. I too acquired a new brain of a millionaire and use their habits to become rich. I took the risk to start my journey to become a millionaire. I trained myself to become an idea machine and exercised my brain muscles to create ideas. I must have trained myself to think well. I became a writer and investor. Both require thinking. By thinking well, I started to enjoy a new path to wealth. You too need a new brain. You need to change your poor brain to a rich brain. You need to acquire the thoughts and beliefs of the rich and successful.

You will think like a millionaire. You need to put into practice the habits and beliefs of the rich. You, too, can become wealthy and fulfilled.

Speaking Well

Speaking well is another important social skill. The basic ingredient is mastering a language, its grammar, diction, vocabulary and expressions. But more importantly is the ability to express worthy thoughts concisely and clearly. What are worthy thoughts? They are simply positive affirmations which help you to grow. Using positive words reflects that you are thinking well. Negative words spring from faulty thinking. Parental influence is significant. The home is a fertile ground to nurture positive affirmations. The water of a stream depends on its source. If the source is dirty, it's difficult to keep the stream clean. Speaking well depends on your initial training and awareness to say what you mean. The home is the source. You may have good grammar and diction but you will not speak well if you have trouble 'saying' what you 'mean'. Parents have an important role to play here. Parents are the first teachers to the children. This awareness of saying what you mean must be taught to our children very early in life. Train them to speak concisely and saying things that are worthy. This is the habit parents must acquire themselves before they can teach their children. Many of our habits of talking and speaking are not taught but actually caught at home or place of work. Parental role model is important. This critical habit must be downloaded into your children's mind and insist that they keep practising it to become autopilot. Being a teacher for more than two decades, I notice that many college graduates can't speak well. They are people with good ideas but they cannot express them. They do not say worthy things and they do not speak what they mean. Many of them are not aware that their environments influence them. Perhaps the lack of training regarding thinking and speaking is the main cause. It is a rare quality for our children to speak well. It immediately separates them from the rest of the group. Remember that if you are critical of others, you are actually criticising yourself. If you keep judging others, you are judging yourself. You keep gossiping about others, you are inviting others to gossip about you. The ability to say kind words attracts attention and encourages friendship. We need to be kind to ourselves but also kind to others. We have no right to judge others. We also do not entertain others judging us. It is better we learn to accommodate others and practise tolerance. Everyone is entitled to his or her opinions. We need to know the difference between facts and opinions. Facts remain facts. Opinions differ. Encourage our children to respect others' opinions. As far as opinions are concerned, there is no right or wrong answer. We are so use to school examination system. There is only right or wrong answer. If your answers are right, you get good grade. So let your children be aware of opinions and not to insist that their opinions are always right. This applies to parents too.

There are a couple of social skills which are equally important besides thinking and speaking. Children and parents have to be aware of these two social behaviours: assertiveness and aggressiveness. Being assertive is another good social skill. Being aggressive to get what you want is not the right approach in dealing with others. Everyone needs to know and differentiate between assertiveness and aggressiveness in our interaction with others. These two social skills will be discussed in detail later. Speaking well gives your children immediate social power. They become more assertive. It makes them look taller, smarter, and better looking in the group. How to teach children to speak well? Since parents are the child's first teachers, we have an important role to play.

First, as parents, we need to have the habit of speaking well ourselves. A child's experience in speaking well comes from their parents. Children have no limit in acquiring skills including speaking well. They can easily learn to be assertive. Be aware that, as parents, we need to speak to our children thoughtfully and we can expect them to do likewise. Speaking well is a habit that must be nurtured as early as possible. This habit is usually caught and is better if it is taught and reinforced. Parental influence is most significant.

Second, parents can encourage their children to speak well by enrolling them in courses specialising in speaking and communication. These can be liberal arts or public speaking courses. First of all as parents, we need to master the art of speaking well first. Parental guidance and example is the best course for our children.

Third, with the digital and video publishing explosion, your children can easily assess programs to enhance their language ability, grammar, vocabulary and the other essential elements for language learning. Speaking well will come with exposure and training. Many video programs are available now. Providing exposure and facility is the responsibility of parents. Give your children a head start by leading them all the ways.

<u>Writing Well</u>

Writing well is an important skill to acquire. I am lucky to acquire the skill and enjoy writing. It gives me my financial freedom. Nowadays, people are not writing so much. They use to send short messages. But they are still communicating and writing. Be aware that writing well is dependent on speaking well and speaking well is dependent on thinking well. So if parents have trained their children to think well and speak well, you do not have to worry much. Your children will eventually write well. To me, writing well is the ability or skill to express worthy ideas clearly and concisely on paper. Writing well demands some additional facilities beyond the skill of thinking and speaking well. Usually, if our children can think and speak well, I believe they can easily write well- unless they are super-active and cannot sit down to write on paper what they think and speak.

How to encourage your children to write well? Just like playing tennis, knowing the various strokes will not make you a good player. You have to practise the strokes during actual playing. The ability to write well follows the same path. Encourage your children to write to friends or pen pals regularly. Encourage your children to keep a record of what they are experiencing. With the Internet facilities, this can easily be done. A certain amount of control is necessary. There are many predators in the Internet. Parental supervision is essential. The ability to express ideas concisely and accurately is a great asset for children to succeed in life. Thinking well, speaking well and writing well will lay the foundation for your children to analyse, assess and solve problems logically and systematically. Including good manners and positive attitudes in their life, your children are on the ways to a successful life.

In addition to the three essential basics, teach your children to purify their hearts and learn to serve others. If you want them to move in the right track towards abundance, teach them to create values for others and they will soon be creating values for themselves. Remind them that if they need help, they have to learn to provide it first. If they need support, they have to do likewise. This is a simple law of attraction. It is analogous to Newton's third law: for every action there is an equal and opposite reaction.

Understanding this simple law of nature, your children will think well, speak well and finally write well. The road towards abundance is well designed and constructed. Doing these basics well paves the way to mastery of any entrepreneur or business skill later on.

Assertiveness and Aggressiveness

Learning is a life-long process. These three fundamental skills: thinking well, speaking well and writing well - have to be part of our lifestyle to attract abundance. It takes a life time and plenty of self efforts to make these three fundamental skills part and parcel of our life. This consciousness is critical for anyone who aspires to be successful. Doing these three basics well is equivalent to charging your electromagnet first before it can attract the abundance you dream off.

A subset of speaking well touches on assertiveness. There is a difference between assertiveness and aggressiveness. Our children should be exposed to these two social behaviours as early as possible. Exposing these two social behaviours to our children is a good start and more importantly, we should help them to download their characteristics into their subconscious mind. By just doing that, it's not enough. Children need to put the characteristics into practice. The secret to succeed in forming the habits of being assertive requires repetition. The more the practice the better your children will do it well. Before we start teaching and allowing our children to practise assertiveness in interaction with others, we need to know what is assertiveness. I accidently discovered this social behaviour when I started secondary schooling in Penang. When I was doing well in mathematics and science in my class, I was approached by two of my own classmates to provide tuition to help them master the two subjects. They wanted to improve their academic performance and I was given the role of leadership. They were weak in the two subjects. This triggered my thinking and I started to think well. The first thing for me was to establish the attitude to be assertive. I did not understand the difference between assertiveness and aggressiveness initially. I started to search for information. I asked my English teacher regarding these two concepts. He too was not sure. So I relied on my observations and my imaginations during meditations. Soon I realised that being aggressive means selfishly pushing for what you want at the expense of others. The tone of our voice is important and the choice of words matter. Remember that being aggressive, we tend to use words carelessly, in doing so, you generate a host of negative behaviours that make others become defensive, angry and even vengeful towards you. Using aggressive words generally creates hostility, threat, gossip and other unreasonable demands. Many people become emotional when they argue with others. They always insist that they are right and others are wrong. My observations reveal that being aggressive may allow you to get what you want immediately but you may not get what you want the next time. For me I will avoid associating with such an aggressive person. I have a strong dislike for aggressive people. So it's important for me to learn the skill of being assertive as early as possible. I was lucky during my school days because circumstances required me to be assertive. I was put into leadership role and I needed to be assertive to carry out my responsibility.

So it's important for our children to learn and understand the concept of assertiveness. What is assertiveness? It means standing up for your rights while respecting the rights of others. It also means using appropriate expression of your feelings, needs, words and opinions while respecting the feelings of others. The tone of your voice should be low, and the choice of your words should be appropriate. It requires you to express clearly what you really want while ensuring that you are not being taken advantage of. Practising this mode of communication soon reveals who you are, not what you do. I began to practise assertiveness when I knew the difference between the two social behaviours. Being assertive is a way of living where you get the most out of life without others telling you how to do it. The secret of success is to keep practising and repeating words expressing assertiveness instead of aggressiveness. You do not have to be obnoxious, pushy or rude to get things done according to your ways. So the earlier our children learn to be assertive, they will gain respect and leadership role. The characteristics of these two contradictory concepts have to be downloaded into our children's subconscious minds before they can start practising them. The path leading you to become assertive is awareness and the key of success is repetition. The more they practise assertiveness, avoid aggressiveness, the more they will gain respect and attract abundance.

Discovery of How to Make a Difference

I must have put these three basics -thinking, speaking and writing well into practice in my early life's journey. These three basic elements paved the way for me to become an effective leader, teacher, administrator, writer and investor. I was conscious of my mission and my destiny. I know where to find meaning and purpose to what I do. These moves really give me a sense of fulfilment my soul craves. My level of thinking is enhanced. And when I found that purpose, I brought it to reality. I knew I do not have to do great things to make my contribution to the world. Simple ideas expressed concisely are enough for me to make a difference in my field of interest. The important thing for me is not chasing after money but to provide service, value and help to others. I have a simple idea of humanising the teaching of mathematics. I try to put on a human touch on each and every mathematical idea. Connecting each mathematics idea with our daily life gives meaning to learning. I had a fair share of fear and doubt initially. I was uncertain. I was not exposed to much research in the field. But I did not allow my limiting beliefs telling me that I am not good enough or smart enough to begin writing. I was aware that a little negative dialogue was going on in my subconscious mind. Just like most entrepreneurs, they too experience fear to play a bigger game. They do not allow such limiting beliefs to paralyse their dreams and stop them from their greatness. They learn to fall in love with their fear and discomfort to succeed. I succeeded to embrace this courageous move. Initially I experienced chaos and craziness because of uncertainty. And soon the concept became clear to me and I began to grow. I wrote down ideas that came to me as I carried out my experimentation. Many entrepreneurs went through such experience of chaos and craziness before they succeeded. Why is that? It all boils to energy. As we are changing and improving our level of thinking, we are moving from the old habits of energy vibrating at a low frequency to a new level of energy with faster frequency. We are entering into a new looking energy. There is certain amount of resonance between these two levels of energies and the space in between them usually cause us some discomfort. Remember the old energy pattern is always there and it may take some time to eliminate it. The period of transition may be short as we put into practice the new pattern of thinking. Consciousness is the key to help us grow and accelerate our implementation to reach our goal. I managed to shake up the old energy level. I began to put into practices what I believe I could do. I have an immediate tool available to assist me. I meditated and allowed my imagination to take over. I began my journey of visualisation. I focused on the moment what I was thinking and paid particular attention on what I intended to achieve. Being mindful is the way to go. It allowed specific intention to focus on the things I was doing. I thought of all possible ways to add human flavour into the teaching of each mathematics concept. After each meditation especially when I reached the alpha state, ideas seem to spring up without much effort on my part. The 'flow' state was achieved. I noted down each process in my notebook and during each lesson, I experimented the humanising process in class and watched the reactions of my students. The students' responses and their attentiveness were amazing. They seemed to appreciate my efforts and appeared to understand better. Refining my technique and improving my presentation became my daily exercise. Writing down the whole process I used to humanise each mathematics concept became my daily practice. After a year, I had a collection of my lessons ready to be transformed into a textbook. I quickly turn my passion into a profitable venture. It took me many years for my passion to show its shoots and I nurtured it well for it to blossom. The significance, connection, truth and the desire to step fully into my purpose of life attracted me. Contributing good ideas not just about trivial things were my desire. I wanted to hack my mind, upgrade my beliefs and habits. The desire to be extraordinary and consciousness of what I want to do were always there. I was awake and I have strong desire to manifest my vision of humanising the teaching of mathematics concepts into reality. Behind all these actions and implementations, a new way of teaching mathematics was born. I long for my soul to express fully through me and shine its light on different human experience in learning mathematics. I wanted to encourage students to think differently from another level. I really enjoyed to rally people around this new vision of connectedness between mathematics and human experiences. I wanted this vision to become a reality faster and more magnificently. The secret of 'tuning' or hacking of the mind becomes my daily quest to make the simple law of attraction work for me. This secret holds the key that unlocks the door leading me to a life of financial freedom.

The journey I took to become a graduate teacher is a long and tedious one. I started secondary school when I was 16 years old. I was patient and determined. I went to university when I was 26 years old. It took me almost thirty years of preparation before I became a graduate mathematics teacher. Many people had helped me in the process. I am very grateful to my eldest sister and her husband who provided me accommodation for me to finish my secondary school. I am thankful to my second sister and her husband who provided me an interest-free loan to finish my university education. My third sister and her husband gave me a helping hand in my investment ventures. To all these charming gardeners who had nurtured my soul, I want to express my heartfelt thanks. I used to harness the amazing power of gratitude to propel me forwards. Every morning before I wake up, I used to spend a few minutes thinking of the things that I am always grateful for in my life. I become more optimistic and joyful that I am alive and enjoy my abundance. At the end of each day, just before I close my eyes to sleep, I used to think of moments of the day I can have gratitude for. All these practices have amazing effects on my life. I have less stress, but also open my mind to positive changes to happen in my life by focusing what are already good. I look back with appreciation what the grace of gratitude has done to my life.

My journey towards abundance is exciting and tough. I follow the traditional path leading me to my destiny. I studied hard in school and got good results. I excelled in mathematics and science. I went to college to be trained as a teacher. I went to university to get my science and mathematics degree. I started my career as a mathematics teacher. I went on to prepare myself professionally using my writing and research skills to get my master and PhD degrees. All these preparations are necessary to help me realise my destiny as a contributor to mathematics education. I also made a little contribution as a school administrator. I served as deputy principal and finally principal of a large secondary school with sixth forms. The school has about 2 000 students. I also served as lecturer for teachers' trainers. I enjoy my career as a teacher, lecturer, administrator and author and later as an investor. The various duties and responsibilities speak to my soul giving me the feeling that I am contributing to a bigger cause and helping to push forwards the human race. Every day of my life is exciting. Work becomes enjoyable. It gives me meaning and it helps me to grow. I enjoy contributing in the exciting learning world. I manage to turn my passion to work for me and it gives me a fortune. I believe you can do the same. All parents desire a better education for their children, a better health care and better job opportunities. My mission becomes clear. It's my destiny. I dreamed of making a contribution in the world of education. I wanted to make a difference and it came true.

The abundance I am enjoying now does not simply land on my laps. It all began when I was a secondary school student in Penang. I had all the time of the world during that period of my life. I did not have to work in the morning, go to school in the afternoon and work again at night. I was free to meditate and began my visualisation. I enjoy the real power of visualisation and I allow all my dreams to become reality. Visualising myself having the thing I desire, the abundance and health I truly want, they soon manifest themselves and become my realities. If you practise visualisation what you desire every day and take action to achieve them, you will find positive changes coming to you in all directions. Remember just dreaming is not enough. A full commitment to action and repetition is necessary to the mastery of the things you do. For true success you need to be a master in what you do.

Overcoming Limiting Beliefs

Psychologists and philosophers, for decades, are puzzled why human beings want something and then subconsciously sabotage themselves from achieving it. It is partly due to our primitive brains which are trained to reject unfamiliar things and stick to those we are familiar. Perhaps it is for our own good. It reduces uncertainty and saves us energy. All of us do not want to wake up every morning to figure out new ways of driving our car. To most people, success is an unfamiliar phenomenon. So it's natural that our brains keep resisting it. How to overcome this limiting belief? What types of transformation are required for us to go out and do something unfamiliar and mentally challenging, proving broad stimulation mentally and socially, to increase our chance of success?

I was doubtful of my academic ability initially. There is no role model in my family. My parents are not educated. They never went to school. All my elder brothers and sisters had received only primary Chinese education. After six years of Chinese primary school, I had to work as rubber tapper in the morning and attending English Missionary School in the afternoon. My parents had a sundry shop. During the night I had to check the inventory of controlled items like tin milk, sardine, canned foods and others during the emergency. I was staying with my parents in a small town in Kedah, in Malaya. Working whole day was the duty call for me when I was 10 to 15 years old. I did not know how to complain. I just followed my father's instruction. The afternoon school caters for weak and averaged students. I was in this situation for three years studying Standard Five to Form One in English. When I started secondary school in Penang, everything changed. I was staying with my eldest sister who is married to a businessman. I did not have to work in the morning, go to school in the afternoon and work again in the night. I was free to pursue my study and improve my basketball skills. I did not want to be dragged down by my limiting beliefs and habits I inherited during my early childhood. Poor self-esteem and lacking in self-confidence were my inheritance! How do I overcome all these disadvantages? I was unfamiliar with success in both sport and study. I did not want my brain to keep resisting using unfamiliar strategies to transform my situation.

I am one of the lucky people who practise meditation. This habit becomes my tool for overcoming my subconscious mind resisting change. While I meditate and I practise visualisation, I allow my imagination to help me. My visualisation is a process of imagining a goal or desire in a way that I am already living in that reality. Soon I realised that my worthiness or thought about myself is only a story I made up. The feeling of unworthy was worrying me because I did not know that worthy is nothing. In the end it does not matter whether I am worthy or not. It is a feeling not a fact. There is no necessity to take courses or lessons to change my worthiness. Entertaining the idea that I have no chance of achieving abundance is also not necessary. I had a disadvantage being a small boy from a little village town with no secondary school. I have no particular talent except I love playing basketball. I also love learning. Initially thinking well was a problem. I was like an eagle brought up with all the chicken. I did not know that in the near future, I too can fly into the sky. I was thinking that success at best is a job with a stable salary with a good retirement plan. So I chose to be a teacher, a stable job and pension when I retired. But after years of meditation and visualisation, I begin to see myself in a new dimension. My new environment studying secondary school in Penang gave me a glimpse of hope for abundance. As I meditated, I began to visualise the life I wanted. I changed my story and started thinking that I am worthy. Thinking, speaking and writing well are my immediate goals. A new positive attitude and an affluence consciousness were ignited. I wanted to be rich, healthy and happy. New experiences, growth and contribution to humanity are my new desires. Changing my habits and limiting beliefs in my subconscious mind was my top priority. I have feelings. They come from my thoughts that are programmed in my subconscious mind. That program will stay in my mind forever if I am not aware of it. What should I do? I had to change my own story. Off course I had to clear the old program and replaced it with a new one, preferably the beliefs and habits of successful people. Becoming proactive was the first step. Creating something to help others became my goal. I wanted to take control of my financial problems so that they have no control over me. I had to establish a right mindset. More knowledge was not enough and not the answer. I had to keep practice the habits and thoughts of rich and successful people again and again until they became my own. The more time I invested in studying and practicing these habits, the more I enjoyed my life then. The more I got involved into meaningful conversation, meditation and interaction, the more my mind expanded. Special thanks to my regular meditation. This practice gave me a crystal clear idea the direction I was heading. Nothing has meaning until I establish my own meaning in it. It is like an addictive drug. My craving for learning habits and practices of the rich and successful people kept increasing. The more I understand the habits of successful people, their behaviours and implementing them daily, the easier for me to fix my financial reality, my happiness and my passion to contribute. I manage to enter the realm of the super-achievers; the gate swing open as soon as I take action. Once I understand why they are different from me, I knew that I was living below my own potential. I started to embrace the powerful strategy of visualising practised by these super achievers. Actually I was enjoying my success as an effective teacher plus providing extra support for those who needed my help. My powerful visualising strategy helped to turn my success as a teacher from one-dimensional picture to a multiple dimensional sculpture. Now I have it all, embracing lucrative experiences as a writer, investor, financial freedom, emotional peace and happiness.

I began to believe in myself. I immediately realised that to become successful, I have to embrace continuous learning and growth. Knowing my model of reality began. My reality is in the form of my mission to provide learning materials to help students succeed in understanding mathematics concepts. Visualising what I wanted to do and what service I could provide began. I was facing the acute problem of getting learning materials to help me learn while I was in secondary school. This problem became my motivation to do something. How do I help? I have to be involved in writing and publishing. I want to bring in connection between life experiences and mathematics concepts that make learning meaningful and easy to remember. My mean goal was a career as a mathematics teacher and my end goal was my mission to contribute ideas and materials to help learning. I have to do something worthwhile. The first thing I visualised was to help in creating materials to make mathematics learning simple. By providing this service, I could become rich and influencing. I also wanted to help others. I started to conduct tuition classes in the weekends to help students preparing for Higher School Certificate of Education. I started writing mathematics textbooks and guidebooks as my contribution to learning. By serving others, I was rewarded greatly. I had to do something else. Venturing into investments like properties, stocks and business joint-ventures became my new mission. Making a difference in the learning landscape was my main aim. Financial freedom was next. Giving back to society what I had benefited became possible. I know what I want in life and I know how to get it. I do not need to be an entrepreneur to accomplish my mission. So it becomes easier for me to get rid of the dirt in the form of negative thoughts in my mind once and for all. I have my own personal dreams and I have to work constantly to transform them into reality. I made changes in my life and I tried a few things differently.

Soon I realised that my life was upside down. This was the feeling I went through and I did not like it. This turmoil might be necessary as part of my growing up and learning. It was normal when I was not thinking straight. I needed a paradigm shift involving my deep-rooted beliefs in my mind. I do not want to be trapped into thinking that I need to be an entrepreneur before I can help to make meaningful changes in the learning landscape. Needing a little bit of passion on something that could help others learning mathematics more easily became my creativity. My passion focused in creating meaningful learning. Thus humanising the teaching of mathematics concept was born. The rest is history.

In the investment world I do not need to be Warren Buffett to be a successful investor. What I need is to make some changes in my portfolio converting losers into winners. Establishing some golden rules to guide me in stock investment becomes my risk management. It's quite another to have global and stock market dreams and ever believe that those dreams can be realised. I did not dream to be an entrepreneur. I only need a humble job as a teacher as a springboard to achieve my mission. I love writing and investing. I take one project at a time. I work diligently, consistently and persistently to move towards my mission. This is a much surer path to my success, happiness and achieving my dreams. I knew that I also need ongoing support from friends and a net-work people working with me. I seek mentors to help me accelerating my learning and implementing my practices. Just like playing tennis, there are only a few necessary strokes: serving, forehand, back hand, volley and overhead. Anyone can easily learn the strokes. But without consistent, persistent and disciplinary practices, these strokes can never become automatic to execute. To be a great player, you need plenty of perspiration and match practices to be able to use the strokes as weapons during competition. Thousands of hours must be put in if you want to be a good player. Similarly knowing the habits and practices of the rich and successful people is not enough. The knowledge will not help you succeed. To be successful you need to keep practicing these habits and beliefs until they become part and parcel of your life. Support and role models can help to accelerate your learning and help you to adopt them as your lifestyle and as tools for your wealth creation. Once that was done consistently, abundance will keep smiling and chasing after you. After many hundred hours of practices, those habits and beliefs become my property. Consequently I am able to retire not only with financial freedom but also enjoying fitness and a healthy life. Now I can say proudly to myself that I am enough. Remember it is not your thoughts but your beliefs that can transform you.

Your mind cannot hold two conflicting belief systems such as poverty and abundance. If you want abundance, you have to replace your belief system of poverty consciousness by that of affluent attitude. You have the power to install the belief system you desire. You have the choice. Just believing in the affluent system is not enough. You have to be motivated to take action repeatedly until such habit becomes part of your behaviour. You will learn to speak the language of abundance and your vibration will resonate with that of the universe. You are dealing with your subconscious mind and your belief system will help you to manifest the abundance you desire. No much effort is required once the affluent system is installed in your subconscious mind. The universe will be forced to respond and provide you all the abundance you commanded. The universe has everything you want and is waiting to give it to you. What you need is to put up your hands to receive the abundance you desire. Remember that we can create everything in the world with our own interpretation. We create every belief about ourselves and our lives. The only problem most of us encounter is that we are ignorant of the four elements of the 'Mastery Formula' to bring our belief into fruition. All of us have the power to change our life story. We are what we say we are. If we do not like our life story, we can change it. If you say that you are worthy, then you have to show that you are actually worthy. Who is the referee in your life? You are. You are everything in your game of life: judge, time keeper, player and everything. There is no body playing but you. The choice is in your own hands. Knowing what you want is the first step towards a life of abundance. The three basics you must have. You are going to create your life story. So choose a good story for your life.

Summary

Do you believe that our children will have a head start if they master the basics very early? The secret of achieving abundance begins with the mastery of the three basics. Could the secret to rapid, effortless manifestation of abundance really be that simple? The mastering of the three basics together with our subconscious beliefs will provide the full equation for our success. Beliefs are critical for success. Remember what Henry Ford famously said, "Whether you think you can, or you think you can't … You are right."

So to achieve abundance we need the mastery of the three basics and change our beliefs. Parents are the most significant persons who will influence their children in learning the language of the basics. It's important that parents know how to think well, speak well and write well. If any parent lacks these basic skills, this book can serve to fill the gap. Parents should also be aware that our conscious mind helps us to set goals but it is our subconscious mind that is responsible for our action or inaction. The natural path of our energy flows in, through and out of our bodies all the time.

Everything is energy. However, that is not true all the time. As we go through life certain negative experiences, unhappy events and emotional turmoil like anger, frustration, fear, guilt and depression cause blocks in our system. These events can cause our energy system from functioning smoothly. These blocks are accumulating in our subconscious minds without us knowing them. These blocks can stay with us forever sabotaging our abundance. This awareness is important if we want to help our children to get rid of these obstacles from preventing them to succeed to have an abundant life. First they prevent them from thinking, speaking and writing well. In order to help our children to master these three essential basics, our children should be made aware of the four elements of the 'Mastery Formula'. The four elements of the mastery formula are as follow:

> First is high-impact learning to cement new skills and habits. Second is high-frequency practice.
>
> Third is ongoing support.

And, lastly it is the inner game involving the subconscious belief.

The three steps actions are simply identify, eliminate and unload good characteristics for implementation. Keep practising them until you achieve your goal.

The basic ingredients of thinking well, speaking well and writing well including the awareness of faulty thoughts, strategies available, and other characteristics we need to explain to our children. More importantly these characteristics should be downloaded into our children's subconscious minds to replace whatever beliefs and habits they have inherited. Repetition and frequent practice is the key for the mastery of these essential basics. Mastering the language of the three basics and be assertive are analogous to mastering the basic strokes of playing tennis. It is not through inspiration but perspiration. Children need to be aware that the mastery of these basics is the foundation for their future abundance.

Last but not least, you need to value yourself and love yourself. If you do not value and love yourself, you will not value your time to do the basic things that will put you on the road to abundance.

After reading this chapter, I hope you have discovered something importance for you and your children to speak the language of the basics fluently. This mastery can bring not only joy of living but also nourishes your purpose of life with good relationship. Every time you interact with others, you enjoy respect and attention. You enjoy mixing with others because you are welcome but there is also harmony between your heart and your mind. The awareness and the choice you give your children by leading them to the mastery of the three basics will be the greatest gift and heredity they ever get. Remember that only 3 per cent of the world population master the three basics well to help them living a life of abundance. 97 per cent of the world population are living in lack. They did not master the basics to give them the advantage. The choice is yours and your children whether you want to be in the former or later.

CHAPTER TWO

DEVELOPING THE MINDSET FOR ABUNDANCE

Introduction to Financial Freedom

You have learned the three essential basics to help you and your children to succeed in life. Learning by itself is not enough to prepare you for life. The importance of achieving success lies in your beliefs and habits in your subconscious mind. You need to know the purpose of mastering the three basics. This will help you to set a worthwhile goal. How to achieve the goal? Awareness and mindfulness are just the beginning. An easy strategy is available. It is not difficult to download all the characteristics of the three basics into your mind and start practising them daily to help you and your children to master them. Your beliefs and habits will activate the motivation part of your brain so that you are driven to take action. A good daily habit is formed. Start cultivating your focus stamina by focusing on thinking and speaking. Keep focus and take one task at a time. Visualising a clear picture of the characteristics of the three basics and the strategies to achieve them will help you in accomplishing the tasks. Once the conception is done, a healthy belief is born. The key is to focus one task at a time before moving to the next task. This habit is nurtured daily and the journey takes a long time. There is no short cut. Mastering the language of the three basics of abundance and having the advantage of being assertive will lay the foundation for good social life. I am very excited to bring passion and joy to your life. Adopting the four steps 'Mastering Formula' strategy with consistent practice will help to cement the three basic skills into yours and your children's lives. Mastering and doing the three basics well can help to bring about changes in your lifestyle and that of your children. Doing the three basics well is your first step towards a good career and a stepping stone towards a life of abundance. Thinking well and speaking will nurture good relationship with people coming into contact with you and your children. They appear taller and more attractive to others. People tend to like them and want to do business with them. Writing well is always a great asset. Its potential is unlimited especially in the era of Internet. The world is within reach and eventually writing well will attract abundance. What is abundance? Abundance embraces happiness, well-being, financial freedom, relationship and being fit and healthy. These variables are interdependent. A healthy body and financial freedom are necessary ingredients for happiness. All of us dream of financial freedom even before we retire. But what does that mean? Most of us focus on financial aspect. We get a job and work long hours to gain good salary. We only concentrate to earn linear or active income. We work for financial security which can easily disappear. Depending on linear income throughout your life does not provide financial freedom as well as time freedom. We have no time for our passions and hobbies. We have no time to enjoy life. We do not have real freedom. Many of us are ignorant about strategies of creating streams of residual income and other types of cash-flow while we are working. The consequence is, the moment we lose our jobs the paycheque ceases to come in. We lose our financial security. Everyone needs to be aware of this consequence. Our lives are affected by the economic cycles. The companies we work are not spare. Depending on your job and paycheque throughout your working life is not a wise move. With the Internet facilities available, everyone can make full use of modern technology to turn any of your passion or hobby into a financial machine. Your three basic skills especially writing and speaking will come in handy. All of us have some special knowledge where others require. Write about what you know and teach others to benefit from your experiences.

Your financial freedom can come from your passions. What is financial freedom? If you start to search for the answer, it is a good beginning. This will activate your thinking and enhance your visualisation.

The Difference between Financial Security and Financial Freedom

You need to understand the difference between financial security and financial freedom. This is just a problem, like all problems which are questions we do not have answers yet. There's got to be better ways to believe something good and practical to turn our passions or hobbies into financial muscles. Our brains are always searching for answers to our questions. We should begin to ask ourselves better questions instead of just affirmation or positive statements. Begin to ask our brains specific questions so that we will immediately start searching for answers. Instead of saying 'I want financial freedom or financial security', ask your brain, 'What is the difference?'

There is a difference between financial security and financial freedom. Financial security depends on our job and paycheque. As long as you have a job, the paycheque is available. You are able to pay all your bills and live reasonably well. Your financial security is tied to your job. But financial freedom does not depend on our paycheque. Financial freedom comes from streams of residual income, cash flow and assets growth. Streams of residual income are recurring income in the form of royalty, dividends, rentals, profits from patents of products created and other cash flow from business. It takes time and efforts to create these types of income. Once they are created, money keeps flowing into your account. These types of residual income and cash flow will keep flowing into your account irrespective of our involvement later on. Can we have financial freedom when we are working? Yes we can. As soon as our streams of passive or residual income and cash flow exceed our monthly expenses; we are already there. So it is not that complicated. I have fulfilled that mission while I was working. My royalties, rentals from my two shops and my dividends from stocks are more than my expenses every month. I was enjoying financial freedom when I was working. My paycheque from my job was an extra bonus to my saving. I want to help others to reach their greatest financial freedom as early as possible. I want you to achieve the same level of wealth and success as early as possible. What we have to do is to think well and create a few streams of residual income that exceed our monthly expenses. This requires planning and using suitable strategies to complement your salary.

To begin with, the things you want to do must not be too time consuming and must not interfere with your main career if you have a job. Otherwise the attempt may be counterproductive. The best thing you can do is to follow your passion and hobby. Do the things you are good at and enjoy doing. Convert your hobby or passion into a financial magnet. Understanding the concept of financial freedom is the first step, pursuing and expanding your passion is the next step.

The journey towards financial freedom is set in motion when you learn how to create residual streams of income structures. Do you have the necessary strategies to do so? Learn from some of the strategies discussed in this book. This book explores many possible ways of creating streams of residual income and cash flow. What are the possible best ones for you? I know my passion. I do not know yours. Pick those that are complimentary to your talents. You can find them in business, hobbies, writing, singing, property or asset investments, stocks, bonds, direct selling, agents for various organisations and many others. Try to learn the best ways to turn your business, hobby or any 'side kicks' into passive income streams. I will share some of my own experiences of creating streams of residual income and cash flow. One of the advantages of financial freedom is time freedom. We have time to follow our passions and choices of life later on. We can have new experiences we aspire; growth we desperately need and make contributions whenever and wherever we can. These are the consequence of the power of financial freedom.

My First Attempt to Create Residual Income

When I started teaching applied mathematics for Sixth Forms after my graduation from university, I caught a glimpse of light shining at the end of my economic tunnel. The light signals to me that there are various ways I can do to make mathematics learning easier if I can connect mathematics concepts to students' daily experiences. The process known as humanising the teaching of mathematics was conceived. This approach makes mathematics learning easy and meaningful for the students. A passion was born and its echo whispered to me that I was moving in the right direction. Humanising the teaching of applied mathematics became my mission. How did I do it? I started to write down each humanising process for teaching each mathematics concept in each topic. After a year or two, I had gathered enough materials to produce my first mathematics textbook using the concept known as humanising the teaching of mathematics. Even mathematics problems given as exercises are designed to be relevant to students' daily experiences. In the process I had also made my teaching strategy more effective. The reactions and the results of my students motivated me further to develop the strategy. Soon my passion paved the way for me to be a mathematics textbook writer. I like it and I enjoy writing. A new chapter of my life was written because I found the area of my calling that is in tune with my spirit, heart, passion and strength. My passion in writing became my calling. This calling created values for students and I was rewarded plentifully. A new stream of residual income was created and it kept flowing for many years. Replication and refinement of my writings are the new drivers for my absolute passion. I kept my writing passion burning and within twenty years, I had produced more than two dozens of mathematics textbooks and guidebooks to my collection. I had also written two dissections, one on instructional strategies and the other on renewal of mathematics curriculum. The first was awarded a master degree and the second gave me a PhD. Streams of residual income in the form of royalties keep flowing and increasing for years. I have created values for students to learn effectively and I also have created values for my financial freedom. Achieving financial freedom within a few years enables me to have the money muscles to help my relatives. Many of my brothers and sisters including my wife's brothers and sister are benefiting from my new calling. With financial freedom, I experience growth in investments like stocks, properties and business joint-ventures. Soon I have a few more streams of residual income and cash flow. I kept investing and ventured into other businesses. Eventually I enjoy plenty of cash flow and real financial freedom.

During my early teaching period, Google was not available.

Research materials were difficult to get. Today we have a different-level playing field. With the Internet facilities, we can easily turn our hobbies or passions into an online digital publishing. Remember time is your greatest friend. Give yourself enough time to practise the habits and beliefs of successful people until they become your lifestyle. This book will provide many useful habits and beliefs of successful people for you to follow. Fear is your greatest enemy. Do not allow the demon fear in your limiting beliefs to sabotage you from implementing the new set of beliefs and practices. Fear sells newspaper but it does not make you rich and successful. You not only deserve to be rich but it's your birth right to have it so that you can be a blessing to many people. That is my strong belief. I will do everything to become rich so that I can help many others who are not so fortunate. This is the philosophy of providing fish for others.

The first step we can take is to convert whatever talents we have or whatever savings we have into streams of passive income. Clarity of your mission is power. The clearer what you want is, it's easier for you to achieve it. If you are not sure of what you want in life, you will most likely to live your life aimlessly. You will hand your future to other people. I experienced such struggle before I started meditation, self-reflection and mindfulness. My journey of visualisation began and it became crystal clear that what I need to do is to manifest my desires. As I am reflecting, I have a burst of insight. The Internet publishing is a good place to show off your gifts and turn them into financial gains. It also helps you to grow and expand your passion. If you have some savings, the money can be invested in many ways for growth and create cash flow. Whatever talents you have, it is good to make your talents secure your financial freedom. Thinking, speaking and writing well are clearly important. If you are interested in writing just like me, then use it to create a stream of residual income in the form of royalty. You can also create your own website to start an online digital publishing. Many entrepreneurs in online digital marketing are enjoying financial freedom. You can be one of them.

If you are good in singing, use the talent to your advantage. Your voice can be trained further, fine-tuned and you can be one of the top singers making a fortune out of your hobby. Many NBA basketball players earn tons of money. The richest among them are Michael Jordan of Chicago Bulls and LeBron James of Cavaliers. They are both millionaires many times. Tennis player, Roger Federal is worth more millions. Once you have the money, it is time to make your money work for you. Stocks and assets will help you build your financial freedom. If you are interested in investment in stocks that works for you, then use it to create another stream of residual income in terms of dividends and portfolio growth. Investment in properties or assets is another possible stream of residual income in terms of rentals and growth. Here we are using good debt as leverage. A good debt is when your rental income exceeds the total expenses per month. It creates a cash flow into your pocket monthly. Building a business based on direct selling can also create another stream of residual income. Other types of companies know as real estate investment trust (REIT), gross domestic product (GDC) and master limited partnership (MLP) are required to pass over 90 per cent of their income to shareholders. They produce great yield for long-term investment. Majority of the people who become wealthy are involved in business, investment, stocks investments, agency for direct selling, Internet digital publishing or through their talents such as great sportsmen or sportswomen and entertainers. Unless you are talented in sport, singing or writing, otherwise using business as a vehicle for financial freedom is a good choice.

Create Cash Flow Using Business

First, if you want to make a lot of money, you need to learn to do something very well. Any profession, the one who earns the most, is usually the one who does his job best. There is no difference in business. Business can create plenty of cash flow if done correctly. Learning the fundamentals of any business by downloading the necessary skills from successful businessmen into your mind is your first step. Just like playing basketball. You must first learn the fundamentals such as dribbling, passing, shooting and lay ups before you can become a good basketballer. Before you pick basketball as the game, you must first look at your own height. Do you have an advantage? If not pick another game if you want to excel.

Just like business, you have to pick the one that suits your temperament and your qualification. Remember doing business is a skill that can be learned. Every successful business man experiences failure initially. Every successful person in sport, entertainment, business, politics, technology, direct selling... you name it, started at the beginning. Even T. Harv Eker failed in his initial business fourteen times in twelve years. He did not give up. He followed his passion in pursuing his health style industry and eventually he found success. Do you need so many years of your life to create your abundance? Do you think is possible for you to have a business that creates true wealth in a shorter time? Yes it is possible now. Most business secrets of successful people can easily be downloaded into your mind and you can start practising and implementing them to accelerate your wealth creation. Go into Google to read about the successful people in the business you have in mind. Learn their philosophy, their strategies, their secrets and their story of success. Once decided, it's time to eliminate all your beliefs and habits in your mind and start downloading new beliefs and practices into your subconscious mind. Get to practices these new characteristics consistently and playfully until they become your own strategies to success. Enjoying the process will enhance your productivity and success will be the only alternative.

Now let us get to the other part of the story. People lose money or make money through various businesses or investments. Every one of these ventures is different. There is no one single system that guarantees success. There is nothing wrong with any of the system that creates passive income. It is the people that screw up or abuse the system. A possible explanation is that if your subconscious mind is not ready to handle money, you're thinking and action will sabotage your success. Inadequate preparation and dedication are the main cause. If the business does not fit your temperament and skillsets, success is usually difficult to come by. Most people fail to build their business because of their mind-set. Their minds are not wired to succeed. Their old beliefs are their mental blocks. They do not do their homework by downloading new practices and habits of successful people in that type of business. Being ignorant and having inadequate knowledge or information, they have nothing to practise. It's the majority of the people not the proven systems that fail. It's important that you enjoy working with the revised system. You need to follow your passion. You can have fun as well as meaning working with such a revised system. If such alignment is found between your mission and work, you can create and perform at your best.

Strategies of Business Mind-Set and Creating Wealth

Remember, the investment market is always smarter than any of us. Show respect for the market. Our limited habits and beliefs will not help us. Get rid of them first. How to do it? I use meditation and visualisation or self-hypnotherapy. Mindfulness can be an advantage. Maybe you need a role model. Start downloading beliefs, practices and habits of the rich and successful in the business into your subconscious mind first before you take massive action to create residual income. To be wealthy, you need to emulate some of the strategies used by successful people in your chosen business. Most businessmen who work hard and only depend on themselves never become really rich. What type of business suits you? The critical thing to do is to identify the service or product you are going to offer. Plenty of research and consultation are needed. Once you have decided on the type of business, then you need to look into the fundamental skills you and your workers required. Look for a shortcut by downloading these skills from successful people in the field for yourself first and learn to use them effectively. To create wealth in any business, you need to hire and train a team of star players. You must know the various skills required to build a business so that you can replicate your business for growth. If you have to spend all your time doing it yourself, you have just got a job. To be wealthy and rich in any business, you need a team of good players to help the business grow. Once proven successful, you can start replicating your business. This is the strategy to be rich and successful. The following characteristics are necessary to expand and grow your business.

First, you need highly motivated people who are great in what they do and committed to perform their best.

Second, you need to systematise your business and know exactly what will happen at each stage.

Third, you need to reduce your time and involvement in the business without affecting its revenue. This will enable you to supervise all aspects of the business. This helps to focus your limited energy to ensure that your effort will produce the maximum revenue. This will help you to achieve financial and time freedom.

Fourth, you need to cut your expenses without affecting efficiency. This will help to grow your business, maximise your profit and serve the market needs.

Fifth, you must know the most profitable customers and who they are. While creating your profit, you must make sure that you make your customers happy. Keep duplicating your successful aspects of your business and cut those that are not profitable.

Since doing business is a skill, strategies used by successful entrepreneurs should not only be noted but also downloaded into your subconscious mind and implemented consistently. You need to think big if you want to be wealthy. You need to step out of your own comfort zone or way of thinking. Coming up with a new business idea is a learnable skill. Identify a booming business now! Which products and services are in big demand now? What are the changes required to boost the product or service? How to create revenue generating elements into the business? Do not forget that the level of happiness of your workers will decide the business productivity. A happy environment and a caring atmosphere will complement productivity. Plenty of visualisation and thinking based on those used by successful business people are the necessary to help to succeed.

Marketing is another skill required for success. Learn and download these marketing skills quickly, otherwise you do not have a business. Learn and emulate wealthy business men's ways of targeting their audience. Learn and implement the most effective way of doing it and the most unique proposition to increase your revenue. Research into strategies used by your peers and pick the best for your implementation. This will help you to visualise better and help you to see more effective ways of doing things. Practising these habits and beliefs will soon make you very wealthy.

Identify the asset of your company and how to leverage it to enhance revenue. There are many business skills you have to master. Learn the secret of negotiation is one of them.

First make a note how good businessmen negotiate. Practice this skill of negotiation as often as possible until you learn the street-smart method of negotiations in the real world.

Second make a note of the successful deals achieved by successful businessmen. Learn their strategies. Increase the number of successful deals as possible and your wealth will grow proportionally. Plenty of research is needed to enable you to master these critical skills.

To expand your business, you have to start training your star players to do the same. Each industry requires its own language to grow and blossom. Whatever business you pick, make sure you learn the language of the business well and speak it fluently. Ensure that your star players also speak the language fluently. Enthusiasm and working happily together will ensure your path to productivity and success in your business.

Follow Your Passion and Do What You Love

Another important factor to consider if you want to be successful is to follow your passion and do what you love. When you do what you love, you create purpose for what you do. With this, you probably increase the probability of success. You have added more energy, enthusiasm and excitement to what you do. Your project or business is more likely to be productive. Being productive, you become more competitive and success is on the way. Many of us in our work suffer from burnout because of interest and lack of enthusiasm. We dislike our work. We go through life feeling that we have missed out on something more. All of us are influenced by the sea of beliefs in our mind. Some beliefs are inspiring and they motivate us to take action. We form our rituals and routines that help us to succeed in what we do. We become passionate in what we do and this motivates us further. Unfortunately not all of us are in this type of situation. Many of us are influenced by outdated beliefs and experiences such as rejection or failures that they form views full of negativities. They procrastinate and they are half-hearted in what they do. They do not enjoy what they do. They suffer under the influence of poverty consciousness. Success is difficult to come by. They believe that this is their reality. What should they do? Many of them are not even aware that they are programmed to fail. Their subconscious beliefs are the real obstacles that prevent them from achieving what they desire. Every effort to work hard to achieve success in their career or project will be futile and unproductive. The purpose of this book is partly designed to help people who suffer under this type of situation. There are solutions to overcome this type of situation. The first solution is to think well. Thinking well requires clarity and help. My situation was overcome using repeated meditations and visualisations. Some people try using transformation hypnotherapy. I tried 'self-hypnotherapy' through meditation. I was determined to eliminate these unhealthy beliefs and habits from my mind. I knew vividly that this process has to be done first before I take massive action. I started to visualise the life I wanted and I started to think of solutions. The easiest solution for me is to unload the beliefs, habits and practices of productive and successful people into my subconscious mind. This book touches on some of the essential beliefs and habits of successful people. Their practices can easily be replicated. This is just the beginning, giving me the direction to move towards my goal. I started to implement these practices consistently, persistently and playfully. I was disciplined to succeed. I added flavour of joy into the process and started to enjoy doing them. These practices become by new habits and the laws of attraction began to favour me. I learn early that if I need helps or supports, I must provide them first. I learn that by creating values for others, I will be creating values for myself. I learn that by providing services for others I will be rewarded. I began to enjoy doing my work and soon I found my passion. My passion is to create values and helps to students' learning. By creating values for students, I am actually creating financial values to myself. It's a win-win situation. It's my contribution to education. This contribution turns into a money magnet for me. I have financial freedom. It enables me to follow my hobbies: travelling, playing golf and tennis, socialising, getting new experiences and keeping myself healthy. Abundance keeps smiling at me as I keep providing services and creating values for others.

It's easier to build our career, hobby or business if we are passionate about what we do. Choose to immerse your life with your passions; there will be no force out there to stop you from achieving your dreams. When you do what you love and love what you do, you become happy. You will do more with great enthusiasm and consequently your productivity will increase. What you need is to identify your passion in doing something. The three steps strategy: identify, download and practise whatever your interests lead you. In addition, use the four elements of the Mastery Strategy to accelerate your skill development. Success in your undertaking is the only way for you.

An Example of Success in Both Sport and Learning

Are you ready to take the first step? Are you ready to make the change? I was ready when I was in my secondary school in Penang - at that time I was where you are right now. I was hungry for knowledge and I was determined to think, speak and write well. Making the change must come from within you first. Dreaming to be a state basketball player became my daily wish. The desire to become an educator motivated me to master the three basics. I wanted to be rich. I wanted be healthy and happy. In short, I wanted to be a successful person embracing the three metrics: wealth, position of influence and good health to enjoy abundance. Enjoying the journey of my life became one of my goals. I wanted to be wise. Appreciating good things and the wonders of the world are my dreams. I wanted to contribute and make a difference in this beautiful world. I wanted not only to control my life but to make a difference in the life of thousands of people. Back then, it seemed to be an unreachable dream. I was staying with my eldest sister who provided me accommodation and food for me to study in Penang. I was not independent but dependent. So what did I do? At first I did not have any idea. I was already 16 years old having the brain of a 13 years old boy. I was studying in Form Two (Year Eight). I did not have a formula, system or direction. The only advantage I had at that point of my life is time and space. I had no room but a camp bag my sister offered me under the staircase. I had to fold up my camp bag before every person got up to go to work in the morning. This handicap became my advantage. Every morning at 6.30 am, I escaped to the basketball court to avoid the crowd at my sister's home. I only came back for breakfast after everyone had gone to work and my sister's children had gone to school. I attended an afternoon private school. I was an averaged student. I was not allowed to attend government-aided school. This allowed me to follow my passion because I loved playing basketball. Because of my environment, I developed a drill strategy to develop my skills in dribbling, shooting and various skills like lay ups necessary to excel in the game. This drill strategy became my routine every morning. Soon all the required skills to play the game well were embedded into my subconscious mind. The secret of my success in playing basketball well is repetition to master various skills. These skills became automated in my physical system. I do not have to think anymore to carry out these skills. I have developed an important weapon to help me excel as a basketball player.

After all the drill practices, I usually returned to my sister's home after 7.30 am to have my breakfast. I took a big glass of lemon juice drink before I started studying. I was in a big trouble because my English was poor and I could not understand most of the subjects. There was no one to help me at my sister's home. What can I do? The only person who could help me was 'me'. Every person has a breaking point and I was reaching mine fast. I used to close my eyes and visualise or imagine what I should do. I did not realise that I had started my journey in meditation. Taking control of my life had just begun. Thinking began to smile at me. I caught my reflection in the mirror. I almost screamed. A solution emerged. I felt something good was about to happen. A good English dictionary was my saviour. A step-by-step self-study approach was born. Every day I learnt new words and I started a collection of new words in English to help me understand my lessons. This repeated habits soon developed into my self-study strategy. Once I began to understand my lessons as my vocabulary improved, I started to prepare lessons ahead. After months of practices I soon developed my self-study strategy of pre-preparing lessons before I came to class. I even wrote down questions to ask my teachers regarding concepts I did not grasp during self-study. I did this consistently, persistently and playfully every morning. I was on the right track. Success seemed to smile at me at the threshold of my academic life whispering to me that I was on the right track. I caught the bull by the hone. This self-study strategy served me all the way in my learning process. I am very passionate about it and I love it. I begin to dream big. I wanted to do something big, leave a legacy and live the life I wanted. My dream finally came true. It is not luck or coincidence. I took relentless dedication and bold perseverance for my dream to become reality. My dream was to be a state basketball player. Another dream was to be an educator, writer, entrepreneur and an investor. I wanted to be rich, healthy and I want to enjoy life. I belong to the type of people who really implement what they know. I do not stop at small obstacles. I share good days as well as bad days. There is no guarantee and there never are. Nevertheless, I just do it. These steps are easily copied, pasted and duplicated by any one. I understand my fear and lack of knowledge. Fear is just a feeling you tell yourself. Knowledge is everywhere. Google provides everything. This book is another source. Before committing to take action seriously with the knowledge available, you need to change your beliefs and habits in your subconscious mind first. If I can do it, I believe you can do it too. An easy strategy for you is to eliminate the outdated beliefs in your mind and download the new beliefs of successful people, implementing them until they become autopilot in your life-plane. Once such habits are formed, you are on the way to a healthy, rich and successful life. By sharing this strategy with you, it can save you plenty of pain, heartache and money. My intention is simple. I want to empower you and equip you with practicable strategy to help you grow. My experiences tell me that once I found a system that works, I am going to repeat it again and again until I become rich. I also use the same consistent system that makes me healthy. I live to enjoy my financial freedom and my magnificent health. I look forwards to every day's excitement and joy. I am full of passion. I sprang out of bed every morning getting ready to welcome another beautiful day. Once you have clarity about your mission, the next step is to find the motivation to make it a reality.

My mission is simple. I wanted to do something to help make a difficult subject such as applied mathematics simpler. I came out with an idea of humanising the subject and making it relevant to students' experiences. I found my purpose. I was inspired by the idea. My contribution in terms of curriculum materials -textbooks and guide books -soon made their appearances. Two dissertations were written to spread the message of curriculum renewal. I started to spread the idea to teachers and students. I taught and lectured to my target audiences throughout the country. I was inspired and I loved it. Joy and happiness began to smile at me all the way. I am still writing and I am still enjoying my writing journey. I also made a fortune out of my passion and mission. In retrospective, I think I have made a difference to students' and teachers' learning styles. I did not set my goal to make me happy or making money. I set my goal to make learning simple and to create value for others. I work from inspiration and that guides my intention. These experiences seemed to provide excitement beyond imagination. My soul enjoys such feeling that no words can communicate. My intuition becomes my greatest guide. I make better decisions and my purpose is intact. I have control over my luck. My vision becomes crystal clear and within reach most of the time. I was liberated from all my past beliefs or hurts and I find myself energised. I was more connected to life and everything appears compassionate and calm. The idea of making a difference to learning applied mathematics inspires me. I enjoy writing and I enjoy adding human flavours to learn mathematics. All these activities enrich my life, add values to my life and lay the foundation of my happiness.

The Mind-Set of Innovative People

My observation reveals that the most successful people are not simply the hardest working but the most innovative. They do not work endless hours on their job. They make full use of their innovative muscles. Most of us work very hard with full concentration on our career, but we never get a breakthrough or experience financial success. The question we must ask ourselves is Why? Innovative people must be thinking differently from us. What are the characteristics of their thinking?

First, innovative people recognise patterns easily. They possess the ability to spot meaningful patterns within random data. They recognise relationship within an industry while others cannot. They have the skill to predict or anticipate a problem and think of a solution which becomes an innovation. They are able to think and put the pieces together to become a picture. They must have acquired the skill of thinking well and thinking creatively when they were young.

Second, innovative people appear lazy but brilliant. Some giant companies prefer to hire lazy but smart employees because these people always think of shortcut or easy way to do a certain job. It boils down to efficiency. Time is money. They know how to work smart but not hard. They think of doing the best product using the fastest route. Time efficiency is money saving. Productivity drives business. This is another tribute to thinking well and thinking creatively.

Third, innovative people are not only observant but they take notes of what they see and hear. They know that their conscious minds can only process a small chunk of information at a time. My reading and observation reveal that most great innovators are fanatic notes takers. History records that Thomas Edison left 3500 notebooks behind. Some of my successful innovative friends carry notebooks wherever they do business. I was able to write so many books because I have the good habits of keeping records of what I read and experience. I wrote down every note involving humanising the teaching of mathematics ideas down before teaching them. The creation of notes helps me to become a writer. As parents, help your children to keep notes of their experiences and ideas they read. This is the habit you can help them to cultivate.

Fourth, innovative people believe in perfection but they practise progress. They know if they discard perfection they embrace mediocrity. But they do not allow perfection to cripple their progress. They embrace progress and reality. Their aim is perfection but they keep their work going through stages of progress. I too make mistakes but I am not deterred by the lack of perfection. I try to be perfect but I know it is impossible. So I do my best and carry on with my writing.

Fifth, innovative people are just like us. They are also affected by fear of failure. They work well with their fear making fear an ally rather than an enemy. Fear becomes an adrenaline rush or push for them to succeed. Fear becomes an awakening force for them to take precaution and avoid unnecessary risks. They turn fear into an advantage to innovate and save cost. They take full commitment to survive at all cost. Fear uses to give me the signal to take precaution and drives me to think through or think of other possibilities.

Sixth, innovative people have an extra creative quality which we are lacking. They understand the four classic creative processes: preparation, incubation, illumination and implementation. Each innovator has his or her leisure way of discovering the creative processes. They have superior subconscious mind capable of synthesising information from the conscious work. Usually out of the blue, they find the solution to their invention after a period of contemplation, visualisation and imagination. I allow my habits of meditation and visualisation to help in my idea creation and writing. I have added a life vision to my visualisation. This helps me to form a final picture of what I desire at the end.

Seventh, innovative people are action oriented people. They do not wait for a thing to break before they start to fix it. In anything they use they always think of a better way to do it. They are constantly interacting and thinking of how to fix it better than waiting for the problem. They do not want problem to exist. They are able to anticipate the problem before it happens and they are able to fix it. The skill of anticipation before things happen can be learned through thinking well. Children need to be aware and start practising such anticipation. Parents are in good position to help children develop this skill.

Eighth, innovators usually have multiple interests. They think differently in terms of alternatives, not only for just extra income but also possible ways of making money. They give themselves opportunities for many projects to break the monotony of single project thus allowing them to expand their knowledge, challenge and overall business acumen. They learn to expand their means especially in business and use leverage to help them succeed.

Ninth, innovative people exhibit confidence and healthy arrogance. Studies reveal that confident people perform better under stressful situations. When we see risk, confident people see opportunities. When we see road blocks or failure in a project, innovative people see opportunity or victory. They are wired differently from us. They may not be the first to come up with an idea but they have the confidence to implement it and have the boldness to come out with the product. A healthy arrogance gives them the courage to take action and produce the innovative products.

Tenth, innovative people embrace all possible thinking. They just do not believe in either black or white, right or wrong, but all other possibilities. They tend to look outside the conventional boundaries and think outside the box. Many of them can hold two or three ideas at a time and still able to function effectively.

To be successful or innovative in your life, you should be aware of the above qualities, be able to tap into your unique strengths, align your vision with your intention and implement these characteristics after downloading them in your mind. You too can join the family of the innovators. As parents, we are in the best position to help our children by helping them to eliminate their outdated beliefs and start downloading these characteristics of innovative people into their subconscious minds. Encourage them to practise these new habits regularly. You never know your children's potential. They may also belong to the innovative class.

<u>Summary</u>

As parents, it's important that we develop the mindset of abundance first before we can influence our children. We need to embrace the new concept of abundance. The best is when we can lead by example. We live an abundant life embracing financial freedom, enjoying well-being and being happy, fulfilled and healthy. Our examples of creating income and cash flow speak louder than our words. Residual income and cash flow begin from an abundant mind-set. Exposure to approaches to create residual income is the right start. Various strategies like writing, singing, sports, business, network marketing, insurance marketing, and others are some of the examples. With the Internet facilities and the popularity of digital publishing and marketing, our children need to develop the basics such as thinking, speaking and writing well. If business is their passion, then it is necessary to expose them to the type of business that can be replicated and expended to create wealth. Otherwise, our children are only involving in business that gives them a job. There is no much room for growth. Planning and awareness are critical when they plan to do business.

All types of skills can be learned, even innovative skills. The important step parents must be aware of is that the outdated beliefs and habits of their children have to be eliminated and replaced by practices and beliefs of successful people or innovative people. It is just not enough to use positive statements or affirmations to change our children's mindsets. Instead of believing in a statement such as I am rich and healthy, we should teach our children to start looking for all the reasons why they should be rich and healthy. I believe this is a far more effective and empowering way to help attract positive things to their lives. This is the new power of affirmations. And we help our children to activate their subconscious minds to start working for them with all the new inputs. As parents, we need to encourage our children to practise these newly acquired skills and beliefs repeatedly until they become their own practices and habits. Parents need to be aware that the hopes and thoughts of your children do not create reality in their lives. Their beliefs and habits will help them to create reality. We need to be aware that their beliefs are wired deep down their subconscious minds. As parents, we are here to help them to shift and rewire their beliefs. Parents are reminded that your children's happiness is critical to help them accelerate how their beliefs create their reality. We can help them to know what reality they want to create. The people around your children especially parents, relatives and peers play an important role to help them create reality. Be aware of all these unconscious elements that can help your children to manifest their reality. Anyone can be successful and innovative when their passion is ignited. There are some practical ways to help your children to be more successful in their studies and eventually their working lives. Remind them to use the four elements of the Mastery Strategy to help them in any skill development. First, help them to get up early each day. Research shows that morning people are more proactive and more productive. This is a good habit for our children. This is the time for them to focus on things of priority and accomplish more. Second, teach them to start moving and stretching their bodies. They will feel better. Movement triggers their bodies to release stress and endorphin. Most successful people know this and take their health seriously. Third, allow them to form the habit of setting time for themselves, disconnecting from technologies to enjoy the activities they love such as playing a game seriously, reading a book, listening to music or spending quality time with friends and family. This will allow them to energise and replenish their mind and soul. Fourth, instil in them that their happiness is their choice, not the external circumstance. Help them to find joy in simple life. Encourage them to see the positive side of everything. They must make the decision to be happy themselves. Lastly, start them to plan ahead. Most successful people map out their days and have short term goals. They will help to develop a clear vision of what they want. This is the power of thinking and nurturing a good mindset. The future belongs to those who think well, speak well, write well and believe in the beauty of their dreams.

CHAPTER THREE

THE LANGUAGE OF MONEY

The First Lesson of Money

When I was a student, I believed that rich people are crooks and actually some are. I always think of some of the rich Indian money lenders whom my father borrowed money for emergence. From my father's point of view, if you have property or asset entrusted to these money lenders and if you are not careful in paying up your interest you can easily lose your asset in the mountain of interest over a period of time. These money lenders charge interest on a monthly basis. Imagine you borrow a thousand dollars at 10 per cent monthly interest. The next month, you owe the money lender $1100 and the following month, you own him $1210. After about seven months, your debt is almost double the amount you owe. This is the effect of compounding if you do not pay your monthly interest. No wonder, Albert Einstein said that compounding interest is the eighth wonder of the world when money is concerned. After a few years you would have lost your asset entrusted as surety. Most poor people like my father do not know the simple principle of compound interest. They borrow for emergence and they are perpetually paying interest for their debts. They do not understand interest rate and they remain poor. This shows the importance of understanding the language of money. The money lenders know the power of the language of money and they get richer and richer. This prejudice lingers on in my mind until I became rich myself. Now I realise that there are far more rich people who are honest, hardworking and trustworthy. Most of rich people are not crooks. They become rich through financial education, innovation, hard work, budgeting wisely, build businesses, creating jobs and values for others, creating cash flow and paying taxes. They speak and use the money language fluently. More importantly, many people become rich because they not only speak the money language fluently; they also set meaningful goals to help them become rich. This is the secret of the rich and famous. If you cannot figure out why you need to earn a million dollars a year, you probably will never make it. Many rich people earn big money because they have their goals worth pursuing.

Truth Path to Wealth

In my observation of people rich and poor, I notice that some people never become rich because they never conceive a meaningful goal why they should be rich. Nevertheless some become rich but they eventually wind up depressed, disillusioned and miserable when they realise that material wealth is all a grand illusion. On the contrary, many people become rich because they not only have meaningful goals, but also think of goals 'bigger than themselves'. Many wealthy people like Bill Gates, Warren Buffett, Ted Turner and many others are actually philanthropists. Warren Buffett pledges to give away 85 per cent of his wealth to charity. How do they become rich? How do I become rich? They are just like me, creating wealth by studying subjects not taught in our educational system. In fact Bill Gates left his prestigious university halfway to pursue his dreams. Most of the rich people pick up their financial education at home or from friends, but not in school. Bill Gates had it in his heart to improve the educational system and to care for the poor throughout the world. He has a meaningful goal to become rich so that he can contribute.

Here is another example. Ted Turner inherited his father's billboard company. He became an instant millionaire. That was not enough for him because he had a meaningful goal in his mind. He went on to develop a global TV news system for the world, particularly for the poor nations. He became a multibillionaire. He cared for the world environment and he donated $100 million a year for the United Nations for the next ten years. So if you want to be rich, you must set your meaningful goal first. Otherwise I am sure you never become rich. Remember: meaningful goals are more superior to just money-oriented goals. To make big money, you need the passion, drive and most importantly the reason for making money. This is the secret you need to master first before you can become rich. I can only speak for myself. When I was working and even now in retirement, I did not buy insurance for fear of losing my money. I always think of creating something which can benefit others in their lives. When I was teaching, I wanted to connect mathematics with daily experiences so that students could be interested in mathematics. I discovered the humanising strategy to help students learn and get interested in mathematics. In my retirement, I started to write motivation books with the intention of helping people living an abundant life. I don't care whether I can make money or not. I ignore the call of my spouse or relatives asking me to take it easy and do nothing to enjoy life. I enjoy doing what I love, I keep my passion alive and streams of residual income keep flowing into my account. My nest egg is still growing in my retirement. I have new freedom to help others especially my grandchildren and relatives in their education. If you want your children to become rich, you need to share with them the common significant thing rich and successful people have in common. Most of them achieve financial goals which enable them to fulfil their dreams of helping others.

This self-help book is written for people who want to give their children a financial head start, study about money, become rich, make contribution and live a happy and healthy lifestyle, which even the best students in schools never study in the school curriculum. Parents are in good position to teach the language of money to their children. I always remember what the late prime minister of Singapore had said:

> Give a man a fish and you feed him for a day. Teach a man to fish and you feed him for a lifetime.

He had just stated what Lao Tzu had said centuries ago. It is just like giving a boy twenty cents and he will come back for his next twenty cents. It is better to teach him how to earn twenty cents by doing some useful work as a reward. Once he learns that skill; he will never come back to ask for money. Perhaps our schools and institutions of higher learning fail to teach people how to fish. Another important aspect of the school curriculum should include teaching students how to grow and contribute by providing the weak with fish. I believe that if our children develop a passion for learning about money, its language and speak it fluently, they will never cease to grow financially. They will be motivated to set their own meaningful goals to become rich.

Dependent Mentality and Attitude

In Malaysia, Australia and even USA, it's glaring that not only the schools but the governments are teaching students that they are entitled to their daily fish. It is why more and more people are so dependent upon their governments and higher institutions for life support even academically. Many questions come to my mind. Our failure to teach our children how to fish can be one of the possible reasons why our economic culture is broken down. Unemployment, being unable to understand communication language in English, financial language, inadequate healthcare, dwindling financial resources, the loss of one's home and the dependent attitude are becoming the driving forces behind corruption, crime, immorality and broken families. Does giving the majority of the population fish in Malaysia or any country increase the people's dependence on government programs? I think so. We are encouraging our children, especially the majority's children, to form the dependent attitude or mentality. Even teachers who were given Malaysian Government loans for their university education refuse to pay back their loans when they are enjoying higher salary as graduate teachers. They even argue that they have good results in the university and therefore they do not have to pay back their study loans. They want their loans to be converted into scholarships. This is their entitlement mentality of the majority of the Malaysian children. These thousands of Malaysian graduate teachers are poor examples for their students. This sums up the troubling trend in the Malaysian education system where the majority of the population have developed the dependent attitude. Many of them are the teachers and lecturers who are going to pass the dependent attitude to their students. Little do these teachers realise they are depriving others of the critical loan necessary for higher education. Selfishness knows no limit and no boundary. I remember when I was at the University of Malaya in 1966, I turned down a state bursary when my second brother-in-law gave me $4 000 loan to finish my university education. I believe the bursary should go to another person who needed the money more than me. It took me twenty months after graduation to pay back the loan. I am very grateful to my brother-in-law for such a help. Our children who go to school and university are taught by people who never know how to fish and worst, they too have the dependent attitude. The majority children are taught to get good grades; join government service and earn a good salary. One good thing is that they are likely to become middleclass who will be paying most of the taxes. Our schools and higher institutions fail to teach students how to fish. There is no need to mention of teaching them to contribute and provide fish for others. Very few entrepreneurs benefit from our education system. Most entrepreneurs learn how to fish or to provide fish from reading, through contact with parents, friends and relatives. I believe that it is now time to teach our children how to fish and better, make them aware of how to contribute and provide fish for the needy. They need to be trained to become entrepreneurs and providers. Hopefully some of them will be in position to provide fish for those who are weak.

When I was in secondary school, I used to wonder why the school did not teach me about money. I wanted my teacher to teach me how to become rich. I did not want to be given fish daily and I wanted to know how to fish. Most importantly I wanted to contribute and provide others with fish. I wanted to be rich. But my teacher told me that he was not rich himself and he could not teach me how to become rich. Instead my teacher told me to study hard and get good grades so that I can get a job. Now I realise that most of my teachers could not help me to become rich because they did not have financial education themselves. They thought that learning about money is not important because they expected to be given a job as employee. Just like the Malaysian Government, my teachers and their unions are helping to spread the gospel of entitlement. They all work to become permanent staff or 'tenure' of the teaching profession or government service. They all aspire to have job security and retirement benefits. I know most teachers are good people. I was a teacher for twenty-three years after graduation. I did not enjoy good salary and I did not have a good pension. I obtain and enjoy financial freedom through other means. I learned financial education from friends and my own reading. Yet I feel disturbed every time a teacher or a government servant mentions the word *entitlement*. Very few civil servants in Malaysia and USA realise that their governments do not have the money to support these entitlement benefits. They are enjoying high salary now and hoping for a great pension. The governments are borrowing money to do it now. How long can this phenomenon last? Part of the money comes from taxpayers, fellow citizens and soon, from our children. It's important that our education system begins to change the entitlement attitude in our children especially children of the majority in Malaysia and everywhere. Every child irrespective of race should be trained to fish instead of being given fish. It will be better if our children are trained to contribute and provide fish for the weak.

In Malaysia, many leaders and ministers are not showing good examples. Their entitlement mentality starts with the prime minister. History tells us that these leaders always voted for their own generous entitlement benefit package and this seems to increase annually. They are good examples of dependent mentality. Another disturbing trend developing in Malaysia is that our ministers are encouraging their followers to strengthen their dependent mentality, claiming that it is the birth right.

A Paradigm Shift towards Financial Education

Education today is one of the biggest industries in USA, Great Britain, Malaysia, Australia and other countries. Parents are spending billions of dollars sending their children to elementary schools, high schools, colleges and universities. Governments are also spending billions of dollars to provide for elementary through university education. In addition the military also spends billions for all types of training to train young men and women to serve and protect their country. A lot of money is also spent by corporations and governments to train future leaders and technicians to repair and maintain equipment including computers, TVs and telecommunications. In spite of such large sum of money being spent for education, our children are facing an educational crisis. They learn nothing about money. They have been taught by teachers who do not know much about money. Most of us seem to believe that the love of money is the root of all evil. They believe that they are religious. They seem to forget that most people perish from lack of financial knowledge. Our educational system provides them with fish but does not teach them how to fish or to provide fish for others. They are fed for a day and become dependent on others to feed them. They are told to study hard and get good grades so that they can get a government job. They do not have to worry, the government will hire them. Our system does not teach them how to fish or provide fish so that they live a life time and helping others. Every student graduating from university is looking for employment. Some socialist governments believe in the economic philosophy of taking from the rich and give to the poor. Our children are trained to become dependent. This book is not about politics. It is about exposing our children to financial education. We don't want the next generation of children to cause another financial crisis in the future.

I had been a teacher for almost twenty three years after graduation. I know most teachers are great people. We are the products of the old system of education. Many people have been pushing to change the education system. But unfortunately the education industry is one of the slowest rates of change. In country like Malaysia and some African countries, their education system is exploited by politicians to remain in power. The lag time for educational reform is always long and tedious. Even with the explosion of information technology, the Internet and Google, we are still adhering to the old ways of teaching our children. With the availability of information, there is no longer necessary to teach history, geography and social science individually or separately. They can be replaced by lessons in thinking, speaking, writing and money management. It is more important that students are trained to think well, speak well, and write well. Students can learn anything about history and geography through projects using the Internet. Google will provide all the information necessary. The education revolution has begun but our schools are lagging far behind. In Malaysia, the government even makes history compulsory for Form Four students to learn all the rubbish which may not be true. The current Malaysian Government objective is control, indoctrination and manipulation so that the party in power remains in control. It's better to teach students thinking, speaking and writing than all the unnecessary facts. Any historical, geographical or social event can come under thinking and project exploration. Learning through involvement and doing in group encourage thinking and writing. At the end of the day, it's only thinking, speaking and writing that are important to our children.

Every child should know the simple lesson in financial education. Most of us who are employees are enjoying an active income known as linear income or ordinary income. Most people are paid hourly or monthly. Most of the poor and middle class people are having only stream of linear income. Some middle class are also enjoying portfolio income. The rich are different. They do not depend on their salary. They enjoy portfolio income, cash flow from business as well, and streams of residual income or passive income from their assets. Children need to know that different types of income are taxed at different rates. When governments raise taxes, usually the taxes of ordinary and portfolio income are involved. The new taxes seldom touch the rich because most of their incomes are passive or residual type. They enjoy cash flow from their enterprises. This clearly reveals that most of the taxes fall on the middle class. So the school advises students to study hard and get good grades so that they land on a high paying job. They work for ordinary or linear income. The governments also encourage and protect the middle class so that they can collect more taxes. Our parents and teachers advise us to save money, and the interest income on savings is taxed as linear income. Many questions appear in my mind. Why is our school teaching students to work for linear income? Many teachers who are earning linear income themselves do not know the different types of income. Students need to know that linear income is just ordinary earned income. Portfolio income comes from capital gain income and residual income is cash flow income like rental, dividends and other recurring income. All students should learn the language of money. Without such knowledge, they can never visualise the possibility of becoming rich. Ordinary or linear income people receive daily or monthly is usually poor people's income because the more they earn the less they keep. I experience it myself. In addition to my salary, I work part time as a lecturer in Colleges and Further Education classes. I managed to earn extraordinary income by working overtime. Earning more money pushed my linear income into higher and higher tax brackets. Again, the more I earn, the less I keep. Realising this, now I teach my children to avoid working for ordinary income. I do not want them to follow my path. Nowadays, I do not encourage my children to go to school, get a job, work hard, save money and invest in EPF (Employee Provident Fund in Malaysia). All these moves only generate ordinary income, the highest taxed of all income. Instead of saving money, I encourage students to invest for another type known as portfolio income or residual income. Middle class investors are counting on their stock market portfolio to keep them alive once they retire. Buying an investment property to produce rental is another source of residual income. Investing in portfolio income can also enjoy 'capital gains'.

All of us need some fundamental knowledge of financial education. Do you believe the politicians when they claim that the new taxes are aimed especially for the rich? The tax increases affect everyone especially GST. It affects the poor most. The rich people do not worry about the 6 or 10 per cent GST imposed on all goods and services. Other increase in taxes aiming for the rich actually affects everyone who works for ordinary income. Remember the rich do not work for money. Taxes are raised on those who invest in the stock market for portfolio income. The poor and the middle class are those who are heavily taxed. Financial education is essential for anyone who aspires to be an active investor in the stock market or the property market.

The rich usually avoids paying extra taxes legally. They work for passive income. The very rich enjoy passive income in the form of cash flow. The rich people teach this type of cash flow education to their children. Rich people have assets, stocks, bonds, and businesses generating plenty of cash flow. Many rich people do not need a paycheque. For example, the late Steve Jobs, CEO of Apple worked for $1 a year. He did not want a salary. He is one of the major shareholders of Apple worth billions of dollars. So technically earning $1 per year, he would be classified a poor man. He was not earning his salary; he has a big share of Apple's profit; and he was actually printing money. That made him very rich. He invested and reinvested his money so that he did not have to pay much tax. So he grew richer and richer all the time. This awareness is important for our children who aspire to become rich. There is an alternative path every child can take towards being rich or just a paycheque if one is equipped with the necessary knowledge. The school does not provide the money knowledge for a child to make the choice. It appears unfair because only parents who have the financial education can advise their children. This book is about financial education, not about being fair. Most of us want our children to get a good education and to get ahead in life. This is part of the reason why many parents send their children to private schools, hoping that a private-school education will give their children a head start in this competitive world. Private education is never cheap. The poor cannot afford. But do private schools offer financial education? Many do by charging parents a fortune. So by paying a fortune, parents hope that their children can get back a fortune when they enter the real cut-throat world. To me education is about more choices in life. If a child knows that it is better to generate passive including portfolio income instead of ordinary income, he has a better chance of becoming rich. They need financial education to help them acquire passive income. They can increase their income and reduce taxes by doing what the government wants done. They enjoy tax incentives and they know how to legally reduce their taxes. They provide jobs and receive tax-breaks. They use debt to invest and receive tax breaks. For example, some rich people receive tax-break by providing affordable housing to those who cannot afford to buy a home. Some drill for oil and they receive big tax incentives. Unfortunately, most students graduating from universities are looking for jobs rather than providing jobs. They leave schools or universities dreaming of buying their own home, rather than providing homes for others. My concern is that our schools and governments in Malaysia, USA and other countries are spreading the entitlement mentality. To bring about a paradigm shift in such entitlement attitude, we need to bring about financial education. I do not blame the students if the governments and schools are encouraging them. If I did not make it rich myself and if I were out of money, I probably would, too. As an entrepreneur, I faced some initial failures. The difference is that I knew I would become smarter and more successful if I solved my own financial problems, rather than expecting others to take care of me. This realisation is important. Our institutions have to start addressing this dependency and entitlement mentality before the country dissolving into a poor country. In my opinion, this has happened to some countries. It will happen to Malaysia or even USA.

Unfortunately, it will be many years from now before our schools start offering financial education. I cannot see the light from the educational tunnel in Malaysia or elsewhere. This awareness is telling parents to supplement their children with financial education. If most parents are not aware of this gap in our education system, most of our children's future earning will go toward funding government's entitlement programs for prime ministers, ministers, members of parliament, government bureaucrats, teachers, police, firemen and other retirees. It's a question of time when the government will become insolvent. Most countries' economic cycles will repeat. Depression will surface and a new government will start transforming and rebuilding for the future.

All students need financial education. At least they should know the different types of income and taxes. If parents understand it, their children will also pick it up. Every child needs to know of someone who has started a part-time business, owns a rental property or assets like oil palm estates, represents a network marketing company and owns value stocks with good dividends. All these revenues can generate passive income helping our children to become rich. Do you want your children to be rich? The hardest part for each person is to get started. I was armed with this financial education through the example of my father and my own reading. I became rich because of my exposure of these revenues. Keep in mind that the purpose of this book is to create financial abundance and to live a healthy lifestyle. I will focus on financial education first. The education choices and decisions a person makes throughout his working life determine whether a person spends his lifetime working for money or if he puts his money working for him. Education is a lifetime process and it is more than just an evening discussion with your child. Remember, the rich are welcome everywhere. And the first step is a solid financial education. So it is important that your child knows the rules of becoming rich and how to become rich. It's important to avoid encouraging our children to believe in entitlement or to wait for government entitlement programs.

As parents, we have many options. If you want your children to study hard and get good grades and find that high-paying job, they will join the middle class. They will work harder and harder to earn ordinary income and pay the highest taxes. The government will be happy to have your children in the workforce. And when your children invest, it is most likely they will invest in stock market for portfolio income or invest in second property for rental income. If you want your child to be in this category, you do not need much financial education. But if you want your child to escape the middle class rat race and become rich, there is an option. The other option is to join the poor. You have the freedom to choose to be rich, middle class, or poor. That choice starts at home. It all starts with the parents. If you teach your child that he is entitled to free fish (the poor), like the Malaysian government's encouragement, or work for fish (the middle class). It would be better if you teach your child to be a provider of fish (the rich). As parents, we have a choice. We need to teach children a better attitude to provide service and provide fish for the less fortunate.

The first step as parents is to do our part to end and to fight this entitlement mentality in our home. Many countries are facing economic collapse because a big proportion of the population have developed the entitlement mentality. This entitlement mentality usually starts in our home. Unconsciously, we are trading money for time or love. This happens in both rich and poor neighbourhoods alike. To keep up with your child's demands to keep up with classmates, we buy our kids high-end athletic shoes, toys or even cars. When your child sees a friend buying a new bicycle, your child feels that he is entitled also to a bicycle. Without knowing the consequence, we are encouraging our child the entitlement mentality. Some sports give every participant a trophy even if he comes last. What are we encouraging our children? That everyone is entitled to be a winner. We need to change our approach in rewarding our children. Instead of the entitlement in the form of money, we need to teach our children that money is simply a medium of exchange. You give something and you get back something in return. And children must learn that the more they give, the more they will receive. So when a child is given something for nothing, we have unconsciously planted the seeds of entitlement. Another quality we need to inculcate in our children is that they should learn to be generous. They should learn to provide help and support for others.

Being generous in words, in kind and gestures should be our nature. They should learn that if they give more they will receive more. If they bless others, they will be blessed in return. In other words they should learn to be givers instead of takers. This generosity of spirit is like a young tree that requires nurture and care before it can grow into a full-bloom tree. Parents are the first examples a child notices and their teaching is the most effective. Teachers are the students' role models. When the majority of our teachers have the dependent mentality, their role models give our children the wrong picture. A shift of mentality especially teachers is urgently needed. Hopefully, after reading this book, many teachers will make that necessary paradigm shift from the dependent attitude to a more generous consciousness. This awareness should be preached to teachers and leaders especially in Malaysia and USA so that they stop advocating the dependent mentality to our students and their followers. They should lead by providing good examples. By creating values for others, you are actually creating values for yourself.

Creating Residual Income Requires a Paradigm Shift

Most of us who hold a job and earn regular linear income never achieve financial freedom. We claim to have financial security as teachers or civil servants. We have an iron bowl. We live from paycheque to paycheque. I was in that situation before I started writing and investing. I made myself a promise that I would start 'side kicks' to give me a long-term payoff. I was lucky because I had already mastered my three basics: thinking, speaking and writing. What are the things I can do? It must not be in a business which distracts me from my teaching responsibility. Anything that does that will ultimately diminish my success as an educator. Something that can complement my teaching career is preferred. Choose something that does not take a lot of time but can give me extra source of income to increase my wealth. Life is too precious to waste by worrying about money. I do not want to retire worrying about my nest egg. Doing something that would ensure my 'never ending nest egg' is a better choice. I make the right choice and in my retirement I still enjoy an ever-growing nest egg from my writing and investments. I have to put into record my discovery of humanising the teaching of mathematics. Writing school textbooks and guidebooks is a natural choice for me. It complements my teaching. When I wrote my first mathematics textbook, I was offered a certain fixed sum to do the work. I did not accept it. I chose to work for free. I wanted to change my mindset instead of working for a paycheque. Working for recurring royalty instead of a paycheque motivated me. I was prepared to create wealth out of nothing. I made the right choice and discovered my talent as a writer and investor. The journey for entrepreneurship began. A paradigm shift from linear income to residual income began. The outdated belief of just earning for linear income was replaced. The creation of more streams of residual or recurring income continued. This shift of mentality provided me with a feeling of calm, compassionate, creative and limitlessly power to fulfil my mission of financial freedom. The feeling of indiscernible connectedness between my intuition and my external universe was given a push. My calling to serve humanity was triggered. I wanted to contribute to human mental growth and provide service to help others. The more contributions I make, the more returns I get. The discovery of the financial paradigm shift whispers to me that I am moving in the right direction. The more I meditate, the more entranced this new belief becomes rooted and the more I believe, the more actions I take, the more contributions I provide, and I soon become rich by creating more streams of residual income. During meditation, whenever I reach an alpha state, my visualisation becomes clearer and my actions become easier.

Today the world is different. Opportunity for publication abounds. The Internet is a new tool for us to get our digital products to the world. Learn to create a website to market your speciality, your passion and your hobby. You have some special knowledge others need urgently. So create something based on what you know best. Look into common fields that are popular. This critical awareness is important. The more competitive and popular the field is the better. Do not worry that you may not have a big slice of the big pie. A small slice of that gigantic pie is far better than you have the whole piece cake when nobody wants. Check out in Google. Many successful entrepreneurs make use of the Internet to become rich. The reward is beyond imagination. Read into the advertisement found in the Internet. The world is moving into online marketing and digital publishing. As parents, it's time to let our children know the importance of mastering the basics: thinking, speaking and writing. Writing well will be an important source to become rich.

More than One Possible Solutions in the Real World

In school, our kids are so used to right or wrong answer. If they score more right than wrong, they pass. They get good grades. If they get most of the answers right, they get grade A. In the real world, that is not realistic and it is not intelligent. Many life problems have alternative or possible answers. In school, there is only one right answer according to the texts or teachers. If most of your answers agree with the teachers' answers, you get good grades. This is the foundation of academic education. But in real life, there is always more than one right or possible solutions. We have to learn to choose the best answer that suits our ability. Can we have the ability to hold two opposed ideas in our mind and still function effectively? If we can, we have a greater chance of succeeding. Many of our children go to school, believing that only one answer can be right. This seems to close a student's mindset instead of opening it. Students are trained to believe in only one point of view, to see only one perspective and only one possibility. I remember when I was teaching Applied Mathematics, I usually challenged my students to think of other possibilities. Is our universe the only one? There may be a possible infinite number of universes! Our universe is made up of the earth, the moon, the stars, the galaxy, the inhabitants and its gods. The possibility of parallel universes is always there. Thinking this way led to my discovery of humanising the teaching of mathematics. The relationship between applied mathematics and human experiences is revealed. This enhances the meaning and learning of mathematics. It connects mathematics to finance and other fields.

Other alternative views are exposed. Many literature books like *Robin Hood*, who took from the rich to give the poor. It seems to condemn the rich and honour the poor. Our students are not taught to see both sides of the stories. Do we need capitalists? Do we need entrepreneurs? Do we need innovators? Do we need people who can provide fish? Do we only want people who only ask for fish? Parents have a choice. Any government has a choice. Do we want only people with the dependent mentality? People have a choice. Our children have a choice. Choose wisely.

The Bible is a great book. Surprisingly money is the most discussed topic in the Bible. Almost half of the forty or more parables told by Jesus in the Holy Bible concerns money. Is the Bible balance? To the believers it serves its purpose. The emphasis on money reveals the importance of financial education to our children. This book is about financial education and financial freedom. It helps to look at money from different points of views. Which point of view is better? Receiving fish daily, catching our own fish or providing others with fish! The choice is for our children. As parents we are here to guide them in making the choice. It is no longer the choice of right or wrong. The school system only provides a linear connection between right or wrong. In real-life situation, nothing is linear. Nothing is simple. In mathematical physics, everything comes in the form of waves undulating back and forth allowing for balance and sometimes corrections. Similarly in real-life situations, we have ups and downs, creating waves of new experiences and courses of alternative paths. Nothing we experience is straight forward. Even the stock market follows an unpredictable path of ups and downs depending on the investors' perceptions and the actual performance of each stock. A paradigm shift for parents is urgently required. We have to allow this paradigm shift in thinking to reach our children as early as possible. This will lay the foundation for them to think well, speak well and finally write well.

The financial journey of our life is never a straight line. Every one of us needs to learn to chart our own financial life. I have done that magnificently, I had celebrated the high points of my life and had also learned from the low points I experienced. Many lessons are learned. There is no right or wrong answer, but rather a wave of choices, from different points of views and different perspectives. Do I live a magnificent life? If a magnificent life resides in the village called innovation, enjoying creative works, enjoying writing, building abundance, enjoying games, keeping fit and healthy, I am almost there. Do you want your children to live a magnificent life? All these information and knowledge, if implemented consistently and persistently, will help our children to accelerate the evolution of consciousness in creating financial freedom and living a healthy and happy life.

This book helps parents to look at financial intelligence and financial education differently. Money has its own language and terminologies. Unfortunately our schools do not teach such a language with its terminologies. A simple way to look at money intelligence is the ability to get out of the trap of a right-or-wrong world that the school system promotes. We need to teach students to look at money from many sides, as many perspectives as possible. We need to look at the highest level of human existence. We need to put aside prejudice, accept facts and there is a possibility of more than one answer. One needs to be a generous giver rather than a taker. Providing help, we get help. A simple law of abundance tells us that if we create values for others, we actually create values for ourselves. This consciousness evolution begins at home with the examples of parents. It's important that we teach our children to serve others and in return the universe will provide abundance. One needs an open mind in learning the money language. The languages of economics and finances are different from the ordinary language. Each has its own definition depending on usage and application. All these extra information will ensure that you operate and help your children to function at a higher state of consciousness.

Understand the Language of Money

The world's greatest investor Warren Buffett has many entertaining quotes which reveal perfect insight into how money works and what it really takes to grow wealth. His humorous insights, colourful commentaries and wise advices have enriched the language of money. He is famous for his two rules in investment. Rule number one is never lose money. Rule number two is never forget rule number one. His quotations are humorous when he said:

> "In investing, you should get high value at low price. Price is what you pay; value is what you get. In investment, losing money can happen when the price you are paying does not match the value you are getting."

A good example is when you are paying high interest rate on credit card debt. Another example is buying things you never use. What value do you get? He encourages us to form healthy money habits.

Warren Buffett added and said:

> Most behaviour is habitual and they say the chains of habits are too light to be felt until they are too heavy to be broken.

But habits are changeable and the earlier we do it the better. Most of us neglect the habits of saving. That's why many of us never become rich. Many of us live with the motto, 'Spend now save later' - believing that we should spend with our hard-earned money while we can and 'You only live once' (YOLO). Please note that the longer we wait, the harder for us to cultivate the habit of saving. After all the longer we get used to the lifestyle, it's harder to downgrade to a more prudent way of living. As parents, we should start teaching our children to pay attention to money habits and help them to strengthen those habits that help their finance and break those that hurt their finance. The habit of saving is important so that we always have cash ready for emergency. Our accumulated saving can play an important role for our financial freedom. The earlier you start saving and investing, the more years for your money to accumulate interest and compounding it over time. Before you start investing in assets or stocks, a wise strategy is to invest in yourself. What does it mean? You can be your greatest asset. Warren Buffet explains:

> Anything you do to improve your own talents and make yourself more valuable will get paid off in terms of appropriate real purchasing power. Anything you invest in yourself, you get back in ten folds; nobody can tax it away; they can't steal it from you.

If we are to examine Buffett's two rules of investment, they appear to be not that useful for us as investors. There is another rule, known as the third rule of investing. It is simple, most great investors like Warren Buffett, Soros and others know the true value of a particular stock before they buy it. Once they know the true value of a stock, they know whether a particular stock is traded above or below its true value. Whenever sentiment is bad, all stocks are oversold and their prices fall. These great investors know the true value of the stocks they are going to invest. The moment arrives, they will scoop up these stocks which are terribly undervalued. They will hold them until the stocks revert to their true vales and more before they start selling them. They will laugh all the way to the bank. This third rule of investment is employed by these great investors again and again. This partly explains why they are rich and wealthy.

Ordinary people like us are ignorant of the third rule of investment. We are ignorant and we remain poor. We are advised to learn more about financial education and how to manage our money. Remember that risk comes from not knowing what you are doing. Many of us do not understand the language of money such as simple interest, compound interest, asset, bad debt, good debt, bonds, REIT, stock and liability. Knowledge is critical before investing. Knowing and using the wonder of compound interest can help to build your wealth. We need to view money and investment as a long-term game. Building financial freedom takes time. There will be challenges all the way. Look at the huge tree in our botanical garden. Someone had planted the tree long time ago and we are enjoying its shade. When you are young, you should start planting and nurturing the seeds of financial success so that you can enjoy later the cooling shade of financial freedom, a secure retirement and the ability to pay for your children's college education. Where do you begin? Learn the language of money first. Do you believe that there is such thing as the language of money? We know the language of the basics: thinking, speaking and writing. We know the language of abundance and the language of happiness. We have just learned the language of fitness and good health. Now you are exposed to the language of money. In order to master the language of money, there are some fundamental terms we have to comprehend before we can understand the larger picture of finance. Here are some of the essential terms which we need to understand.

Types of Debts

I never learned the language of money when I was a student. My dad taught me a little bit about the language of money when I was 12 years old. When I started as a graduate teacher at the age of almost 30 years old, I remember what my dad told me that if I depend on my salary, I will never become rich. I did not understand the meaning of good debt from bad debt when my dad explained it. I started reading into the issue when I started working. When we borrow to consume like credit card debt, we spend money before we earn it. This is bad debt. The interest is high. My father used to borrow money for doing business when he was short of fund. He told me that was good debt because the money he borrowed generates money for his profit. He also borrowed from the bank to buy his first real estate. That is also good debt. The income from the real estate exceeds its mortgage. Now I know that money has its own language. There is bad debt and there is good debt. In doing business and real estate investment, my dad needed management and people skills. My dad told me that by investing this way, he is using debt and taxes to his advantage. The difficult part is managing the real estate or business and profitability.

The language of money can be complicated. The English language has almost a million words. We do not need to know all the words to use the language effectively. In fact knowing about ten to twenty thousand words is enough for me to write this book. Similarly our children do not have to know everything about the language of money to be able to become rich or enjoy financial freedom. I believe knowing the common words used in money transaction will enable them to have a good start in financial education and intelligence. This implies that our children will have plenty of room for increased intelligence related to the vocabulary concerning the language of money. The following will introduce some of the common terms or words we usually hear during daily conversation.

Income

Every child should know that there are basically two different types of income. When you are paid hourly or monthly, the type of income is linear. Linear income is also known as ordinary income or active income. Your salary full time or part time is a linear income. If you are paid royalty repeatedly for the products you produced or other forms of recurring payments like rentals, profits and dividends, then the streams of the income are known as residual type. Residual income includes portfolio type as capital gains in investments.

Linear income will not make you rich but streams of residual income can. As parents this vital information must be made known to our children. The intention of this book is to make available strategies to create residual income and cash flow to help our children to become rich.

Expenses

Expenses are also known as liabilities. Expenses take money from your coffer. For most families, expenses come in the form of housing, food, clothing, transport, medical care, education and entertainment. Note that your home can also be your liability. It takes money from your pocket in the form of mortgage,

assessment, quit rent, electricity and water bills, furnishing and maintenance. The only advantage you enjoy later on is capital gain. But not all home owners enjoy capital gain. The last housing bubble burst in 2007 in USA caused many million people to lose their homes without capital gain. In fact they abandoned their home because the mortgage they got from the bank is higher than the worth of the house during the bubble burst. Teach your children regarding this concept that your home can be a liability. Do not encourage your children to buy their first expensive house to create their first big liability. It's more logical to buy a small house as the first home and upgrade as the family demands after a few years of working. Financial planning is the key towards financial freedom. Do not be convinced by sale agents that your house is your greatest asset. It may turn out to be your greatest liability when you lose your job in any recession.

Simple Interest and Compound Interest

Normally when you save money in any bank you receive a certain percentage of interest. The bank uses your money, pools it with other people's money and loans it out at higher rates. The bank may pay you 5 per cent interest rate and charge the borrower 8 per cent interest rate. When time is good, you get 5 per cent of interest annually on your deposit. Every thousand dollars you save, you receive $50 as interest at the end of the year. This is simple interest for the year. If you allow the interest and capital to accumulate, by the end of the second year, you receive another 5 per cent on the accumulated capital $1 050. The total amount you have at the end of the second year will be $1 102.50. If you allow your interest and capital to accumulate for five years, you are actually collecting compound interest. How much do you have at the end of five years? Do some thinking! Albert Einstein called compound interest the eighth wonder of the world.

Nowadays governments are talking about implementing negative interest rate. Japan is practising negative interest rate to stimulate its economy. What does it mean to you? Negative interest rate simply means that your bank is going to charge depositors (you) a fee for storing your money. Is it a perversion to saving? I think so. Instead of stimulating the economy, governments are stimulating disaster. I think forcing people to pay banks to hold their money is a tax. Where do you put your money? Governments want you to spend or invest in assets to stimulate the economy. What do you do? One possible answer is buy gold or silver as an alternative. These precious metals will not charge you interest or corrode. Its price will be forced to go up.

Assets

Anything that adds money to your coffer is an asset. If you buy a second or third property to rent out, it can become an asset. If you buy an oil palm estate, it is also become an asset. What you need is managerial skill to turn the asset into a profit. The revenue generated from the asset must exceed its expenditures. Otherwise you may end up buying a liability. A real estate is also a challenging asset class. Buying an asset involves debt, a good debt if managed properly. The ultimate goal of any asset is profit or cash flow. You need to learn a new property management language. There is no room for failure and novice real estate investors get into trouble. If you speak the language well, the benefits and rewards can be very attractive. You get both capital gains and cash flow. My own investment experiences are good examples. When I started working, I bought a simple double-story terrace house for $32 000 as our first home. I put down a down payment of almost $5 000 and the rest I borrowed from a bank. The mortgage per month is manageable. I knew that my first home is not an asset. It was a liability for five years because it took money out of my pocket. With some saving, I upgraded my home to a semi-detached house costing about $72 000. It took the developer two years to complete the project. After my family had shifted into my new home, I was ready to sell my first house for a profit. I was aiming to buy an asset in the form of a shop-lot to maximise profit. Residential property usually does not generate good rental. Timing is in my favour. When I put up my first property for sale, the price of real estate had tripled. I sold my first property for a big profit which enabled me to purchase my first shop-lot. This asset provides my family with a recurring income for many years. I have got a goose that lays a golden egg every month in the form of rental. After a few years, I bought another shop-lot next to my first shop. I have got two geese laying two golden eggs every month. I kept these two golden geese for almost forty five years until I sold them. The capital gains plus the rentals in the form of cash flow for forty five years come to a few thousand times the amount I paid for the investments. I believe many parents are keen to teach their children about liability and asset. Information and knowledge are critical to use them correctly for the sake of financial freedom.

Paper Assets or Stocks

Paper assets usually refer to stocks, mutual funds, bonds and Real Estate Investment trust (REIT), which are saleable in the stock exchange. Many stocks and REIT produce dividends or income sharing which is a form of residual income. Some of the dividends are frank meaning that the tax is paid by the companies. These forms of investment do not enjoy tax and debt advantages. Any capital gains are subject to tax as ordinary income. Most of the millionaires of the world hold paper assets. With inflation at about 4 per cent annually, one of the safest investments we can have is still stocks. Buying shares of a company or stock is actually investing in a business. Knowledge is important. Investing in any growing business will make you rich when you retire.

Commodities

Commodities include oil, coal, gold, silver, coffee and other food stuff. Each commodity has its own language. They are also traded in the commercial market. Many of them enjoy tax advantages. Gold and silver are serving as insurance when the market is facing uncertainty. In USA, with so much money printed under quantity easing (QE), I believe some commodities are good insurance for your money in the future. Every commodity has its own economic cycle within years. Each cycle is analogous to the sea waves going up and down in a period of time. Understanding each economic cycle will be an advantage for your children if they invest in commodities-related companies. For example in 2014 to 2015 the price of oil is affected by glut and it's falling. Investors need to be careful when investing in oil stocks. The period of glut will last longer than we expect. Patience is the key if you are thinking of investing in oil stocks.

Businesses

Many of the rich people are usually involve in businesses and stocks. If you want your children to be rich, business is a good alternative. To be an entrepreneur, you need to learn to speak many languages such as the language of engineering, law, accounting, marketing, leadership and more. You need not to be fluent in all these languages. You need to be a generalist, able to understand the basic to these languages that support your business. Our institution teaches us to be specialist and narrows us to know less and less about the universe. Entrepreneurs are generalists who speak and understand many languages of businesses and professions. They mingle with people of various fields and work with all types of workers from A students to C students. As parents, if we want our children to be businessmen, we need to expose them to many languages of various industries. This will give your child a good start. My observation is that many children tend to follow their parents' footsteps regarding business.

Liabilities

What are liabilities? Anything that you do which takes money from your pocket is a liability. You buy a home to live in, you pay mortgage, it is a liability but a necessary one. Your credit debt is a liability. Your car payment, the bills you pay every month and expenses are liabilities. But you must know that when you buy a rental property, the debt is not a liability. It is usually covered by the rental. It can turn into an asset if the rental exceeds the mortgage payment and other essential payments like quit rent, assessment and others. Taxes, mortgages, assessment, quit rent and others are liabilities. When buying a rental property, the cash flow is important. If the rental exceeds all the liabilities, you have a positive cash flow. You need to be a competent entrepreneur to make sure that you invest in assets which put money into your coffer. If you do not manage well, an asset can turn into a liability.

The Two Faces of Debt

Any debt that takes money from your coffer is a liability. This is the bad face of debt. In your family account, you have many liabilities. Your credit card debt is the worst. If you forget to settle the debt in time, it incurs interest, another form of debt. Our schools do not teach children about debt. Most students who leave schools are deeply in debts with education loans and credit cards. When I left university after my degree, I was $4 000 in debt. It was a loan given by my second brother-in-law. I was lucky the debt did not incur interest. With financial education, children will learn that there are good debts and bad debts. But not all debts are liabilities. Some debts are assets. This is the good face of debt. Good debt makes people richer and bad debts make people poorer. A money lender lends someone $1 000 at 5 per cent monthly interest, that debt is his asset but the borrower's liability. As mentioned earlier, the debt of buying a second property for rental is an asset. An entrepreneur makes use of this unfair advantage. Since debt is the new money, a financial education will be necessary to use debt as an advantage. If you want your children to be rich, they have to learn using debt to acquire assets such as real estate or properties. We need to teach children to be generous to choose a type of investment that serves the real need of society like providing affordable housing. By doing such act, they can earn passive income and pay less taxes.

I learned early that I can use debt or other people's money to buy assets and make money. This type of unfair financial education can bring infinite benefits. Most rich people use other people's money to build their fortunes. This is a tool you can introduce to your children if you want them to be rich and happy. You must be aware that if a debt is not managed well, then it becomes another liability.

Cash Flow

Most rich people understand the power of cash flow. It is the most important financial word. In any household budget, it is important that you have a positive cash flow. In simple terms, your income per month must exceed your expenses or your assets must be larger than the liabilities. For rich people, their income springs from businesses, real estates, paper assets, commodities and capital gains. Capital gains occur when the value of an asset or stock increases in value. I bought my first property at $32 000 and sold for $140 000 after five years, I have a capital gain of more than $100000. Capital gain in a stock is the aim of most investors. The actual net cash flow is the total profits minus expenses including the capital, taxes and commissions. But not all properties or stocks you buy will provide cash flow. If you sell your property or a stock at a price less than your purchasing value, you lose money, then it becomes a liability. Our home can become our liability. Robert T. Kiyosaki created this controversial saying that our home is not an asset. He is partly right and partly wrong. Many Americans experienced the liability during the housing bubble burst. But I experienced capital gain when I sold my first house or home for five years. To me the home is a relative asset that is not all homes are assets. So management, timing and strategy of investment are important to create cash flow.

The Choice of Money Language

Every one of us is different. The money language each of us speaks will be different. Rich people speak affluent language and poor people speak the language of lack. As parents, we think differently. All parents want their children to speak at least a middle-class language or the rich man language. So it's our responsibility to expose our children to different careers and life experiences. Remember that most habits are not taught but they are actually caught as children grow up. My own experiences tell me that if I want my children to be entrepreneurs, knowledge of business, stock investments and real estate investment are the necessary fields for them to understand. They will learn real-life experiences necessary for them to become a professional in these fields. My real-life experiences just reinforce this belief. They need financial education, managerial skills, dedication and resilience. If our children are not interested to be an entrepreneur, then paper assets, properties and commodities are better investments for them. Many grades A and B students will do well because the skills involved are similar to classroom skills. They can sit in front of their computer screen and trade the world. They do not require interpersonal skills, leadership skill, emotional intelligence but they too require financial education. If parents just want their children to have a well-paid job, then it is enough to get good grade and get a good job. They will earn linear income and mostly likely become middle class, paying the most taxes. If you want your children to be poor and live with a dependent mentality, then you do not have to teach them anything. Just tell them to enjoy themselves, and the government will take care of them when they are old. You can help them to dig the grave of poverty and develop the dependent mentality. They will live on the fish provided by others.

Expand Your Means

We are so used to the idea that we should always live beneath our means. With financial education such an idea may not be very good. There are many wonderful things in life we want our children to enjoy. So living beneath their means can kill their entrepreneur spirit. When a child leaves home, he faces many expenses such as rent, food, clothing, transportation, entertainment and many others. All these bills are usually paid using their credit card. It depends on the size of his paycheque. He needs to learn how to balance his budget. When he gets married, extra burdens in the form of extra expenses are incurred. Unless there are two or more streams of income, the balancing of the budget can become a problem. They will tell themselves that they should live beneath their means. They want to work hard to become debt free. Being debt free from the angle of consumer point of view is a good idea. But without financial education, very few people know that they can actually use debt to acquire asset to generate cash flow to expand their means. Parents should encourage their children to make use of this advantage to expand their means. This will provide outrageous opportunities to be creative and build extra wealth. I did that successfully. First I added extra streams of income by working part time and working during night time to increase my income. With a little bit of saving, I took advantage of debt to acquire an asset to generate a positive cash flow. After a few years, I manage to use further debt to acquire my second rental property to increase further my cash flow. From assets I ventured into paper assets to enhance my cash flow until I became wealthy. You see all us can use good debts to expand our means. Most people fear debt because they have been indoctrinated with the fear very early in their life. Parents and even teachers without knowledge of money always advise children not to get into debts. They are right for us to avoid credit card debt. But most of them are ignorant of good debts that can expand our means and enhance our cash flow. This limiting belief regarding debt is deeply planted in our subconscious mind. This explains why most of us never become rich because we fear debt, even good debts. Before we download strategies to expand our means and using good debts into our mind, we need to be aware that we have to eliminate our outdated beliefs about debts first before downloading a new set of beliefs and practices using good debts to help us to become wealthy. How to do it? My tool is simple. I use the process of meditation until I reach an alpha state of brainwave vibration. During this state, I usually experience deep relaxation of the mind and body. My problem-solving ability increases and my creativity moves to a higher level. I reach peak performance and even my immune system improves. My subconscious mind becomes more malleable and it is easier to eliminate limiting beliefs which have been holding back my life. For example, adolescents take on new beliefs more readily than adults because the former experience more alpha state on average than the latter. So if you feel that there is a gap between your life now and the ideal life you want to live, then it is time to start unloading characteristics of innovative people in investing into your subconscious mind. One of the strategies is to make use of good debt to produce cash flow and extend your means in creating wealth. Other means can come in the form of creating streams of linear and residual income to help in building funds for investing in stocks. Implementing these characteristics takes time and patience. Keep practising these strategies until they become parts of your thinking and beliefs. Soon all your fear, doubt and uncertainty will disappear. Procrastination is forgotten. Confidence will start to smile at you and wealth creation is on the way. You learn the meaning of leverage and the powerful force of compound interest. Regardless of your intention, if you want to be wealthy, the following terminologies are essential for creating wealth.

Entrepreneur and Technological Inventions

The world is totally transformed by the advancement and globalisation in information technology (IT). Who are responsible for all these advancements? We have to thank many of the billionaire entrepreneurs like Bill Gates, Steve Jobs, Elon Musk and many others. While enjoying the technologies, software and applications of IT in the various forms, people are expecting new technology and products that are going to make their appearances. Very soon many of us will be driving rechargeable electric cars using lithium battery. At the present moment, we are witnessing web applications, online shopping, trading and services, mobile applications, social networks and calling services. IT has also become essential services to engineering, medicine, business administration, mathematics, accounting and finance. Soon every aspect of business and human life will be touched by using IT products, services and applications. Entrepreneurs are in big demand especially for linking interdisciplinary and cross disciplinary fields. Opportunities for IT professionals and entrepreneurs in all fields are just the beginning. We are just witnessing the new technologies involving mobile phones and handheld and pocket devices with intelligent systems and applications. The world is now in our pocket. With a single touch, we are connected through social networks like Twitter, Facebook and Linkapp. We can call or send a message to anyone using services like WhatsApp, Viber, Skype, Vimeo and Line. Any news reaches everywhere within minutes. Besides our PC and laptops, smart phones and tablets can also do the same tasks. These inventions are getting cheaper and cheaper through economy of scales. People have plenty of choices. Smart phones like iPhone, Galaxy, Huawei and others are available everywhere. These technologies and services are no longer luxuries or fun anymore. They become a necessity for almost every person, company, business, job, household and employees. The availability of the support of WiFi, LiFi, 3G and 4G services have totally transformed the widespread usage of smart phones and tablets. A large number of smart, interactive and lightweight mobile applications for all types are available to more and more people. This is the beginning. Many banks, companies, government departments and social networking websites are offering their services and applications to smart phones users. All these advancements enable us to make payments and needs easily through our smart phones.

Our life especially for our children's life will never be the same again. These technological evolutions have completely changed the trends and preferences of all sectors of economies and societies. Every child is not spared. The earlier your children are exposed to these advancements and usage of IT technologies, the better they are prepared for their new world. Teach our children how to fish by allowing them to use the essential tools in school first. Include financial education such as accounting, cash flow and budgeting when our children start their usage of smart phone and computer. Be aware of abuse and excessive expenditures involving these tools. Initial parental guidance is critical to avoid exploitation and predators. Children have to be guided on the correct path of using these fantastic tools. There are plenty of rooms for entrepreneurship, professional growth, services, business and applications.

Summary

Money smarts is a vital lesson not taught in our school. What drive the economy? Most of our perceptions are actually wrong. The world economy is driven by the people. Our children are the people who will drive the world economy. We have just seen what drives the American economy. The baby boomers (about one third of the American population) are responsible for American prosperity over the last fifty years. They control over 70 per cent of the American wealth. They are retiring in batches now and they are liquidating their assets preparing for retirements. The result of the real estate bubble in 2007-2008 is one of the consequences. The same phenomenon prevails in many developed countries. Many other disasters are coming as they exit the workforce and the stock markets. Whether we like it or not, we are likely to determine our kids' future prosperity. The language of money should be taught at home as early as possible. A first lesson is to make our kids earn their pocket money. Children will learn quickly that money is earned not awarded. We will have avoided creating a false, destructive expectation. It would be great if we encourage our children to work for their pocket money. Another exposure for young children is to discuss money on the menu. It would be good if we can chat about our family finance over dinner. Children will learn the income coming in and the expenditure going out. Money is finite and has to be managed. It would be great if we can share our financial goals with our children and how we are going to achieve them. Teach the wonder of compound interest and other money terms. Children will learn that delaying gratification yields larger rewards. For example they could be millionaire by 60 if they put aside $6 a day from the age of 15 at an interest of 8 per cent. Sorry if they are 40, they need to put aside $58 per day. This may become impossible. Besides teaching children to live within their means, we also need to teach them to expand their means if they want to be rich. Credit card debt is the worst form of debt. Buying with credit will always cost more. Management of smart mobile phone and expenses are essential to know the value of money. They must know the difference between cheap and value. Choose and buy right; they only have to buy once. Think of examples to illustrate real bargain from the rots. Wealthy parents teach their kids to be rich while we teach our children how to survive. So children should be taught to avoid inheriting their parents' limiting beliefs. Encourage entrepreneurship and teach them investment smart strategies. If parents are lacking in these types of skills, then get this book to help them. Encourage our children to share their talents, money, and others. They will grow to be responsible, self reliant citizen in this global world. Encourage our children to speak the language of money fluently as early as possible. Financial literacy is necessary for your children to catch the bullet train to financial freedom.

CHAPTER FOUR

THE LANGUAGE SPOKEN BY HEALTHY AND HAPPY PEOPLE

The Language of Healthy People

No one can be happy if he or she is not healthy. Being healthy is one of the elements of abundance. How to live a healthy life? You need to know that a goal without a plan is just a dream. A plan without execution is equally useless. You may not have figured out how to be healthy and fit. It's simple if we are disciplined to follow a simple lifestyle. Just look at people around us who are healthy and fit. Learn to speak their healthy language and get involved in similar activities. What do they do and eat to be healthy? What do they do to be fit? They are ordinary people like us. They live on a nutritious diet; they have enough sleep; they exercise regularly; they have good relationship with others; they enjoy working and they enjoy their life. They cultivate healthy thoughts. They know that their thoughts have significant control over the cells of their bodies. We can easily start planning similar activities to boost our health and become fit. One easy way to enjoy your exercise is to take up a game and play regularly. They not only enjoy their productivity habits but also their healthy lifestyles. They speak healthy language and conceive exciting thoughts. Just be active and learn their healthy language. You can easily be one of them.

I am passionate about good health. How do I achieve it? It's simple. I replicate the habits, practices and lifestyle of healthy people I know. I learn to speak their healthy language. In our computer language, I actually downloaded the beliefs, habits and practices of healthy people into my subconscious mind. Before I start practising these habits, I have to eliminate those outdated practices and beliefs about lifestyle in my mind first. If you are unhappy and living an unhealthy life, the main reason is that you are suffering from the preconditioned programming in your mind. How do I overcome it? I have a simple tool called meditation to assist me. Once I bring my brain waves to an alpha phase or better theta stage, the brain becomes responsive to my intention. So the process is elimination by dislodging the rubbish beliefs and practices permanently in the unconscious mind. A vacuum is created. My imagination and visualisation take over. I begin to unload those habits, practices and lifestyle of the healthy people into the mind. What are these good habits and practices? They came from my observations and reading. The first in the list is my diet. The second important thing I need to obey is to have enough sleep and rest. The third thing I need to follow is to have regular exercise. The last thing to cultivate is a positive attitude towards life. I need to enjoy working and love my work. I need to have good relationship with others. Last but not least, I need to elevate my level of conscious thinking. True self-love is the foundation of a happy and fulfilled life. The essential key is giving love and receiving love. Forming the habit of nourishing myself, I am able to put my best self forward in my personal and professional life. I follow my passion and I plan my destiny. My mission is to live a long, happy and healthy life.

Once I know what I want, I will start visualising those pictures in my mind's eye when setting out to achieve my goals. First I need a plan and make a commitment to carry out daily. This is just like what I do when I visualise making free throws, lay ups and making a winning shot at the final second of my basketball game. This is the first time I realise the importance of a clear picture in my mind's eye what I should do. Have a plan and take time to visualise those goals. Concentrate my energy and focus on those practices necessary to bring happiness, fitness and good health in my life. Carry out these activities regularly until they become my lifestyle. A healthy body helps to build an active mind leading us to conceive healthy thoughts necessary for our cells to function optimally.

Happiness is slightly different. How to activate it? To get in touch with my intuition to achieve happiness, I need to find the answers to the following areas every day. Think of three or more things I am grateful for and the things I do for myself. Showing gratitude has profound effects on my well-being. It enhances my self-esteem and helps me to sleep well. Constant practice of this habit encourages good things on my lap. Acknowledging things I have done for myself and appreciating them help to boost self esteem. Showing love to me and looking forward to the day are my daily practices. Love yourself first and the rest will take care of itself. And what are the things I do that make me happy? Showing kindness to me and others activates my consciousness. This helps to see kindness as the natural thing for us to do. Understanding my subconscious mind helps in the goal-attaining process. Always live at the present moment. The past is gone and the future is not here. Clearing all issues will pave the way for love and understanding to begin. The visual cortex is part of my brain that helps to shape my goal into concrete image. This will help me to turn those ideas into my visions for me to move towards certainty. Writing down the steps I have to take every day activates my visual cortex. Clarity is needed. And I need are crystal clear steps to take and a clear vision or image to follow. I will start imagining what I will look like when I achieve my goal. By taking these steps, my thoughts, emotions or feelings and behaviours will begin to change and align with my goal, setting me on my path to attain happiness, fitness and good health. Discipline is the key in following the steps consistently, persistently, and playfully until I achieve what I set up to do. I have to watch my diet, my sleep, my regular exercise, my attitude and my overall lifestyle. I love to play my game tennis and I enjoy playing. Getting enough exercise is no longer a problem. I must also make sure that every muscle of my body is tuned up every day. While doing all these intentionally to be fit and healthy, the next important thing to watch is my diet.

Good Diet

My first mission is to make my health a top priority. There are so many things in life that need my attention. We can be easily distracted by so many things that we forget to put our health at the top of the list. For me, work and family always seem more important than working on my health, but I have to convince myself that I'm better off for my work and my family if I am happy, fit and healthy. This conscious awareness is critical for me to keep myself fit and lean. In my younger days, I needed stamina and fitness to play my favourite game, basketball. Now I play tennis and I have to be fit to last two hours of play each time. So fitness is always my top priority. So I need to exert my heart to pump vigorously for at least half an hour by running or weight lifting every day. By doing this feat consistently, persistently and playfully, I always keep myself fit and lean. Being fit by getting involve in regular exercise also improves my metabolism and enhances my immune system.

The food I eat daily have the power to renew my body, revitalise my health and even reverse or delay my aging process. This is conscious awareness that the cells in our body renew completely in less than a year and our body is literally brand new every two years or less. The diet I follow is most critical for my heath. The food I eat every day must have the nutrients that can help in building a brand new, healthier, stronger and even younger body. More importantly, eating a balanced diet helps us to build and strengthen our immune system and builds a strong protective system against diseases including cancer, heart disease and other mental diseases. I am in my seventies. A good diet every day is a good routine. I can do most of the things persons in the fifties do. Being disease-free and never get sick are my enjoyment. I still have a laser-sharp memory. Looking much younger than my age is a reward. I still have inexhaustible supply of energy. Playing tennis for two hours without feeling tired speaks well for my stamina. I can still do most of the things I did when I was in my forties. Having never been hospitalised is my advantage. I owe all these to my choice of living on a clean and good diet. I enjoy using food as my medicine and my medicine is in my food.

Dr Sin Mong Wong

Cholesterol Does Not Cause Heart Disease

I am in my seventies. Many people including doctors, warn me not to eat more than two eggs a day because cholesterol is bad for the heart and also the brain. I used to eat eight eggs a day when I was at the prime of basketball career. Sometimes I had to play soccer match in the afternoon followed by a basketball match in the evening. Being the key player for both of the games I could not avoid them. My service was important to both of my teams during my college days. I needed all the nutrients to give me the energy level. I am 76, I never experienced heart disease and stroke. Keeping active most of the time helps to avoid heart disease. My doctor must be lying to me without knowing it. After reading many research findings into cholesterol, now I realise that cholesterol has nothing to do with heart disease. Studies reveal that almost half of the people in USA suffering from heart disease have low or average cholesterol levels. Dr David Eifrig Jr argues that cholesterol cannot be bad for us because our livers are making it regularly. I concur with him absolutely. It does not make sense to me that cholesterol is the cause of heart disease. This myth is so engrained in our medical dogma that doctors who slack and do not keep up-to-date with medical findings still believe that cholesterol is responsible for heart disease.

What is cholesterol? It is a type of waxy fat we have throughout our bodies. It is the building blocks for many parts of our anatomy. Each of our 37 trillion cells has a membrane surrounding it. The membrane is made up of cholesterol. It is also a necessary component our bodies use to make some hormone. Cholesterol also covers the end of our nerve cells in the brain. There are two types: dietary cholesterol and blood cholesterol. The former comes from the food we eat and the latter is made by our liver. Structurally both types of cholesterol are the same but the former has no effect on the latter's levels. Please note that dietary cholesterol does not affect our blood cholesterol levels. In 1999, a study at Harvard School of medicine reveals that eating an egg every day did not affect the blood cholesterol levels. Next time, if you have high blood cholesterol and your doctor tells you to avoid eggs you can ignore his or her advice. Your doctor does not keep up-to-date information. For your information, eggs are packed with protein, zinc, iron, copper and vitamins A, D, K, B6 and B12.

Many other heavy-cholesterol foods like butter, shrimp and fish are full of vital nutrients that are beneficial to our health. This information does not imply that we can eat any type of food we want. We should avoid foods that are high in trans-fat and sugar. Trans-fat food include margarine, fried food, baked processed food like cookies, biscuits, cakes, fatty meats, food cooked in highly processed cooking oils and others. But we should not avoid eating eggs. Sugar and all types of preserved foods should be avoided at all cost. Otherwise our liver will be overworked to produce cholesterol in response to these trans-fat foods and sugar. Please take note that cholesterol is there to protect us. Sugar and excess carbohydrates are dangerous for our heart and brain.

If it is not cholesterol then what causes heart disease? Doctor David Eifrig Jr explains that heart disease is caused by a process called atherosclerosis. It means that the arteries that carry oxygen rich blood to parts of our body become less flexible and start to form hard, sticky plagues inside their walls. This can constrict blood flow to parts of our body which causes a rise in blood pressure. Sometimes the plagues can break off and block small arteries. If the arteries happen to be close to the heart, blood cannot reach the tissues causing the muscles of the heart to cease functioning. This is heart attack. Plagues breaking up can also travel to the vessels in our brain. If they get stuck in any brain vessel in our brain, oxygen is cut off from the brain cells. The brain cells will die without the supply of oxygenated blood. This is stroke. The common belief is that cholesterol causes these plagues. But it is not true. An intensive study in 2012 reveals that inflammation is the main cause of the arterial plagues. It is not the cholesterol that makes the plagues which then triggered inflammation. So it is not cholesterol but inflammation that we should worry about. Although cholesterol makes the plagues, but it is not the reason we get plagues in the arteries. What is inflammation? Inflammation is simply the response of our immune system to any irritant like trans fat or sugar. It can be anything like a cut, a scrape on your hand to viral infection like flu to autoimmune diseases like rheumatoid arthritis and others. We feel it when we get a cut. The body tries to heal itself. It is the red hot feeling we get when any cut is healing. Similarly when any part of our arteries is hurt due to irritant from trans-fat, sugar or other toxins, our body increases blood flow to the area. The blood carries extra immune cells to the area helping to heal and repair the injured parts. In the process, any break-up plague containing partly cholesterol will get stuck there because of inflammation. What are other factors causing inflammation? Smoking causes chronic inflammation at our airways. And many trans-fat foods, sugar and toxic materials also cause inflammation especially in our arteries. Our bodies cannot break up trans-fat or toxic easily. They upset our immune system and easily trigger inflammation. And it is also true for refined carbohydrates like white bread, sugar and additive preserved foods. How do we avoid inflammation? The first step is by avoiding food loaded with trans fat ingredients, white bread and white sugar. The second step is to eat more anti-inflammatory foods like fruits and vegetables. These phytochemicals like lycopene found in tomatoes, beta-carotene found in carrots, anthoxanthins found in banana and others are helpful and beneficial to our health. Many types of berries, coffee, cocoa and dark chocolates contain antioxidants can help to combat inflammation. Many studies show that regular exercise and maintaining healthy weight also reduce inflammation. Brushing our teeth and flossing are important. Studies show that keeping good dental hygiene not only is a good habit but also protects the heart and brain too. The germs and bacteria living in our mouth can contribute chronic inflammation in our bodies. I am a living example. I used to brush and floss my teeth after every meal. I still do. After seventy-five years my teeth are still intact and I am as healthy as ever. As parents, these valuable information and new discoveries should be made available to our children.

Habits, Lifestyle and Aging

Our fast pace of life and our diet are the main causes of our aging process. Most of us are aging faster than we should. How do we slow down the process? Here are some of the habits that can help us to slow down our aging process. As parents it's important that we pass these information and lifestyle to our children. We are the first examples that our children will notice. Living this great lifestyle will not only slow down our aging process but also give our children a head start.

First, eating healthily is the first step we should take to slow down our aging process. Aging is the decadence of our organs and is usually reflected through our skin. The logical thinking is to provide our organs with healthy foods to slow down the aging process. Where do all the necessary nutrients required by our organs come from? Most of these rich nutrients come from vegetables, fruits, nuts, eggs and other forms of organic foods. They provide nutrients like beta carotene, zinc, selenium, vitamin C, vitamin E, B12 and antioxidants necessary to help in the production of collagen and elastin which help to keep our skin wrinkle free.

Second, make sure that we have enough sleep. Beauty sleep is not a myth but a truth. Most people who do not have enough sleep will develop dark circles under their eyes and their eyelids will be tired. This helps to make you look a few years older. Most people who are sleep deprived usually look stressed and tired. Stress is one of the causes of high cholesterol in our blood system. Many health problems like high blood pressure, weight gain, diabetes, and others are linked to deprivation of sleep and stress. Our body will be thankful to our habits of getting eight hours of sleep daily. It helps to slow down your aging process. You can help to reduce stress before you sleep by intentionally thinking of three things you are thankful for the day and three things you are grateful for. Do these regularly and soon become a new habit and you will sleep well and reduce stress.

Third, regular exercise not only helps to control your weight but more importantly it helps to slow down your aging process and helps to prolong your life. You need to know that exercising regularly helps to boost production of testosterone, dopamine, and other beneficial hormones which help to keep you healthy. In addition, exercising regularly helps to improve your blood pressure and mood, keeping you strong and flexible. Staying active can also boost your energy level and slow down your aging process.

Fourth, drinking plenty of water will keep your skin and your body younger. Water helps to moisturise our skin and receive necessary nutrients. This helps to prevent having wrinkles on the skin. Water is also essential for the health of all the organs and the entire organism of your body. Fruits like watermelon, cucumber, tomatoes, and others contain plenty of water and also nutrients our body requires. So it's important you keep hydrated every day for good health and to slow down your aging process.

Fifth, avoiding sugar can help us look younger and prevent other health problems like diabetes, heart disease and strokes. Sugar in the blood stream is usually linked to the formation of molecules that are harmful to our body especially our skin. If you are addicted to sweets, try to take dark chocolates which contain less sugar. By avoiding refined sugar and processed foods with addictive ingredients your body will be thankful and you will look younger.

Sixth, do not pick up the habit of smoking. If you want to stay young this habit must be avoided at all cost. Many diseases like heart disease, stroke, dementia, and cancer are linked to smoking. Smoking produces irritants that can cause inflammation in your blood vessels. Smoking also tarnishes your skin and makes wrinkles more obvious. Cigarettes contain plenty of toxins which cause inflammation of your arteries, make your vessels contract, and deprive your organs from enough oxygen. The production of collagen on your skin is reduced and the skin gets thinner over the years. More wrinkles will form and you will look much older than your age.

Seven, avoid drinking excessive alcohol. A little of alcohol is good for you. But it's difficult to control. So drinking alcohol daily is not healthy for anyone. It dehydrates you, and in the process it takes away vitamins and minerals from your body. Sometimes, impurities are present in alcoholic drinks and your liver has to do extra work to eliminate everything that is unhealthy. Extra alcohol adds extra stress to your organs and the whole organism. If you like to drink, practice moderation to one or two glasses of wine or beer a day. Anyhow, by drinking alcohol, you are not helping to slow down your aging process.

Eight, protect your skin from overexposure to the sun. Wear sunglasses when you are in the open. A little bit of morning sun can be beneficial to the production of vitamin D and your general health.

Lastly, keep yourself happy most of the time. The most important ingredient is good relationship. Parents are critical examples to our children. Good relationship between father and mother is the most invaluable relationship children can emulate. Availability and dependability of parents and their examples are the most valuable lessons children can treasure. Happy parents set a good role model for others. When you smile, you usually look younger. You can smile only when you are happy. How to be happy? Your thinking is important here. If you are tired, stressed, and sad, you usually look older. To achieve happiness, there are a few simple things you must do daily. Live a life of love, avoid grudges, forgive others, show gratitude, develop positive attitude and think positively. It is easy to say but difficult to accomplish. This book provides you with the characteristics of happy people for you to follow. Unload all the unnecessary beliefs and habits of your stressful life and get rid of them. Start to download characteristics of happy people into your subconscious mind, visualise your goal and start implementing them to gain happiness.

The purpose of this book is to introduce these happy characteristics for you to understand and digest so that you too can implement them in your life. Here is an important finding for you to digest. Robert Waldger, a psychiatrist and the fourth director of Harvard's longest study (lasted seventy -five years) of happiness, concludes that good relationship, not money or fame is the surprise factor for happiness. The most critical relationship between husband and wife is based on dependability, security and trustworthiness. Most old happy couples do not agree all the time. They hold different views on many things. They like different things. They enjoy different foods. They may argue and fight over certain issues, but they can depend on each other. That security, dependability and reliability are the necessary ingredients to their health, their long lives and their eventual happiness. Relationship with a network of relatives and friends adds values to their lives and their happiness. This critical information should be passed over to our children. They too can start building their network of friends and enhance good relationship with their relatives and friends.

The Danger of Dietary Supplements

Dietary supplements are big business. Supplements sales are billions of dollars per year. The reason most of us take supplements is understandable. A big proportion of people take dietary supplements to improve their health and another big proportion of people take supplements to maintain their health. Only a small proportion of us take dietary supplements on the advice of our doctors. Many of the people are just ignorant. They are not only wasting their money but also doing harm to their bodies. Many of us think that taking these supplements implies that they are medical treatments for our health. Remember that these supplements are not regulated like medicines. Nobody is checking the health claims of these supplements. Many of the claims are pure marketing gimmick and fiction. And worse, many of these supplements contain ingredients and substances that are different from the labels. This awareness is important when you buy supplements for your children. To be certain, consult your doctor first before taking them.

An Example of Liver Damage due to Ignorance

Many people are keen to slim down quickly by taking green tea extract pills and suffer from liver damage. The danger is more acute for children. Do not encourage children to take this pill. By taking concentrated green-tea extract in the form of pills to burn fat can lead to liver failure. An obvious effect is immediate. Your face and eyes turn yellow. A hospital report shows that about 20 per cent of all drug-related liver disease is due to green tea supplement pills. Green tea contains molecules called catechins. In brewed tea, the catechins are at a safe and diluted level. But a big concentration of catechins in pills can cause liver damage especially with an empty stomach. Do not practice such habit of taking pills. Just drink your brewed green tea in dilute form regularly to avoid such a liver damage.

The Most Dangerous Disease in Developed Countries

This disease called diabetes mellitus kills more people that breast cancer and AIDS combined. It can lead to blindness, kidney failure, debilitating nerve pain, heart disease and even stroke. In USA alone, about one third of its population is suffering from this disease and many are not aware of it. I remember when I was in my thirties; my doctor told me that my sugar level was high. If I do not take care of my diet and exercise, my chance of getting diabetes mellitus is high. This awareness motivated me to take my regular exercise seriously. The next step is to reduce my intake of sugar and carbohydrates to control my blood sugar level. Remember sugar is not the only enemy, many carbohydrates are equally dangerous. For my own health, I began to form the habit of eating carbohydrate-rich foods moderately. I avoid white sugar totally. The cakes and biscuits we eat contain a certain amount of sugar. I enjoy these foods but always restrict myself to a few pieces. To get a better idea of which carbs to eat and which to avoid, look at two things: glycemic index and glycemic load. The glycemic index is a scale of 1 to 100 that measures how much of the carb in certain food increases your blood sugar. For example, cooked white rice ranks 89 and brown rice ranks 50. Foods high on the index spike your blood sugar more. And repeated spikes can kill you. The amount used is only 50 grams of the carb. More important is the glycemic load which takes into account how much your blood sugar rises based on the serving size. Some foods have less than 50 grams of carbs per serving. Foods with more carbs per serving will have higher glycemic load, giving a more accurate indication.

Another thing to help your blood sugar control is to eat foods rich in fibre. There are two types of fibre: soluble or insoluble in water. Our system can't break down insoluble fibre but its helps food and waste move through our digestive system. Soluble fibre helps slow down the absorption of sugar, meaning our blood sugar will not spike so much. Forming the habit of eating a high-fibre diet can help to control your blood sugar level.

The spice found in your curry known as cinnamon helps process glucose and stabilise bloodsugar levels. A compound in the spice called methylhydroxychalcone can mimic insulin's action. Ginger also has blood-sugar lowering properties. Cinnamon and ginger have certain enzymes affecting the pancreas to produce insulin which serves to lower blood-sugar spikes after meals. It's a good idea to include cinnamon and ginger in your regular diet. Regular exercise together with diet awareness can help you avoid diabetes.

Natural and Nutritional Foods-A Better Choice

I believe strongly that in most cases we are better off without these supplements. Only take supplements on doctors' advice due to deficiency. Instead we should turn to nutritious foods like vegetables, fruits and whole foods for our nutritional needs. Many vegetables are packed with phytochemicals and nutrients that can protect our bodies and maintain our health. So the whole food is a better alternative than dietary supplements to supply our bodies with the necessary nutrients. A research study in 2013 published in *New England Journal of Medicine* involving 12 000 people reveals that taking supplements of omega-3 fatty acid from fish oil supplements does not produce the same effect as the placebo group taking it from whole foods. Getting omega-3 fatty acid from fish reduces significantly the risk of suffering from heart disease, stroke and other cardiovascular diseases. The study shows that the nutrients in whole foods like fish and vegetables are far more superior to dietary supplements. There are many researches showing the health benefits of phytochemicals from whole foods. The most recognised phytochemical, lycopene, found in red vegetables and fruits, is found in abundance in tomatoes. Many research studies show that taking enough red foods containing lycopene will significantly reduce the risk of lung, stomach and prostate cancers. It is known that lycopene helps to fight off free radicals that damage the cells. Lycopene also protects our DNA from damage, a problem that can lead to cancer-causing mutations. A significant contributing factor to cancer, heart disease and stroke is inflammation. According to the American Cancer Research, many types of vegetables like broccoli, cabbage, Brussels sprouts, kale and turnips can help to protect against colon cancer. These vegetables contain a chemical compound called glucosinolate which can reduce inflammation. They also contain high levels of folate that protect our DNA from damage. Eating enough vegetables and fruits will provide us most benefits. Although many of the photochemical from fruits and vegetables are not well understood, there is also a possibility that they may interact with each other and produce greater beneficial effects. Research studies reveal that eating up to seven servings of vegetables and fruits per day will provide all the protection and reduce our chance of dying from any cause. What is each serving?

Each serving is just half cup of cooked vegetables or a cup of raw vegetables. So for four servings of vegetables and three servings of fruits, you are well protected from all types of diseases. I concur with these findings. I always make sure that I have enough vegetables and fruits each day. I used to add avocado and tomatoes for my afternoon sandwich. I am 76 years old and I still enjoy vibrant health. I still take my morning walk and play my regular tennis.

The power of our immune system is usually underestimated. Modem medicine still has no cure for the common cold. Yet our immune system can overcome a cold's symptoms naturally in a matter of days. This discerning and powerful army of our organised cells protect us against attacks from foreign invaders. But most of us forget to strengthen our remarkable immune system because of ignorance. Instead we look to vaccines, antibiotics and other medical interventions to protect our health. Although each medical intervention has its certainty, overreliance on them can be costly not only on our pocket but also on our immune system. Sometimes it can be deadly. So it is more logical to learn to support our immune system with healthy lifestyle choices and nutritional foods that can give us confidence for our health. Avoid sugar, trans-fats, processed foods and artificial chemicals in our diets. This will save our immune system from working overtime to deal with them. Instead, our immune system will have its power to deal with diseases and invaders. We will be more resistant to infection and diseases.

Remember that chronic stress attacks our immune systems, inhibiting the body's ability to defend itself against infection and disease. Learning to manage stress effectively through relaxation or meditation and physical activities can help balance the nervous system and improve our immune system. Ultimately, the best defence against disease is to support our immune systems so that they can function at their best. Our vitality in life will be noticed.

Overcome Joint Pain

I had been a keen basketball player for almost fifty years and now I am in my seventies, I still play tennis regularly. I have enough experiences of knee joint pain. I do not know what to do and I live with it by exercising and walking daily. I keep playing tennis even with my knee joint pain. I tried everything possible to strengthen my muscles around my knees by walking up the hill and walking backwards down the hill. The slight pain still persists. One day by chance, I read about a special report prepared by Dr Eugene R. Zampieron, an authority in chronic pain, introducing pain fighting Vital3 Drops. I tried the liquid, three drops at a time, for a few weeks and was surprised that the pain has gone. Now I am more flexible and I move well. I do not know how long this pain free period will last. I am still trying to find out. I do not know whether there is any side effect taking this miracle liquid.

According to Dr Eugene, new research shows that most of the supplements we take to repair our cartilage, target at the wrong thing. They do not stop the cause of joint destruction. Now we have scientific evidence that in cases of joint pain, our bodies' own immune system mistakenly attacks our joints. This explains why most of the supplements used to repair our cartilage cannot do their work. Every time they try to repair the cartilage, it triggers an alarm to our immune system to rip it down. So it continues to erode our joints and worsen our joint pains. Researchers spent a vast resources and time to find way to turn off the joint destruction switch. They found the secret in a liquid formula that flips off the 'attack cells' aimed at the cartilage. I do not know what is this liquid. The solution, according to Dr Eugene, has been proven effective and is patented. The solution stops the cause of joint degradation and it removes the source of our joint pain. And it gives our cartilage the chance to repair and rebuild naturally. The breakthrough is called Vital3 Joint Solution. With just three drops of this miracle liquid a day, it delivers more relief than the glucosamine supplement I had taken. In ten clinical studies using Vital3 Joint Solution, the following results are published:

(i) Subjects ooze their stiff fingers
(ii) Subjects greased creaky knees
(iii) Subjects eased stubborn backs
(iv) Subjects relieved hip discomfort
(v) Subjects improved morning stiffness
(vi) Subjects erased joint tenderness

Some tests even saw their subjects' symptoms vanish completely. Dr Eugene has witnessed the miraculous successes his own patients have achieved using Vital3 Joint Solution and has staked his professional name on the integrity of the product.

Another simple exercise using a pillow to strengthen the muscles around my knee joints is shown to me by a friend. It's simple exercise and it can easily be carried out every morning. First place your pillow on the floor and knee on the pillow. Place your two hands in front on the floor and stretch forward as high as you can and follow by sitting on the pillow as low as you can. Repeat this exercise thirty or fifty times each morning to strengthen the muscles around the joints. I did this exercise every day for almost a month and now I can play tennis without using my knee guides. If you are suffering from knee-joint pain, you can try this simple exercise every morning.

The Importance of Adequate Sleep

Many of us experience dozing off during a meeting or worse at the wheels during driving especially long distance. Many car accidents are caused by sleep deprivation. It can be fatal. Remember, sleep deprivation impairs memory, alertness and concentration and can lead to serious injury or even death. Research into sleep requirement reveals that most of us require about seven to eight hours of sleep a day. It is just an ideal range of numbers. Some of us need more and others need less. This conscious awareness can help you to live a healthier life. Adequate sleep helps to reduce stress; to maintain a healthy weight; to reduce chances of catching cold and lastly, to reduce your chance of developing diabetes and cancer.

How do you get enough sleep? The first step is to develop good sleeping 'hygiene'. This is simply a set of behaviours that affect the quality of your sleep. Here are some of the ways you can easily adopt to improve your sleeping hygiene.

First, stop drinking coffee or any caffeinated drink five or six hours before you sleep. To many people, it is obvious that caffeine will keep you energised and make it harder for you to sleep. Its effect can last for six hours. I advise you to do what I do. I only drink coffee in the morning. Forming good drinking habits is important to help you sleep well.

Second, make your bedroom a place for rest. It's obvious but difficult to follow. I make sure that my bedroom is a sanctuary, a place for sleep and sex only. I do not read or eat on my bed. I also avoid argument or discussion in bed. A clean, tidy and comfortable bed is the first essential requirement to sleep well.

Third, remove all electronics like TV, computers, out of the bedroom. All these electronic devices emit blue light that is the most disruptive for the circadian rhythm. It signals our body to do things. It prevents the release of the hormone melatonin that makes us sleep. I usually shut off all my electronic equipment half an hour before I go to bed.

Fourth, keep the room dark and cool. Light can easily disrupt my sleep. Keeping the room dark helps my body adjust to its natural circadian rhythm. Light can prevent your body from producing melatonin and disrupt your sleep. Various ways of blocking out light from your room are necessary. You can use darkening blinds or shades or eye mask to block out light. A cool temperature lowers your body's temperature and it triggers sleepiness. A warm room results in raising body temperature triggering wakefulness. You may even be awake while lying down resulting in deprivation of sleep.

Fifth, do not eat just before you sleep. I believe that eating just before bedtime increases weight gain and disrupts your sleeping cycle. Digestive sugar spikes and the production of stomach acid can wake you up from sleep. Alcohol can be worst. It causes bouts of wakefulness as your metabolism starts to work. I follow a good habit. I stop eating or drinking two hours before I sleep.

Sixth, schedule your sleep. It's not easy. Many people work well during the night. They are night birds. I usually go to bed before 11.00 p.m. And I follow the schedule rigidly. By following the schedule, it tells my body to get ready to start getting sleep when the time comes.

All these behaviours and habits are easier said than done. It requires discipline. I hope I have brought you to a higher level of awareness and consciousness. It's time to download these sleep hygienic behaviours into your subconscious mind and start implementing them. You need plenty of practices before these behaviours become your sleeping routines. By making these changes, I can be sure that you will not fall asleep during meetings or on the wheels. Your quality of life and your health will improve. It's also important that we pass this information and practices to our children so that they too will not suffer from deprivation of sleep.

Regular Exercise Helps Prevent Cancer

Your energy level is usually determined by your activities. People who are active usually have more energy. The most active people like cyclists, middle distance runners, marathon runners, Olympians and professional sportsmen have one thing in common. They are able to supply oxygen to their bodies' cells constantly to enable them to enjoy optimal performance. They have good stamina and physically well built. Many studies have confirmed that these top performers have 40 to 50 per cent less chance of getting cancer than ordinary people. What is the reason? Many think that it is because they do not smoke. But most studies cover all types of cancer, not only smoke-related cancer. Do you want to know the reason why? The cancer industries do not want us to know the real reason. Researcher Dr Otto Warburg suggested that the major reason is that they are able to supply oxygen to the cells in their bodies; destroying any 'cancer plague' before it is formed. This was discovered 100 years ago by Dr Warburg. But such secret is hidden from us. Most people are not aware of this important discovery. You do not have to be an elite sportsman to defeat cancer. You may not have the time to train like an elite sportsman but you can still defeat cancer by getting more oxygen to your cells. According to Dr Warburg, healthy cells are aerobic. They live by respiration, burning oxygen to create the energy they need to function. But cancer cells are deformed cells and are different. They are anaerobic and they survive by fermentation. This discovery should have been the turning point in the fight against cancer many years ago. But it was covered up by commercial cancer industries, a big business for more than 100 years. Dr Warburg had laid the foundation to fight cancer and other researchers simply confirm his work. In 1953, USA researchers proved that Dr Warburg was right about fermentation. The researchers kept some tissues under normal atmosphere. Other samples were periodically switched to nitrogen atmosphere. Deprive of oxygen, the tissues began to use fermentation to survive. They began to produce abnormal cells and they became malignant. This agrees with Dr Warburg's prediction. The cells under normal atmosphere remained healthy even after more than two years. But in 1960, only one type of cancer cells hadn't been proved to survive by fermentation. This exception was taken as an excuse to ignore Dr Warburg's discovery. Now researchers realise that Warburg is right all the way. We know what causes cancer and know how to stop it. Regular exercise is one of the strongest strategies to fight cancer.

Other strategies are available. A new vaccine called 'Alpha Cells' therapy uses the idea of mobilising the body cells to combat cancer cells. It's similar to strengthening our immune system. This is analogous to regular exercise; the therapy supplies plenty of oxygen to our cells mobilising them to fight cancer cells. Why do the medical science industries not use such discovery? Cancer remains the second cause of death across the world. Oxygen is free. But free does not make the drug industries money. Many medical industries giving treatments to cancer continue to prosper by ignoring Dr Warburg's discovery.

Warburg lost his mother through cancer. He devoted his whole life to beating the disease. One of his discoveries is the importance of respiratory enzymes supporting cellular respiration. There are certain nutrients promoting their production. When we get enough of these nutrients, our cells operate efficiently. The body's cells do not have to turn to fermentation to survive. Dr Ralph Steinman, the Nobel Prize winner, discovered the active cells known as Alpha Cells, which can combat cancer. This 'Alpha Cells' vaccine actually activates the normal cells to kill all types of cancer cells. This vaccine not only kills cancer cells but also prevents normal cells from turning cancerous. Besides this vaccine, the nutrients that come from a balanced diet with plenty of vegetables and fruits will also activate the normal cells to combat cancer. Remember that oxygen is your number one friend and is the number one enemy to cancer cells. Studies reveal that oxygenated cells do not turn cancer but your body's cells starved of oxygen will. This awareness, though hidden for a century, is enough for parents to encourage children to take up a sport seriously. Regular exercise and a balanced diet are the good habits we must instil in our children as early as possible. Parental examples will be caught easily by most children. Remember, parents are the children's first teachers and role models.

Other Benefits of Regular Exercise through Simple Movements

All of us know that if we can move, we are alive. So movement is one of the most powerful ways to improve our health. Everything from burning calories to strengthening muscles comes from simple exercise. Regular exercise also helps to elevate positive moods. The benefits will be greater if you can add enjoyment to your exercises. Playing a game regularly or taking up a movement exercise like yoga is one of the best ways to improve your health. All these exercises protect our heart. It's good to know that simple movement exercises provide four essential health benefits.

First, regular exercises reduce stress. Stress is detrimental to our health especially our cells and on the protective caps of our DNA known as the telomeres. These caps wear down each time our cells divide and they are destroyed as we grow older. Stress causes the telomeres to shrink faster than normal. Soon, the telomeres are gone and the cells stop dividing and die. A host of age-related diseases begin to develop under stressful condition. Regular movement exercises like yoga, dancing or others help to reduce stress and protect our telomeres.

Second, regular movement exercise protects our heart. Research into yoga, dancing and other movement exercises reveal that they decrease blood pressure and heart rate. They improve our physical strength and relieve stress. They help to regulate our regular heartbeat thus avoiding atrial fibrillation, a condition of irregular heartbeat leading to stroke and blood clots in the heart.

Third, regular movement exercises like yoga strengthen our brain. Especially by playing a game regularly, the amount of coordination and conditioning are significant for the brain's function. All of us know that as we age, we lose our grey matter. These clusters of nerve cells are activated by regular movement exercises and live longer. Regular activation improves the brain functions, including muscle control, memory, vision, emotion and decision making. Regular exercises like yoga seem to increase our grey matter. Remember having more movement exercises not only help to increase grey matter but also increase our energy levels. Last but not least, exercises like yoga, dancing or others help to relieve arthritis. Especially yoga, stretching and exercises relieve stress in our joints, providing relief to arthritis. Exercises providing facilities for gripping and stretching seem to improve our strength in our fingers and joints. Our flexibility, stability and movement are enhanced by regular exercises like yoga. For people over fifty, regular exercise helps improve our posture and reduces joint or back problems.

Everyone is encouraged to take regular exercises like yoga, dancing and playing a game seriously if you want to live long and healthy life. The journey to a healthy life begins today. You are encouraged to take up a movement exercise like yoga or a game regularly to help you achieve your health goal.

Take the Supplement Coffee Three Times a Day

I am generally sceptical about taking supplements. Most of these dietary aids are sold on the promise that they provide incredible health benefits. Most of these promises are actually empty and they lack scientific evidence. I am introducing you a natural supplement that you can add to your diet today. It will help to protect your heart and brain, help you live longer and even boost your sex life. What is this supplement? This supplement, known as coffee, offers a host of scientifically validated benefits. It's fragrant, delicious and is good for you. Millions of people around the world drink it daily. I drink almost two to three cups a day. According to Dr David Eifrig Jr there are dozens of chemical compounds found in coffee and provide many health benefits. The three main benefits are listed here.

First, the chemical compounds in coffee fight inflammation, the main cause of heart disease and stroke. Coffee is packed with antioxidants like caffeine that soothe inflammation. Inflammation damages cells and causes plague of cholesterol to deposit on the arteries resulting in stroke, heart disease and even cancer.

Second, the chemical compounds in coffee may protect your DNA directly. Damaged DNA can usually divide without end, leading to tumours. Although it is not clear how this subdivision takes place research suggests that the compounds in coffee stimulate an enzyme that fights DNA-toxin.

Third, the caffeine in coffee blocks adenosine receptors. Adenosine is a neurotransmitter in our brains that sends signal to our body. Its primary role is to signal when we need sleep. That's why coffee keeps us awake whereas decaf coffee doesn't.

So there are good reasons why we should take this supplement daily especially in the morning. It reduces many types of cancer, cardiovascular diseases, stroke, dementia and migraine - soothes an upset stomach - protects the skin and fights erectile dysfunction. If caffeine disturbs your sleep, try to drink coffee only in the morning and noon. Coffee is available everywhere. The choice is yours.

The Language of Happiness

After learning the languages of the basics, money, good health, the next thing to master in life is the language of happiness. The world we live in can give us infinite ways to convince us to be happy or unhappy. There is dissatisfaction everywhere. My observation is that most poor people speak poor language resulting in lack of happiness. They are not happy at the moment. Some of us believe that dissatisfaction of our level of life now will motivate us to strive harder and satisfaction will not motivate us to strive higher. Well that is not quite true. Many of us believe that dissatisfaction leads to motivation, to action and to success.

Remember that such a philosophy might work for success but not for happy success. You will not be happy along the journey to success. The dissatisfaction lingers on from one success to another. This is not a good strategy for happiness. A better way is to be motivated by progress. It is better if you are motivated by your passion instead of dissatisfaction. In other words you must be satisfied right now. You must be contented right now. You do not have to be thrilled every minute to be happy.

Being contented right this moment provides the harmony with the present moment - knowing that even under tough situations you still have confidence in yourself. You will find a way to overcome any obstacle. Being contented brings happiness and happiness drives productivity. Remember unhappiness encourages procrastination or inaction. Happy people take a balanced approach to life: the good, bad and ugly. They find joy in whatever life gives. They are contented with what they have. Contented people are generally happy people who tend to use positive words. They know the power and importance of words. I use to hear from poor people that they cannot afford buying certain thing. Most people who live an abundant life want to know why they cannot buy such a thing that they wanted badly. They will not say that they cannot afford it. They live a rich life. Rich people use rich words. Words have the power to build people up. As parents, our responsibilities are simple. Our role as model is to show the way. We expose our children to the languages of the three basics, money and health; now we need to expose them to the language of happiness. We have to keep introducing new positive and inspirational words to our children's vocabulary.

It is easy to look back and focus on regrets, mistakes and missed opportunities. Remember that a negative outlook on the events of the past year can set us up for failure in the next one. So instead we should focus on the happy things that we are grateful for during the same period, we will be amazed how we can change our perspective. Practicing gratefulness does not come naturally. They have to make a conscious effort. They need to be aware that being grateful is necessary for them to be thankful for all the good things happening to them. Just ignore the unhappy things happening and focus on the help you get, the health you enjoy, the love of your spouse and a fulfilling job. Being grateful for all the small things happening is a good feeling. It's time to download the beliefs and habits of happy people into your subconscious mind and start implementing them to be happy. There is no need for us to change the world to accommodate us we just need to change ourselves and our perspectives. Learning to love and enjoy ourselves, we have already started to change the world.

The Beliefs and Habits of Happy People

Why are some people not happy most of the time? We want our children to be happy. So the sooner the better if our children learn the language of happiness. Before learning the language of happiness, we need to be aware of the beliefs and habits of happy people. Is it true that poor people are not happy? Is it true that rich people are generally happy? I do not claim to know the answers. I want my children to be happy people. If you observe carefully, many people have power, wealth and prestige but they are not satisfied. They seem to be discontented. Why? They want more control, more rebellion, more money and they forget to replace all these with virtuous deeds. They are not conscious of replacing this viscous cycle with the virtuous one. They ignore the fact that they must have a purpose to be rich. They have experiences, growth but no contribution to humanity. Happiness does not include them. The poor lack thinking ability. They do not understand the importance of the language of the basics. They remain poor and usually unhappy. They look at most things from the perspective of lack. They feel that they are the victims of society.

After giving our children the unfair advantage of the languages of money and health, now I want our children to have the head start in using words spoken by happy people. The examples we bring about in the home will give our children a lifetime of rewards helping them to be happy. What are the beliefs and habits of happy people? Can the transformations of poor people to middle class or from middle class to become rich bring happiness? I do not know. If you want to know, you need to find out more about happiness.

What is happiness? How to measure happiness? A simple measure of happiness is the language we speak. Happy people speak happy language. Just like rich people speak rich language and healthy people speak healthy language. They see the universe from the point of abundance. Everywhere they see opportunities. Every challenge is an opportunity. They tell interesting stories. Unhappy people speak unhappy language. Open your ears, you will hear the language spoken everywhere. Sad people tell sad stories. Unhappy people are grumpy and tend to blame others, the environment and the government. They see the world from the point of lack. They become pessimistic. My life experiences tell me that if I enjoy doing something I like, I feel happy. I keep myself happy by doing the things I like. I like the game - basketball, tennis and golf I play and I enjoy playing each of the games. I like the excitements, the competitions and the exercises I get. After each game, I feel happy. I become fit and healthy to enjoy each day. I believe this is one aspect of my life that adds to my happiness. I know I have to make a living and I need money. I started my life with only ordinary income that is my salary as a teacher. I learned the language of money quickly. Adding extra streams of income enabled me to transform my ordinary income to portfolio income and eventually passive income. The process of transformation from linear income to residual income including capital gains appears to make me happy. Happiness is a process and doing more things I like, I become happier. The moment I achieved my financial freedom, I moved on to follow my dreams. New experiences, growth and making contributions became my goals. While pursuing my dreams I did not forget many people who had helped me. I am grateful to my parents providing me the first language of money and love. I am grateful to my relatives who rendered me financial help while I was a student. The grace of gratitude makes me happy. Providing moral and financial support to my younger brothers, sisters and my wife's brothers and sisters became my immediate priority. I also rendered financial support and accommodation for others including my relatives under my care. By doing all these generously, I really feel happy. Embracing the generosity of spirit adds happiness to my life. I move up the ladder of needs, from basic to safety, and finally to self-actualisation. As I progress, my happiness begins to increase by leaps and bounds. I begin to become generous because my needs are well taken care off. The more I give, I experience something else. I seem to be getting more. I begin to give support unconditionally for good projects and I am excited to know that I am actually getting more help and support. Generosity behaves more than Newton's Third Law. For every action there is more than equal reaction. I supported many schools and ministry projects personally. When I was given the responsibilities to organise charity projects for my school and the education ministry, I was amazed at the support I got. I really feel happy after each project.

  I read about the generosity of Elvis Presley. In one story, I read about a woman admiring his diamond ring. He gave it to her with a smile. He was rich and he was prepared to share his abundance with a stranger. I met another rich and generous man from my hometown. He saw a poor old man lying on the side of the road. The old man fell from his bicycle and was slightly injured. His bicycle was partly damaged. He stopped his car and carried him and his bicycle to his home. He gave him some money to repair his bicycle. The next day I saw the rich man in a coffee shop. The poor old man was having his breakfast there. The rich man told the manager of the shop to include the old man's bill into his account. This rich man is generous and willing to bless others who are less fortunate. He saw the needs of others. This observation reminds me to follow his example of giving and sharing my gifts and talents. The more I give, the more I receive and I become happier.

Many people believe that money does not buy happiness. I do not entertain such an idea. I believe the luxuries of life are to be enjoyed and shared. Living beneath our means does not always make people happy. I think so. Rather than living beneath our means, I would prefer to teach our children to go for the good life, expand their means and become richer. I would encourage them to use their dreams of life's luxuries to drive them forward, giving them the ambition and incentives to live their lives' dreams. To enjoy the journey of my life is one of my dreams. Happiness seems to smile at me all the way. You can even buy liabilities and become richer using assets to pay for them. All you need is having financial education and managerial skills and the ability to speak the languages of the relevant fields. You need success intelligence in the form of emotional intelligence, a form of delayed gratification. It's always better to buy their assets first and then buy their liabilities. Success intelligence is encouraged first.

There are many different paths to wealth. You can marry for money; you can win a lottery; you can be a professional athlete; a good singer or you can become rich using financial intelligence. Most of the temporary rich lose their wealth in a few years. They do not have good reason to be rich. I pick financial intelligence to become rich. I have a purpose to be rich. I knew I do not have exceptional academic, singing, acting or athletic talents. When I started as a graduate teacher, I fell in love with my calling.

I knew my calling will not make me rich. The 'side kicks' from my calling in the forms of writing and coaching others will make me rich. I knew my service will be in great demands as a mathematics tutor and writer. Serving others bring great rewards as well as happiness. I have learned that the more I give and produce, the more I receive. Our children do not know this and they don't believe that it is true. They will not believe that they can raise capital; they can lead people; they can design business and use debt to make more money. As parents, our duty is to show the way. We have to be well educated financially. Most importantly, they must have a reason to rich. This book will open the way for parents to give their children a head start. I have two professions: one for teaching and one for making money. My main profession is teaching and my money's professions are writing, real estate investments, stocks and businesses. Both are providing service and value for others. When I became principal of my school, I learned leadership skills which became important for entrepreneurship. I was a good follower when I was a teacher. I learned cooperation and support for my leaders. These qualities helped me to become good leader. In the process, I became happier. Doing your work happily increases productivity and generates more wealth. The process generates happiness in return. It is a happy cycle.

General Habits of Happy People

There are some general habits that make people happy. Here are some of them. When I feel happy and great, it does not mean that I will only feel them for just a few hours. The feeling of continuously being peaceful for who I am and being grateful about everything as the way it is. First, I choose to embrace a positive attitude towards everything I do. This positive attitude comes from a long process of self-examination through self-awareness. When I was in secondary school, I started the journey of self-examination through the process of daily meditation. After each meditation, I used to list down the things that I had done each day. I would separate the things that I enjoy doing and the things that I had done wrongly. The things that I enjoyed doing and felt happy, I will repeat them regularly to become my habits and practices. The things that I did not feel happy, I would try my level best to avoid them. Things such as being rude, using unkind words, telling a white lie and many others, I would try to avoid them intentionally. This awareness is critical for me to have a clear conscience for who I am. The process is not easy and I have to be consistent and determine not to repeat these unhappy things in my life. This awareness strategy that I applied to my daily life gave me a new journey in my life. I did it consistently, persistently and with great discipline, soon my conscience became clear. I feel happier each day as the things I wanted to avoid become less and less. Even in the game basketball that I played passionately; I kept reminding myself to embrace gentleman behaviours in every game I was involved. Showing good sportsmanship in every game I played is my top priority. Repeating the habit brings happiness. I learned to smile even when my opponents committed a foul against me. This habit eventually became my trademark and most players seemed to notice it. The experience of respect from most of my opponents adds happiness to my life.

With less and less things that worry me, I began to embrace optimism, enthusiasm and contentment. With less and less things that I needed to change, my life began to take on a new dimension. My academic achievement began to show improvement as I adopted my self-study strategy of pre-preparing lessons before attending classes. My optimism growed as I intensified my self-study strategy daily. This optimism also applied to my basketball game as I intensified my drill strategy to improve my dribbling, lay ups and shooting skills each day. These skills began to show their effects when I competed in most of the basketball tournaments. When I was performing well in most of the tournaments, I was treated with great respect from team-mates and also my opponents. These things added fuel to my optimism as a state basketball player. I enjoyed all the excitements and all these add value to my life. Feeling great most of the time adds happiness to my life. I learn because I enjoy it. I play my game and I enjoy it too. I become more optimistic in my life and I want to excel in both, academics and sports.

My simple philosophy gives me direction and it adds enthusiasm to my life. When I do a thing, I always follow this simple procedure. If I like it, I will enjoy it. If I do not like it, I will avoid it. I also realise that in life, there are certain things that we do not like, but we cannot avoid them, so what must we do? There are a few things we need to examine. First if we can change them, then we should. But if there is no possibility of changing any of them, then we should change our attitude to like them. By changing our attitude to like them, we allow enthusiasm to take root because we can do them well. Life is always a choice. Once we can do a thing well, we will grow to like it and our enthusiasm will be kindled. By adopting this attitude, I seem to feel great most of the time and happiness follows.

Another element that helps me to feel great and happy is contentment. Contentment in everything I do is important. I always adopt the attitude that for something that I am not contented, I will try to make changes so that I can grow to like them. Contentment applies to everything: relationship, finance and health. Relationship requires plenty of attention. There will be difficult situations most people encounter. I use to love myself and I also love others. It's natural that if you hate yourself, you tend to hate others. Relationship with others is just a mirror of you. So embrace the grace of love for everyone. You will feel happy loving others.

Another element of life I have embraced is that I have stopped judging others. Before this realisation I used to constantly pass comment or judge people, things and situations. Once I stop labelling, I succeed to free myself from emotions and expectations that can prevent me from enjoying my life to the fullest. Embracing this attitude opens the gate of happiness for me.

All of us are influenced by the emotion called negativity. Most of us are not aware of its limiting beliefs and perceptions. I was stuck in this situation during my adult years unable to create the life I dreamed of. Negativity can be in the form of feelings, emotions, actions or behaviours. These emotions are caused mostly on my own internal circumstances. Awareness is important. First I recognise it. So what is going to be my reaction? For me, once I understand where negativity comes from, I will allow my feelings to flow instead of expressing them, I usually am able to detach myself from such negative thoughts and move on. I do this consistently, persistently and with discipline; repeating such a process until negativity ceases its influence on me. I do not want negativity to sabotage my abundance including my happiness. I started to unload positive thoughts, beliefs and habits of positive people into my mind. I started to implement these characteristics daily. Surprisingly, because of my efforts for a few minutes daily to positively work for myself, I am able to achieve the goal I envisaged. Whatever age you are does not matter. Just like any successful people, I do not accept that negativity is normal but I choose to embrace a positive attitude. I wanted to create my new reality. Instead of settling for being average, I decided to make a new decision to be extraordinary. I have the strong belief that I am already extraordinary and what I need is to discover the truth. Soon I have developed a new positive attitude towards negativity helping me to overcome its effects on my happiness and others. These intentional practices soon became my habits. They allow the ray of happiness to shine into my life. I began to adopt a new philosophy in life.

These are some of the wise words I come across and I intend to follow.

'Behind every problem, there is a question trying to ask itself.
Behind every question, there is answer waiting to surface.
Behind every answer, this is the solution we hope to have.
Behind every solution, there is action to accomplish the goal.'

To bring in sunshine or rain in my life, I just use my mind to imagine and take advantage of thinking well. Look at the blue sky for a few seconds and enjoy the sunshine. The sunshine represents hope and the blue sky represents happiness. What is your choice? I speak for myself. I choose hope and happiness. The weather changes all the time. I do not have to complain about it anymore. I allow hope and happiness to shine in my life.

Turn Failure into Success

To some people the energy of failure can be overwhelming and they stop trying. To me, many of my failures turned into my successes. I was not discouraged by any failure. I consider the period of failure as the time to sow the seeds of my success. I kept trying until I experienced success. Even in the game I loved, I met failures many times, but I persevered and kept practising the basic skills until I succeed. Every one of us experiences failures in our lives. In fact, people who fail the most are the most successful people in life. Many successful people like T. Harv Eker experienced fourteen failures within twelve years before he succeeded. Most people who failed and then succeeded have different mindset. They are constantly trying new things, taking new risks and never giving up. It is not the things that we do that make us regret later on, but the things that we do not do. We need to find our interest, passion and follow it.

Are you one of the persons who never fail? People who sit on the side line and never go down the court to play the game of life are the people who seldom fail. They never achieve their dreams either. They keep complaining about life without success. They choose not to play the game of life to the fullest. Instead they retreat and continue to live their routine lives. They feel it is safer and easier to just keep things the way they are. They rarely fail because they never try.

To me, it's okay to fail, as long as you fail smart, you fail forward and you fail with enthusiasm. What do you mean by failing smart? Every successful person had faced failure before. The difference between learning from failures and getting stuck with failures is failing smart. Successful people know how to move on after a failure and learn the lessons from it. A successful person uses failing smart as a stepping stone to his success. He learns to make changes and plans for another project next time and he seldom repeats the same mistakes. He will analyse his mistakes and find the causes. If the main causes are his thoughts and beliefs in his mind, he will start to look well into the matter next time. He will learn the strategies of successful people. He will visualise the new steps he has to take. He will look into the practices and beliefs of successful people and download their characteristics into their subconscious minds. He will start practising them repeatedly until they master them before venturing into another project.

Failing forward is another way of saying that despite a failure, it encourages him to try harder using another approach. Failing forward teaches him to be more careful in planning and executing his strategies. Failing forward serves as a warning that he is not well prepared for the project. Due diligence is necessary for him to try again. Failing forward becomes his turning point and he starts to examine alternative strategies used by successful people to help him succeed.

Failure with enthusiasm is an attitude of moving forwards despite failures. The spirit is strong and he is willing to spend more time to learn the right strategies leading to his success. Failure is viewed as an opportunity to learn. Many successful people consider the season of failure as the time to sow the seeds of success. It may hurt a little bit and just stop overthinking about it. To them, both success and failure are temporary waves in the ever-changing ocean of life. They are neither permanent nor final. Winston Churchill said: "Success is stumbling from failure to failure with no loss of enthusiasm."

So we need to be aware that in our life journey, we are going to meet failures once in a while. Learn to fail smart, fail forward and fail with enthusiasm. The period of failures is the season where you cultivate the land; getting ready to throw your seeds of success!

Accepting the process and deeds, everything will respond to you. Learn to love yourself and you will realise that you will not find someone more worthy of love than yourself. Try to surround yourself with people having positive energy so more energy will be created. You will move up to a higher level of energy. You will be motivated to go out to meet people who inspire you.

My own experiences tell me that you should not do one thing all day, all week, all month, for the rest of your life. For my life, I mixed them up: games, teaching, writing, investing and having fun with friends. I learn to read books, meet people, spend time with relatives and friends. I try to look for new experiences all the time. I also need time to rest and think. My mind is such a wonderful machine that is capable of combining ideas without me thinking about it. Usually after enough rest, I will go back doing what I love to do, I usually do it better.

Remember, all our possibilities and limitations are self-created. Both fear and confidence are narratives we tell ourselves. If you want to change and improve your life, shift your thoughts and beliefs to the story you prefer and stick with it. Everything you experience including failure is essential to your growth. Every one of us is looking for experience, growth and contribution. Learn to live at the present for it is the foundation for success and happiness. Learn to make full commitment to relax, to work and to enjoy your life. Remember that you need a centred mind to have creative thinking. Whatever the moment brings, embrace it and cultivate peace of mind. The present moment is the ground in which the game of your life happens. I do not allow my past to influence me and I do not worry about the future. I know I cannot change my past. I only focus on the moment and I will do my very best to do better than yesterday.

Lessons on Habits of Happy People

Looking around, I notice the difference between happy people and others. Why are these people happy and enjoying their lives? My observation reveals that happy people are totally excited about life and looking forward towards each day. Unhappy people are different. They drag to get up from bed. They spend their time longing and hoping for better days. Happy people embrace certain habits and practices. They have bounce in their steps, a smile in their face and a sense of purpose in their heart. They have good relationship with others. They are creative and they do work that matter to them. They live a life of purpose and meaning. They enjoy their work. They usually have some degree of financial success. I used to suspect that happy people have advantage because they come from an environment of good upbringing. I also used to suspect that unhappy people come from poor or horrific upbringing. Research into this issue reveals that there is no correlation between these two assumptions. The truth is that happy people can come from all different backgrounds. This awareness is important. To be happy, we need to be sensitive and pay attention to the longing of our heart. This shows that we can learn and practise these habits to attain happiness. We can learn the skills and habits leading us to experience happiness. Once you have acquired them, you must start practising them daily to attain happiness. Discipline or repetition is the key to experience happiness.

The search for happiness is well wired in our brains. Our duty as awakened human beings is to find and strengthen the network to experience happiness throughout our journey of life. To many people, happiness can often be mysteriously elusive. Why is it so difficult for many people to look for positive habits to help them increase their level of happiness? This is partly due to ignorance. Most of the skills leading towards happiness can be learned. It's easily said than done. We are emotionally affected by our experiences. Most of them are engrained in our subconscious mind and they affect our habits and actions. In spite of our massive steps taken to be happy, they are not effective. Happiness seems to be elusive. So what must we do if we want to live a happy life? There are many strategies to help us to eliminate our past experiences, beliefs and habits from our mind before we unload new habits and beliefs of happy people into our subconscious mind. Guided-hypnotherapy is one of them. Mindfulness is another one. There are many other strategies you can follow. I use meditation until I reach an alpha stage to help me to eliminate these outdated beliefs and practices from my mind. Nowadays I use Quantum Jumping and my powerful visualisation technique to download the characteristics of my doppelganger who is a happy person in another parallel universe. I write down all the possible habits imaginable and start to practise them daily to attain happiness. The following habits are imagined to be practised by my doppelganger to become a happy individual. If we want our children to be happy, we need to make them aware of the following habits and learn to practise as many of them as possible regularly. Here are some of the important characteristics our children should learn to embrace.

Accept What Cannot Be Changed

My doppelganger shows me that he never makes an effort to change his past. He only makes changes to his life under his control. I follow his example. I will make every day a better and more productive day than yesterday. I need to accept things that cannot be changed. Everything in life cannot be perfect. What had happened during childhood, during schooling life, working life and family life had passed and cannot be changed. I will accept injustice and setbacks in my past. Instead, I invest my energy and thinking on changing what I can control for the better and make everyday a better day for me and my family. By practising this new habit, I will ensure that every yesterday will be a day of great memory and happiness.

The present moment is what I have. Value the moment is the beginning. What I can control now is to free my heart from worry and hatred. Try to give more and expect less. I make a commitment to be happy when I get up from bed daily. This is how I arrange my mind and I already decided to embrace it. As parents, this approach, accept what cannot be changed, needs to be made known to our children. This is the first step to help them living a happy life.

Let Go of Grudges

My doppelganger tells me that grudges are bad for happiness. He shows clearly that he just lets grudges go and cremates them. My imagination reveals that holding a grudge against anyone encourages resentment, anger, hurt and other negative emotions.

These are standing in the way of my happiness. Practising forgiveness helps me to feel peace and to regain my happiness. This is not going to be an easy thing to do. Think well and know what I want. I need to practise it consistently, persistently and regularly until I achieve my goal. I meditate regularly to gain clarity of thought and soften my mind to let go of grudges. Letting go of grudges in my mind frees me from negativity and allows more space for positive emotions to fill my subconscious mind. Children learn faster than us. The earlier we introduce this habit to them, the better chance for them to be able to let go their grudges and the better chance for them to live happily.

Treat Everyone with Kindness

My doppelganger is such a kind person. A kind person shows compassion and love. Compassion comes from the heart. He loves himself. He cares for others. He is concerned of others' welfare. Usually, a kind person is a giver, not a taker. Kindness is compassion in action. He is smiling most of the time and I think he must be very happy. Happiness is contagious and I also felt happy after meeting him. I immediately realised that I need to pick up the habit of being kind to every person I meet if I want to be happy. I need to learn to say sorry whenever I make a mistake and learn to say thank you whenever someone does me a favour. I learned to give a helping hand when someone is in difficulty. It's natural, giving help to others and you get help. My conscious mind reminds me to practise giving and provide support to others especially the weak. Kindness not only is contagious but also makes me happy. A study reveals that when you are kind to others, your brain produces feel-good hormones and neurotransmitters like serotonin and you are able to build strong relationships with others, fostering positive feelings all around. Kindness is a language everyone can hear and understand. All of us admire the quality called kindness and long to practise it consistently. What is kindness? It is a trait not easily defined. It is a general term referring to a cluster of more specific skills which essentially involve a specific thoughtfulness displaced towards someone. Many actions such as caring for children, elderly people or animals are considered as kindness. An act of giving a helping hand to someone in difficulty or pay for someone who cannot afford a meal is considered kindness. You need to be kind to yourself before you can be kind to others. Many characteristics such as thoughtfulness or considerate behaviours are also common traits of kindness. For me, to be kind, I need to be considerate and mindful of other's well-being. I need to learn the unselfish act to get the focus off myself and on to others. The world will be a better place if we are kind to each other. We will be happier. As parents, this is the first element we need to teach our children. The earlier our children exhibit this trait, show kindness and love for everyone, the better chance for them to be happy. I learn that kindness begets kindness. So it's important that we show kindness and love to anyone we meet. But kindness should not be abused by anyone, even our love ones. We need to practise firm kindness if such an act of compassion is abused. Compassion is from the heart and it expresses itself with a language that is unambiguous, firm kindness for you and the person who might have crossed the boundary line. You need to teach the person to stand on his own feet by saying 'no' to repeated kindness when money is concerned. You need to teach him how to fish instead of keep giving him fish.

Express Gratitude for What We Have

My doppelganger impresses me with his gratitude towards others especially those who have rendered help to him. I share his trait. I am very grateful to so many people who helped me throughout my journey of life. I share his habit of writing down things that he is grateful for in his journal. I keep a gratitude journal by actively writing down things I am grateful for each day.

I have a good record of many people whom I am grateful of. I am very grateful to my eldest sister and her husband who provided me accommodation and food for me to finish my secondary school in Penang. A few of eldest sister's children are not doing well now. Whenever I meet them, I will show my gratitude by giving them financial and moral support. I am grateful to my second sister and her husband who gave me an interest-free loan to finish my university education. I showed my gratitude by providing her son accommodation and tuition in his academic pursuit while he studied at the University of Malaya. I receive help and I give help in return. I am grateful to my third sister and her husband who provided me financial help to acquire my second investment property. I am also very grateful to my girlfriend who helped me to buy my first car. She is now my wife. There are many friends who helped me in many things in my life and I am very grateful to them. All these memories have been linked to my happy moods, greater optimism and better physical health. Many people are not aware of this trait. They take for granted whatever help they receive. It's time to teach our children the beneficial effect of showing gratitude. Knowing is not enough; get them to practise gratitude regularly and it can become a good habit. Knowing to say thank you for any small favour will make parents happier. People who show gratitude are usually happier. This is a good start to encourage our children to do this important trait and they will become happier now and in their later lives.

Don't Sweat over the Small Stuff

My doppelganger is always cheerful. He always lets go any unpleasant event in his daily life. He does not want this small event to affect him. I learned from his example not to sweat over the small stuff. Every day of our lives, many things happen. Some are pleasant and some are less pleasant. I learned not to sweat over an issue that I am mad about. I will let it go. It will be irrelevant soon in a matter of time. Happy people like my doppelganger and me know how to let go life's daily irritations and allow them to roll off our back. I learn and practise this habit to avoid being drag down and become unhappy. Many people are caught with such unpleasant issues every day and they cannot let go. The result is that they are always unhappy. I have a choice. I choose not to sweat over the small stuff. I want to be happy every day. Our children need to be aware of this reality. The earlier they learn not to sweat over the small stuff, the better they can perform things that matter to them. This habit requires regular practice to become autopilot. Hopefully, they learn to lay the foundation for their happiness.

Speak Well of Others

My doppelganger is a typical optimist and he always has some kind words for others. I must make it a habit of always speak well of others. Avoid gossiping and talking negatively about others. Doing such things is like taking a bath in negative emotions and my body will soak them up. Instead, I should talk positively and use nice words about others. By practising this habit, it will help me to foster more positive thinking in my life. I become happier after each practice. As parents, we need to avoid gossiping, judging others and passing unnecessary comments about others. We have no right to such activities. It's more important that we learn to speak well of others and be a role model for our children. By encouraging our children to practise this habit, they can become happier too. When our children speak kind words of others, we too will be happier.

Regard Problems as Challenges

My doppelganger faces many problems in his life. He seems to accept each problem as a challenge. I learn immediately from him that I too need such an attitude. I need to change my internal dialogue so that anytime I have a problem; I will view it as a challenge or a new opportunity to change my life for the better. I need to eliminate the word 'problem' from my mindset. Happy and successful people like problem. They see it as a new challenge to exercise their thinking muscles and make creative innovation for a better outcome. I have a good weapon. Whenever I face a problem, I meditate first to gain clarity of thought. I need a calm environment to think well. I usually let my imagination and visualisation explore all possibilities before I make any decision. I allow my thinking muscles to do all the analysis. It's a challenge and I need to be innovative to think of a solution. I will lay down all the facts, data and information on the table and consider all the probabilities before I make my decision. Once a decision is made, I will stick to it until I achieve my goal. As parents, we need to inculcate such an approach to our children. The earlier they learn to regard their problems as challenges, the better they are prepared for real-life situations. I have passed through the three stages of my life and every stage has its own problems. I learn to solve problems as they emerge. They are good challenges keeping my idea muscles tuned up all the while. I feel happy every time a problem is overcome. I believe our children will be happier if they are well prepared to see problems as challenges.

Dream Big

My doppelganger has big dreams. He dreams big and he accomplishes his goals. He is a successful writer and he has many bestselling books. I learn to dream big as well. I hope to accomplish my goals. I have faith in the infinite power of my mind to achieve virtually everything I can dream off. I must make it a habit of dreaming big. This will help to open my mind to more optimistic and positive ideas. There is nothing to lose by dreaming big as long as it makes me happy. Hope is the mother of all men. Dream with actions is the driving force for achievement. Many children are not aware of dreaming big. As parents, we need to start them early and teach them to set goals and dream big. There is nothing wrong to be ambitious. In fact the actions and efforts caused by dreaming big can enhance motivation and happiness. Dreaming big gives them direction and points the way for their future. They learn to expand their means and make extra efforts to accomplish them. The activities and involvements are usually the ingredients for happiness.

Avoid Making Excuses

My doppelganger is very firm in his decision making and he seldom makes excuses. I learn and practise his habit not to make excuses. It's easy to blame others for our life's failures, but doing so means we are unlikely to rise past them.

Happy people take responsibility for their mistakes or missteps and use the failure as an opportunity to change for the better. As a parent, I need to pass this habit to my children so that they too will not make excuses for their mistakes. Learn to admit any mistake and learn the lesson from it. Give enough thought for the mistake and think of a strategy to avoid such a mistake again instead of making excuses. My experience tells me that by admitting my mistake instead of making excuses, I usually feel happy. All of us make mistakes and we must be ready to learn from each mistake. A mistake encourages me to think. I need to think well. I will avoid the habit of making excuses. By doing so, I have planted another seed of happiness for my life. Children need to learn this habit. As parents, we should encourage them to practise this trait regularly. They need to be honest to themselves to be happy.

Live in the Present

My doppelganger always pays attention on the importance of living at the present. The past is gone; the future has not arrived and we only have the present. Learn to live well in the present. All of us have different past experiences: some were pleasant or positive and some were unpleasant or negative. I learn not to allow my past negative events to replay in my mind. I also learn not to worry about the future. I follow my doppelganger by immersing in whatever I am doing now and take time to be in the present moment. Committing to practise this habit every day and enjoy what is going on opens the door to future happiness.

The present moment is what I have. Making a habit to make today the best day of my life is the beginning of a new chapter in life. Doing so consistently, I have made every yesterday a memorable and happy day. Children are affected more by their past incidents. Many of the children are so affected that these unpleasant incidents blur their thinking. It's time for parents to intervene and make them aware to live in the present. Introduce interesting projects for them to do and keep them active and involved. By working enthusiastically on the present, it will lessen the effects of the unpleasant past. Cultivate this habit of always living in the present, our children will feel happier.

Don't Compare Yourself with Others

My doppelganger does not compare himself with others. Although he is successful and happy, he does not compare his lifestyle and happiness with others who may be more successful. He does things to improve himself and measure his achievements in terms of his own initiatives and efforts. He never forms his judgemental language and develops ill feelings like envy. I learned a good lesson from him and my imagination helps me to realise that each of us is unique. I am unique and I do not have to compare myself with my relatives or friends. By adopting this attitude, I manage to reduce stress and judgemental feelings. Even developing the feeling of superiority or inferiority comparing with my peers is detrimental to my happiness. I learn to measure my success based on my own progress and not that of others. Practising this habit seems to increase my happiness. Many weak students feel inferior when their results are compared with others. As parents, it is important that we measure our children's success in terms of their own efforts instead of others. Teach our children early not to compare their achievements relative to others. This will avoid superiority or inferiority complex. They will be happier if they can practise this habit of not comparing with others. They will learn to strive for themselves and for their own improvements.

Wake Up at the Same Time Every Morning

My doppelganger and I have the same habit of waking up at the same time every morning. I formed this good habit of waking up early by circumstances. I was living with my eldest sister's family in Penang. There was no room for me and I had to sleep on a camp bag under the staircase.

Every morning, I woke up at about 6.30 am to avoid the crowd going to work and my sister's children going to school. I did this regularly every morning and this habit helped me regulate my circadian rhythm and I felt more energised. I have formed a good habit. I escaped to the basketball court behind my sister's house to train my basic skills. This partly explains why I became an outstanding basketball player. The secret of mastering any skill is repetition and drill. I was an outstanding player in dribbling, shooting and various skills of lay ups. I was the star player for my team for many years.

My doppelganger is a happy and successful person. Most successful people have the habit of getting up early and this habit enhances productivity and focus. Getting up early regularly is a common virtue of successful people. My experiences as an administrator revealed that I got more work done in the first two hours in the morning than four hours in the afternoon. I used to get the best work done without all the distractions and interruptions. My focus is at its best in the morning. It's a simple thing to get up half an hour earlier than others, but over time, the benefits can be dramatic in making you more successful than the next guy because your productivity increases.

One of the most important things you can do to change your life is get to work or train your passion half an hour early. My doppelganger and I belong to the group of disciplined people. We have another good habit of brushing and flossing our teeth after every meal. I used to keep a spare toothbrush in my pocket wherever I go. After a snack, even tea time, I used to brush my teeth. This habit lives with me until now. I am in my seventies and I still enjoy a full set of beautiful teeth. By practising these healthy habits, I enjoy good health and feel happy. Children learn the habit of going to bed early and getting up at the same time easily. The habit has to be cultivated as early as possible. A little bit of encouragement will help. They will be happier and have better energy to do things they enjoy.

Surround Yourself with Positive People

The choice of friends has a great influence on our happiness. I notice many of my good friends are always surrounded by successful and optimistic people. They learn to speak a positive and happy language. I learned this approach early in my working life. Most of my friends are my university mates and also my basketball playmates. Talking, interacting and listening to them helps me to soak in their wisdom and their healthy language and I follow their happiness mindset. Happiness is contagious and I soon develop the habit of positive thoughts. Thoughts are important to good health and happiness. Healthy thoughts also help to quiet my own mind and enhance clarity of thinking. Healthy thoughts influence the cells of our bodies to function well. I learn to be selective in choosing friends. I usually avoid people who are grumpy and pessimistic. I know their influence is not good for my happiness. I prefer friends who are optimistic and happy. I enjoy sharing their positive energy and their successes. Adopting the belief 'Birds of the same feather flock together' gives me more energy to be happy. Children are influenced by their peers. Teaching them early to mix well will lay the foundation for their happiness. It's important to teach our children to be selective in mixing with friends. Peers' influence can be one of the important factors in deciding the behaviours and beliefs of our children. Make them aware of the importance of surrounding themselves with positive people. Their thinking and speaking are influenced by the people surrounding them. Ultimately, their happiness will be affected. Happiness is contagious. The happy language we hear can influence and affect us. Words of encouragement and affirmation are powerful. They influence not only our mood but also our thoughts. We learn to speak the same language. The surest way towards happiness is to surround ourselves with positive people whose energy and enthusiasm will resonate with us.

Take Time to Listen

I notice that my doppelganger from a parallel universe is always very attentive when his friends speak to him. He takes time to listen to others and he seldom interferes when others are speaking to him. I did not have this quality of listening attentively before partly because nobody sensitises me regarding this trait. I was not aware of such a good habit. I learn a critical lesson after this encounter. I have many friends who are successful and optimistic. I learn from them by taking time to listen to their wisdom, their thoughts and their opinions regarding daily issues. Learning to think well and speak well earlier gives me an advantage. Now I discipline myself to listen attentively to different perspectives and different opinions. The new discovery of taking time to listen adds ideas to my thinking and helps me to speak and articulate from different perspectives. My wisdom and judgement seem to improve and my relationship with others improves, too. I grow to become more considerate and more polite in speaking. Consequently, I feel happier. By taking time to listen, not only we benefit from the wisdom of others but it also helps us to gather information and alternative views. Awareness is not enough; our children need to be trained to listen carefully if they want to learn more instead of missing valuable information and knowledge. They will be better equipped and gained more from others. Knowing more and respecting others' opinions will pave the way to enjoy happiness. People will tend to like them and communicate with them.

Nurture Social Relationship

My doppelganger not only listens to others, he also makes an effort to nurture social relationship. He has many friends with similar interest. They feel at ease with each other. They can discuss issues and jokes. They play together and enjoy common interest. I have good social contact because of my enthusiasm in games. When I played basketball in my younger days, I had many good friends who enjoy the same sport. Now in my retirement, I play tennis. I enjoy meeting friends with the same interest. I also keep in touch with friends from the academic circle. We have gathering once in a while to enjoy foods and share common interest regarding current affairs and issues. We are gregarious animals and we need to embrace the trait of interacting and exchange ideas regularly. Sharing and helping each other keeps our social relationship alive. I always make time to visit friends, family members and significant others. All these positive relationships are keys to build our happiness. As parents, it's our responsibility to introduce hobbies or sports to our children. Most sports or hobbies require participants. This provides the platform for our children to socialise. Common interest seems most effective to nurture social relationship. Our children will be happier through these groupings. Once our children learn to think well and speak well, they normally socialise well. They stand tall because they think well and speak well.

We Do Not Need Other's Approval

My doppelganger is an independent achiever and he has the habit of acting independently without seeking other's approval. He listens to advices and he considers different opinions or views, but he follows his own dreams and goals without letting naysayers stand in his way. I learned an important lesson regarding my own dreams and my desires. I want to be happy so I will follow what happy people do. They stay true to their hearts' desire and do not get bogged down with the need for outside approval. Once I learn this critical habit, I begin to practise it regularly. Whenever I plan a project, I will consider all possible perspectives, listen to others' opinions and advices, but I will make my own decision on how to execute my plan without seeking other's approval. As a parent, I need to impart this habit to my children. They do not need other's approval to be proactive and take initiative. They need to form this independent attitude after considering the views and advices of others. They learn to follow their hearts' desire. They do not have to live under others shadows. This independent attitude will ensure their confidence in decision making and feel happier.

Be Honest

My doppelganger has a very strong trait that he is always honest in everything he does. This strikes me greatly. Before this realisation, I used to give excuses even telling white lies to cover myself. Now I realise that by not being honest to myself, I reduce my own happiness. Honesty becomes the most critical habit of my life. Honesty is now the best policy for me to live a happy life. My past experiences tell me that whenever I lie or cheat my stress level increases and my self-esteem crumbles just a little bit more. Not being honest does not help my happiness. My conscience was not clear whenever I told a lie. I realise the danger that when others find out that I am a liar, it will damage my personal and professional relationship. On the other hand, telling the truth is always a good habit. It boosts my mental health and allows others to have trust in me. After practising this habit regularly, my relationship with others seems to improve and my happiness strengthens. Children learn easily. As parents, this particular trait is critical to share with our children. They need more than just knowing that honesty is the best policy, they need to practise this habit regularly until it becomes part and parcel of their life. I believe most honest persons are happier people. Our children will enjoy self-respect and happiness if they master the behaviour of being honest in dealing with others.

Establish Personal Control

Self-control is an important trademark for my doppelganger. notice that he does not allow others to dictate the way he behaves and lives. He enjoys independent thinking and personal self-worth. The only person important to you is you. Nobody can live the life for you. You are the only person who decides who you want to be. You are the player, the referee, the judge and the only person in your game of life. Your destiny is in your own hands. I learn a great lesson here. I am the only person who will decide my dreams and goals. No one can dictate the way I live and the way I go about achieving my goals. I need to be independent in thinking and action. My self-worth is only a story I can tell myself not somebody else. I need to be the player and the referee in the life game I play. My destiny is my own responsibility. Developing my personal control in everything I do is critical. No one can dictate to me how I live my life. I will take responsibility of what I do and no one can tell me to go after my dreams. Personal control is the key. Sharing this trait known as self-control with our children is a priority. Self-control needs to be taught and practised as early as possible. Once our children master this trait, they will be more responsible for every one of their action. They will not form the habit of looking for somebody to blame for their action or failure. People with self control are usually happier people.

Exercise Regularly to Keep Fit

My doppelganger is a healthy and fit person. Healthy people exercise regularly because they love their bodies and they enjoy an active and happy life. Exercising regularly is crucial for your health and well-being. It not only keeps you slim by losing weight but it improves circulation, memory and it boosts your happiness hormone or serotonin levels. My doppelganger and I are active sportsmen. We are both slim and fit. We enjoy our healthy bodies as well as the excitements of competitive games. To us, excitement and active participation in games bring happiness. A healthy body is essential for me to live an active life. Even now, I discipline myself to play tennis at least three times a week to enjoy the game and maintain my stamina. I am lucky to be living at the foot of a mountain in Brisbane. I climb the mountain every day to keep my leg muscles tuned up regularly. This allows my heart to pump vigorously and keep me fit to enjoy life. It improves my cardiovascular health including lowering my blood pressure. I keep myself lean and my weight under control. It boosts my muscle tissue and increases my metabolism. All these regular activities seem to boost my level of health-promoting brain chemicals like serotonin, dopamine and norepinephrine. All these chemicals are produced to help me to buffer some of the effects of stress and also relieve some symptoms of depression. I am happy because I am stress and depression free. These activities partly explain why I always feel happy. I use to share this lifestyle with my children and grandchildren. Healthy people are happy people. Other benefits follow. Regular exercise helps to improve my bone mineral density and I live a life free from arthritis. Little do I realise, I pass motion easily every day. This is partly explained by regular exercise that increases gastrointestinal transit speed and it reduces my chance of getting colon cancer. As parents, it is our duty to pass this information to our children and get them to exercise regularly. Get them to form the habit of regular exercise by picking up a game and play seriously to enjoy it.

Eating Well Increases Happiness

My doppelganger impresses me regarding his diet every day. He eats plenty of vegetables, fruits, fish and other types of protein. I share his eating habits to keep me on a balanced diet. I allow my food to be my medicine and medicine to be my food. I learn to eat moderately and avoid sugar and trans-fat like animal fats and preserved food. I prefer fresh foods. I always remember that what God provides in terms of fresh food, I eat plenty of them and what humans do by adding unnecessary additives to the food, I avoid them. My choice of food serves well for my well-being both physically and spiritually. Healthy living is necessary to happiness. We need to share this vital information with our children. Encourage them to eat well as their bodies renew themselves regularly. Eating well improves our immune system and keeps us healthy to enjoy an active life.

There are foods that can help to keep our brain active and alert. Fish is known as brain food. Eating fish regularly will certainly help. Eating plenty of fruits and vegetables will also help. There is another type of fruit called avocados which can help to build your brain's muscle strength through its monosaturated acids. Though fatty, avocados are full of unsaturated fats which keep cell membranes supple. Another food found in dark chocolate known as coco is a good stimulant of the brain. Do not eat too much to avoid obesity. An array of condiments including salsa, mustard and horseradish are all good for the brain provided they are wheat and gluten free. A vegetable such as broccoli is a versatile food containing vitamin K which strengthens cognitive abilities. It also enhances your immune system preventing diseases. The folic acid in broccoli helps to prevent depression and reduces risk in Alzheimer's disease. Fruits like blueberries help to repair nerve damaged cells and enhance short-term memory loss. Eating raw garlic, ginger, cinnamon and onion allows your body to consume helpful probiotics. A perfect meal that consists of three to four ounces of protein served with moderate amount of vegetables will do wonders to your brain. Essential fatty acids (EFC) are necessary for the brain to function efficiently. Fish like salmon, trout, mackerel, herring and sardine contain plenty of EFC. They help not only brain function but also our joints. We need to be active; eat well and live a healthy and happy life.

Living A Simple and Orderly Life

My doppelganger is such a successful man and yet he lives minimally. I live an orderly life. I avoid clutter which has a way of sucking the energy right out of me and replacing it with a feeling of chaos. Clutter is a habit providing unrecognised source of stress prompting anxiety, frustration, and distraction. I live a life free from clutter by getting rid of excess papers, files and other stuffs that not only take up physical space but also take up my mental space. Just like my doppelganger, I learn the skill of placing things in orderly manner and organise my space to suit my lifestyle. Orderliness and organising ability saves me a lot of headache and time. I am helping to create more space for happiness.

As parents, it's important that we train our children to live a simple and orderly life. Getting them to practise this habit early can save them time and money. Avoid clutter and avoid disorder habits starting at home. An orderly life is important. Placing important items in their orderly places saves time and avoids unnecessary frustration. Orderly arrangements look nice and encourage happy moods. An orderly home or office is necessary for efficiency and productivity. A lot of time is saved in looking for things in the house or office. Ultimately, this simple and orderly life is necessary for happiness.

Increase Your Spirituality

My doppelganger is spiritual but not religious. I, too, believe in spirituality but not being religious. I have practised meditation for many years and I seem to gain clarity of thought and increase my spirituality. My consciousness evolution begins and my conscience starts operating well. I become aware of others' needs and become more considerate. I long to contribute to others' well-being and needs. I am excited by new experiences, growth and I develop the urge to contribute. I am a Born-Again Christian but I must admit that I am not religious. I admire the wisdom and teaching of Jesus. I want to follow his teaching to enhance my spirituality. But I do not follow the rituals of Christians. Now I have found a new way of meditation called Quantum Jumping. My imagination and visualisation take on a new dimension. I manage to keep my mind focused, calm my nerves and keep my inner peace. All these mental games in the form of meditation or prayer seem to provide me with physical changes in my brain, enhancing spirituality and make me happier.

Do you want to be happy? Do you want your children to be happy? I believe all of us want the feeling of happiness throughout our lives. It is proven that our performance in our job or project is enhanced if we are happy. The journey in this pursuit of happiness will be worth every effort you put in. Your productivity will pick up if you work happily. Your success will improve while you are happy. Working happily throughout the journey of your life, the abundance you dream off will be the end result. What are the steps you can take to help yourself and your children? Simple, teach your children to embrace spirituality either in the form of meditation, prayer or hypnotherapy. Whatever process you choose does not matter. The important thing is to be happy. I choose this simple three-step procedure to achieve abundance.

First, get rid of the outdated beliefs, habits and practices that make you unhappy from your mind. You can choose whatever method you want. This pre-reloading of all the rubbish beliefs in your mind must be done first.

Once the pre-reloading process is done, a big space in your mind is created and this space can be loaded with the characteristics of happy people. Learn each of the characteristics listed above carefully and discuss it with your children. Some explanations are necessary and you can start the process of thinking well in them. Mastery of the elements needs repetition just like practising the strokes of tennis. The more practices you do the better leading to mastery and play well.

Get your children to practise these beliefs consistently until these habits become their lifestyle. This is analogous to practise the strokes of tennis under playing condition. I believe all the efforts will benefit both parents and children alike. Once these happy elements gain autopilot stage, they have found the key that unlocks the secret of happiness.

The manifestation comes in the form of their smiling faces. They are excited about their lives and look forward to each day. They can forget about spending their time hoping for better days. The happy days are here.

They have bounce in their steps, a cheerful look all the time and a sense of purpose in their heart. They have mastered the habits for happy people. They will be more productive in whatever they do. The journey towards abundance has just begun.

Imitate Some Good Habits of Happy people

I use to look around and mix with happy people. I am very interested in the habits of life and I want to follow their good habits to be happy. I also manage to contact my doppelganger in another parallel universe to share his habits of living a happy life. The following are some of the observations I notice and I want to follow. First, most happy people are fit and healthy. If you tell me that you are happy and you are not fit and healthy, I will never believe you. People are happy because they love their bodies and they understand the connection between body and mind. They have a positive attitude and they exercise regularly. They probably enjoy their sex life. They have children and they love them. Regular exercise helps to enhance their happiness hormone or serotonin levels. It's simple, the happier your body, the happier your mind thinks.

Second, most of the people around me are happy with their lives and they take ownership of their happiness. They know that they alone are responsible for their own happiness. There is no one else to blame. This simple positive attitude reveals that happy people not only think well but also speak well. Many of my happy friends are intellectuals and I believe they write well, too. They enjoy their experiences, their growths and make their contributions. They are aware that creating services and values for others they have created values for themselves.

Third, most of the happy people I know think well. They do not believe everything they think off. They are aware that their minds are capable of throwing negative thoughts, fears and anxieties. So it's natural that they do not have to take every thought seriously. They are capable of self-discipline to focus on their positive thoughts and act on them. They are able to let go the rest of the negative ones.

Fourth, happy people exhibit compassion and their kindness is the act of their compassion. They let love lead them all the way to happiness. Their life is surrounded by love and they give love freely. Most of them love their jobs and they love helping people.

The more help or support they render, the more they get in return. There is certain risk while doing all these acts, but they know the rewards far outweigh the risk. They understand the principle that the more love they share, the happier they become.

Fifth, most of the happy people I know appreciate the wonders of the world. They are grateful and thankful for all the wonders they receive every day. They enjoy the free sunlight, the free air and many nature gifts to us. Some of them believe in a power beyond and others have their own methods of attaining spirituality. They have faith in the universe and they witness their goals and dreams manifesting. They live with hope and they take action to achieve their dreams.

Sixth, most happy people are inspired and feel that they are drawn to a bigger purpose than themselves. They share the two important days of their lives: the day of birth and the day they found their purpose of life in the universe. They respond to their calling knowing that they are here to serve others. By creating values for others, they create values for themselves. They seem to have discovered that the bigger their dreams, the more people they will impact and the happier they become. They enjoy new experiences, growth and contribution. They begin to enjoy spirituality that comes naturally.

Last but not least, most of the happy people enjoy good relationship with people around them and the environment. They put in a lot of efforts to build relationship with special focus on relationship rather than getting it. They believe in rendering help to others, saying kind words about others, praising their works, supporting others and showing love all the way. The consequence is that the more they give, the more they receive and the happier they become. Rendering help, you will get help. Give and you will receive. All these natural things are analogous to the physical laws of Newton especially the third law stating that for every action there is an equal and opposite reaction. These natural laws of attraction are analogous to physical laws.

Overcome Past Unhappiness

Throughout our lives, we have encountered many issues and we have to make decisions regarding our career, the car we buy, the house we live, our relationship, where we live and the size of our families. We make many decisions. Some are good and some are not so good. However, the one and most important decision we need to consider is regarding our happiness. I do not allow external factors which are beyond my control to make me unhappy. Most of us are affected by past events. There are many unhappy events we experienced. These unhappy issues and happenings are unconsciously programmed in our subconscious mind without us realising them. And they are affecting our life, our beliefs, our thinking and our perceptions of the world. Do you allow past issues to make you unhappy? How do I overcome these unpleasant issues?

In this modern world, your doctor may suggest that you consult a psychologist or a hypnotherapist to help you to overcome these past unhappy issues. For me, I always have a ready tool in the form of meditation called Quantum Jumping. It only takes me a few minutes to meet up with my doppelganger who is psychologist and a counsellor. As soon I merged with my twin-self, I acquired his rhythm, energy and frequency of vibration. My imagination and visualisation began its exploration. I immediately obtained a glimpse of my vision through the lens of my doppelganger. Instead of getting external influence to change my belief system, I knew immediately I had to do it internally. When I reached the alpha state of mind, I had the advantage of clarity of thinking that I had to get rid of all these unhappy issues that stuck in my subconscious mind. I allowed these unpleasant issues to dissolve and I began to get rid of them from my mind. I sensed that I had a big space in my mind for me to fill. I took the opportunity to unload the characteristics of happy people to fill the vacuum. What are these characteristics? I must get rid of all the conditions I was thinking before. My happiness does not depend on an apology, a letter of admission, a good partner, a good job, an expensive house, or getting a big sum of money. I make the commitment to be happy right now. This powerful intention to follow the characteristics of happy people will eventually transform any disharmony because of my past issues to feelings of peace and bliss. Some of these characteristic of happy people are simple, such as accept what cannot be changed, let go grudges, show kindness, speak well of others and do not compare yourself with others.

I am committed to be happy. I have to keep reminding myself to practise these habits of happy people daily. Practising these habits of happiness is analogous to practising my tennis strokes. The more practice I have will help me to become a better player. Similarly if I keep reminding myself of these happy habits and practise them regularly until they become my own habits, I will definitely be happier. It only takes me a few months of constant reminder and practice and I am on the way to live a happy life. Now I must make sure that I keep practising these habits consistently, persistently and playfully. I enjoy doing them and my happiness seems to be growing. As parents, you can also start to help your children to inculcate these happy habits in their mind and teach them to practise them regularly so that they will enjoy happiness. These three simple approaches will help you to hack your subconscious mind, to create a new brain which has the quality of instant recall, unbreakable focus, motivation on command and clarity of mind. While you are practising and adhering to this proven strategy, I believe that nobody can prevent you from the smile of happiness.

The Marriage Effect on Health and Longevity

Recently I come across a longevity factor which is more powerful than food. I have been concentrating on good diet, regular exercise, meditating, prayer, getting enough sleep, eating plenty of fruits and vegetables to keep me healthy and hope to live to see my grandchildren finishing their university courses. I have overlooked the marriage effect on my health and longevity. After a few verbal clashes with my wife, I suddenly realise that there is another factor which will affect my longevity and good health. Now I see clearly that a happy marriage is an important factor for me to live healthily and enhance my longevity. This is an important consciousness that I want to share with others. All of us want to live longer, enjoy physical and mental health and improve our immune system to recover from sickness quickly. A study in 2007

reveals that the rate death of single men over the age of 40 was twice as high as that of married men. It shows that marriage for men is a life saver. This marriage effect is found to be only for happy married men, not those in partnership without the commitment. Oprah calls this effect the 'Marriage Whisperer' applicable to only happy married couples with safety, security and trustworthy. Men in partnership do not enjoy such safety, security and trustworthy, the most profound human needs. This triggers the awareness that we all need to work for our security knowing that the payoff is longevity and a more stable lifestyle. Take note of the good news for married men and women that sex can save your life. All married couples who want a healthy and happy life, make sure that you have regular sex, the more the better for your health and longevity. The finding of sex expert Dr Pepper Schwartz of the University of Washington is good news for women as well as men. In his studies of women in happy marriage, he found that regular sex lowers anxiety; provides more vitality; enhances a higher quality of life and helps in the building immunity. For men, sex one time a month or more will reduce the risk of dying by over 60 per cent. The men who have sex twice a week or more are least likely to die because sex provides protection against cancer and heart disease. The bottom line for happy married couples is that a sexy marriage is one of the keys to a long and healthy life. My new resolution after having a few verbal arguments with my wife is that I want to invest my time and energy into my relationship with her. We should stop trying to be right all the time. Making assumptions and speculations are not healthy for happy marriage. We should support each other rather than try to put down our spouse because of different perceptions and different interests. Each one is encouraged to pursue his or her passion. I believe that the investment into a good relationship between husband and wife is worth all the efforts for healthy and long life.

Summary

Teaching our children to speak the language of healthy and happy people as early as possible is a good sign for our own sake. The habits and practices of healthy and happy people can be learned. The three-step procedure is a good strategy to use. First is identification. Find out why you are not happy. Usually our happiness is affected by our past and environments. This awareness is important for you to eliminate them from your subconscious mind which is the controlling machine. Find a tool necessary to accelerate the eliminations of these beliefs and habits. The next step is to be aware and learn the characteristics of healthy and happy people. Download these characteristics into your subconscious mind and start practising them regularly until they belong to you. The more you repeat and practise them, the better. Follow these steps consistently, persistently and playfully, soon you will belong to the group of healthy and happy people.

CHAPTER FIVE

THE LANGUAGE OF THE MIND

Introduction

This chapter introduces the language of the mind. It focuses on the common terms such as conscious mind, the unconscious mind, the conscious gap, conscience, intuition, conscious fear, unconscious fear, emotional brain, intellectual brain, perceptions, perspectives, beliefs, reprogramming of the mind and others. Familiarity of the language of the mind will provide the advantage of understanding your actions and inactions towards your dreams. Most of us know what we want to achieve in life. We all want to be happy, healthy and wealthy. We want meaningful relationship. We want to be a great parent and be connected to our children. We want to be a greater lover. We all want to be fit and healthy to enjoy our journey of life. In short, we all want a life of abundance. How do we achieve abundance? We are aware of the bits and pieces of the necessary steps we need to take in order to achieve a particular goal. We know the end, bits of the middle but we do not have any clue how to start off a journey towards abundance. Our education system does not help. The aim of education is to enrich our life but there is a big gap. The necessary steps of moving towards our dreams are not taught in our schools. Being conscious of these dreams does not help us either. We need to know that success in areas mentioned above will decide whether we live a normal or extraordinary life. I hope this book will serve to fill the gap most of us are lacking.

The Evolution of Consciousness

What will decide our success or failure to accomplish these dreams lies in our subconscious or the centre of the mind. First we need to know that the universe will provide abundance to anyone who seeks it. It is interesting that our perspectives will shape our reality. If we see the universe as the gracious provider of everything; we need to be fit and healthy, happy and wealthy, then the universe will be the place that helps us to achieve our dreams instead of a place that deprives us from reaching our goals. What we need is our imagination and creative visualisation to see our lives' visions. We need to learn to tap into the creative force within us. The quote from Henry David Thoreau says it all. The quote is as follows:

> I know of no more encouraging fact than the unquestionable ability of man to elevate his life by conscious endeavour.

Another quote by the late Steve Jobs echoed the same sentiment:

> "Everything around us was created by people no smarter than you… and you can change it."

This awareness triggers the power of consciousness that directs our life. Do not let others telling us to be realistic from reaching our full potential. This is the quantum leap in the evolution of our visualisation and imagination. Visualisation is a concrete method that can make our dreams and desires become reality. By adding life vision to our visualisation, we move from reactive to proactive and this will enhance our chance of success. This helps to show the direction and points to the destination we desire. It's important that we align our thoughts and goals when we 'innercise' or internal exercise to visualise. Creative visualisation is a mental process of forming images of what we want in our life. Even sportsmen and top executives use it to enhance their performance. We get moving and stay moving! We keep our motivation centre active. With it, we can experience any kind of success. It is a proven technique to tap into the full power of our subconscious mind. The spiritual teacher, Esther Hicks said:

> "Seventeen minutes of focus, pleasurable visualisation is stronger than 2000 hours of working to obtain a goal."

First, we need to say goodbye to our stubborn limiting beliefs. These beliefs in the form of destructive habits, fears, anxiety, negative thought patterns and other internal blocks are holding us back. Life is never a smooth path. We come into contact with people. Each one of them is unique. Most people are good and kind. They are willing to go an extra mile to help you. But there are some people who are different. They do not care for you. Some are actually big bullies. They do things or say things that can hurt you. All these experiences will live with you. Are you going to be affected by this small group of people? I learn to ignore them. I do not want their behaviours to affect my life and my happiness. How do you do it? I choose to forgive them by not associating with them. I choose my friends with common interest. I choose to mix with positive and happy people who can help me to grow. I want to make contributions to make the world a better place for all. This awareness is critical to help me in eliminating anxiety, anger, fear and even hate in my conditioned mind. It is not me. Once these chatters are eliminated from my head through internal and intentional process or meditation, replacement process can begin. How? It is simply unloading characteristics of successful people into our mind and starting to implement them daily to experience the success we desire. Every intentional effort will be richly rewarded. Remember that our efforts will be futile if our desires are not aligned with our subconscious beliefs. The earlier we communicate with our subconscious mind with creative visualisation the better for us to achieve our desires and dreams. This communication will trigger a radical shift from inside out that can change the way we perceive reality. Soon these intentional practices become part of our habits, practices and thought patterns. This consciousness exercises will trigger our thinking to the next level. We will not get stuck to any absolute model of reality like being disconnected with the universe, being disillusioned about our environments, living with fear and hostility. We need to learn a new language of the mind.

The Language of the Mind to Achieve Abundance

Mankind has all the potential for an incredible future. All we need is a higher level of thinking. Most of us are operating at a static level of thinking that needs to be updated. The world needs more people who think well and can help to push humanity forwards. All of us need compassion, healing and consciousness elevation. Compassion is the driving force for kindness. Consciousness directs the course of our actions. Our life vision describes our desired destination. The journey towards abundance is exciting. Repetition of good habits, beliefs and practices of successful people can help us to activate an autopilot attraction and repetition that etch a crystal clear idea of a future abundant life we envied. Many of the practices and habits will be dealt with clearly for you to download into your mind. Practise them regularly like what we do in tennis strokes to gain mastery. Eventually, your reality will be forced to match the picture of abundance you created. Our education system fails to address this aspect of human aspiration. The following suggestions will serve to help us moving towards a life of abundance.

First, if we learn to see the world surrounding us as full of abundance, our life will be filled with abundance. So it is important that we begin to see the positive side of the world. The poor think that the universe is against them. The reason many of us are poor is because we have poor contexts or beliefs in our subconscious mind. We think that we will never be rich. Some of us even think that the rich will not go to heaven. We think we will be happy when we hold the perception that money is not important to us. In most welfare countries, people think that their government will take care of them. This partly explains why so many lottery winners are soon broke. People think differently. People in the middle class have different thinking from the poor. To the middle class, there is a shift in priorities and values. Their contexts are different. They think of getting a good education, securing a high-paying job and they will have job security.

They earn and spend. They never become rich. The wealthy people think differently. They cut their spending and save money to invest. They invest in financial education. The rich men contexts are different. They own business, stocks and assets; take challenges and learn more about money. They do not want a fixed salary. They want more free time and financial freedom. They are capitalists. They know how to use other people's money or good debt to build their wealth. If we want to be rich, we need to learn to use debt, good debt instead of bad debt, to become rich. I wanted to be rich, so I have to change my contexts or the beliefs and practices in my subconscious mind. When I started to change my poor man context to middle class context and then to rich man context; I had changed my view of the world. I begin to see the world from the lens of the rich. One thing I notice is that rich people use rich words, middle-class people use middle-class words and poor people use poor words. They speak different languages. It is always true that what we think about or what we say about always come true. Poor people say that they can't afford it but rich people say how they can afford it. The middle-class considers the pros and cons of buying it. To change our life, we first need to change our spoken words and more importantly change our beliefs in our subconscious mind. We need to learn the language of the mind by embracing the language of the rich and successful.

Second, according to my experience, once I have internalised the practices, habits and beliefs of the rich, my view of money begins to change. I begin to speak the language of the rich. I have learned the power of sharing, investing, giving and expanding my means. My paradigm shift in education from academic to finance helps in the transformation. I need to learn in sharing whatever abundance I have. What is sharing? Money is not the only one thing we need to share. If we can, it will be fantastic. We can also share our talents, our love, our attitudes, our experiences and our happiness with others. We need to grow together and make our contributions in whatever way we can. By sharing, we will have mutual benefits. Even if we do not feel that we have all the abundance we need, we can still share as if we have everything we need. Giving support, we get support and giving help, we get help. If you create value for others you create value for yourself. These simple spiritual laws behave like Newton's Third Law: for every action there is an equal and opposite reaction. It would not be long before we are blessed with more abundance as we share with those in need. I realised that if I wanted to change my life about money, I need to change my context. I know immediately that if I want to transform my life, I need to learn to transform my income from linear to residual. The poor and middle class work for linear income which is their salary. The rich work for streams of residual income (rentals, royalties, dividends and commissions and portfolio income as capital gains) and cash flow. The rich use cash flow as their income creation and they become richer. You need financial education to help you become rich.

Third, do not allow others to dissuade us from our goal of abundance. Remember that there are always people who will be critical about our pursuit of abundance. They will tell us to be contented and be realistic with what we have. We need to be polite and respectful of their beliefs and habits, but we must not be influenced by their opinions. Never give in to negative thoughts and emotions. Keep our emotional mind under control and keep our focus on positive energy to help us get everlasting abundance. Make sure that we implant this powerful flow of energy and positive abundance in our subconscious mind. Make every effort to keep the energy flowing and the positivity deeply implanted. Our goals of abundance will be granted. Another quality to embrace is to learn to be generous. Remember, the more people you serve the more effective you become. You can also become a capitalist. Before you can do that, you need to become rich. The Bible says,

> "Give and you will receive. Your gift will return to you in full pressed down, shaken together and make room for more, running over and poured into your lap. The amount you give will determine the amount you get back."

Most of us tend to violate this principle of generosity. We want more pay, do less work and retire early. Are we generous? So if more and more people are generous and are willing to share their abundance, the world will be a different place. By giving our children another point of view by discussing the principle of generosity, they will learn sharing instead of being greedy. They will be more likely to be inspired to be generous and have a new perception that not all capitalists are greedy. They will soon learn to serve others and are more receptive to financial education.

It's important to teach our children the languages of money and mind. Without such understanding, our children will face many unpleasant consequences. When our children buy their first house, many salespersons will impress on them that their home is their greatest asset and biggest investment. So they should buy the most expensive house they can afford. If your children are not financially savvy, they will certainly believe. According to Robert T. Kiyosaki, your home is not an asset but a liability. Remember, your home does not add money to your coffers. It takes money out of your pocket. There are many bills you have to take care of to maintain your home. My advice is that do not buy a home that is too costly. Buy a small house first and upgrade your home after four or five years as your income increases and the family grows. If you are not careful, your home can turn up to be a liability when you lose your job or any recession sets in like what happened in 2007-2008 in USA. Many Americans learned a bitter lesson considering their homes as assets by refinancing their mortgages. Always be prepared when you buy your first home. Buying a second property is different. It is going to be an asset producing rental, adding money to your coffer. Remember that any salesman will always tell you what you want to hear when you make an investment. For example, investments in REIT will give a return of about 8 per cent per year on average. Those gains occur during the boom years. They will use words and information that support their sales. They will not tell you what happens during the period of recession. We need to teach our children the language of money in order for them to be financially savvy. They need to understand and not be deceived by many of the sales slogans such as your home is the greatest asset; diversification is a way to reduce risk and invest for long term. All these words are not financial education. Remember when an investment planner advises you to diversify your investments in stocks or properties; they are telling you that they do not know which one will do well and which one will fail. It's great if our children start to learn the language of the mind and also language of money together with us.

I share my experiences of using the step-by-step strategy of elimination, replacement and implementation of habits and practices of successful people to help me to move to the next level of abundance. I use a simple weapon called meditation and visualisation to help me achieve my goals. The process is tedious and it requires consistency, persistency, discipline and playfulness. Playfulness will ensure interest and joy to enhance productivity. You can choose to follow me or use whatever strategy you prefer. And today, I live a life that literally inspires me to get out of my bed each morning, filled with energy and purpose. I want to accomplish something every day. The new beliefs in my central mind act as the driving force to activate more love and passion in my thinking and doing things. I want more fulfilment and more vitality. I want to make more contribution to better mankind. Knowing the important role of the subconscious mind is a great blessing to me and I want this blessing to be shared by as many people as possible.

The Conscious Gap towards Abundance

Abundance is not just financial freedom but it includes well being, happiness and good health. The body's immune system will be rejuvenated from within and the healing process accelerated to keep us healthy. There are other benefits when our subconscious mind is activated. Our inner energy level increases, resulting in better memory, enhancing learning skills and changing unwanted habits. Our journey towards abundance begins. But do not forget our happiness. A lot of people think that they will be happy when they achieve a goal in their future. The problem is when they achieve it; they have another goal to achieve. So they are never happy. They created a happiness gap for themselves. Do you suffer from this gap? It would be more logical to compare where you were a few years ago and now! You were in bad shape a few years ago and now you have achieved something better. So you should be happy now as you look back. This will remind you of your reverse happiness gap. A sense of gratitude is invoked and you should feel happy now. For me, I feel it strongly. When I was a student, I slept on a camp bag under the staircase. This was the courtesy provided by my eldest sister to enable me to pursue my secondary education in Penang. Now I have a beautiful bungalow surrounded by trees and a beautiful surrounding. I have a master's bedroom with attached bathroom. This reverse gap is big and I feel very happy now. Just thinking about it, I have no reason to be unhappy now. I would encourage you to think of your reverse gap this way and be happy now. Happiness will accelerate your productivity and manifestation in every aspect of your life. You will be motivated to be fit, healthy and wealthy.

Meditation to Activate Your Subconscious Mind

An easy tool is available to all of us. Learn the power of imagination through meditation, mindfulness or prayer. Practicing meditation, mindfulness or prayer every day is like brushing our teeth daily. Such brushing habit makes our teeth clean and healthy. I practice brushing my teeth every time after each meal. I still have a full set of teeth in my seventies. Similarly, practicing meditation, mindfulness, or prayer is food for our imagination. Practice it as often as possible. It becomes the food that nourishes our emotional well-being. Such practice daily ensures well-being for every part of your body. Imagination is the ability to create an idea, a vision or an image of something new. In creative visualisation, you use your imagination to create an image of what you want to accomplish in your life. Whatever you want, you imagine the desired outcome in your life. That becomes the life vision of your visualisation. You become aware of where you want to go. It's important that you repeat a positive affirmation or life vision about your goal in the present tense. By asking why and how to achieve it, such imagination is your beginning of creation. And ultimately, it will lead to your final creation of what you desire. You can be sure that creative visualisation will enhance your dreams of abundance.

It will be selfish on my part if I do not share my successful journey to financial freedom and good health. I have found a new purpose in my life. Helping anyone who wants to transform his or her life to find financial freedom and live healthily becomes my mission. Sharing many of my secrets and experiences in creating abundance including good health is my duty. I have discovered an easy way to do just that. You can easily implant these characteristics into your mind if you are open and willing to follow your desires. Be aware of the space in your subconscious mind which has been occupied by outdated beliefs and habits. They have to be eliminated first. This part of the consciousness engineering has to be done first. What are the tools available? Religious people trust their God and they pray for salvation and divine help. I also use prayers occasionally. I prefer to use a simple tool called meditation. Nowadays I use Quantum Jumping, a new format of meditation discovered by Burt Goldman. When I reach an alpha state, these toxic beliefs and practices can easily be dissolved and get rid of. I do not understand why such phenomenon takes place. But I always manage to achieve what I intended. The process can take some time depending on your energy level and your commitment. I do not intend to teach you. I want to share with you a tool so that you can learn to acquire abundance yourself. You will no longer living in lack because of lacking in knowledge to shape your reality. You need to be aware that the brain works best when it can link up with different ideas. This is the first step of your journey towards financial freedom. This is also the beginning to live a life fit and healthy. You must have the will and desire to start this journey. It will be exciting for you, if you know why you think, react and act in a certain way. You need not be hold hostage to the programming of your early stage of life. We are aware of the quote from the Greek playwright (496-406 BC):

> There is no witness so terrible and no accuser so powerful as conscience which dwells within us.

This conscience does play an important part directing our behaviours and practices. These beliefs and attitudes may come from many sources. They may come from our significant persons like parents, relatives, peers and teachers. It is also possible that this conscience is inherent in us. This nagging little voice in the mind makes us feel ashamed or guilty when we do something we shouldn't have done. Things like stealing, cheating, telling a lie or insulting a friend make us feel ashamed and guilty. I believe that all of us are born with an innate sense of fairness. This quality can be strengthened or weakened depending on what happens in our lifetimes.

Most of us have enough of a conscience to realise that some actions or demands are regarded as anti-social behaviours.

If we have committed such actions or behaviours, we have strong tendency to hide them from others. Most of us will never declare that they are going to lie, steal, cheat or belittle others. We want acceptance and we want to live with others. What happens if we were caught telling a lie or cheating by our parents or teachers? The memories are still living with us. It's difficult to forget! We still remember our fathers' fearsome wrath. Those memories are stored in our subconscious mind, training our conscience on the virtues of honesty. But our conscience can only be burdened with so much. If we keep repeating one lie to cover another lie, the habit can become our practice. This will encourage us to tell a bigger lie. After a while, we begin to believe our own lies and pretend that we never do anything wrong. Many people who steal and rob others have such a feeling. They stop reasoning and care only for themselves. Their needs are their priority. Others' welfares are not their concern. I have experienced this phenomenon myself during my childhood days. It became impossible to keep track of every lie I told. Eventually, our parents or teachers or friends will find out. It became a terrible strain to my life. I could not look anyone in the eyes after telling a white lie. Many a time during my childhood days, my stories based on lies were never convincing and my hands were shaky. My conscience, that nagging voice, was telling me to change and stop lying. This consciousness realisation is important. I need to adjust my inner compass that tells me where true north is so that my authenticity does not becomes muffled or ignored altogether. I am lucky to have parents and teachers teaching me the values they practice. I learn to obey traffic lights because it is a good thing to do. Do you get angry when you see people who don't obey traffic lights? Do we need traffic cops at every junction to see that we obey traffic lights? The more people having conscience the safer we are on the roads. Our conscience will reflect our beliefs, habits and practices. If your system is faulty, it's time to replace them with those of the healthy, wealthy and others with the right conscience. Do you want financial freedom? Do you want to live a life free from conscience? Do you want to be fit and healthy? The journey towards these goals begins with refurnishing your subconscious mind. Once this is done, our intuition will serve as our GPS guiding us in the right direction of our dreams. We usually have the inky feeling when we somehow compromise ourselves in our integrity of friendship or working situations. When we are in an argument with others, we hear the little voice telling us whether we are going to say that because we may regret later on. The little voice from our subconscious mind is directing us to be authentic and asking us to take certain action to improve our life. This awareness should be shared with our children, giving them direction to think well.

The Power of Intuition

When we allow our intuition to speak to us, we feel good, whole, fulfilled and on track to achieve our dreams. Intuition is a sacred gift we must not forget. We honour our rational mind because it serves as a faithful servant to us. Intuition is not only real but also a latent skill, a fundamental survival skill which can be developed. It is the ability to understand something immediately, without the need of conscious reasoning. It refers to communication or perception outside the boundary of our five senses. Studies have given solid evidence to such a skill or gift. All of us have this ability but some of us are able to use it more effectively than others. So if you believe in human intuition, you are not alone. More and more people are experiencing it, including mental healing. The unbelievers and sceptics are doubting it. But even among the well educated people, they believe in the sacred gift. The more intelligent you are, the more likely you will believe in a world beyond the five senses. The intellectual mind is more open. I do believe in this gift and I also believe that it can be developed in our journey of life. Everyone has certain degree of intuition. The greater you believe, the more likely that you will develop the intuitive ability. Remember that your mind can influence matter at any distance. Some of us possess telepathic abilities and telekinetic powers. It is true that not all of us have these abilities. Scientific evidence of these abilities is gathering momentum. So intuition is real. A little cautious is required regarding this little understood phenomenon. If anyone claims to have this ability and want to charge you for his service, you better be a cautious believer rather than a true believer. Make sure that we keep practicing this skill all the time even on the little decisions and questions we face each day. The more we tape into this little voice, the clearer we can hear it when we need it urgently. Life will get better as we expand and change with it. We will not sweat the small stuff but feel more confident that we are doing the right things towards financial independence and live a more healthy life. So if we learn to respond to our intuition and act accordingly, we will discover that it guides us in making choices that are aligned to our goals. This is true relating to our financial freedom, happiness, relationship and well-being. I strongly believe that if we tune into it and trust it, we will always move in the direction of our new beliefs and habits imprinted in our mind. Let us not get confused between intuition and thinking well. We need both to function optimally.

Optimisation in Reprogramming the Mind

When you start to write a new program for your subconscious mind, you want to have as few steps as possible. This is called optimisation to reprogram your mind towards your abundance. If you can reprogram your mind with the beliefs, habits and practices of the wealthy and healthy people and implement them consistently, you can have financial freedom and a healthy body easily. Most successful people know that continuous learning and growth are the hallmarks of extraordinary people. Do you want to be one of them? Yes, you can be one of them. If your mission is clear, your motivation will make it a reality. You will find your purpose. Your belief in living a mission-oriented life is going to be exciting for you. You will be excited to get up every day and love what you do. Once the characteristics of wealthy and healthy people are planted in your mind, what you need is to practice them intentionally, consistently, persistently and playfully. Your dreams will unfold before your eyes and manifestations are a matter of time. Try to follow the following simple steps to get immediate results.

First, before you reprogram your subconscious mind, identify the mental blocks first. Try to trace the root cause and give your current interpretation in your favour. Be proactive to shift immediately to current reality so that you are feeling the present moment. The past is no longer relevant.

Second, reprogram your subconscious mind to help you to shed your negative beliefs immediately. Use any practical tool you have: prayer, meditation, mindfulness or guided hypnotherapy. Repeated practices may be necessary to help you to manifest what you truly desire.

Third, try to raise your vibration frequency as high as possible so that you are connected to your higher self to feel inner peace and tranquillity.

Fourth, regardless of what life is throwing at you, you are motivated to practise the beliefs and habits of successful people you have programmed into your subconscious mind. Make use of the four elements of the 'Mastery Formula" described in chapter 1. Repetition and plenty of practice hold the key to success. Make those habits and beliefs part and parcel of your lifestyle and soon abundance will be smiling at your doorstep.

An Extraordinary Example

Have you seen the show 'Matrix'? I remember the scene when Neo leans back and plugs a giant black tube into his head. From that tube, he downloaded confidence, leadership and the best of all, Kung Fu skills. All of a sudden, he jumps up of his chair and he is a new man. He is now ready to take on any villain instantaneously! This scene inspired me to think of something similar, making use of our subconscious mind by reprogramming. The burning desire is sparked in my mind to figure out the best way to imprint skills of abundance on people's brains. Here abundance includes financial freedom, happiness, relationship, well-being, fulfilment and others. The main focus of this book is on wealth creation, a healthy body and a happy life. All of us want to live happily, healthily and enjoy financial freedom. Everything around us that we call life is made up by people. We just take things for granted and assume that what we see and do are the norms. Most of the ways of life are passed down from generation to generation. Our beliefs, attitudes, habits and practices have never been questioned. The ways we learn, work and live are not created through a rational thought process. I started thinking whether we can change all these for the better. Can we challenge all these norms we inherited? If we can, what type of mind-set do we want? Is it possible to download the beliefs, habits and values of rich and successful people into our brain? Can we also download the habits, practices and behaviours of the people who are fit, healthy and happy? The real secret of becoming rich, happy and healthy resides in our subconscious mind that is our inner game. Our old beliefs, attitudes and practices need to be eliminated first. This process provides space for new habits and practices to take root. Can we replace our limiting beliefs with more empowering ones? You can start reflecting on how you picked up these limiting beliefs in the first place. I believe that you did not pick them up through rational choice. The people around us are the most likely influence. How do we overcome all these thoughts as our dormant power? Armed with your imagination, I believe that you can imprint a new program in your subconscious mind and start implementing them to help you become happier, healthier and richer. Is there a technology that can transform us to become a money genius in a short period of time? Can this be our new belief? Yes, we can. We need to be aware that our subconscious mind is so powerful that it will help us to live the life we desire. The journey begins with creative visualisation and realisation. You can easily reprogram your subconscious mind and expand your comfort zone. Our mind affects our performance. We have seen people achieve remarkable things by imagining and believing them with clarity and conviction. In my own experience of playing golf, I used to imagine my swing with a follow through repeatedly until I was able to carry out automatically. Surprisingly, my repeated practices with visualisation seemed to help me achieve my goal faster than expected. Research reveals that athletes who did the most mental training including visualisation improved the fastest. Dr Garfield said:

> 'During mental rehearsal, athletes create mental images of the exact movements they want to emulate in their sport. Use of this skill substantially increases the effectiveness of goal setting, which up until then had been little more than a dull listing procedure.'

If this mental training can have such a profound effect or impact on athletes, it can also have some effect on your learning and practices to become rich, happy and healthy. Can you use the same principle to improve your attitude, confidence and skill? Can you use visualisation to build your abundance?

First thing first, it is easy to vividly imagine the thing you want to have such as financial freedom, happiness and being healthy in all stages of life. Why you need to be happy, healthy and rich? Explore all possible reasons why you want them. Learn 'how' and 'why' to create such types of income which keep flowing into your account year after year. Before you keep the motivation and inspiration going, you need first of all to release the subconscious blocks to money. You must replace them intentionally with higher level of attitudes, beliefs and practices of the healthy and wealthy. Knowledge and information of the characteristics of successful people are important. Be emotional about such moves and take action to make it a reality. Keep repeating such moves using creative visualisation and make commitment until your dreams come true.

This rewiring and retraining the subconscious mind is done through creative visualisation. The meditation process is practised and repeated until you reach the alpha phase, lowering your brain vibration frequency. Further practice can lead you the theta stage, when your brain vibration frequency reaches four to seven hertz. Using music at this range of frequency helps to accelerate reaching the theta stage. This is the stage when you are almost hypnotised. At this stage the subconscious mind is in a plastic stage and it can be moulded to any shape you desire easily. Even at the alpha stage, you can easily eliminate your old beliefs, attitudes and values. You will begin to challenge those outdated rules and beliefs that chained you to a life of scarcity and poor health. Once this scarcity consciousness is eliminated, your subconscious mind is ready to receive new beliefs, habits and practices of successful people. These values will be absorbed easily under such situation. After that, your mind is rewired for success. What you need subsequently is to keep practising such values and habits until they become your lifestyle. My personal experiences tell me that whatever I visualised repeatedly; I began to invite them into my life. I begin to take action to achieve my dreams. Soon most of visualisations became my realities. I realise I need to share my story. So I set out to share my experiences with the world on how to use the power of creative visualisation to people who are still struggling and especially those who need a tool to accelerate the result of their meditation.

Our brain's neural connections are stimulated through repeated visualisation or stimulation and the transformation will change the ways we behave, perceive and react. Our attitudes towards money will be renewed and rejuvenated. We are inspired to take action. The choice of action is instantaneous. Just like Neo in Matrix, new skills and practices are implanted. He is inspired to take action immediately because he has the new skills and tools necessary to help him achieving his mission. This book will provide plenty of materials to help you to achieve your dreams of financial freedom and live a happy and healthy life. They will provide the foundation for your end goals: to experience, to grow and to contribute.

Overcoming Rejection

All of us experience rejection in our life. The effect can be dramatic when we are kids. The experience of rejections stays in our subconscious mind forever as long as we do not take a step to get rid of it. This can become a massive block to our future career and advancement. This awareness helps us to identify the cause of each of the rejections and understand it. There are many possible reasons for each of the rejections you experienced. Sometimes, it can be misunderstanding and sometimes, it can be wrong interpretation. Whatever the reason for the rejection, understanding it is critical. A change of attitude and a paradigm shift all begin with the mind from inside. We need to eliminate the rejection phenomenon by reprogramming our mind with positive affirmations and beliefs to empower us to think well and interpret things to our favour. These positive affirmations have to be practised daily to become permanent in our lives. Meditation with visualisation and guided hypnotisation can be useful tools to help us in accelerating our transformation. They can provide power and confidence to shift our self-esteem, making the transformation from within.

Instead of seeking help from hypnotherapy and psychotherapy, an easier 'self-therapy' is through meditation until you reach the alpha stage, where your brain is more receptive to your desire to make the transformation. Continuous practice and repeated effort will soon replace your rejection belief with more positive ones. You can reprogram your mind to get whatever you want and keep it. You can also install emotional well-being, self-esteem and unshakable self-belief into your subconscious mind. A tool available to all of us is a simple 'Quantum Jumping' into a parallel universe to meet with your doppelganger who is a hypnotherapist. Now your imagination will take over and your visualisation will do the rest. Our visualisation is a powerful technique raising our level of consciousness. By practising this technique regularly, we can level up to a new state of consciousness. This consciousness will reveal the relationship with life and how we, as souls, create within this life.

It only takes me a few minutes to be in deep meditation. Soon I am at the quantum door ready to jump into a parallel universe to meet my doppelganger who is a renowned hypnotherapist. He is cheerful and ready to give me advice how to get rid of my rejection experiences when I was a little kid. He told me that my mind cannot hold on to two conflicting beliefs. To allow new beliefs of self-esteem to be planted, I have to eliminate the rejection experiences which are already there in the subconscious mind. Rejection is one of the greatest fears that I encountered and it damaged my self-esteem. These experiences have corrupted my thinking and weakened my approach towards others. My confidence towards my career dived. I want to regain my self confidence and self-love. What should I do? My doppelganger wants me to let go the fear of rejection immediately. I cannot control people rejecting me but I must not allow them to control my thinking and give in to their interpretations that I am not good enough. The concept of rejection in the primitive society means death. The rejected person became the food for the wild beasts. But this belief is no longer relevant. If some organisations reject me, it does not mean that I will die. Other better opportunities are out there. What I need is to grow and improve my knowledge. Another organisation will hire me or I will create my own opportunity.

When my doppelganger uses hypnotherapy on me, something magical happens to my brain. The perception of my rejection changes and my interpretation of the rejection alters. The belief of rejection is no longer important and the fear seems to vanish from my mind. I have a new understanding of my rejection which can be interpreted in my favour. Rejection is not permanent. It's only a perception and an interpretation. I do not have to accept people's perceptions. The truth is that we are born to live our lives to its full potential. No one can have everything they want. No one can have acceptance by everyone. Every one of us is different. There will be someone who does not like me. A rejection is not the end. There are many people around who will accept me. There is no reason to fear a rejection because we can always accept ourselves with open arms. Self-love and self-belief is the way to go. My doppelganger impresses me that I have to make my own choice and build my new belief to enhance my self-esteem and my well being. We need to build bulletproof armours against rejection. I do not have to entertain someone's opinion about me. Changing my thinking and my perception of rejection begins. Any rejection will not hold me back and hurt me. Now I am different. I am no longer that little kid now. There are always people out there having different opinions about me. I must begin to believe in myself. Agreeing with their opinions is my choice. Understanding myself and knowing what I am doing is the way to go. The inner transformation will begin. I no longer have to listen to what others say about me. I will not allow others to reject me. The only person who has the power to reject me now is me. I can provide everything I need. My words are important. I have the talents and the skills to succeed; understanding what I do and want is the beginning of my life. Making extraordinary beliefs is critical. Not allowing others to control me is equally important. I will create experiences with my new beliefs. Cancelling those outdated beliefs provides space for new beliefs to grow. My thoughts will not decide who I am but my new beliefs will. I have to make sure that my actions are aligning with my beliefs. I have to create my new reality and my new confidence. Setting goals and using intention, you can send a crystal clear signal to the universe to hand deliver to you the abundance you most desire. A few rejections will not affect your life but help your inner resources to better manifestations of abundance.

Overcoming Conscious and Unconscious Fear

One of the obstacles that keep you stuck from achieving your abundance is fear. What is the science behind fear? Fear is an emotion which is a thought of like or dislike to a certain degree. What is the opposite of fear? People seem to confuse and think that the opposite of fear is courage. But a person who has courage still has fear. His courage emerges because of positive expectation exceeds his degree of fear. Fear is a negative expectation. Faith is a positive expectation. Therefore, the opposite of fear is faith. Are you suffering from conscious and unconscious fears? Many of our conscious fears are actually good fears. They are there to protect us from harm or injury. We do not jump from a tall building or a moving vehicle for fear of breaking our legs. We can classify our fears into good fears or dangerous fears. It's important that we recognise and notice these good fears keeping us safe in the process of achieving our goals. Some of the conscious and unconscious fears like fear of failure, fear of success, fear of public speaking, fear of height, fear of asking questions and fear of disappointing yourself are holding us back. These illogical fears cause us to doubt, procrastinate, stuck in our comfort zones and never take action to achieve our goals. Most of these fears are buried deeply in our subconscious minds. Most of us are not aware of the illogical fears and they are responsible for our inaction. We never live to our full potential. The purpose of this book is to help you activate this consciousness. The simple tool we can use is meditation or prayer. The power of imagination and visualisation will help you to uncover parts of yourself buried so deep in fears that you never knew existed. We can overcome these fears and turn them into fuel or energy to help us achieve our goals. This book will help you to regain clarity and confidence that comes with fine tuning to guide you towards your goals and dreams. Every illogical fear is an opportunity for expanding your consciousness towards a greater realisation of your true self. We will help you to understand and transform any unpleasant event or memory in your life to catapult yourself to greater heights of development.

Many of our unconscious fears are actually illogical fears we pick up during our childhoods. These childhood experiences have profound impressions in our subconscious minds. For examples, I was told again and again by my grandmother that children must not interfere or ask questions whenever adults are talking. This experience is deep-rooted in my memory and I developed the fear of asking questions even I did not understand certain things explained to me. I used to listen to haunted stories told to me during my childhood and I developed the fear of darkness and abandoned houses. My grandmother instilled the fear in me from climbing tree to protect me from injury. I did not understand her intention. Instead, I developed the fear of height even when it is safe to be at such height. All these emotions including fear live with us as we grow up. Now I recognise that I have many illogical fears such as fear of asking questions, fear of public speaking, fear for the unknown, fear to try new things, fear of meeting strangers, fear of height and many others. How do I control my fears and turn them into fuel to help me achieving my goals and dreams.

I have discovered a good weapon. I use meditation and visualisation known as Quantum Jumping. Within a few minutes, through meditation, I am able to reach a doppelganger that has great experiences in mastering fears in another parallel universe. I will merge with him and acquire his energy and learn his techniques of overcoming many illogical fears to achieve success.

Overcoming the Fear of Public Speaking

Although I have mastered the basics-thinking and speaking early in my life, but I still have the fear for public speaking. This fear appears to be deep rooted in my subconscious mind because of my childhood upbringing. There was not enough exposure to public speaking while I grew up. I was only involved in conversation involving two or three people casually. I have no problem talking to others. But when I became captain of my basketball team, I had to speak to ten or twelve players to motivate them; I seemed to be affected by fear in talking to them. The fear kept coming back whenever I spoke to them. I also remember when I became principal of my school, I was also facing fear whenever I spoke to the staff and to the students during school assembly. I was determined to get rid of the fear of public speaking once and for all.

I have a good weapon called Quantum Jumping, a unique form of meditation discovered by the great Burt Goldman. My intention is clear. I wanted to get rid of the fear of public speaking. This fear was programmed in my mind without knowing it and it was affecting me whenever I had to speak to the public. Whenever I was invited to speak in public, I used to meditate first using my newly acquired technique called Quantum Jumping. Just before my engagement, I followed my usual procedure of meditation introduced by my mentor. I sit comfortably on my chair. I close my eyes and relax. When everything is quite and calm, I start counting the number three, three times in descending tone that is three, three and three. Then I start counting the number two also three times that is two, two and two in a similar descending tone. Then I start to count the number one, three times in a similar way. I remain quiet for a few seconds and I start counting backwards from ten to one that is ten, nine, eight... until one. The purpose of this ritual is to wake up my subconscious mind to begin its exploration. In this context, my intention is to overcome my fear of public speaking.

Now I imagine I am walking through a great hall, going towards a quantum door so that I can jump into another parallel universe to meet a particular doppelganger who is a great public speaker trainer. As soon as I reach the door, I open the door and jump into that particular parallel universe to meet up with my twin-self. I allow my imagination to do the rest. In this particular jump, I merged with my twin-self to acquire his rhythm and energy. We were then vibrating with the same frequency and our thinking was at the same page. I had a new clarity of the requirement for my reality. The first thing I learned was to get rid of the illogical fear for public speaking due to my childhood's low self-esteem. I was in an alpha stage of mind and this mental stage made it possible to eliminate the fear easily. As soon as the space was created, I started to unload the confidence and the procedures adopted by my doppelganger whenever he spoke. I began to write a new story and a new chapter for my public speaking. Since we were vibrating with the same frequency, I was able to tap into his style of public speaking. I could visualise his style towards public speaking. He smiled to the crowd before he introduced himself and he stated clearly the topic of his speech. It's simple he just focused and talked to one of the members of the crowd. He spoke with ease while smiling at him. Then it dawned to me that I can do the same because I am good at speaking to any individual. This visualisation seems to stay with me whenever I make a public speech. I keep practising this style of communication when I make a public speech. After many repeated attempts, I soon forget about my fear of public speaking.

A new chapter of public speaking is written for me. This secret has given me my new quantum power and confidence to stand in front of a big crowd and just talk to one of the members at a time and then another. So public speaking is simplified to just talking to any individual member of the crowd one at a time. Now I have developed this strategy of public speaking by just talking to one member at a time and then to another to cover as many as possible. This awareness that I am talking to one person at a time is the root of my new confidence in public speaking. I have mastered my basics in thinking and speaking and now I am extending these basic skills to public speaking. The foundation I have anchored well for my new creativity and growth in public speaking.

Overcoming Fear of Asking Questions

My fear of asking questions lived with me for almost fifteen years. When I started my secondary school in Penang, I managed to overcome such fear when I was doing well in my study. As I mentioned in my first motivation book, *The Journey through Four Seasons of Life*, that I developed my self-study strategy out of circumstances. I was very weak in my command of English and I had to catch up or drop out of my study. The struggle was intense and I managed to come out with my self-study strategy to ensure my success. I learned to write down questions regarding concepts which I did not understand well. This encouraged me to ask questions during regular lessons. I was full of fear whenever I asked questions. I had illogical fear that my classmates would be laughing at me. I might look stupid. After many attempts of asking questions concerning difficult concepts, I was treated with respect. I was ahead of the class. This repeated style of learning concepts and facts seems to accelerate my understanding and remembering them. I discovered a secret to succeed in my educational pursuit. I did well in secondary school and two of my classmates showed exceptional faith in my ability. They approached me to guide them. I was given leadership role and I learned to be assertive. I started to think well and speak well.

Whenever I am outside the classroom, I still live with the fear of asking questions about things I am not certain. I want to overcome this fear of asking questions about things that I am not certain, once and for all. I closed my eyes and followed my regular procedures in Quantum Jumping. It only takes me a few minutes to reach my doppelganger in another parallel universe. We merged immediately and we began to vibrate at the same frequency. I acquired his rhythm and his energy to share his attitude and confidence in asking questions. His rhythm struck me immediately that I have to get rid of all the illogical fears of asking questions. The fears such as people may think that I am stupid or they may laugh at me are just imaginary fears. Getting rid of these beliefs and habits will create space for more encouraging beliefs to replace them. A new belief is born. My doppelganger showed me that when he asked questions politely and gracefully, people seem to entertain him with polite answers. I also noticed that whenever he asked questions, he put on a smiling face. I began to unload these habits of asking questions into my subconscious mind. This awareness was put into practice regularly whenever I did not understand certain things either in public or with friends. The habits of asking questions politely and gracefully are nurtured and repeated regularly. Soon I have developed my style of asking questions and I enjoy the polite responses regularly. My knowledge and understanding seem to grow exponentially. I have uncovered an effective way of finding out things that I am not certain of. A new dimension of life is added and I find more happiness and well-being. When I became principal of my school, I used to encourage others to ask questions after my explanation or speech. I have formed the good habit to ask questions politely and encourage others to ask questions whenever I give my speech.

Overcoming the Fear of Height

My grandmother had a protective instinct telling me the danger of climbing tree. Repeated warning from her might have caused the fear of height in me. This emotion creates a thought of dislike for height. This appears to be a good fear to protect me from injury. I lived with this fear for the first fifteen years of my life. But when I am in a tall building, it is very safe. But I seem to be overwhelmed by fear of looking down. This becomes an illogical fear. This fear seems to discourage me from mountain climbing and rock climbing. I am determined to get rid of this illogical fear in my subconscious mind.

How do I overcome this illogical fear? I have a meditation weapon called Quantum Jumping. It only took me a few minutes to catch up with my doppelganger in another dimension. He is a mountain climber and a very adventurous person. My intention is clear. I want to get rid of the fear feeling when I am at some height above ground level. During this jump, we merged and my doppelganger took me to a high platform overlooking a great green forest. The scenery was amazing and I enjoyed the panoramic view. I forgot that I was standing on a narrow platform over the trees of the forest. The slow rhythm for height because of my fear seemed to dissipate and be replaced with a high rhythm filled with excitement. I kept moving along the narrow platform enjoying the new adventure. I enjoyed the bird's-eye view of the natural environment. With a few more Quantum Jumps of these scenarios, my fear for height seems to have vanished in thin air. I begin to enjoy good views from higher places. My life has made a great turn and I seem to enter into another level of living, enjoying the higher grounds.

Natural Healing Using Our Subconscious Mind

The most important things I have learned about staying healthy and wealthy came late in life. It was not a formula or a therapy. It wasn't even advice people gave me. The most profound lesson I have ever learned came from years of reading and my own experiences in life. After years of experiences through my own struggle and my reading about the human body, I come to the conclusion that it works differently from my previous perception. The Japanese's concept of sticking to a company for life and the company will take care of your retirement is found to be no longer true in our modern world. Depending solely on a salary is no longer insurance for a good retirement. We are advised to create other streams of residual income as well. Just like depending on a doctor for any small injury or even when you are not feeling well is no longer necessary. There are many other natural healings our body will do. There is overwhelming evidence that creative visualisation can accelerate our bodies' healing power. Doctors in Australia are using this technique together with modem medicine to help patients recover quickly. It can be coincidence that patients who use visualisation experience faster recovery. In addition, there is something more incredible happening when you use creative visualisation. People who practice creative visualisation not only enhance their emotions, skills and body healing but also influence the outside world beyond their physical control. In other words, creative visualisation can spawn amazing coincidences which lead you towards your goal. These coincidences are seemingly unconnected to you and beyond your control. I believe in all these manifestations because I have experienced them myself. I believe that you can use this technique to accelerate your healing, gain inspiration, start a business, find a dream job and live a healthy and happy life. My own experiences reveal that when I visualised something, I would write it down every day until such an event happened. It normally takes about a couple of weeks when such a coincidence happened. This shows that our mind is such a powerful tool that can literally bring wonderful or tragic events to bear within weeks. Most of us do not tap into and control this powerful force. On the contrary, many people have their mind working for them in negative ways. Doctors call this illness 'psychosomatic', caused by a person's negative belief system. Most people are not aware of their negative belief system and continue to live with their sufferings.

My realisation is at once striking and obvious for both health and employment. I never look at health and income the same way again. Better health is a critical part of our manifestation; looking great and feeling great are part of what make us whole. Having financial freedom creates time for us to pursue our new experiences, growth and contribution. Is there a common factor in the two different realisations? The common factor is deep down in our subconscious mind. So before we take action to achieve our abundance, we need to put our mind-set in the correct perspective. We want to embrace the attitude of forgiveness and practice gratitude. They are powerful forces working for us. We want to liberate ourselves from past hurts. The limiting beliefs and practices are draining our energy. We are not free to do things we are passionate about. A new attitude is necessary for us to be free from these burdens. We need to sharpen our intuition to help us in making good decisions so that we can move on with more confidence. We want to be free for a new lease of life. We want to feel connected to the universe. We want to nurture good relationship. We want to feel irritated less and feel calm and confident as we move towards our new reality. We will feel lucky and begin to see the world from a new lens. All of us aspire to grow, to have new experiences and make our contribution to push humanity forwards. How to begin?

Yes, we need to have our correction set points and our correction procedures in place. For example, if my optimum weight is seventy kilograms, for me to be fit and healthy, I need to make sure that I maintain this weight. That say after a long holiday I manage to put on a few kilograms, my health is affected. The weight exceeds my non-negotiable set point. I feel less active and my energy level is dropping. Immediately I will start my correction procedure such as changing my diet with less carbs and increasing the intensity of my exercises until I maintain my optimum weight. I will do it consistently, persistently and playfully with discipline until I regain my set point. Another example is my financial position regarding my savings for the rainy season, investment and for retirement. I have my set point for my saving every month or every year. If in a certain month or year, I spend more than my set point, I have to start my correction procedure the month or year that follows. By sticking to my nonnegotiable set point, I can ensure my annual saving will be maintained. By consistently following my nonnegotiable set points, I will be able to accumulate reasonable amount for the purpose of investments. You have to be aware that your mind moves in the direction of your dominant thoughts. Having your nonnegotiable set points in health and finance will soon become your habits. You set the right intention; you will create the day's experiences that please you. Note that the best intention is full of details, emotion and descriptions. So when you fill your intention with detailed scenario, you will find yourself doing things that are committed to your intentions. These habits will become your unconscious patterns of life and eventually they become part of your character. When you create a habit of positive intention each day, you will create a powerful swing in your quality of life. You will train yourself not only desire but command the best. These good habits require great discipline, consistency and persistence to develop. This attitude is developed with the desire to be healthy and rich throughout your life. Remember, education is the most important weapon you can change your world. This book serves partly to help you live a mission-oriented life, helping you to reach a higher level of consciousness. Perhaps this will lead you towards a limitless powerful way to achieve your mission. The way towards bliss and flow is open up. New experiences and growth will follow in whatever you do. You will be excited to get up every morning and do what you love to do. A new life without limit is dawning on you. A new empowerment is born for you to meet challenges and help you to live a life of abundance.

Let us look at health first. My own experiences tell me that the human body is designed to renew and perfect itself all the time. My old perception of the human body to that of a new car which starts out perfect from the factory, but over time, it breaks down and eventually falls apart, is no longer true. The perception of our body as a machine, like a car, requiring regular maintenance, is what most of us think. We require a mechanic in the form of a doctor who will keeps us running and fix our parts when they go bad. My readings and life experiences now tell me that this mechanical metaphor is misleading. This is the reason why we run for a doctor whenever we feel uncomfortable or sick. Now I come to realise that doctors play only a very small role in healing. My experiences of my own health and many research findings tell me that more than 90 per cent of the time our body heals itself, with or without the intervention of doctors and the medicine they prescribe. A few observations like a bruise on your leg or a cut on your finger will heal in just a few days without medicine. Your body just cures and heals itself. I notice that damaged skin is replaced by new skin which is healthy and perfect. The same is true when you break a bone. Once it is put back into position, the bone will heal itself. After healing, the bone is strong or even stronger than before. This is a great realisation that the body wants to renew itself and will do so as it is allowed. The process of healing and renewing any part of the body which is injured always continues constantly. You can use creative visualisation to help in accelerating the healing process. Your belief system and the power of the subconscious mind have the final touch for healing.

Even older people can grow new skin, bones and muscle, if it is given the natural nutrients and time to heal itself. This is how the body works. Yet this idea that the body has the natural ability to heal itself is anathema to the medical and drug industries. The body does not require intervention and regular maintenance like a machine. I live for the last seventy six years without being hospitalised. Most of my injuries and sickness healed themselves. The most important thing for me is to keep myself fit, have enough sleep and a balanced diet. Many interventions for small injury or sickness are part of the world's greatest con games for financial gain. The business of medicine, services and pharmaceutical sales are very large and powerful. The primary goal of these businesses is to convince you that you are sick and you need their services or prescriptions. But this is not the end of it. The medical industries are in collusion with food industries which manufactured products you are encouraged to consume. What we are told to eat by doctors and our government is based on the results of studies financed by the food industries. Many of these processed foods are unnatural foods that continue to stress our natural bodies. Many of the products and therapies do not work as mentioned. You should be careful when you take them because of the many side effects. The habits of eating natural foods with good nutrients will do the healing for your body over time. I am aware now that many of the so-called health foods or prescriptions drugs are made for commercial purposes. Remember, our body can regenerate new cartilage, restore clogged arteries and strengthen our bones at any age. Remember, your body can renew and perfect any part which is injured. But the medical establishments do not want you to know that because they will lose revenue. We should, instead, look for alternative to 'medicalisation' like natural healing through foods with the necessary nutrients allowing our body to heal itself. The following awareness is useful for self-healing. A simple change of diet can improve prostate health. You can fight diabetes by eliminating starchy foods and avoid heart disease by having a low-carb diet. Drinking a moderate amount of red wine can actually reverse the signs of aging. All these natural cures work the same way by stimulating the body to do what it is designed to do: regenerate itself, minute by minute, on a cellular level. Remember, the body wants to heal itself and many of the natural cures take effect in a matter of days. When I had lower-back pain, my doctor suggested surgical procedure to mend one of the discs. Instead of surgical solution, I seek the help of a yoga therapist and practiced the art myself. Within a few weeks, my back pain disappeared. It is an amazing natural cure. Even my chronic pain because of the ligaments and tendons problems at the knees and joints healed themselves over time with good nutrients and natural therapies.

Most of us have great fear for getting cancer. Do you know that cancer cells are always present in our body? They are present in millions. Most of us do not succumb to cancer because our bodies have billions of anti-cancer molecules swarming around in the blood system, killing cancer cells as they appear. But when the immune system of a body is weakened, these cancer cells will eventually established themselves and the disease takes over. This message is important to us. We need to keep fit most of the time, have a balanced diet and maintain our good immune system. In all the years the medical industry has been fighting cancer; it has made very little progress. In fact, natural therapies and natural foods can do better to combat and prevent cancer. A Mexican doctor has a breakthrough treatment using the technique called hyperthermia. This natural technique is safe and has been practiced for thousands of years. It originated from ancient Egypt. Although it is natural; it is based on science, on the fact that cancer cells are weaker than healthy cells. Cancer cells are more sensitive to heat and the technique drives them from their hidden places and eventually eliminated. Clinical studies confirm the effectiveness of such therapies. Another cure for cancer is on the way. A vaccine called 'Alpha Cells' therapy is about to end its clinical trial in 2016. FDA approval for such vaccine will soon be a reality. It's a powerful vaccine that stimulates our body cells to fight cancer cells. It acts like a general leading the healthy cells to combat and can easily eliminate various types of cancer in just a few doses. We will wait and keep an eye on its development.

A simple way to keep our immune system functioning optimally, we need to have enough sleep, exercise and a balance diet. A minimum of seven to eight hours of good sleep is necessary for most of us. Exercise will improve our metabolism and strengthen our immune system. A balanced diet rich in fruits, vegetable and protein will enhance and protect our immune system. Always be aware that any sleep deprivation or malnutrition is a serious problem for your health. As we age, another disease known as Alzheimer's frightens most of us. The best thing we can do is to live a healthy lifestyle, eat a healthy diet rich in vegetables and fruits to prevent inflammation. Study shows that people who eat fish regularly could fight off the disease. People who eat plenty of fish have fewer 'plagues' in their brains. Plagues are common signs of Alzheimer's where there is too much clamping of a brain protein called beta amyloid. It's important that we eat regularly real fish and not fish oil supplements. A little example is to eat a Mediterranean diet full of fruits, vegetables, whole grains, olive oil and plenty of fish. Another step to take is to exercise regularly and have plenty of sleep. Keep using your brain for productive work or start learning a second language.

All these consciousness, information, knowledge and clarity of thoughts will help us to ascend to new height of bliss and understanding. Religious people use prayers to activate their consciousness towards a life of abundance. Spiritual people seek the help of meditation, mindfulness and affirmations with purpose; they can have effortless success in multiple dimensions of their lives. We can follow them. We will also enjoy a more intuitive, compassionate version of ourselves and be surrounded by an abundant, energetic field of love that nourishes our souls.

Consciousness and Financial Freedom

Every one of us aspires to become financially independent when we retire. Our realisation is that depending on our salary will not guarantee our financial freedom when we retire. We no longer can depend on the company that hire us to take care of our retirement. The possibilities are too many to mention. You may be retrenched when any economic cycle turns bad. The company you work for may not be there in just a decade or two. Employment for life is no longer relevant. I would like to help you debunk a myth that when you take massive action and concentrate on your career; you will eventually have financial freedom. Most self-help books and seminars encourage you to work hard and learn more about your job to help you achieve your goal of financial freedom. Now I realise that this suggestion, on its own, will not transform my life. This is an important realisation. The action taken in concentrating on your job may turn out to be counterproductive. Yes, you should aim to move in the direction of your goals. The truth is, a whole of inner work of reprinting your brain needs to be done before you start taking action. Otherwise, you will experience negative states such as procrastination, anxiety, stress and even self-sabotage, every time you try to move in the positive direction. This is not your fault before this realisation of the power of your subconscious mind. If you only set goal for your financial freedom at the conscious level, then there is a limit. There is a limit because the conscious mind only plays a minor role to help you reach your full potential. Research reveals that the conscious level limits you to only 1 to 5 per cent of your potential resources. The lion's share of your potential resources is decided by your subconscious mind. It is your subconscious mind that will decide how much financial freedom you can enjoy. The first step you need to do before taking any action is to change your subconscious beliefs, practices and habits. Without this realisation, it is a fatal mistake for your financial independence. Just like Neo in Matrix, you can imprint new programs in your subconscious mind to enhance your creative visualisation. You can transform any aspect of your life, so you experience more abundance or any kind of success you desire. In fact you can get result faster and with less effort. Even right now, you can use your imagination to eliminate failure from your life, multiply your success and start creating a life you are truly inspired by. Just like the first realisation that the body is always ready to heal itself. The brain is always ready to make new cells in the form of neural connections all the time. Once you allowed the brain to do its work by providing adequate nutrients and practices, more neural connections will be established. They will directly change your deepest beliefs, thoughts and programs. This realisation tells you that you can reprogram your subconscious blueprint and expand your comfort zone. Is this possible? Yes, it is now possible by allowing your neural connections to grow continuously daily. You can now imprint into your subconscious mind the beliefs, habits and practices of rich and successful people. What are these characteristics of the rich? This book will help you to acquire them so that you can implant them in your mind. Learning and practicing these beliefs and habits will move you faster towards your financial goal. You need to know that your action and your achievement are dictated by your subconscious blueprint. It is your comfort zone. Once you are out of your comfort zone, you experience stress, tension, anxiety and even self-sabotage. So it is critical that you reprint a new subconscious blueprint using creative visualisation and widen your comfort zone. In simple terms, creative visualisation is simply using your imagination to create whatever you want in life. Practice this imagination every day preferably through meditation. Learning how to use creative visualisation can help you become someone with the creativity, vision and resources to enjoy a truly epic life. What is visualisation? It is simply imagining what you want to experience. There is nothing new, strange, or unusual about visualisation. We use it almost every day. It is the natural power of our imagination. In a deep meditation, we can paint a picture in our mind or form an image of our desire. The first attempt may not give you a clear picture. With repeated practise, you can reach the alpha phase or even better at the theta stage, the paintings or images can become clearer. What you need is that you have to be aware of such a powerful subconscious mind you have. To use creative visualisation, you must first become clear and specific about your desired reality, in this case financial independence. How to double or triple your income? What are the opportunities available? Can I download these characteristics from proven sources? Knowledge is the key and implementation regularly your visualisation in its subconscious stage, your brain is ready to be moulded. By storing new beliefs and habits, your subconscious mind will be rewired according to your desires including creating wealth. For example, every one investing in the stock market has the same intention. They want to make money. Not all of them achieve their aim. Why? You have a choice. You either follow the losers or the successful long-term investors. All successful investors have used the same method. They ignore the fads of the day and tried to answer the question. What is value and how do I determine it? They follow the value metrics created by economists such as price-earnings ratio (PE), price-to-book ratio, price-to-earnings growth and many other technical terms used. These characteristics give them the power to compare one company with another in the same sector. The rich people have a simple method of investing. They don't chase stocks. They look at the numbers to find under-valued companies. They buy them and wait for the market to agree with them. They have patience and they follow the economic cycles. Whenever any hot trends emerge after a long period of bad news depressing prices, they have the cojones to make the move and enjoy an incredible upside. When the market is overheated, they know when to come out and take their holidays. These inputs can help you in your creative visualisation trying to replace your old beliefs and habits of investing by this set of new discoveries in your subconscious mind.

After that you must remain firm and persistent about your desire. Make the commitment and take action. What is your end goal? Before you start to visualise, just observe the habits, practices and attitudes of the rich. Explore the reasons why they have financial independence. Try quantum jumping and visit the quantum library to gather information through imagination. Just like tapping into Goggle for any information you need. The characteristics of rich people will provide some inputs for your imagination. Do they just work for their salary? Most rich people do not depend on their salary to have financial freedom. They are rich because they own assets such as stocks, properties or business that generate consistent residual incomes and cash flow. For you to create your financial freedom, visualisation is the key. You can start painting pictures of activities of rich people in your subconscious mind. What are the possibilities of creating residual incomes? Knowledge through reading from experiences of rich people will add flavour to your creative visualisation. You will begin to paint a better picture of the activities they are involved in. Visualising something you want is the beginning and inviting such thing to happen in your life is what you want. So if such invitation is for financial freedom, you will begin to take action creating as many possible residual incomes in your working life. You begin to make commitment and begin to see what you must do. The journey of your financial freedom begins. The techniques of creative visualisation will be exposed to you in the subsequent chapters. You can write your own future soon. Nothing will work unless you decide to make it work. Just like nothing has meaning until you give it meaning. This book will teach you a new process of meditation called Quantum Jumping invented by Burt Goldman. This concept will be discussed in detail for your experimentation. I have also added an additional concept making available the Quantum Library for the purpose of generating new ideas and strategies to help you reach your goal. This new concept not only teaches you how to get rich but also how to be able to download valuable values and habits into the software of your brain. The quality of delayed gratification can also be downloaded into our mind. Practicing this can help to manage your consumption habits and pave the way for your saving power. Controlling our spending on unnecessary items will help us save. The culminating effect is slow saving and money accumulates. Once a certain sum of money is there, you can look into more important things like investments and others. We need to develop strategies to help us develop this quality called delayed gratification. An easy way is to limit or avoid the use of credit card. It's removing the temptation like taking out sugar when you are on diet. When shopping in supermarkets; stick to the list of requirements you intend to buy. Delayed gratification gives you time to think and understand what is right for you. Do not buy on impulse and purchase things you do not need. It should be applied to all facets of our life if you want to succeed financially. Once these beliefs and habits are made aware in your subconscious mind, then you can make full commitment to practice them to secure your financial freedom. You will start thinking differently, regaining your confidence and certainty regarding your financial freedom. You will change totally the belief about yourself. You will learn a new word or idea or belief to step outside many rules that restrict and hold you back in life. Many of these beliefs and rules are what people see and follow for years. They are not necessarily the truth. There are others which are more empowering ways of gaining financial freedom. By changing our mind-set, we can break free from these restricted rules for a better life. Soon you will not only have total financial freedom but also control over your future.

In simple term, creative visualisation is an essential component for you in manifesting. You have to see something in your mind before the process of manifestation is triggered. Whatever thing happened to us, we use this to give our interpretation. We create every belief about ourselves and our financial freedom. All our beliefs are stories we make and we have the power to change them at will. If you admit that you are the only player responsible for where you are. You can easily change your belief about yourself and your life. Many people seem to say, 'I am not a big deal.' They hold that belief because at some point of their lives, somebody ran them down and made them feel less worthy. Their self-esteem is eroded on purpose or accidentally. I encourage you to change that belief into, 'I am kind of a big deal.' It is not egotistical or proud to make yourself relevant to the universe. Do not sell yourself short. You are important at least to yourself. You can easily be a role model for people like you. Change your story and change your life. You set your own rules and nobody can stop you except yourself. You have a purpose and an intention for such a vision manifesting in your life. Take this simple similarity. Whenever I visualise what I want, I think of placing an order at a restaurant. I tell the waiter, 'I want an eye-fillet steak.' If I do not specify the cooking condition and the sauce I want, I may not get what I like. I may get a medium well-done steak instead of a well done cooked steak. I have to be specific. But the trouble is that most of our visualisations are incomplete. We do not see the details, just a big picture. To visualise your financial freedom, you need to feel happy first before you can imagine what types of works you have to create for residual incomes. Familiarities with various works available in your community can help you in creating images and expanding your mind for free-flow ideas; helping you to get answers to your questions. You cannot expect to achieve something if you can't see it for yourself. It is only by visualising what you want that you are able to give yourself a clear destination to steer life towards. Always imagine and open to unlikely solutions to help you achieve your goal. The first rule you need to follow is to infuse your mental images with feelings and sensations.

Applying Visualisation to Basketball Game

I remember my own experience in visualising my own deceptive moves in basketball. I had been practising dribbling every morning when I was a student. I became an expert in ball control during dribbling. This exceptional skill helps me to create my own chance of penetrating the opponents' defence. I imagine the single fake: dribbling the ball to my left and sensing the opponent follows me to the left reflexively to intercept me, I will cut him with my lay up on the right. This will leave him lunging in the air, missing the interception. I also imagine that I can only do this dribbling fake once or twice before the defender sensing it and change his tactics by going in the opposite direction and intercept my ball. This is my single dribbling fake. Then I start to visualise doing a double fakes dribbling. First I will fake dribbling to the left and sensing the defender only follows me to the left half way, I will do a second dribbling fake to the right, sensing that the defender has the past experience to change direction, he reflexively tries to intercept me on the right, I will cut him on the left and do my layup. This becomes my double dribbling fakes. I keep visualising this single and double dribbling fake deceptions many times. But this visualisation cannot become a reality unless I put the vision into practice. I may not succeed in my first attempt because it involves skills, senses and timing. With repeated practices I soon automated these single and double dribbling fake deceptions technique. After many practices, this technique becomes a conditional reflex or autopilot; it becomes a weapon for me during important matches. When this dribbling fake technique is done correctly, it gives me split second of advantage to pass my opponent, giving me the space and time to do the layup. The success of the single dribbling fake relies on the defence acting reflexive rather than having time to think of what is going on. The second double dribbling fake is used when the defender is thinking intentionally to go in the opposite direction knowing that the first is intended to be a fake. Again, the defender is deceived acting on the opposite way he purposely intended. Having alternative dribbling fakes can put any defender in confusion. I realised that it's important to have a clear picture in my mind's eye when I make a single or double dribbling fake. Secondly, whenever I visualise something, I claim and own it. Just like my single fake and double fakes deception dribbling technique. I put myself into that visualisation. I always remember that my subconscious mind cannot feel the difference between the images created on my imagination and those created by my senses. Both are equally real. I always choose the best-case scenario and practice it to fascinate my manifestation. Thirdly, I need to be persistent. I keep on practicing my single fake and double fakes' deceptive dribbling technique until I can carry it out automatically without thinking during a game. I used my senses and timing effectively. This positive reinforcement changes the neurological pathways in the brain so when a single fake fails, it is automatically replaced by the double fakes' strategy. This higher level of development requires plenty of rehearsals and practices before execution become smooth and automatic.

Similarly if you want financial freedom, you need to meditate and visualise your ideal situation to create streams of residual incomes and cash flow. If you focus on financial freedom, your visualisation will begin to generate paths of getting there. Any path or method in a vision requires action and time to carry out. Showing only interest is not enough for such vision to manifest. Full commitment and action are necessary to help your vision become reality. Lastly it is important to put your emotion and feeling into your visualisation. For example, to gain accuracy in my basketball shooting, I used to visualise that whenever I elevate myself, I need to roll the ball in the path of a parabola. I keep visualising that move that requires coordination of strength and judgement. Shooting accuracy is the most critical part of winning any basketball game. This is a true catalyst. Such strong desire and positive emotions will drive me to take action. As I visualised it I also fell in love with such a vision. It felt good when I was able to put the ball into the basket consistently. As I visualised each day, I put in more practice and this seemed to complement each other. Over a short period, such shooting becomes automatic without me knowing the complexity of coordination. I was surprised when my level of play started to change in such an amazing way. Armed with the same emotion in visualising financial freedom through residual incomes and cash flow, you can imagine the moves you make. Seeing the images of success will drive you into action. The journey towards creativity begins. Choose the work you are passionate about and enjoy carrying out your creation. In my personal case, I enjoy teaching mathematics, writing, investing and having business-joint venture. I can visualise my journey in writing my first mathematics textbook in three steps. My first vision is to follow the syllabus closely by sequencing the topics in each chapter from easy to more difficult. I imagine that each mathematics idea can be related to our daily life. Second, I imagine giving examples for using each concept to be relevant to human daily life. I began to visualise that exercises in the form of questions have to be created to reinforce understanding each mathematics concept. Third, I imagine that I need to summarise all the important concepts at the end of each chapter, followed by giving a miscellaneous exercise at the end to consolidate all the concepts covered. This creative visualisation becomes my standard presentation for each chapter. I see my goal, focus on my goal and the path to get there will reveal itself in time. Once I visualise the steps to be taken, I make full commitment to carry out my vision. I put everything I have, time, passion, emotion, knowledge, style and dedication to accomplish my mission. It is just like planting a young tree. It has to be nurtured and cared for, and over time it will grow into a full blossom tree. The concepts and ideas of my creative visualisation are like the missing pieces that tie together everything I have learned in my games or life lessons for my personal growth space. I have distilled and compressed the teaching of years of experiences and discoveries into this simple book, helping you to lead a healthy life and enjoy financial freedom. I believe these two ingredients are necessary for you to live a successful life of experience, growth and contribution.

My life story is interesting and amazing. It took me over twenty years of working life as a humble teacher to create my abundance. If you are interested in my journey creating my abundance rich life, all these struggles are revealed in my first motivation book, *The Journey through Four Seasons of Life*. I am a successful, healthy and happy man now. My success in life is based on three basic metrics: wealth, position of influence and being healthy including happiness in the three stages of my life I went through. All these wonderful stories are revealed in my last book. It took me thirty years to prepare for my career and twenty three years of working life to accomplish my dreams. My secret of success is meditation and creative visualisation to help create residual incomes and cash flow to help me achieve financial freedom. Now I realise that I was actually using the technique of transforming my subconscious beliefs, habits and practices though meditation and creative visualisation. I must have downloaded many of the beliefs, habits and values of successful people into my subconscious mind. My means and goals are simple. I just have to conform to what society demands of me. I was expected to get good grades in school, college and university and get a government job for financial security. My end goal is different. I wanted to grow intellectually and make a contribution to the world. The important vision for me is to have financial freedom and a healthy body to pursue my dreams. Money is just like fuel to my car. It is useless if it just sits in my bank account and I just stare at it. But wealth and abundance can fund what I want in life. I have to learn how to create abundance, especially wealth. Changing my beliefs and attitudes at the conscious level will take many years or even decades to reach my goals. Another possibility is that I may never be able to do it at a conscious level.

On the human development area, there are dramatic changes taking place every minute. In 1937, Napolean Hill laid down thirteen success principles to help us to become rich. Not many changes take place until Natalie Ledwell starts her new matrix movie to innovate these principles. She claims the breakthrough by reprogramming the subconscious mind. A brain retraining system that will help to switch the brain to a higher receptive point, which is capable of replacing outdated beliefs, values, attitudes by those of more successful people. It is like reprinting the subconscious mind by scripting a new system for success. Armed with the beliefs and attitudes of the rich and taking actions, my journey for financial freedom began to transform. I discovered this secret very early in my working life. To achieve my dreams or end goals, I have to keep myself consistently happy to enhance my creative visualisation, changing my inner game or the subconscious mind. How do I do it? In the film Matrix, Neo got it instantly. I did not achieve my transformation overnight. It took me twenty three years to reach my end goals. Before I started practicing creative visualisation, I learned to be happy and acquired the state of flow first. This precondition is the key for quick manifestation of my dreams.

Stay in the State of Flow

The journey towards my end goal is long and challenging. How do I enjoy that journey? These are the steps I had taken. First I choose to be happy every day. With that choice, I find myself lucky to be at the right place at the right time to help me remain consistently happy with my current working situation. Soon I realised that the universe is not against me but want me to create an ideal situation on earth. I do not allow unnecessary things to hold me back. With meditation each day, I slowly become a true master of manifesting. My vision of financial freedom and good health is my heart's desire. I have always kept in mind things that are important to me. These include the following: spirituality, wealth, career, health and family. How do I attain such a state of flow so that I enjoy each day of my life? I have a simple exercise called meditation to get my mind on the right track and with creative visualisation; it helps me to clear my brain of clutter. I used to imagine my best perfect day and tried to paint that magnificent picture again and again in my subconscious mind. This helps to tell myself what I want to experience each day. Each day I feel energised, feeling optimistic and feeling energy circulating through my veins. I feel abundant happiness magnetically attracted to my body and mind. I had my dream job as a teacher and I was ready to make my contribution to my students' learning. Even after a hard day's work, I arrived home feeling more energy to have fun with my family. When I played game with my friends, I enjoyed the excitement and friendships. I was happy and I was able to create and visualise the financial images to coincide with my desires. I used to picture the dream house and the abundant wealth which will enable me to pursue my end goals. Whatever I dreamed of, I could really see it. I use to think about the feelings, the purpose and the accomplishment behind it. This visualisation helps me to create my flow. I learn to harness a focused flow state where I feel less stress and more advancement towards my goal. As I inch closer to my dream, I experience every moment is a blessed occasion. Confidence and happiness seem to follow. I remain focus on my big goal: enjoy the ride and realise that life is about now. The satisfaction of knowing that I am a powerful human being is just the beginning. Every effort to remain in the state of flow is activated. Soon I realise that my flow is an important state of mind which helps me effortlessly draw towards my end goal. Enjoying happiness and feeling expansive in my growth are allowed to unfold. I discipline myself to stay in that state of flow. The feeling that the universe has my best interest at heart is invigorating. I feel that the universe is backing me, I experience more coincidences and synchronicities that help to build my desired life. The imaginations of the amazing occurrences effortlessly pulled me closer and closer to my end goal. With more practice with creative visualisation, I soon begin to receive blessing and abundance. My consistent state of flow brings me luck every day. I used to think of a happy day in my life, a day where everything goes as planned. Enjoying my life and my work comes naturally. I used to wonder why some people enjoy an epic and authentic life while others experience more share of heartache and struggle. Now I realise that I need to join the group who enjoy a state of flow. What drives flow? Now I know it is happiness. And with creative visualisation, I begin to see that happiness is really the new productivity. I have to make an effort to combine my vision with my happiness. I cannot have one without the other. I realise that if I have a vision but I am unhappy, I would have created a lot of stress and discomfort, preventing me from reaching my goal. My three fundamental needs are simple: new experiences, growth and contribution. Using creative visualisation empowers me to give back to the world, help others and be of good service to others. I need a vision to direct my progress and back my thoughts and actions. Being in a state of flow is about consistent happiness that I feel all the time. I know very well that happiness must come first. I am going to create a better future for myself and my family, but not at the expense of the moment. Looking back, I can see that happiness fuels my manifestation and it is never a distraction. It is the positive energy that helps me towards my end goal. I choose to be happy while keep focusing on my vision, I find the magic miracles happening. So happiness must be attained before I can achieve my goal. Happiness is the most essential part of my journey towards my end goal, not the end result. The goal pulls me forward and tells me where I must go. I must keep myself happy all the time. The truth is that the universe is overflowing with abundance of wealth, love and happiness. And there is no limit of prosperity I can invite into my life. I must not do anything that will prevent them flowing into my life. I observe the following happiness rules by living my life moment to moment.

First, when I am happy, the road to my end goal becomes clear.

When I experience flow, it inspires me to take action.

Second, my inspired action feels effortless. Productivity increases when I am happy. Happiness helps me to get more out of my creative visualisation.

Third, happiness allows me to let go my limiting beliefs and thoughts easily. Replacing them with new beliefs and values of successful people enhances the process of manifesting.

Lastly happiness spawns intuition, a vital component of the mind to get everything I want out of life. I allow life to go on. Enjoying the ride and enjoying every moment are my choice. I dream and live at the moment. Avoiding living my life in the future or the past gives me peace of mind.

My simple philosophy is to enjoy the journey of my life. At the end, I want to stand back and enjoy the masterpiece I have painted. I also want to saviour every little moment and miracles that come my way. I am engaged in my life that is when the process of creative visualisation becomes more fun and more efficient. I know exactly what I want and am happy with my intention. The result is that I become happier with my current life. Eventually I am able to harvest the manifestation I desire. I read that most successful people built their success through happiness. When everything is right with the world, you are at the best. I too experience the miracles of being alive. I share all these experiences so that you too can have these miracles. But you must ensure that you too are always in the state of flow. Your creative visualisation equates to your happiness. Create your own flow and allow happiness to help you toward your life vision.

I was happy while I was working. I practiced creative visualisation daily. I became a very creative person and within the span of about two decades, I had written more than two dozens of mathematics textbooks and guidebooks. I have just added two motivation books to my collection. The first book is *The Journey through Four Seasons of Life*. This book is my second. There are many more to come as long as I am living.

The habit of meditation and creative visualisation also helps me to become successful in investments both in properties and stocks. I go on to become a successful business man and an entrepreneur. The secret of visualisation also helps me to become fit and healthy. I was able to reprogram my subconscious mind with new beliefs, habits and practices to enable me excel in the game basketball which I love. My creative visualisation enables me **to enhance my dribbling skill and shooting accuracy through** repeated practices and visualisation. I was focused and fully committed to practise my playing habits regularly. The various skills developments are enhanced further through daily creative visualisation. This is just reinforcing the result of research that athletes who use creative visualisation in addition, perform better than those who just practice without involving their subconscious brains. They have added mental strength and are able upgrade their skills with visualisation. Soon all these activities become automated and I was able to carry them out in matches without much thinking.

Never Too Late to Dream another Dream

Now I am tired of sitting comfortably in my new home looking into the horizon. I do not want to feel trapped or burnt out in my life. I do not want to join people who feel an impending doom every day. Living a better life is always a choice. Keeping busy and happy requires initiative. To add extra feathers to my writing skills, I added two dissections (one for my master's and one for my PhD) and two motivation books to my collection. This book is my second motivation book. My third book is almost ready. "Enjoy Eighty Five years of Abundant and Productive Life" is under production. Now I am ready to share my journey of exciting positive transformation and teach people how they could get there too. You can also create your own passion-filled abundant rich life. The top priority is a healthy body to enable you to enjoy the time and wealth you are going to create. Winning the game of money creation is equivalent to plugging into the matrix just like Neo. I believe strongly that values, habits and practices including beliefs can be imprinted on people's brains if they have recognised things to follow in their transformation process. According to Natalie Ledwell, there is always a number invisible glass barriers that are keeping us from achieving our success. She suggested a powerful strategy to help us remove those barriers permanently by reprogramming our subconscious mind. When we reprogram our subconscious mind with new empowering beliefs, successful mental models and positive affirmations, it's like putting a new carpet across those old barriers. Everyone uses different strategies. I use meditation called Quantum Jumping. There are a handful of buttons in my room. Each button is for an important area of my life. If I am stressed and can't see the path to peace and serenity, I just press the right button and jump into a parallel universe. My doppelganger is there to guide me. Natalia uses different strategies. She claims that this can be done quickly. How? She uses the Mind Movies Matrix, a process which is fun, simple and incredibly effective. According to her, it takes only a few minutes a day to be successful in getting everything you want in life. Mind Movies Matrix combines one of the most powerful tools ever created with the best subconscious programming technology in the world. She claims that this process allows you to supercharge your way of reaching your goals and desires faster than you could possibly imagine.

Each Mind Movie Matrix lasts three minutes of video snapshots of the life you dream off. It contains powerful positive statements and uses EEG (electroencephalography) technology. The visual image of successful you with sound technology inducing you to an alpha, theta and delta waves stages helping to download beliefs and success habits directly into your brain. The EEG can measure your brain vibrations from the surface of the scalp. When we are highly active and focused, our frequency of vibrations is from 13 to 30 Hz. During meditations at alpha, theta and delta brain stages, the frequencies of vibrations are respectively, 8 to 12 Hz, 4 to 7 Hz and 0.5 to 3 Hz respectively. It is believed that when we are in the alpha brain state or below, the reprogramming of personal successes becomes smooth and easy. It is a powerful technique to reprogram our minds. It involves seeing the 'successful self' in your eyes not from the conscious mind. In this stage of meditation you are using the subconscious alpha-state of your mind while the conscious mind is at rest. There will be no contradictory logical responses. Consequently, the reprogramming will be accelerated.

This is a revolutionary concept helping you to put your success on autopilot. Perhaps it is worth trying if you want a fast way of reprogramming your subconscious mind. I encourage you to try this new technique in addition to meditation and visualisation.

This book is written especially for people who long to have financial freedom and live healthily to enjoy their life. Now if you could plug into the matrix and learn any skill or practice you want for financial freedom, which approach would you choose? I suggest that you should learn the game skill of wealth building through creative visualisation by creating as many residual incomes as possible. But before you take action to accomplish your goal, you need to use creative visualisation to balance your body and mind. By taking an inner transformation process, you will instantly feel unlimited clarity and inner freedom. Many of us have experienced a lot of pain because of poor health and financial difficulty we suffered. With creative visualisation, you will discover that your natural state is one of perfect health and mental balance. Your body is created to self-healing itself and your mind's neural networks are recreated continuously. A healthy lifestyle is necessary for self-healing to function continuously.

A reprogrammed blueprint for your subconscious mind is required for the brain to keep renewing itself. They must be allowed to function as they are created. The purpose of the various approaches to residual income of rich people is to provide inputs to help you in creative visualisation. You would have more recognisable familiarities to explore further your power of creative visualisation. If you learn early to imprint the abundant mind-set, values, practices, attitudes and beliefs of successful people, you can have pretty much everything else. At the same time, you are able to get rid of your old beliefs, thoughts and perceptions about finance. You will have a new mind-set to drive you into actions. Resistance and opposing forces holding you back will start to dissipate. You will require less effort and struggle to have what you desire. You can have better health, education, relationship and wealth. Do you believe all these? Money may not help you to have better relationship. In fact, money may be the cause of divorce. Remember money is not the root of all evil. The love of money is.

But if you practice the power of gratitude and embrace the spirit of generosity, you can change your habits and actions towards good relationship. Using money wisely can bring joy and happiness to others. Can money buy you happiness? I know at least money can buy you trips, adventure, a car and even a nice home. All these may help you on the way to be happy. What if you could imprint on your brain approaches and habits of creating residual income? Would you do it? How can meditation and creative visualisation help your brain? Remember your present financial reality is just an illusion. You can use your creative visualisation to recreate your new financial reality. You can reprogram your beliefs, habits and mastery of approaches of creating residual incomes to lower the fiery threshold of doubts, anxieties and fears to financial freedom. I want to introduce you to another approach to meditation. Meditation through Quantum Jumping can lead the way how to be more coherent with your goals and dreams. My success of financial freedom took thirty years of preparation and twenty three years of implementation for abundance to happen. If I had discovered creative visualisation using Mind Movies Matrix or Quantum Jumping in my early days, I would have shortened the duration of reaching my goal. The concept of Quantum Jumping and the imaginary Quantum Library in another parallel universe can provide you with all the necessary beliefs, values and habits. What you need to do is just action and full commitment to realise your dreams. After reading this book, you may not have to struggle such long periods to achieve what I had done. It took me many years to realise my passion and purpose. With creative visualisation, you can easily get in tune with your passion. You will discover early what you are really here to do even if you have always felt your sense of purpose has been missing. I discovered my passion and purpose as an educator because I enjoyed teaching and financial freedom. I felt happy because I finally found what I meant to do in my life. I was empowered and used my full potential to become what I wanted to be: a writer and an investor. My life experiences pursuing my passion can add flavour to your visualisation. This book provides all the approaches and ingredients of creating residual incomes necessary to help you achieve your dream instead of living from pay cheque to pay cheque. In order to succeed in gaining financial freedom, you need to follow the natural instincts of successful people. They do not depend on their salaries to gain financial independence. Their natural habits allow them to create residual income besides their regular salary or they are doing business of their own. Why do some succeed and others don't? It is not because some are smarter or work harder. Maybe we don't need both! It is also not because they are lucky. There are many other factors contributing to their success in gaining financial independence. I can only speak for myself. Just like Neo, in Matrix, I reprogrammed my subconscious brain to change my beliefs, practices and values to help me succeed. Beliefs are ingrained in our minds from the time we are kids by our parents, teachers, preachers and lifestyles of others around us. Yes, we carried all of them into adulthood. These beliefs, habits and behaviours are our paradigms. They are deep inside our subconscious minds. They control our thinking, our actions and our lifestyle. They govern how we make money, how we love, our happiness, our sex life and our ability to grow or stagnate. If these paradigms are faulty, we are unlikely to move towards our goal of financial freedom and live a life of abundance. I was lucky to be aware of this situation because of my hardship during childhood. I urgently needed a paradigm shift in my subconscious mind. The tool I have is meditation and creative visualisation. I was committed totally and took action to realise my dreams. I used my imagination and visualisation wisely. I tried many approaches to help me all the way. I dreamed to become a state basketballer, I visualised my plan and reached my goal. I made full commitment to become a teacher, writer an investor and an entrepreneur. I achieved what I visualised. You can make use of the strategies in this book to build a system of creative visualisation to create your own streams of residual income. For example, if you want to make more money in the market, you are advised to follow a proven, profitable method for picking stocks. Following a proven strategy that works can help you achieve your goals. After practicing the strategy, you are more likely to stick or improve on it. Similarly, investment in properties requires knowledge of locality and rental potential. The lessons from this book go beyond creating residual income. You will learn to believe in yourself as I do and benefit from other aspects of abundance. A healthy body is essential for you to enjoy the life you desire. Creative visualisation is a key to help you eliminate the blocks that hold you back from living fully. Many of us are hurt badly in our life mainly because of our financial status and poor health. These limiting beliefs we picked up during childhood and we held on to these 'mental blocks' into adulthood. They can cause us a host of problems in many areas of our life including career and finance. We spend without knowing where to source. We procrastinate on many important things. We seldom think before we act. Lacking training in thinking is the cause. We even make our decisions based on the ground of fear instead of from the position of abundance. These limiting beliefs are so deeply implanted in our subconscious that we do not realise that they exist. So most of us are not aware of the main cause and consequently we experience lot of struggle in our life. They are poisoning our daily thoughts, habits and practices in relation to our financial freedom. How to replace these limiting beliefs by more empowering beliefs? Many of us are ignorant of the tools available to help us achieve financial freedom and a life-style that helps us to keep fit. By reprogramming our subconscious mind towards giving more love we will make a move to receive more in return. Such inner transformation will make you not only happy but also more productive in your works. Allow one of these pearls of wisdom to resonate within you. Once empowering beliefs are unloaded into your mind, it's time to take action. Many strategies work best when you practice them repeatedly. The more you use them, the more confident you become, making it more likely you will keep repeating them to achieve your dreams. You will soon find the recipe for success in investments. Just like when you dance, your goal is not to reach a certain place on the floor, but to enjoy yourself and be fit. Dancing your way while you take action, your energy level increases. You will open up your energy flow and you will quickly let go of all resistance to abundance including financial aspect. Everything is energy. You will find it easier to eliminate energy blocks and allow the best experiences of life to flow freely. Your desire for financial freedom and healthy life will be accomplished. These good strategies will also help you to overcome your greatest obstacle, your emotions. These characteristics of successful people, if implemented effectively, can touch our hearts profoundly and transform us into a money magnet. I was touched deeply. I share my experiences here.

Firstly, I never doubt myself. I realised early that if I doubt myself regarding my abilities, I will miss many opportunities. I do not believe in sabotaging myself and living with one foot on the brakes. I know that any self-doubt in my ability to create extra residual incomes could unconsciously stop me from living the life of my dreams. Depending only on my salary alone will not provide me with financial freedom. I need to make use of my subconscious mind to help in my creativities. Meditation changes my brain by reprogramming my beliefs and habits. My success does not come overnight. It took me many years of preparation and implementation for success to happen. I believe that being aware of this can inspire you to do the same.

Second, I do not go at it all alone. I have a lot of help from many people especially my close relatives. Without the support system I have, I do not think that I would have succeeded. I have provided plenty of supports for others and I get more supports in return. Having the right people helping me all along, I am able to fulfil my dreams of financial freedom.

Third, I do not fear future failure. I do not wait for everything to be perfect before taking action. As the saying goes, the fear of failure leads to 'paralysis by analysis.' I would not have left my comfortable job as a college-trained teacher at the age of 26 to pursue my science degree in the University of Malaya. Fearing future failure is like waiting for all the lights to turn green before leaving for a new venture. I was prepared for failure. But I did not doubt my own ability.

Fourth, I do not fear success. I reprogram my mind for success. It usually stems from fear of criticism. I am not afraid what others may say about me. I have to do what I need to do. I need to strive where I want to be. Life will not provide me a second chance if I missed the opportunity to create residual incomes while I am working. There is no second chance for my working life. I cannot rewind the clock of life.

Fifth, I do not tolerate clutter. I learned early to organise my life. To me disorganisation is clutter. It causes unneeded delays, creates a feeling of overwhelming and unnecessary stress.

Sixth, I do not ignore the big vision. I acknowledge that I do not need to be the best or the richest man in the world. What I need is a plan and direction. I only need financial freedom and a good retirement free from worry. *I take my own* sweet time to step back and reflect on the big picture of creating streams of residual income for my financial freedom and not depending solely on my salary.

Lastly, I do not act without thinking. I learned to think well when I was young. My plan is important but it is just one part. I am aware of faulty thinking. I acknowledge that the road to financial freedom is full of road blocks and I need to embrace changes and to improvise strategies instead of following the plans of someone who succeeded before. I have to modify, improvise new formulae that will help me to financial freedom.

I must admit that when I was introduced to creative visualisation, I told myself initially that such stuff work for others but not for me. But when I unloaded those habits and values of successful people into my subconscious mind and began to practice them daily, things began to change. Now I know that I have to share the new way of inner transformation before taking actions. I set out to share my achievements to others who are struggling and they especially need this new tool to accelerate their process to acquire financial freedom and physical fitness. Practicing a skill with the help of visualisation will multiply and expand its result. If you share the same goal of achieving financial freedom while you are working, you can follow the same path of creative visualisation I practised and avoid the seven fundamental things most successful people do not do. Creative visualisation is more than a method to help you achieve your goal in financial independence. It allows you to use your brain power to change not only your own destiny but also the lives of your love ones. What goes on in your brain can affect your future reality such as your desire for financial freedom. If you care to focus on your end goal, everything you desire will unfold exactly as you conceive it to be. But you must know exactly what you want in terms of financial freedom because you will get nothing more and nothing less than what you visualise. By practising creative visualisation today and every day in your working life, you really start thinking about the financial reality you want to achieve. Never settle for anything less than what you truly desire. Your dream of wealth will come to life when you implement creative visualisation into your life. You must know that your thinking will shape what happens in your real world. If your life were a book, you are the main character and you are also the writer of the story. Your viewpoint is born from your beliefs, readings and experiences in life. Many of us have deep-rooted beliefs about our financial abundance. Most of them are set in our minds through the social media and childhood indoctrination. Some of the limited beliefs originated from our own wrong inexperienced assumptions about the world when we were younger. These beliefs lie in our subconscious mind and we are not aware of them. Unfortunately, these blocks stay with us until our adulthood. And they can sabotage your career, your pursuit of purpose of life and ultimately, your abundance. One of the energy blocks is that you cannot make money doing the things you love. My experiences tell me otherwise. I love teaching. Many of my close relatives told me that if I take up teaching as a career, I will remain a poor teacher. I love teaching since my secondary school days. So I responded to my calling which did not pay well. Through creative visualisation, I created parallel careers to complement my financial independence. I did all that successfully through services to others, through writing, business-joint ventures, and investments. My journey in life is just one of the many examples which can help you overcome this energy block. After reading my story, I hope you will be inspired and you will understand that no matter who you are and where you come from, abundance is just a mind shift away. Just be happy doing the things you love and invest your energy at the right place, abundance will flow in your direction. Let your imagination and creative visualisation do the rest. This book will provide some clear applicable inputs into the software of your brain, refresh and renew your connection with inspiring ideas that may shape your reality of financial independence. Your mind will begin to make judgements about the world and the goal you desire for financial independence. Your interpretation may be unique and different from another person; but the ability to take action for your financial well-being based on familiarity will be built. Financial reality is built by what is recognisable. Do you find your desire for financial freedom out of reach? Do not inherit this problem? Limited beliefs create limited possibilities. This type of roadblock is undesirable. Do not blame your circumstances. Every one experiences these circumstances every day. Do you wonder regarding the meaning of the word 'circumstance'? It means to stand around. That is you are in the centre of an infinite circle and your creations or circumstances stand around you. You are the main actor or writer of the circumstances. And with creative visualisation, you can rewrite yourself out by creating a new reality for your financial freedom. You are the designer of your own financial reality. So look at your own working life from a new scientific lens for a moment. A series of thoughts lead to you choices of projects and they lead you to take action. You can trace every result in your working life back to your thinking patterns. This can be incredibly humbling and also empowering. You know that everything ever being created started as a thought. To put this idea into your life, think about the inventions: the phone, the Internet and others were all born from thoughts. The inventors used creative visualisation to upgrade the software in their mind and put them into the operation system to manifest new ideas which never existed before. It is an imagination with a purpose. It is a spark to increase your creativity. It encourages out-of-the-box thinking, helping you to find a solution to your intention. The more you practice this, the more you will imprint the idea in your mind as something important. It will soon open the door to unexpected solution. It is more than creating images in your mind. It calls for all your five senses to be involved plus one extra. It helps you to paint a picture of your dream. If you want to be a writer, imagine seeing the mental image of a draft of your book you intent to write. Then you can start adding details to your ideas. If you keep seeing and adding ideas and their details you want to see this will arouse your emotion, sensing that people appreciate your ideas and your style of presentation. Emotions will drive your action. As you visualise what you want, prepare to be astonished by the awesome ideas that come to you and you want to get them done. Allow your emotions to gather momentum and as you act on them, you will manifest any desire you want. Daily practice will help your imaginations and manifestations. This tells you that you can shape reality either consciously or unconsciously. So if you do not like your financial reality now, you have the brain power to change those circumstances. Showing interest is not enough. Commitment is the keyword. You must be committed to create what you desire for financial freedom. This book provides part of the awareness that you can use your creative visualisation as the cornerstone of your dream to financial security. The thought of creating residual income and the commitment you make, while you are working, can transform your financial freedom, thanks to creative visualisation. If that is what you want for a good retirement, you should begin to direct your focus on creating that goal. Your mind is the most powerful muscle that can create that reality. Since you are aware of the approaches now, you can use them effectively to manifest the financial reality you want in time. The strategies work for many others and it can also work for you. Many people get stuck to where they are for life because they are not aware of their ability due to their ignorance regarding their limiting beliefs in their subconscious mind. They are not aware that they can rewrite and reframe their story in life. They forget that certain challenges and people who are presented to their lives are there to open up their hearts and to help them grow. If they were to imagine that their life is like a novel, they can choose how each chapter unfolds. Awareness is so powerful that it helps to write your life story, your attitude, your relationship and your weaknesses. It steers you on the path towards success. By accepting and embracing these changes unloaded into your mind, you can overcome negative aspects of them and become successful.

    Every one of us has our own potential. When I bought a new car, the maximum speed of the speedometer is 200 km per hour. But I have never driven close to the maximum speed because of two glaring factors. First I do not have the skill and confidence to drive at that fast speed on a racing track because of my conditioning on ordinary road. But I believe that if I practice driving the car on the racing track every day, I would have the skill and gut to drive my new car close to the maximum speed. Another factor is that the car has a governor set at an optimum speed of only 110 km per hour to fulfil the governor set maximum speed on the highway. The governor is a mechanism used to control the speed of the car. Regardless of my effort, the car will not exceed the set speed. So no matter how hard I try, I will not be able to reach the maximum speed of the speedometer. Do you know why I choose this analogy? This analogy has a strong message for you because you will never live to your own full potential. You may not be aware that you may have the same governor in the form of financial block restricting your income monthly or annually. Most of us are not aware of this limitation.

This awareness tells us to reset or rewire the subconscious governor by reprogramming the software of the brain to a higher level of achievement. The process of practising creative visualisation every day and taking action with full commitment will slowly add skills and knowledge moving you up the level of wealth creation. Just like practising driving on the racing track to reach the maximum speed of the car's potential. Knowledge has a level playing field now because Google is available to everyone. The only difference is the ability to use our creative visualisation and take action to recondition our subconscious mind to move us up to the next level of financial independence. We are conditioned by our beliefs, values and our perceptions. We need to control our emotions and perceptions to enable us to take action. Do you think it is possible? Do you want some extra money to do things that matter to you? Can you make twelve months of your income in six months? It is even better, if you can make your annual income in just one month. Do you ever conceive that thought? You need to upgrade your mental software and take action to accomplish your dreams of financial freedom. You need to gather all the necessary tools available like mindfulness, guided hypnotherapy, self hypnotherapy through meditation using creative visualisation and others. Make full commitment to achieve your dreams. Interest, commitment and knowledge will produce dividends in life's success, especially financial freedom.

Happiness Drives Productivity

To be productive in our creative visualisation, we have to be in good mood and also be happy. How to be happy? We can make use of simple practice of daily gratitude, which will provide fuel for our desired manifestation. The healing power of gratitude is always underestimated. Creative visualisation is more than just expanding our life. It is about creating a better reality such as good health and financial freedom, as a new reality. This includes our current surrounding. You will ask what you want with abundance so that the universe will respond to your request. You want to be happy at the moment and also in the future. You also want to have more energy; enjoy fuller relationship and be able to sleep well at night. Obviously, you want to be less anxious, have fewer headaches and do not feel depressed. You want to have the forgiving attitude and be more fun-loving. You want to be a person of high emotional intelligence. Your desires are to improve every aspect of your life including financial, spiritual and emotional including relationship. The manifestation of all these will depend on the focus of your desires.

First thing first, these desires must not come from the place of lack. It must come from abundance with special focus on happiness. So it is very important that you start to take notice of the many delights surrounding you. How you feel is critical. Do you feel thankful every day? Your subconscious mind responds to your happy feeling than your direct affirmation. You do not want to fall victim to 'the pain of new desires' because your gratefulness falls by the wayside. All because something new comes along and the current environment becomes toxic. As you know thankfulness is a foundation for creative visualisation. The goal is happiness. But without gratefulness, you begin to resent what you do not have such as financial freedom. It is easy for us to forget to be grateful for what we have, while adding happiness with new desire. So be aware to practice gratefulness in all aspects of your life. It is a natural progression with the fulfilment of your dreams. It is critical that in any unhappy situation, we need to find a way to turn it around. To create happiness again, you need to find elements of your current life that you appreciate such as laughing at a joke with a friend or having a good meal with a friend. You need to actively seek your happiness first before you search for something better through creative visualisation. There is always something that you can be grateful for. If your goal is to become fit and healthy, be grateful right now that your body is capable of healing itself of any injury.

Be grateful that you are able to walk up the hill without any help. Always think of something to be grateful for.

Financially, if you are broke and your goal is to become wealthy, be grateful that the financial situation has taught you to live within your means. Be grateful that you have learned patience and perseverance. You can have many examples from your life experiences to help you in turning any negative situation into something you can cherish. When you start to cherish every single day, you begin to live a happier life. There are many areas of your life. If one area is not ideal, you can be grateful in another area. Always allow the happy events of your life to be your main focus; you will create your desires from a place of abundance instead of lack. You will find that daily gratitude does not only improve your temporary mood but also enhance your foundational attitudes. You have more energy and a better forgiving attitude that allows you to let go. You would have few headaches, less anxieties, no feeling of depression and have a higher emotional intelligence. Your daily gratitude opens up to incredible abundance and joy. Each night before you sleep, think of many things that you are grateful for. This practice will prompt your subconscious mind to find solution to your obstacles. You will learn that gratefulness is foundational on your path to the reality you wish to create. Your life will take on a fresh, bright, and new meaning. Truly that is what your creative visualisation is all about. Be thankful every day and when you do, new opportunities to create what you want will reveal themselves.

In our life, we come into interaction with many people. Every one of them is unique. We are likely to encounter people who are rude toward us. There will be misunderstanding and others who may be more serious. When you hold a grudge against someone, you are harbouring a negative charge. If you hold on to the negative charge, it will begin to negatively affect you. It can spoil your day or even weeks as long as you hold on to it. People will notice that you become more irritable, less patient, more reactive, more stressed and more emotional.

Luckily there is a cure. It's forgiveness. Similar to gratitude, forgiveness is another powerful way to positively transform your life. Being able to practice forgiveness can reduce stress, revitalises you and give you a more positive outlook. You need to be aware that a lion's share of forgiveness is compassion. The ability to forgive brings in compassion, which can significantly improve your health, your connection with people and your well being.

    This important habit and practice have to be planted into your subconscious mind through creative visualisation. This is a choice you command your mind to react unconsciously to anyone's unkindly actions against you. You become stronger for forgiving someone's unkind acts and this can be empowering for you for being able to control your emotional reactions or responses. You need to visualise the person who upsets or hurts you. This is the source of your negative charge. This is the person to whom you are directing your anger and negativity. Asking this person for forgiveness may be counterintuitive. Remember, you are connected to the person and what he does to another person he does to himself as well. Your negative thoughts and feelings toward this person affect you negatively. By opening your heart to compassion, you can forgive this person whose unkindly actions came from his inner pain. Once you can practice compassion, you move from judgement to caring, from isolation to connection and from dislike to understanding. The beauty of practicing this exercise is that you apply the concepts both to the person who betrayed you and to yourself. It's difficult but rewarding if you practise it often. You are sending positive energy and radiating unconditional love to this person. As soon as you practice this, you will feel the love radiating out of you and feeling love throughout your body. The person may not deserve such love, but the source may come from his great pain reflecting in his behaviours. The person has acted out of his pains. Anyhow, be prepared to give him an energetic hug. You will feel better. Remind yourself that you do not have to condone such behaviours. You do not have to have such a person in your life. However, once you have forgiven the person, then you release the negative charge you associate with that person. You will regain your balance and feel free. You naturally become stronger, more empowered and have formed an automatic positive response to any unkindly act. You will feel happier because such a negative charge is eliminated. The truth is that your perception is your reality and you can literally create your own reality. So you want to create the life you want to lead. Start taking action today towards your ultimate happiness and let go of things that are not serving you. Remember the elements required to make you happy.

Do you want to know why you think and act in a certain way? Usually, there is nothing wrong in the way you think and act in a certain way. Being aware that was part of the programming of your childhood years and you need not be held hostage by such beliefs. You can start unloading a new positive programme so that you can have everything you wanted. Open your eyes to all possibilities before you can see them.

Three Fuels Helping You in Achieving Your Dreams

Now we are going to focus on the tools which can help you to be healthy and be able to work smartly in achieving financial freedom. The three elements are desire, belief and expectancy. To build the life you want, you must make sure that these three elements are allowed to work in harmony to facilitate your manifestation. From my own experience, when I desire something such as financial freedom, it is because I was struggling and that is part of my reality when I started working. My problem is that this desire came from a place of lack. It did not come from a place of abundance and hope. This confused thought has the power to cancel out the manifestation. To correct this thought of lack, I have to enhance my own expectation. Desire is not lack. There is no such belief that what I want, I cannot have. This dormant power in the subconscious mind has to be activated first. I started to experience desire from a different point of view. As I acquired little confidence and lived my life with hopefulness, the lack and frustration slowly disappeared. I used the intense desire to propel myself towards my goals and after repeated practice, I was able to manifest my vision.

I began to expect the best and ensured that my actions correspond with my goals. I started implementing the three elements on the things I wished to create so that I would have constant inspirations. My desire for financial freedom began. Why I cannot have it? First, I noted that at that point of time, it was not part of my reality. I wanted financial freedom because of lack. I realised that most probably I had misclassified my desire as a by-product of lack. I might have sent conflicting thoughts to my mind. The feeling of lacking creates confusion. The steps I had taken towards my financial freedom seemed to cancel one another. Then I realise that my subconscious mind is a powerful thing and when I send a signal of lack, it ensures that my thinking becomes reality. The subconscious mind reacts based on feeling not what I tell it directly. I started to change my approach as I started reading and writing.

As my financial standing improved, I began learning to desire from an abundant place. I started to control my thinking and began to expect goodness that will come my way through creative visualisation. I managed to overcome this internal battle brewing in my mind. I started to influence my subconscious mind of what I want from the point of desire. I knew straight away that my vision of financial freedom will be built based on my feelings, not my affirmations. So I became aware that I am the creator of my own reality. Whatever I want will come to me. I am able to go beyond my belief stage and into the expectancy stage. My belief is the core element and it is more than an affirmation. It is more than something I wish for. Belief that I can have financial freedom is something I accept as truth. So I expect it to happen because I believe it will. I expect it to happen without question or doubt. So it goes beyond what is possible and becomes what is definite. I expect it and I know I will have it. By practicing creative visualisation regularly, I take control over how I live my life and what will happen. It's only a matter of time before manifestation of my financial freedom and my biggest goal. I use this analogy of ordering a meal in a restaurant. I know the meal will come within time. There is a similarity in my creative visualisation of financial freedom. My expectancy tells me that what I want will come to me. If I am confident that something is already mine, it helps to send the feelings of lack out of my life. Expectancy is important to help me get what I want. Remember, what you expect will always come true. I know very early that if I expect to fail at my dream of financial freedom, then failure becomes my destiny. The feelings and thoughts I have become the commands that my subconscious mind listens to and reacts to. So I always expect what I desire and I will manifest it without cancelling out what I order from the universe. I expect my way towards manifestation. I remember my first attempt to date a girl. I expected her to say 'no' and she did. Similarly if you think that your dream is too far-fetched or impossible, then you know you do not deserve it. My experience tells me that I have to overcome my past negative expectancy. Now I need to recalibrate my thinking of what will happen. If I will it, it is no dream.

If I expect an excellent life, then that is exactly what will happen. What I expect is based on my beliefs which I know are the truth. Sometimes, our expectancy does not always come from ourselves. Your circumstances and others influence how you view the world and what you expect to get from it. For example, when I came to Sydney the first time, I was told that the area Parramatta in Sydney is a dangerous place filled with gangsters and rude people. So when I visited the place, that became my expectation and I attracted a lots of negativities unconsciously. Even the fruit seller's loud voice was taken to be rude. When I saw a group of youngsters gathering around, I expected them to belong to a gang. I did a study on secondary students' attitudes and found that if their teachers expect them to be lazy and disrespectful; I found that this reality manifested itself because the teachers unconsciously treated them that way. When teachers find that the students are curious and hardworking, they rise to the occasion. In a way expectation is always self-fulfilling. When parents expect their children to do well, positive energy is always created. Their subconscious minds will alter their behaviour to correspond with the expectation. Some of us use to expect the worse and it usually happens. When the worse happen, they say, 'I told you so.' Be aware that with your expectation, you change the outcome. My own experience in game shows that when I expect the best, I create the best. When I was at the prime of my basketball career, I went into every game, expecting to win. This prophecy had resulted in my club team winning the state tournament five times in a row. If you find that is difficult, you should learn to create positive expectancy. If you are used to pessimism, try to begin with small steps. Each small step can create small manifestation and you will improve on your positive expectancy. After some practices, you expectation will be in upward momentum. Try to use these three elements: desire, belief and expectancy as your immediate tools to facilitate your manifestation in building the life you want. If you still have faulty beliefs, negative desire and negative expectancy in your subconscious mind, creative visualisation is the solution. When you are familiar with the implementations of these characteristics, your desire for them will start to unload them into your mind. Make sure that these three fuels work in harmony with one another to help you in your manifestation. Remember, when you order your meal in a restaurant; you have to specify clearly what you like to get what you want. Similarly, in your visualisation, you have to paint a clear picture of your financial freedom through the paths of many streams of residual income and cash flow. Once you have done all these, you will start moving closer and closer to the reality desire. So in implementing your strategies towards your financial freedom, you need to follow the three-part code to expect the best and achieve the best.

First, you must have a very strong desire which is capable of replacing the faulty one. It must be a heartfelt desire not a minor financial gain. This desire must encompass everything you want including wealth and being healthy all along.

Second, you must believe that your financial freedom will manifest without questioning or doubt.

Lastly, you must expect your financial freedom to happen during your working life.

As you begin to design your paths to residual incomes and giving commands to your subconscious mind to implement your moves, you must always expect positive results. Positive expectancy will help you to overcome lack. By allowing the three fuels to provide the positive energy, you will bypass lack desires and you will change your beliefs. Everything will bend to your desire. You have to remember that if you expect your financial independence to turn out the way you want it to be, the path to the manifestation of your vision will not be blocked. The three elements will be the foundation of your financial freedom. Your abundant desires will move you closer and closer to your goal. Do not allow the lack desires to hold you back. Keep your focus on your goal with positive expectations and make sure that your actions match your visions.

There is no such thing as neutral attitude. The ways we act like the clothing we wear are never neutral. We dress conservatively or otherwise, we are putting on a show. Specific characteristics, traits or design details of clothing we wear are cues to communicate certain messages. People cannot help it because of programme wiring in their subconscious mind. Just like when a man put on torn, faded jeans, he seems to suggest that he has a careless and lazy attitude. If a man put on crumpled, un-ironed shirt to work, he gives an impression of a person who does not pay attention to details. If you put pants that are too tight to work, you may suggest that you are not bothered about his company's image or setting. Similarly if a lady puts on uncoordinated outfit or clashing colours, she gives an impression of a disorganised and unprofessional person. A lady going to work in a conservative profession by putting overly trendy clothing might give the impression that she cares more about fashion than her work. Be aware that wearing frills, ruffles, laces and florals to work may make you appear immature and less ready for an important career. A lady wearing low-cut blouse and too-short skirt may portray her as lacking of self-control. People tend to think that she is not aware of appropriate dress code. A lady wearing ill-fitting clothes may display poor taste and is unaware of her physical liabilities. So it's important that when we go to work, dress well and dress right. To me, I always think that if a person dresses respectfully, he or she attracts respect. So pay a little attention to your dressing attitude.

The Winning Attitude and the Losing Attitude

What is attitude? Our attitude is revealed in our words, actions, body language and thinking. It is our habit of thoughts. So if we want to change our attitude, we have to change the way we think, act and speak. All of us want to be successful in life. Success in life is our universal set. There are many subsets contributing to success in life. One of them is financial freedom; another one is power or influence. And another one is our overall well-being including happiness, giving and wisdom. All of us want new experiences, growth and contribution. First, we need to think well, speak well and write well to allow us to acquire this habit of thought. Every one of us has a key in our hand that opens the door to untold success. You choose whether or not you want to open that door. It's our choice. I realise that I am not determined by my look, where I live or who my parents were. Who I am is a function of specific choices that I have made. I am where I am now and what I have because of the dominating thoughts in my mind. We are what we think we are, not what we appear on the outside. Our overall pattern of thinking is generally positive or negative. Remember, the pattern you choose has profound effect on your life. It affects your beliefs and your potential of success. A negative attitude causes you to doubt your ability to achieve, while your belief in your potential will affect your action or inaction. Your attitude determines how you perceive any challenge. A positive attitude causes you to see any challenge as an opportunity while a negative one causes you to see a threat. It determines your confidence. It enhances your chance of success. A positive attitude opens your eyes to see opportunity and you can choose which challenge to face. Negative attitude serves as a dark cloud preventing you from seeing opportunity. How is attitude formed? Everything since birth is used by our subconscious mind as input. This explains the influence of significant persons like parents, relatives and teachers affecting our attitude. The Bible in Romans 12:2 tells us that we can only transform ourselves by renewing our mind. It leads us to believe that these outdated inputs have to be eliminated before we can download inspiring fresh inputs to help us in forming positive attitude. Changing an attitude is possible but it takes time and implementation. We must first make the choice to change. The following principle shows us the way. If we sow a thought, we will reap an action; if we sow an action, we will reap a habit; if we sow a habit, we will reap a character and if we sow a character, we will reap a destiny. The three major changes are our thought, speech and behaviour. Avoid saying that we can't. Always tell yourself to look again and try to give the opportunity a chance. Change our speech pattern from negative to affirmative. Always use positive words in our daily interactions. Make a conscious effort to modify our behaviour. Since your personality is unique and your abilities are different, always give any project a try first. Soon a change in behaviour is on the way. There is a creative force inside all of us that can make our dream or desire a reality.

Do you think you can imprint the beliefs, attitudes and habits of the wealthy and successful people so that you can attract abundance effortlessly? Yes, you can. You can rewire and retrain your brain to higher levels of attitudes, beliefs and habits around money and health so you can have the income and the lifestyle you deserve. You can also release your brain's old thought patterns and habits like poor organisation, poor dressing attitude and procrastination that have limited you financially. By imprinting new characteristics of the wealthy, replacing your limiting beliefs, into your subconscious mind, they will motivate you to achieve a greater financial freedom. You can reprogram your brain to filter the inner conflict, resistance, anxiety and problems that are holding you back from your happiness and financial freedom. Happiness is the gasoline that drives your productivity to meet your vision. Teach your brain to think systematically by using strategies and models of the rich to help you to become an unstoppable force in wealth creation. You can reprogram your brain for automatic success. Get the help and support of the mastermind group. They can help, encourage, support and nurture you to shatter the glass ceiling of your financial income. Lastly to fulfil your dreams, you need to imprint in your subconscious mind the reason why you need to take each of your steps towards creating residual incomes. It is critical that you cultivate the winning attitude in your subconscious mind. Circumstances and significant persons have influenced your attitude. You may have developed unconsciously a winning or losing attitude while you grow up. Can we make use of the infinite power of our brain muscle to transform it into a winning attitude? Can we activate a winning attitude in our subconscious minds? People think that it is impossible! Now it is possible. The tool is simple creative visualisation through mindfulness, guided hypnotherapy or Quantum Jumping. Let our imagination do the rest. Start the journey of gathering information and acquiring knowledge. The investment in knowledge pays us the best dividends when it is used productively. Most of us are living below our potential. Give yourself a chance to explore all possibilities.

First, you need to develop the attitude of dreaming big. The size of every one of your dream does not matter! They are equally easy to manifest. Thinking bigger is about taking action. It's about the act of taking the dreams and constructing a reality around them. Can you remember your childhood dreams? Allow yourself to dream like that again. A financial reality you can see happening.

Second, you need to know that qualification does not affect the results of your dreams for financial security and abundance. Everybody can assess Google nowadays. We have a level playing field now as far as information is concerned. So your results of financial freedom are not affected by how much you know, but by your actions, beliefs and habits. Replacing our outdated beliefs with those of successful people, we can start implementing their habits, beliefs and behaviours to pave the way for our success towards abundance. The ability to shift towards empowering beliefs, behaviours and habits will determine our outcomes.

Thirdly, you need to know that you are not 'hard-wired' for anything. Limiting beliefs and habits that hold you back can be eliminated. We can retrain our brain through creative visualisation and reconnect our neurons that strengthen our motivation circuits to move us forwards our dreams. Do you believe that you can achieve them? Do you believe that you have the tools to accomplish them? Do you believe someone else can do it but not you? These questions are not necessarily true. You know you will get your dreams and your financial freedom. You can do it. So think bigger and get the necessary tools to get there. This book can provide inputs and strategies to help you in your transformation.

Fourth, you need to make the commitment that will deliver the result leading to financial freedom and living healthily. Just showing interest is not enough because it can encourage excuses. There is a difference between wanting financial independence and committing to financial freedom. There is also a difference between wanting to be fit and committing to fitness and living healthily. If you are only interested in achieving the goals, you are more likely to think of every excuse why you cannot accomplish them. But if you are committed, I am sure you will do whatever it takes to achieve financial freedom and be fit and healthy.

Fifth, your belief system is critical. If you believe you can achieve financial freedom and live healthily, it has already happened. The secret is that you already believe that it will happen. You think, feel and act like it has already happened. Such winning attitude is important. By believing that you can achieve financial independence and total fitness, it is already guaranteed.

Last, time is money but money is also time. Having financial freedom can provide you more time with your loved ones, to travel and contribute more to others. By being fit and healthy, you are in better position to take care of your loved ones. You need to remember the potential of money is a powerful motivating force for you to attract abundance into your life. Living a life of fitness and health will enhance your happiness. These are ways we obey natural laws to attract abundance.

How do you develop the winning attitude? First, you need to transform your beliefs, values and actions from a losing attitude into a winning one. How do you do it? There are many ways you can do it. Religious people use prayer. You can practise mindfulness or meditation by exploring possible ways to acquire positive attitudes. I prefer to contact your doppelganger in another parallel universe through Quantum Jumping. He has the power and the experience because he has already imprinted a winning attitude in his subconscious mind. What you need is to get his rhythm, his energy and his technique and you are on the way of attaining a winning attitude in your money game. By imprinting the habits, values and actions of your passionate wealthy doppelganger into your subconscious mind, your power of imagination is born. What is your financial goal? Why do you choose that goal? Your winning attitude begins with a plan and your direction. You deserve as much financial abundance as you think you desire. This will trigger your realisation that your salary alone will not bring home the abundance you desire. You need to create alternative incomes preferably residual incomes. What constitute a residual income? Let your imagination run. Consult your successful doppelganger who has implemented successfully many streams of residual income. How does he achieve them? Let him take you to his Quantum Library so that he can help you to download beliefs, attitudes and practices of successful people into your brain. Find out from all sources including creative visualisation. This book can provide you with some inputs. Creative visualisation has transformed my life. It can make the paradigm shift for you, too. Your losing attitude will emerge when you begin to doubt yourself. The only limit is the limit you impose on yourself. Research reveals that the majority of so-called lucky people, who won lotteries, lost their money in just three or four years. Why did such a thing happen to this group of people? Most people who dream of winning lottery have money problem. They have flawed beliefs and habits around money. In other words, they have losing attitude or suffering from poverty consciousness regarding money. People who have problems with money have a very low financial set point. Unless they upgrade their financial beliefs and habits to those of the wealthy, they never attract outrageous abundance. They may strike a small lottery but they are unable to make the amount grow. Instead their losing attitude will cause them that sudden good fortune to disappear. To overcome this money problem, they need to upgrade their beliefs, attitudes and habits not at the conscious level but at the subconscious level. This awareness is critical if you want to attract abundance. This will help to you see your greatest desire unfold in the months and years to come. You can write your story and you can write your own future. Your success will begin when you start visualising your dreams. The secret lies in changing your subconscious beliefs and thus changing your daily habits of doing things. As you visualise every day, your subconscious beliefs begin to shift from the losing attitude to that of the positive one. You will feel more confident, creative and empowered. It will help you make progress in the area of finance, which matters most to you. Think about your life of abundance as a series of time frames. What do you want to achieve in each time frame? In creating each residual income, you begin with the end in mind. You know what you want. Once you picture the end product, start thinking about what you need to do to make such a residual income happen. You know the end products are creating recurring incomes for retirements. You will write a personal mission statement to yourself to affirm your goals. This may take many years, but it is going to be a good guide for your financial freedom.

In the process of creating your financial abundance, you need to put your priorities in place. Put your career first while building other streams of income. First, you need to be dependable and responsible. Never allow your extra streams of income to jeopardise your career. The ability to compartmentalise your time for the various types of responsibilities is critical for both your well being and happiness. Your conscience must be clear and avoid any conflict of interest. The ability to classify various tasks into compartments either urgent or important is important. This will help you to plan and spend your time wisely while you build your abundance. There is nothing wrong that you want to be competitive. Healthy competition may serve as a drive to help you to succeed. But relationship with others matters, too. So always remember not to do unto others what you do not want others to do unto you. Think of the best way to compromise so that everyone is happy. Do things that are fair to others. You will be happier if you have peace of mind. It's important that you seek to understand then be understood. As you listen to others, also listen to your rejuvenated subconscious mind. Learn to synergise with others by working together with them. We can see synergy happening together, in both manmade world and nature. We have no choice but to work together with others to make life easier and smoother. Division of labour always makes a project easier to accomplish. Remember that the best thing does not happen overnight. We need to remind ourselves what we have to do to be at our best. We need to renew our beliefs and habits by first replacing the old ones in our subconscious mind and sharpen our skills to carry out the tasks towards abundance. It will help to clear our mind and improve ourselves, go for a run, learn something new out of interest to maintain our positive attitude. I know everyone wants to do something to achieve many things especially abundance, but one has no clue where to start. So the journey of self-discovery begins from renewing your beliefs and habits in your subconscious mind. Once this renewing is done, then it is time to take action. This transformation will overflow into other areas such as relationship, happiness and health.

As Lau Tzu says, the journey of a thousand miles begins with the first step. If you follow the awareness strategy describe above, the first step to improving yourself is to realise that there is more than one way of looking at things and there is also more than one way of changing your attitude. All of us are wired to resist change. We need to be information literate. So awareness of information and willingness to take intentional process can help to make change possible. Before you can go through a paradigm shift to positive abundance consciousness, you need to be aware of your limiting beliefs buried deep in your subconscious mind. Make sure that these beliefs have to be replaced. This critical information is important. We need to respect intelligence and scientific information. We need to acknowledge scientific findings. What are the options on the table? Taking a small step each day by loading positive values and habits of affluent people into your mind-set and starting to replace your limited beliefs with more positive ones, you have started your journey towards a paradigm shift. By thinking that it is possible, you have made it possible. My own experiences tell me that by taking small steps each day, I was able to change my paradigms so that they become positive. It is about taking small steps each day. Try to implement these values and habits consistently, persistently and playfully. We can easily transcend our past belief system and open the way for positive values to flow. Sharing valuable information is a way to help humanity to change for a better life. This can become one of the powerful straggles you can adopt. When I was young, I did not like to eat vegetables and fruits. Once I was convinced that vegetables and fruits are good for my digestive system and prevent pimples on my face, I was determined to add these foods in my daily consumption. By adding more vegetables and fruits into my diet each day, I began to like them. Now I am enjoying the tastes of vegetables and fruits. So taking the first small step is important. The fundamental steps you take are the ones you make for yourself. Think of them as the beginning of a journey of self-discovery. The process of each strategy for the transformation will be discussed in later chapter.

The process of replacing our limiting beliefs in our subconscious mind requires us to be proactive. To be proactive simply means to have initiative to do things. As adults, we are trusted to make our own decisions instead of waiting for others to tell us what to do. Unfortunately many of us are not aware of this leeway to be proactive or to possibly be reactive. A reactive person as opposed to a proactive person might prefer to do nothing once a project is over. A proactive person, on the other hand, might suggest to his boss what other extra additions or improvements he can help to make the project more attractive. He thinks of adding values to the project. Everyone enjoys a certain amount of free time other than our responsibility in the job. Being proactive, we can use this free time to create a parallel career without jeopardising our job. The possibilities are infinite. We can also be proactive in our own personal lives. The decision to be active and healthy starts in our subconscious mind. We must be ready to put on our exercise shoes and head for the tennis court or the gym.

Consciousness of Social Standards

All of us want to be accepted and become influential in our society. So we need to let our children know the social standards that are acceptable. This consciousness awakening will give our children an advantage when they start interacting and mixing with other children. Even in our working environments, such social standards are also essential.

First, people are drawn to others who are physically attractive, not necessary good looking or at least, not physically repulsive. So it's important that we teach our children to eat right and exercise to stay fit and lean.

Train them to dress neatly and be well groomed. And impress on them to pay attention to personal hygiene.

Second, people feel better with people who are deemed to be 'real'. Teach them to be ordinary people who are cordial and friendly. Teach them to avoid pretensions of any kind. Teach them not to pretend to be interested in tennis if they are not. Teach them not to talk about basketball when their friends are only interested in football. Let others talk first to find out their interest. Speaking well is always an asset.

Third, people feel comfortable with people who are like them in some ways. You do not have to be exactly like them. Teach your kid the trick of identifying one thing in common with the other person. It can be tennis, basketball or a movie. Then use that as an anchor to create a connection with the person. So you have something common and worthy to talk about.

Fourth, people respond to people who listen attentively to what they are saying. Teach your children to develop their listening skill and be able to remember what the other has just said. Look at your physical endowment: two ears and one mouth. Logically you should listen twice as much as you talk.

Fifth, people are drawn to accomplished people who are humble. So when people ask about your accomplishment, you should let others know that they, too, can do it. You are not special. Explain the other reason why you do such a thing.

Sixth, people are impressed by people who are productive. But you should be tolerance of others who are slower in their works.

Seventh, people tend to associate with people they respect and admire. Speak politely and be patient. Talk about worthy things of common interest. People do not like you if you are rude. Always act kindly to others.

Eighth, people like to do business with people they like and people who keep their words. Teach children the skill of being likeable. Talk less about yourself but focus on others. Teach them the importance of making a promise and act on it accordingly. Always do it before the dateline you promised.

Ninth, people trust others who are honest especially about their own shortcomings. Teach our children to admit things which they do not know.

Only speak confidently about things that they know. Teach them to resist the urge to speak more than they know or they are.

Tenth, people want to listen to advice of real experts, not pretenders. So only advice on things you really know. Do not pretend you know every field.

Last but not least, people can be fooled sometimes, not every time, not forever. So when you practise some of the skills listed above, do them sincerely and honestly.

Financial Knowledge

To many of us, money is usually an off-limit topic and we do not like to talk about. But it is the most necessary thing we need to know. To succeed in life, finance is one of the most necessary metrics and we have to do it right. Without financial freedom, we can't claim that we are successful. I have read a few financial books. They are too complicated and I will literally never understand most of them. It appears that I have to memorise a thousand theories and principles to know what finance is. A sudden inspirational idea tells me that I only need to understand a few basic core principles that will shed light in the field of finance. The majority of theories on finance are just the various combinations of these core principles. Just knowing these basic core principles will be enough for us as investors.

First, make your investment simple. A friend of mine in USA just bought a low-cost S&P 500 index fund in 2003 and earned a 97 per cent profit when he sold it in 2012. He does not need technical analysis or portfolio management skills. During the same period, many fund managers lost their clients' money. So if you want to make investments in stocks, just follow the simple philosophy in buying value stocks when nobody wants them. You need to be patient and wait for the right moment to buy them. You also need to know the concept of value stocks. Value stocks are companies that are making profits, plenty of cash, good dividends and potential for growth. You need to do your own research. Investing should not be complicated like your computer. It should be simple and basic.

Second, you need to know the concept of compound interest that will make you rich. Here, time is the secret. Buy good stocks when their prices are low and hold them for a long period. Reinvest their dividends and let compound interest and growth to help you become rich. The earlier you start saving, the better for you to benefit from the power of compounding interest.

Third, buy stocks that are making good profits and are growing. Future market returns depend on the following multiples: profit, dividend and growth. These valuations are the core ingredients for any company. If a company gives a 5 per cent dividend this year, we can only guess that it may provide 6 per cent or more next year. The changes of earnings multiples are totally unknown. What people think is usually uncertain. What is certain is the year-to-year performance of the company. The health of a company is determined by its revenue and profit. If they keep rising and the dividend keeps increasing, we know that the company is growing. Our investment in such a company is usually safe and we are going to make money.

Fourth, if you believe that certain stocks will produce superior long-term investment, you need to hold on in spite of volatility. The fluctuation of a stock price is the normal phenomenon.

Fifth, do not listen to others, even your brokers. The industry is dominated by cranks, charlatans and salesmen. Most of the financial products are sold by people whose only interest is the fees you pay. Remember that most financial pundits do not need experience, expertise or common sense to make noise. The louder the noise they make, the more likely that they will be wrong. Do your own due diligence and research before you put your money in any stock.

These few things listed above are the basic core principles for theories of finance. Make sure you understand them before you start investing in stocks.

The Wisdom of Residual Income

Most wealthy people have created many streams of income different from us. They have more money and time than most of us who depend on a salary. Most of the streams of income of the wealthy are residual type and they do not depend on a salary. So they have the time to spend on anything they want. Before we discuss the wisdom of residual income, first we need to be aware of the difference between residual income and linear income. They are not equal. For every hour of work, how many times are you paid? If you paid only once, then the stream of income is known as linear. This type of income is also known as active income. If you are employed by a company, organisation, government or institution, your income is linear. You only get paid once for your effort. Any part time job you are engaged and are paid by the hours, your extra income is also linear. The moment you do not show up for work, your paycheque vanishes. On the other hand, if you work hard for a period of time and you create a steady flow of income for months or even years, the type of income is residual. You get paid over and over again for the same effort. It is wonderful to get monetary reward many times for the same effort. What type of works will generate this type of recurring income for years?

For example, I wrote a mathematics textbook in 1975. It took me almost a year to complete the book. I spent almost a few thousands of hours to produce the book. I was not paid by hour for the writing. Kids working at Kentucky Fried Chicken outlet are paid more than me. But I was not looking for linear income for the hours of work. Instead of looking for a paycheque, I was aiming for royalty. So I was willing to sacrifice my precious time. It took over one and a half years before the money started to flow. It is worth waiting. When money started to flow into my bank account, it kept flowing for many years. In fact, this residual income flowed for almost fifteen years before the book was replaced by a new book. Once the writing train starts moving, soon I had many other books rolling out into the market. I have now earned millions of dollars in royalties. And the cheques are still flowing year after year! That is the power of residual income. It keeps on coming without me lifting a figure now.

Here is another example. Have you ever bought any music CDs? My nephew and his wife are both well-known singers. They performed on stage functions and sang their way to become rich. They were rewarded during each appearance. They also have many recordings of their popular songs. I was told that they became wealthy not because of the performances but the residual income from their CD recordings which are sold like hot cakes years after years. Their stage performances serve as advertisements for their CDs. They do not have to sing any more but the residual income keeps flowing and flowing.

Another example is the inventor of Duracell battery. It took him many years to conceive the idea and perfected his method of creation. Although his idea was rejected by many companies, he persevered and finally Duracell recognised his genius. The company agreed to pay him a few cents per battery pack for his idea. A few cents of royalty per pack soon became a few million dollars per year for the inventor. Now it has become a raging river of residual income for him. It never stops. It keeps flowing year after year as long as Duracell battery is in the market. This demonstrates the magnificent power of residual income. Once you have established your financial freedom, you will be in better position to seek your end goal of experience, growth and contribution. Time is money and money is time. All of us know that time is money. We are paid by the hours we work. But only few of us realise that money is time. With our residual income flowing into our accounts, we will have time to do what we want. We would have more time to spend with our loved ones. We would have time to pursue our hobbies. Time is our own. We will no longer sell our time. We would have more time to think. What types of experiences do you want in your life? What type of growth do you want for your life? What contributions do you want to give the world?

Leverage, Cash Flow and Residual Income

Most people who depend on their salary never become rich. In fact a family with a single stream of income may not be enough to make ends meet. Most families need at least two streams of income to live comfortably. On the other hand, wealthy people do not depend on salary. They own assets such as properties, stocks, bonds, businesses and others. The wealthy has a few secrets we need to learn. They appear not working. Their streams of income are usually residual type. They have all the freedom of time and money to enjoy what they like to do. They enjoy them because they have the time to spend on anything they want. They know that time is money and money is also creating time. They understand the concept of compounding to grow their wealth. They also know that their money buys them time to do what they like. They also understand the concept of leverage. They may have a personal service business in some way. They know that if such business can't function without their presence, then their freedom is restricted. They have to train others to do the things needed so that they can replicate the business elsewhere without his involvement. They plan to use leverage so that they can move away without affecting the running of the business. They learn to systematise the business so that someone else can do it while they are away. They never get stuck to earning a living by doing it all by themselves. What is leverage? It is simply doing more with less. They understand that they can get more income, more values without putting much energy and efforts on their own parts. This is one form of leverage, using others, using technology or other ways of delivering portion of the services without their direct involvement. People want their problems solved or the services provided. They do not care who is providing it to them. If anyone can provide such a good service or solve their problem, they will just take it. You have to train someone to do it. So leverage means you do not have to be there all the time. Once you have done that, you enjoy the leverage of others, technology or other leverage points for your business, so that you have the real chance of scalability. They become rich because they know how to systematise and leverage their business. It's simple as that. If they do not use such leverage, then they are just earning a living. They never become rich. You have to learn to put on your thinking cap.

For most people depending on salary, their income is usually capped. They have to clock in and clock out according to the company's or organisation's time table. Even doctors and dentists have a capped income according to the number of patients they can see each day. All of them have to be there five days a week or more. All of them are on the treadmill just like the rest. Their income is linear. Most of them do not enjoy residual income. So it's important that we create residual income while we are on the treadmill. So while we are working, remember to put aside part of the income for saving and eventually for investing. This is the beginning in the journey of creating residual income. Another possibility for such a move is to create parallel careers like writing, CD recording, insurance sales other direct marketing such as Amway and herbal medicines distribution network. The possibilities are endless.

So it is important to include a few streams of residual incomes in our working career. It would be wonderful if we can start shifting our income streams from linear to residual. Most wealthy people own assets that provide them with residual income. We can do the same. This will give us the time freedom and time to do what we want when we want. We should at least commit ourselves to start creating a new residual stream of income every one or two years.

Strategies of Creating Residual Income

There are many ways you can create streams of residual income. Have you ever heard of Robert T. Kiyosaki, the author of *Rich Dad and Poor Dad?* He advocates the concept of the most powerful form of leverage using the mind. In his book, *Retiring Young Retiring Rich,* he believes that the leverage of the mind can make any one rich. Rich people use rich words and ordinary people use poor words. All of us know that our brain can be our most powerful asset or it can be our most glaring liability. Rich people use leverage but poor people are afraid of leverage. Words of affirmation are not enough for rich people. Rich people are not satisfied by saying, 'I can afford to buy this.' They want to know why they can afford to buy such a thing. They search for reasons and work on them. They get what they want. Poor people say that investing is risky. So what they think becomes their reality. They become the biggest losers. But rich people not only think that investment is safe but they also begin to find reasons why certain investments are actually not risky. For example, rich people use leverage to buy an asset; they do their due diligence to avoid any risk. They are not satisfied by such affirmation that buying such an asset is not risky. They want to find out why such a purchase is not risky. They make full use of the most powerful leverage of their mind to make them rich. Using the concept of leverage to buy an asset such as a property is a good strategy to create residual income and cash flow eventually. An asset does not necessary mean a house or any property. An asset can be in different forms such as a franchise or a small business.

There are other ways of creating residual income. You must have heard of the greatest investor of all time, Warren Buffett. How does he become so rich? A great investor like him sees into the future better than others, he believes in buy today where the profit will be tomorrow. I consider him as the smartest stock picker in history. His strategies of creating wealth became well known. But can we imitate some of his ways of investing to help us create residual income? Investing in value stocks that pay good dividends is a way to create residual income. I believe in the power of dividends. Dividend investing is a powerful way to achieve solid return for our investments. Indeed, investing in companies which offer solid dividend yields can leverage the power of compound interest especially when the dividends are reinvested into the stocks. This is very attractive in countries like Australia and USA where interest rate at this moment is very low. In Australia, companies like Telstra, WestFarmers, and the top four banks are offering high percentage of dividends. These companies are solid and their profits are generally increasing annually. This is a great opportunity for investors wanting to create residual income. Most of the dividends are enjoying franking credits. These franking credits represent an amount of tax already paid by the companies, helping us to reduce our tax bill. It sounds great. But we need to be aware that not every company that pays high dividend is a sound investment. Mining companies like BHP Billiton and Rio Tinto are paying low dividends now. Their revenues and profits are falling because of the slowdown in development in China and other developing countries. The stock prices are falling. Timing is important when buying stocks. The wisdom of Benjamin Graham should be noted:

> No intelligent investor, no matter how starved for yield, would buy a stock for its dividend income alone.

Investors need to scrutinise the strength of the underlying business to assess how attractive the companies' dividend payment is. Look for companies which are maintaining their growth, strong balance sheets, exceptional profits, strong cash flow and a possible increase in dividends.

Can you also become rich? Why do you want to be rich? I can only speak for myself. I think I can. It is not about money but to improve my family's quality of life. I want to give my family the true gift of financial security and freedom. And whether I want to buy a holiday home, a new car or pay the fees for my children and grandchildren's further education. It's simply not possible without money. Investing in stocks is one of the best ways to create that kind of wealth. I must learn to take my investment in stocks to the next level. Knowledge followed by actions will provide the greatest dividend. There are basically two approaches to become rich. We can use the aggressive approach or the conservative one depending on the station of life you are in. You should be aware that these approaches can also make you poor. Knowledge is the deciding factor. Anticipation always brings uncertainty. Many people lose money in stocks. It even happens to me when I started investing in stocks. I can only speak for myself. How do I get ahead? It's simple. I adopt a system of buying tomorrow's profit with a margin of safety today. That is my essence of investing. The key is being able to look into the future and visualise how the story will change. A stock has its true value at any time. If the trading price now is below its true value; the stock is considered undervalued. On the other hand, if the trading price exceeded its true value, the stock is overvalued. Any stock which is considered undervalue in relation to its upside today will be my favourite. A quality business selling at bargain price is an anomaly I can usually assume will eventually get corrected. I do not mind to be few months early than to be one day late. I have more winners than losers. I learned my lesson quickly. When I lost in a stock, I did not stubbornly hold on to it and lost everything waiting for the 'dog' to turn around. It is easier to say than do. Remember, scientific studies reveal that we are all wired to lose. So it's not our fault. I have established some golden rules which serve to navigate risk and maximise profit. They are my disciplinary master. My loss in any stock is capped at 15 or 20 per cent and my gain is usually allowed to run as high as possible. I have to discipline myself to let my winners run. I do not give in to this evil temptation. I will avoid acting irrationally and prematurely closing a big winner by asking myself these two critical questions.

First, is the original investment idea still valid? Second, have the share become fully valued?

Every stock has its own cycle. Even Apple or Microsoft obeys the cycle. Any dip of 15 per cent from the peak triggers my selling discipline.

Following this approach, I always keep my big profit less 15 per cent. I keep repeating this style of investing and it makes me plenty of money. I stick to my inner scoreboard. I only measure my success according to my own yardsticks, not those of others. My inner scoreboard is also my philosophy of investing. In short I am a long-term business-focused investor. I do not worry regarding my valued-stocks price fluctuation. I stick to my golden rules risk management philosophy. My goal is to make money.

I read about Warren Buffett's strategy of buy-and-hold for life with great interest. He bought about 60 per cent of Coca Cola in 1987 to 1989 because it is a safe and growing company. The company enjoys capital efficiency and big profit. Even when the stock was traded far more than fifty times its PE ratio in 1988, Warren Buffett did not sell his share. Its dividend was good and its growth is still intact. But one thing people never realise is that he sold his 'put option' at the height of the stock's price instead of selling his share. He did that to many of his companies which he bought and held until today. He harvested big profit from his 'put option' when the stock price reached its equilibrium again. This awareness is important if you intend to buy a stock based on the buy-and-hold principle. There is a flaw in this buy-and-hold investment philosophy. Like Warren Buffett's strategy, this investment strategy success requires something that most us cannot master: an unwavering commitment to hold for a long period. It fails to include a safety mechanism that will ensure that we do not lose all our money. Our human behaviours are irrational and we are no good at risk management. Little do we realise that we are our own worst enemies. Our resources are limited and we have to look seriously at our own capital preservation. This is the missing piece in the buy-and-hold strategy. Some investors using this buy-and-hold strategy landed in the investment graveyard. Be aware about such critical consequence will save you from great pain and big loss.

It is true that from 1950 to the present, the investment in stocks in USA had never produced a negative return when you hold them for over twenty years. Many buy-and-hold investors enjoy their long journey in investments because the price of a value stock always climbs higher, because it always has. The same echo applies for housing market. Over a long period, house prices will always go up. These beliefs for both equities and properties are generally true in the long run. But this phenomenon does not necessarily apply to individual company or individual property. Many developed properties which could not be sold had gone to zero. Similarly many companies listed in the stock market had also gone to zero. Over the years many companies are delisted from the stock market. The companies went bankrupt and went completely out of business. So if you buy-and-hold any such company, you face total capital annihilation. So remember individual stock does go to zero. This piece of information is a harsh reality that individual stock does go to zero. I will still advise you to stick to my first two golden rules to gain profit without limit but to cap your loss to only 15 or 20 per cent at whatever peak or buying price.

Investors with great vision about the future needs of society usually make a fortune. Those who anticipated the technological boom before it happened made thousands times their investments. Similar anticipation of biotechnologies and medical stocks also made their fortune. The anticipation continues. Knowledge is the key to such anticipation. What will be the next big technological trends that could revolutionise our day-to-day lives? Robotic technology, electric cars and lithium or metal oil to generate energy will be the current industrial revolution. New surgical techniques using digital technology will be the common phenomenon. Over the next ten years, big data on human habits and medical care will be the next important technology trends. Can you imagine walking into a restaurant and the waiter, as soon as she keys in your present, is able to know what you are going to order for your dinner. Internet shopping is the new fashion for the young and rich.

Imagine that you are shopping for a new pair of pants and when you key in, the website shows the only items in your size with the colours and styles you like. Such anticipation is like walking into a cafe and having your pumpkin spice latte ready for you. Everything you need is custom-made for you. Your habits and preference data are stored ready everywhere to make life convenient for you. Your medical needs are at your figure tips at any hospital. You do not have to repeat your life medical history to any doctor any-more. And it is no more a science fiction. This emerging trend in data storage through cloud computing will be the future trends for us. It is just like the songs we are listening. This incredible storage of the amount of data will be the trend for our future. With all these data, businesses will be able to predict the behaviours of each customer's needs before he or she even knows them. The doctors will be able to anticipate accurately your medical needs before you even know it. This information revolution is taking place now. Information scientists are creating programs and algorithms to crawl through data around the clock with the intention of figuring out your preferences of lifestyles and your medical needs. The gathering of more data about you will enable the programs and algorithms to learn more about you and what you like. These will include what you eat; what clothes you wear; what types of purchase you make; what supplements you take; what medical care you seek and what you do during the weekend. As you browse the Internet, you can see advertisements tailing to things you are searching. Imagine that type of experience in the world around us. Many decisions of lifestyles will be made for you. That's the future for you. As an investor, such knowledge is important. Companies which have control of the explosion of data will make billions in the process in the next five to ten years. The blue chip company IBM has already started. The product called Watson is a computer that uses big data to answer questions. Integration between Watson and Apple's smart watch has been endorsed. The medical field will be the next great beneficiary. IBM is collaborating with health care giant Johnson & Johnson in the field of knee and hip implant division. IBM is also working with many other medical companies on medical devices using the new trend of data technology. So it's natural that many conservative investors will buy IBM shares to gain from this long-term megatrend. IBM, such a giant company, will have difficulty to double or triple its share price. To be more speculative to make big money, I would suggest that you invest in smaller companies which are working to create cutting-edge applications using the storage of big data. Google will provide information of such software companies like Infoblox, Neustar, Jableau, Splunk and many others. You should look well into the matter before you invest. Yes, if there is no risk then there is no gain. Even professional investors know that these early-stage businesses are full of risk. Knowledge is important. If you know what the companies are doing and their financial status, you can eliminate much of the risk. The returns will be great if you choose wisely. So whichever strategy suits you, this envision of the big data trends creates financial freedom for the rest of your life.

Summary

Most people are not aware that our subconscious mind affects our everyday choices. The centre part of our brain or the subconscious mind controls 95 to 99 per cent of our thoughts and beliefs that drive us to action or inaction. The simple act of setting a goal activates the centre of the brain. This awareness is critical for those who dare to dream big knowing that their problem will become small. To be successful, this activation itself is not enough. It is critical that our outdated thoughts and beliefs have to be eliminated permanently from our mind first. This is critical because beliefs are like muscles, they can be strengthened and weakened through emotional and mental exercises. The centre of the mind has to be loaded with new beliefs and habits of successful people to replace them. We need some tools to help us regarding this consciousness. I use meditation and self hypnotherapy to help me accomplish this transformation. You can use mindfulness or prayer to accomplish your mission. Once the centre part of the brain is loaded with the new set of beliefs and habits, I make use of the four-steps Mastery Formula to intensify and consolidate these beliefs and habits until they become my routine practices. Practising these new habits consistently and playfully will enhance excitement and anticipation generated by visualising your goals. This is the inspirational act that cements these new beliefs into your life. This is your secret mirror that attracts abundance from inside out. The beauty of the four elements of mastery formula is analogous to the goal of lifting fifty kilograms. You start off by lifting lighter weight and add little bit at a time. You keep practising your muscles until you succeed. The brain operates the same way. When I was working, my visualised goal was financial freedom, that is, my streams of residual income and cash flow must exceed my monthly expenditures. I was focused; I took inspirational actions and began to work on high impact money-making activities. I started creating streams of linear and residual income one at a time. If you read my last motivation book, *The Journey through Four Seasons of Life,* you would have read the strategies I carried out to achieve financial freedom. I did that and the result is that I enjoy abundance in my life. I believe you can achieve the same result; if you follow the step-by-step procedure and the Mastery Formula, you can also have abundance.

CHAPTER SIX

ASSETS TO CREATE RESIDUAL INCOME AND CASH FLOW

Introduction

This chapter introduces you to the language of asset investment. You are familiar with terms like linear income, residual income, cash flow, debt, bad debt, good debt and leverage. Many more terms used in asset investment will be exposed. If you are not a businessman; you don't have any asset or saving for retirement and you are in your early thirties; you are likely to live your later years in poverty. Yes, life is tough. Many people hardly earn enough to pay rental, mortgage, car payment and living expenses. How do you find a solution to financial freedom for your retirement? How much do you need if you retire at 65 and live another 15 years? In USA or Australia, to retire comfortably, you need about a million dollars. The first lesson you need to learn is the difference between linear income and residual income. If you are following this book, you probably know the difference now. I was in that situation when I started my career as a graduate teacher at the age of 30. I was struggling to provide for my extended family. I started to create a few streams of linear income and residual income for my extended family to survive. I was lucky by working hard using my spare time; I managed to have some surplus every month. I started saving to accumulate some fund for investing. I follow the footsteps of successful people by developing the 'keep learning and growing' attitude. I started with inspiration intention and took action on almost every idea that came my way; I managed to create a few streams of linear and residual income and ended with financial freedom when I retired. The importance of creating residual income is critical when you are at the prime of your career. There are two easy ways of creating residual income through investment in assets: second property and Real Estate Investment Trust (REIT). The home you stay in is not an asset. According to Robert T. Kiyosaki, anything that takes money out of your pocket is a liability. So the home can be a liability. For first home owner, do not buy a very costly house. Your debt will be a great liability. The home requires maintenance, mortgage, quit rent, assessment, water bill and electricity bill. There is no cash flow for you. To generate cash flow, you have to buy an asset in the form of a property or land. The debt in buying your second property can become a good debt if it provides cash flow into your pocket. This form of asset is a good way of creating residual income. There is another way of investing in properties in the form of REIT. The trouble with most of us is finding the initial sum to start investment in either form of these asset investments. We are familiar with the saying, 'It takes money to make money!' Too many of us are looking to build wealth through investment, unless a windfall or inheritance is on the way, the only way, only real way to accumulate money is through savings.

The Difference between Spenders and Savers

There are two types of people in this world: the savers and the spenders. Which type do you belong to? The savers naturally live a lean lifestyle. Regardless of income level, they spend less than what they earn. They build up savings. Spenders struggle to avoid debt, let alone have regular savings. These habits are either caught or taught. Most saving habits are usually taught by parents who had experienced hardship. Many self-made wealthy people are great savers. They know how to balance their needs to become rich and economically productive with their choice to enjoy life. They understand that they cannot enjoy an abundant life if they are addicted to consumption and the use of credit. They neither borrow nor earn just to consume. They are usually not credit dependent and many lead a simple life. This simple frugality lays the foundation for their saving habits. Their children are taught these habits very early. In fact many of these habits such as 'managing your debt and not allow debt to manage you' are not taught but caught by their children. They learn to spend wisely and get maximum value for their money. They continuously work to increase their income and save the surplus for investments. They are aggressive savers far outpacing their peers. They have great disciplined investors. They understand the difference between asset and liability. On the other hand, many spenders are addicted to their habits of spending. They may earn a lot but they have no saving. When they spend, they feel good and they continue to spend. If you are one of them, I am sure you have nothing to save for investment. This spending habit has ruined many individuals. Many of them are not aware that their working life is short and soon their power to earn will diminish. Once the working age is passed, their trouble begins. I think this partly explains why there are so many old people sleeping on the five-foot-way in many big cities in many countries.

Consciousness Approach

Many of us have wasted many years of our life chasing after our goals and dreams, accomplished very little, or worse, nothing at all. Most of us are struggling with drought; some of us have given up in despair, leaving behind a struggling family. As we know, despair is caused by the loss of hope and a sense of being abandoned by the government. This book is written to help children and parents who are willing to make a drastic paradigm shift to a new dream. They need to understand the power and influence of their subconscious mind on their dreams. Negative thoughts and a sense of despair are affecting your well-being including finance, relationship and success. Corrective measure through the subconscious mind is critical. First, we need to understand where this negativity comes from. We need to understand that negativity is a defence mechanism that we develop to feel safe. Understanding negativity this way allows our feeling to flow instead of expressing it. We can detach ourselves from the negativity by unloading positivity of successful people and move forward. What do successful people have? The answer is passion. Their driving force comes from their subconscious mind and their passion. Remember that you may work hard and make money, but if your brain and your heart are not working together, eventually you will be screwed. All of you want to make money but what is your passion? We need the courage, the zest and understanding to live it. So it's important to find something you love doing. You must have the courage to try something you love. Just like me, I love playing basketball and I love learning. So I made sure that I embraced these three fundamental skills: thinking, speaking and writing well. Eventually, I discovered I love writing and it becomes my passion just like my game. I started looking for opportunities in publications. Eventually, I have a collection of more than two dozen of mathematics textbooks and guidebooks to my credit. I became wealthy by removing money out of my life equation so that I can pursue new experiences, growth and contribution. How about you? What do you love doing? Try to work hard in the area you love and you will able to meet the balance of success and fulfilment. Once you find a place to focus on, something you love and enjoy doing and start thinking from there. You will work without knowing that time is on your side and apply your passion to any business success, no matter how big or small.

Never underestimate the power of your subconscious mind. Even our spending habits can be changed. The addicted spenders need to imprint a new belief and habit to start changing their habit of spending. First they need to know that there are two types of savings: saving to spend and saving for wealth. The former is saving for short-term or medium-term spending goals, taking a holiday or buying a car. For many spenders, this is a difficult task. They will most likely buy on credit with an extra burden of interest to bear. To compare saving versus debt, consider this: a saver with 8 per cent annual interest and with $200 per month payment in a managed share fund, a saver can build up a saving of $20 000 in just six and a half years. Do you see the wonders of compound interest? No wonder, Albert Einstein once stated that 'compound interest is the eighth wonder of the world.' Capital gain is not even considered. On the other hand, a debt of a car loan $20 000 would take thirteen years to repay at $200 per month. Depreciation and maintenance of your car are not even considered. After thirteen years, your car will most likely to be worth $500.

Saving for wealth is the regular accumulation of money that builds long-term financial health. Without significant saving, it is not possible to build wealth. The money making process begins when you put your savings into a home deposit, stocks, managed fund or salary sacrifice into superannuation. These amounts will eventually add to your personal wealth. The recipe of building wealth is a combination of time and disciplined savings into productive investments. There are two ways of investing in properties: Asset and REIT. The details will be discussed later.

For the spenders, there are many ways you can change your spending behaviours. The habits and practices deep rooted in your subconscious mind have to be eliminated first. Mindfulness or meditation and creative visualisation with life vision in mind can be a useful tool to help you implant new beliefs and habits of thrifty but rich people. A guided meditation leading you to the alpha level, a deep level of relaxation, can be an important tool to help transform your spending habits. You can mentally reprogram your attitudes, kick bad habits and influence your practices. This practice is not intended for a day. Regular mindfulness or meditation is essential to reduce stress and to improve your immune system so that you are more energetic and healthy. Soon you will realise that you have a powerful way to tap into your mind to change habits, solve problems and practice creative visualisation. You will learn how to exaggerate your imagination resulting in better creative visualisation. A non-negotiable set point saving system needs to be implanted in your mind and you need to carry out consistently to build wealth.

First, you need to know where your expenditure goes. Do you need to take drastic actions? Keep a record of your spending for a month and list those which are essential like rent, mortgage, foods and utilities. List also those that are not necessary like eating out on the weekends and other luxuries. Start to visualise strategies to overcome your spending habits especially the nonessential ones. If it is necessary to save, look for alternative marketing instead of buying from the supermarkets. You can easily save up to 30 per cent of your food bill. Start with two saving types of accounts: one for later spending and one for wealth. Create an automatic spending limit for the first type and never touch the saving for wealth. You can start small and stick to the non-negotiable set point. You will be amazed how your savings build up in a year. Practise this new strategy consistently until you have accumulated enough money to begin your investment journey.

Then it is time to look for the new process that money makes money. Put your savings into stocks, managed fund or asset such as REIT. Keep building up your saving for wealth. So spenders do have options. The choice is theirs. If they are realistic and take positive action by setting non-negotiable limit spending on luxuries, they can change their spending behaviours and can make a big difference to their financial future. Do it at the prime of your working days. You cannot buy time and your working days are limited. The earlier you start to create extra streams of linear and residual income, the safer for you and your family during retirement.

Some Money Mistakes to Avoid When You Are Young

When we are in our 20 to 35, our lives are filled with milestones such as learning to drive, finding a partner, building the foundations of a career or starting a business. The decisions we make during this period can make a difference between financial success and living paycheque to paycheque down the road. Here are some financial pitfalls we should try to avoid.

First, we forget to put aside money for emergencies. If we do not have cash for any emergency, we are likely to borrow money and run into trouble paying interest. We may run into trouble such as losing our job. So it is advisable to have at least six months' worth of living expenses in our savings account.

Second, we are tempted to buy an expensive car. This is perhaps one of the greatest mistakes young people will make. Cars depreciate in value and are expensive to maintain. If having a car is necessary, buy a second-hand car first to avoid heavy payments of instalment. Putting $20 000 into a REIT or index fund when you are in the twenties, instead of buying a new car, could add hundreds of thousands of dollars to your wealth when you retire even at modest returns. Think first before you buy a new expensive car.

Third, many of the young people get into credit card debt early and start accumulating by having many cards. A bitter lesson of mounting debt with interest compounding can easily lead you into a personal bankruptcy.

Fourth, when we are young, we tend to forget setting financial goals. Having a financial goal gives us direction to save and plan for the future. It's important to start budgeting, saving and monitoring our investments so that we have some achievable financial goals in mind. Identifying goals and measuring our progress make it easier for us to focus on the steps we have taken. We may think that our retirement is a life time away. But actually, our working life is usually short. If you are not very healthy, it can even be shorter. It's critical we start saving early and let the compounding effects do the rest. For most millionaires, they start very early and let their money works for them.

Fifth, many of us do not talk about finances before getting married. This can be a costly mistake resulting in many divorces. Argument about finance is one of the main causes of divorce. Money is a touchy subject and if we want a happy marriage, you and your partner have to be on the same page. So it's important to talk about financial situation, set financial goals together, make savings plan and discuss responsible spending before tying the knot.

Sixth, many of us tend to spend too much on weddings. Unless you are rich, otherwise do not start a huge pile of debt which is an unnecessary stress on the marriage.

Seventh, many of us thought that our house is an asset and we tend to buy an expensive house to live in. We think that we are involved in forced saving. My advice is never stretch your finances too thin. A big house usually requires heavy upkeep and big mortgage. Worst if you lose your job, your big house becomes an immediate liability. Most Americans experience this bitterness during the housing bubble in 2007 to 2009. It's advisable to diversify your finances in stocks and a second asset. Only when your finances are sound then you update your home. Buy a small apartment first when you just get married. Planning is important.

Save Money by Shopping Alternative Sources

Everyone who starts a family will have to struggle for the first few years of their life if there is no help from parents. I went through that for the first few years of my marriage life. There is no help from my parents. Instead, I inherited an extended family. My brother and my sister depended on me for support for their further education. My wife's brothers and sister also required her support. We had extra responsibility and we accepted it willingly. Our meagre incomes were not sufficient to support our extended family. Luckily, I was thinking well and I had the means to create other streams of linear and residual income for us to not only survive but also prosper. Initially, our lives were tough and we had to exercise prudence to save money. Without saving, there is no way for us to invest for our retirement. We learnt to shop like an investor. We used the same value investing skills to buy stocks to buy groceries. We saved money on our weekly shop and this helped to grow our savings. This provided us with money to invest later on. I share this experience so that you need not have to pay more on your next shopping.

First, we did our research and we got organised. Buying groceries are analogous to researching companies before we buy the stocks. By putting a little more effort into our weekly shopping, we managed to save a few hundred dollars every year. We developed our meal plan and wrote down our shopping list. By doing this consistently, we avoided impulse buys and avoided wasting money on items we did not use and would never use. We did not have loyalty for any brand. We bought items we needed on the most competitive prices. We usually bought our groceries from alternative sources instead from the supermarkets.

Second, we did not follow brands but bought from private label. Just like stocks, a higher share price is no indication of higher intrinsic value. This applied to groceries. What's important is the value of the goods not the brands. We knew that many of the private brands are made by the same people under the favourite brands anyway. So why should we pay double the price for the same product.

Third, we learnt to buy discounted products in bulk. In the share market, whenever there is a big dip, we added shares to our portfolio at a cheap price. Similarly, in groceries, we buy in bulk to take advantage of cheap price. When Milo or other tin products are on sale, we bought in bulk, two tins at the price of one. Building a stock pile also saved us valuable time during our initial working days.

Last but not least, there is always price discrepancy for any item in various shops. Keeping items we need to buy and their prices gave us an opportunity to compare prices in various shops we frequently visit. You will be surprised at the price discrepancy in the different shops. There are always items on sale to attract customers. This explains why some people are spending more than others on groceries. Comparing unit price by buying in bulk is also a good way to save money. Maximising the value of every dollar we spent initially gave the power to save more money for investments later on. The power of leverage will not apply if you have no fund or money to start investing.

The Power Leverage in Properties Investment

My father had a big family: eight boys and six girls. I remember when I was a small boy; my father was able to use the leverage system to acquire his first asset in the form of thirty-two acres of rubber small holding. Besides his sundry shop business, my father had a few other revenues of income. He operated a very traditional way of providing transportation using animals like bulls and buffalos to pull carriages. He also reared chickens and pigs to increase his sources of income. With as little as a few hundred dollars, he put down payment for his asset. He made full use of the land planted with rubber trees to generate recurring income daily and used any vacant land to plant sweet potatoes and banana plants to produce other sources of income. His leverage system worked out as planned and he was able to settle his loan within a few years.

My own experiences of using leverage to acquire my two business properties show that leverage can be a powerful tool to create wealth. I bought my first shop investment property by putting down payment about sixteen thousand Malaysian dollars and a loan from the government. The property was rented for forty over years and I sold it at 1.25 million Malaysian dollars. I had collected rentals for forty over years, a surplus of over a thousand dollars for fifteen years and then full rental of four thousand dollars for the rest of thirty years. How much rentals have I benefited? I think it is over millions. I have a second shop investment property bought a few years later than the first. I also held on to it for over forty years and sold it over a million Malaysian dollars. The rentals I enjoyed also exceeded over a million for those forty years. If I calculate the money I made over the actual amount I paid for the two properties, it must be over a few thousands per cent. You can see clearly the power of leverage if it is done correctly and properly.

The Danger in Commercial Property Investment

Not all investment in properties will bring benefits. Investment in rental properties especially commercial properties can also be risky. Most commercial properties are usually costly and it requires a big initial sum as down payment and subsequently mortgage payment as monthly instalment. So planning and management are equally important. Another critical factor to consider is location and availability of tenant. If the property is left vacant for a long period, it will cost you interest and expenses such as assessment and quit rent. If such problem is not managed properly, it can cost you a lot of money and can also lead to bankruptcy. Before you start to buy such an asset, you have to consult experts and put all facts on the table before you invest. If you are just a wage earner depending on your paycheque and saving, you have to aware of the property cycle. For example, in USA, from 2011 to 2015, commercial real estate takes a dive of almost one third of occupancy. This period is not good to invest in commercial properties.

An important story in USA commercial properties is a good example. From 2011 until 2015, the demand for commercial properties took a dive. From 2000 to 2011, commercial properties provide a consistent return of rentals because of demands. From 2015 onwards commercial properties are under attack. The awareness of important information is necessary to ensure that your investment timing is right. From 2016 onwards, the demand for commercial properties will slide further before any recovery takes place. For commercial properties investors, patience is the key word.

I will only start investing in commercial properties when the demand starts picking up.

Here is another alternative interpretation for the demand of commercial properties. The intention of description instead of drawing a chart is to enhance your visualisation and imagination. The demand for office space per worker in USA from 2000 to 2010 increased gradually from 320 square feet per worker to 370 square feet. There is a gradual increase about fifty square feet per worker. You can easily download this information into your subconscious mind. This information and awareness is important telling you that commercial rental properties are increasing in demand. What happened from 2011 to 2016 is just the opposite. From 2011 to 1016, the office space per worker decreases from 370 square feet to 270 square feet. A dramatic decline is about 100 square feet. What is the implication? You must not assume that less square footage per worker means more workers than in the past and everything is okay. More importantly is that the sharp decrease in square footage implies a lack of demand for commercial real estate. There is a surplus of commercial properties and less demand. In USA, developers had overbuilt during the boom period from 1983 to 2007. What should you do now? A good investor will exercise patience and wait for the occupancy rate to pick up before start investing.

Another factor that investors in commercial properties should take note of is the economic cycle of the country. For example, in USA, many investors in commercial properties in 2015 and 2016 will sit on the side line because economic factors are beyond control. The US debt was 2.54 times GDP from 1983 to 2008 indicating that there is no continuous expansion. The oil price is on a downtrend. Affordability and business are slowing down. There is no sign of inflation indicating that business is stagnant. The consuming power is in tatters. The consequence is deleveraging and coming depression.

The comparison of USA debt growth relative to its GDP growth is significant. The US debt was 2.54 times GDP from 1983 to 2015. The percentage of debt growth is far too big compared to GDP

growth. All these indicators do not speak well for commercial properties investment from 2016 onwards. All signs are pointing to a contraction and a depression in USA commercial properties. So investors must be well informed before you make any commitment to buy commercial properties during this critical period in USA. What is going to happen in USA regarding its commercial properties and its economic growth will have a ripple effect across the world. In developing countries like Malaysia, there is also a glut of commercial properties because of overdevelopment. If you care to drive around some of the towns in Malaysia, you will see a big number of unoccupied commercial properties. The surplus of supply in commercial properties and high-rise properties indicate the mismatch between supply and demand. The rate of growth of most of the countries' economy is slowing down and investors in properties have to take note.

There is an oversupply of commercial properties in USA and many developing countries like Malaysia and China. In USA many millions of property owners were affected during the properties bubble burst during 2007-2008. The recovery from 2009 to 2015 was slow and many of the properties are still under water. In Malaysia and China, inflation is affecting most of its population especially the poor. The prices of properties both commercial and residential are too high and not within reach by the majority of the population. The oversupply of properties will soon be felt as the economic grow rate slows down. Investors should have a second thought of investing in the property sector from 2016 onwards. I feel strongly that the property bubble in USA, China and Malaysia is at its critical stage. I will sit out and wait patiently for a big correction in property counters and will only start investing in property stocks in USA, China and Malaysia when the uptrend begins. I will apply the CHU strategy aggressively to property stocks in a few years down the line when the uptrend begins. Remember in stock investment, what goes up has to come down and what goes down has to come up for any value stock or good property. Even value stocks like Apple, Microsoft, IBM, Johnson & Johnson and many others will repeat their economic cycles many times in the last twenty or thirty years. Similarly, investment in Real Estate Investment Trust will also follow properties cycle. Knowing properties cycle will always be an advantage.

Real Estate Investment Trust (REIT)

One possible place where investors want to get a return of 6 to 10 per cent is REITs. At the current low interest rate, investment in REITs is a good alternative in Malaysia and USA. It generates good income rate and a slight capital growth. In USA, during the past seven years of the economic recovery, into the first quarter of 2015, a great majority of REITs perform quite well. Since the second quarter of 2015 onwards, performance has been more selective. The REIT index, tracking eight brick-and-mortar REITs, gave the following relative weightings.

Diversified REITs	7.2%
Health care REITs	11.90%
Hotel and resort REITs	6.6%
Industrial REITs	4.5%
Office REITs	14.1%
Residential REITs	16.90%
Retail REITs	24.3%
Specialised REITs	14.5%

A group of REIT sector has been paying dividends but struggling to deliver capital gains. However, specific brick-and mortar REITs using lower level of leverage have been enjoying upside share price movement. In this high nervous market where dependable quarterly revenue and income are paramount, selective REITs in the classes of self-storage, skilled nursing, shopping centres and data centre operation are emerging as winners. As investors, this awareness can help to generate good income under the present low interest rate. My experience in investing in REITs since 2012 until now is quite encouraging. After selling my two shop lots, I put most of the fund into these types of REITs to generate a 6 to 10 per cent return of my fund for my children and grand children's education needs. The returns have been quite consistent until 2016. The future is unknown. I am watching the situation especially the occupation rate of the REITs I invested.

Summary

A good way to generate residual income in the form of rental is to make use of debt as a leverage to buy a second or third property. Buying an asset like oil palm estate is equally good provided that the revenue generated is more than the expenses including mortgage. This requires initial saving, planning and management. Understanding the concept of good debt is just the beginning. Timing and management are just the other factors for success in using assets to become rich. Investing in REITs usually involved commercial properties. Understanding the demand of commercial properties in terms of the footage per worker is also important. Keeping an eye on the occupation rate of the properties invested is equally important. Following the property cycles can help to avoid a lot of headache.

CHAPTER SEVEN

STOCK TO CREATE RESIDUAL INCOME AND GROWTH

Introduction

We don't have to be an expert to invest in stocks. We also do not have to be rich to invest, yet many of us fail to get started in managing our money. Why? Some of us are intimidated and many of us do not know how to start. But investing is crucial for our retirement. Inflation lops an average about 4 per cent off our money value every year. So it appears that investment is one of the only ways to grow our money fast enough to outpace inflation. Investment can take many forms. One of them is stock investment or paper assets. Others to consider are property assets, mutual funds, bonds, land and business. Remember that investing in stocks is always a risk. Many believe that you should not invest your funds which you need in a year or two. You may not have time to recoup your funds when the market goes down. With any surplus money, the earlier you invest is always an advantage. Time is your advantage and compounding your interest will be in your favour. Losing money initially is very likely but you can easily recover and make back later on. It is never too old to start investing as long as you do not take unnecessary high risk to make up for lost time. It would be good if you have an investment goal in mind.

Another alternative way to invest is through option. Most people are scarce when they hear the word 'option'. It is a new language. There is nothing to be scarce off! Knowledge is important, but it is insufficient to help you make money. Playing option has an advantage because you have the choice to buy a 'put' or a 'call' option. When you buy a 'call' option, you are expecting the stock price to go up and you make money. When you buy a 'put' option, you are expecting the price to go down and you make money. The advantage of selling a 'put' option is that you get pay or premium first without putting any money in. Any wrong speculation, you will lose money. The details of this type of investment will be dealt with later on.

The idea of investing in stocks or options conjures different vision and emotion. For those who are very successful, it's going to be new cars, yachts and holidays. For others, it is full of bad memories of getting burnt following hot tips. To them, it may be just the last time they ever invest in stocks, option or any other paper assets. My own experiences tell me that investing in stocks needs not be any or none of those pictures. It is best done slowly, boringly and potentially profitable. We should learn to avoid some of the regular traps people fall into. Actually, investing in stocks is not difficult as you are told. Some helps and advices from friends can be useful initially. The important thing is that you should know the company you are buying. Do not be fooled by any get rich scheme or top tips. Do your own research and due diligence before you invest! You do not have to wait for the right time to invest. Buy a company that has potential, good cash flow, increasing revenue and profit and good dividend. Warren Buffett famously said,

> "It's far better to buy a wonderful company at a fair price than a fair company at a wonderful price."

I concur with his view. I will buy a company with a rock solid balance sheet, plenty of domestic and international growth potential, increasing profit and good dividend. A good example is investing in the company 'WestFarmers Ltd' in Australia. In three decades since the company was listed in 1984, the company generated a return of 20.9 per cent annually. Mathematically, the company has turned $1000 into $300 000 in just thirty years. Is this profit impressive? I think it is an impressive feat by any language. If you have invested in this company over the years, your retirement is well taken care off.

When I invest my money in stocks, my intention is to own the companies for a medium or long time. A good strategy is to look out for stocks that are undervalued. Never touch any stock that is overvalued. How do you know? My philosophy is to look well into the matter. Numbers seldom lie! Every stock has its true value which can fall between small range of values. You have to find your own criteria to determine this range. Some indicators are revenue growth, profit quarterly, cash flow, value per share estimated by the company and potential of the company. All these numbers will reveal the true value of a company. For example, if the true value of Coca Cola is $100 or in the range from $95 to $105, and if the stock drops to $80, it is now undervalued. It is time to buy. Similarly if Coca Cola rises to $180, it is overvalued. It is time to sell instead of buying, though it is a value company. Knowing this important concept whether a stock is overvalued, undervalued or at its true value can be critical to help us make the decision to buy or sell the stock. Another extra knowledge regarding the company's management is helpful. The calibre of the team of managers and its CEO of a company is also important. If the majority shareholder is running the company, it's a plus point. This technique has been used by investors like Warren Buffett, Benjamin Graham, Bill Spetrino, James Altucher, John Templeton, and others successfully. Do not expect immediate result when you invest in a good company. The important thing is your medium or long-term result. My intention is always buy and hold for a reasonable period. Any value stock will eventually revert back to its true value. I am not going to trade all the time. I always remember the game of averages. Not all the stocks I pick will make money for me. If six out of ten stocks I pick make me money, I will be successful as an investor. I have risk management in place. My loss is capped at 20 per cent and my gain can be anything 50 per cent or more. Strictly adhere to my golden rules of investment will ensure that I will make money in the long and medium terms.

Follow Investment Leaders

The investment landscape is often difficult to survey or read. There are so many factors or multiple things we have to consider. Factors such as economy, politics, world events, earnings, valuations, cash flow and others affect the market. There is always a diverse of opinions where the market or stocks are heading next. We cannot be too dependent on the interpretation of any single individual to help us in investing. Most successful investors develop their own strategy and they keep repeating their approach as long as they make profit. An easy way for us to benefit when we do not have time to do our own research is to follow well established investors like Bill Spetrino, James Altucher, Sean Hyman, and many others. Their advice is not free. You have to pay certain amount of subscription to follow their picks. But it's worth it. I follow Bill Spetrino and I made reasonable investment returns. But it is always better if we can develop our own strategy so that we do not have to follow the shadow of others. It is important to tap upon the wisdom of many experts. We also need to be aware of the various cycles affecting the economy. According to Harry Dent, we have the ten years Boom and Bust Cycles, thirty-nine years of Generational Cycles, thirty-six years of Geopolitical Cycles and forty-five years of Innovation Cycles in most developed countries. Be aware that the beginning and ending of each of these cycles can add extra information and knowledge to our investment success. During each cycle there will be certain sectors performing better than others. The ability to identify the relevant sectors during each boom and bust cycle can be invaluable for investment success. What are the worst performing sectors during a boom period? What are the best performing sectors during the period of recession? For example, during the energy glut period in 2014 and 2015, the price of fuel is low, companies related to airlines, tankers, logistic transportation, plastic industries are benefitting. Every accounting year is divided into four quarters. Knowing each sector's performance during each quarter can help in our investment choice. All these information and knowledge are critical for us to identify stocks to own or avoid. Roughly, we have the following: consumers' sector, health sector, oil and gas sector, technology sector, trade and service sector, manufacturing sector, and others. The history of Warren Buffett's success can be great lessons for all of us. According to Warren Buffett, the greatest investor of all time, if your grandfather had bought $40 worth of the stock Coca Cola in 1919, he held on to the stock, your inheritance today is worth $10 million. You see the power of patience. The amount $40 in 1919 is adjusted for inflation and others is now worth about $540. In Malaysia, if you had bought 1000 shares of Genting or Public Bank at its inception in the 50s and hold it until today, your share is worth more than a million Malaysian dollars. All these harvests are still unimaginable. Are you able to find such a wonderful company to invest now? I think it is still possible! So timing is not that important. Finding a right company at a fair price, you should buy immediately. But what is a right company? To me, investing is not the same as a putting a bet on the number 19 on a roulette table for an immediate fortune, but buying a tangible asset for long-term investment. Buying a stock as investment is actually buying a piece of tangible business. My experiences tell me that if I buy quality companies at sensible prices and if I have the temperament and patience to see the value recognised by the market, I always do well in the fullness of time. It is important to understand the relative price you are paying for the business. It's not important as whether you are buying at the right time as it is always an arbitrary imagination. But reference bias is a psychological flaw that leads us to assume that our own experiences are representative of the wider one. We need to be aware that someone we know, smokes until his 90 and was fit as a bull. So you conclude that smoking cannot be bad for you. But be aware that he is exceptional and not representative of most people. Everybody knows smoking is bad for you. Similarly in stocks, it can lead you to make terrible mistakes just based on your own experiences. In the words of Warren Buffett:

> If you are right about the business, you will make a lot of money. With a wonderful business, you can figure out what will happen; you can't figure out when it will happen. You don't want to focus on when; you want to

focus on what. If you are right about what, you don't have to worry about when.

On this strength, when I buy a good stock, I am not influenced by what the chart says. I will pay a fair price to own a part of the wonderful business. In Australia, I will buy TPM or Telstra when the relative price is fair or there is a big correction. In USA, I will buy Apple or IBM when its price dips. I can be for sure that I can sleep well at night holding these world-class stocks. I will get good dividends and enjoy portfolio gains.

Simple Guiding Principles

The following simple guiding principles based on the true value of a company are important. Relative to its true value, when a stock is overvalued, do not touch it and when the stock is undervalued, it's time to pick. How do you know the true value of a stock? You have to establish certain criteria based on its cash flow, profit, revenue and growth. What is cash flow? Cash flow is not the same as having cash on hand. Having cash on hand is like having money in saving. It's great for the company. In fact, the more cash the better. But ideally, we don't want the company to dip into saving to operate or run the business. Instead, we want the company to have positive cash flow. Cash flow is the money a business generates from its day-to-day operations. When a company has a strong cash flow, it is able to keep up with its debt payments. It is able to grow its business either through acquisition or investing in new products or developing new lines of business. And it is able to return money to shareholders in the form of dividends and stock buy-backs. All these are revealed in the cash flow statement, just like its revenue and profit. This document tells us the company's earnings from its day-to-day operations, how much is borrowed, how much is invested in capital expenditures and how much is given out as dividends and to buy back stocks. The natural value per share given by the company may not be very reliable. However, it is a good estimate of the true value of the company. The true value of a company has to be determined based on the above financial statement.

There is another alternative view to look at the true value of a stock. A stock is easily classified as cheap or expensive based on the four states of the market. When a stock is cheap and on the uptrend, it is time to buy it. When a stock is expensive and on the uptrend, it is time to stay long. Do not buy expensive stocks that are overvalued. When a stock is cheap or undervalued and on a downtrend, do not buy or short it. When a stock is expensive and is on a downtrend, it's time to sell or short it. Simply, the market has four distinct states based on trend and value. Understanding these basic principles can help you make good profits. Remember the quote of Roger:

> Markets often rise higher than you think possible and fall lower than you can possibly imagine.

The principle is, do not fight the trend! Bet against weak stocks... in weak sectors. Buy strong assets and sell weak ones. Embrace this flexibility to capture opportunities while stocks are falling. It also opens up opportunities to boom time for stocks, commodity markets and foreign currencies. In investments, when you get it right, you make a lot of money. On the other hand, if you get it wrong, it can cost you a fortune. I will share two simple ways in helping you get it right and two simple ways of getting it wrong in stock investment.

Let us examine evidence supporting Roger's first quote, markets often rise higher than you think possible. During the period 2010 to 1015, many analysts and other investors are predicting a bear market for years. Such prediction is almost always useless for me as a long- or medium-term investor. Every investor or trader is entitled to his opinion about the market. Do you have to follow their opinions? The important thing for me to do is to examine their opinions and form my own conclusion. I notice that many investors pulled out of the market in during the 2010 correction, the 2011 correction or 2012 correction have missed out an enormous gain. Even if you pull out of the stock market at the end 2015, you may stand to miss another big gain to come. Many analysts and investors think that the prices of stocks are going to fall off the cliff in 2016 onwards before recovering in 2020 or later. I do not believe such a fall is coming. In USA, 2016 is the presidential election year. Normally this is the year where stock market will shine especially just before election. Can this election year be different? I will still hold on to my value stocks where profits are intact, dividends are good and the potential of growth is there. I will avoid energy related stocks in the medium terms. I will invest in airline companies, tankers related companies, plastic industries, biotech companies, Internet companies and some uranium companies for their potential growth. Whatever happens, I do not worry much. I have my trailing stop strategy in place for any of my stock. If the price of any stock falls about 15 per cent below its new peak, I will sell to avoid any big loss to preserve my profit and capital. This is the strategy telling me to sell a stock. There is no emotion involved and no opinion is needed. This is my decision made when I buy any stock.

Another approach I take is to follow the long-term trend of any stock in my portfolio. Instead of following others' opinions, my investment behaviour is guided by the long-term trend. A 200-day MA is used as a gauge of the long-term trend. It is a simple technical analysis anyone can use.

This is a simple principle using a little bit of technical analysis. This is another visualising exercise for you. All of us in the investment game are familiar with the S&P 500 index chart. If you were to look at the S&P 500 index chart plotted against its 200- days moving average (MA), you will see a clear picture of a bull and bear market. What is the 200-day moving average (MA)? It is simply the average of the average of the closing prices of the stock market over 200 days. Every day, the price of the first is dropped and the price of a new day is added and a new 200-day MA is calculated. The first thing you will notice is that when the S&P 500 index is above the 200-day MA (from 2004 to 2008 and 2001 to 2015), the USA market is in bull territory. When the S&P 500 index is traded below the 200-days MA (from 2001 to 2003 and 2008 to 2010) the bear is in charge. For individual stock, by plotting its index against its 200day moving average, you will notice the same trend for bull as well as bear situation. In 2016, the S&P 500 index is beginning to move below its 200-day MA telling us that the USA market is in serious trouble in the years ahead. As smart investor, you should avoid buying stock from 2016 onwards.

What do you notice about the general trend of a bull market? From 2010 to 2015, the S&P 500 index is mostly above the 200- days MA. This period is the uptrend for American market. This tells me an important uptrend regarding any of my stocks when its 200- days MA is below its stock index. This reveals a general trend that during a bull market, the price of any stock is generally above the 200-day MA. What does it imply when the prices index of any stock is below its 200-days MA? This is the period of correction or bear market from 2007 to 2009. So the direction of the 200-days MA (either above or below the price index) is a good indicator of the long or medium term trend of any stock.

Another observation reveals that in August 2015, the 200-day MA has drifted below the S&P 500 index. What does it mean? Perhaps it's telling us to be careful that a bear market is in the making and you should avoid buying new stocks. But the index rebounded after that and now the index has fallen below again.

Without getting too complicated, the moving average convergence divergence (MACO) indicator can provide an early warning sign of a bear market. In any chart showing the S&P 500 and the 200-days MA, the bottom indictor showing when the black MACO line is traded above the red line, we are heading towards the bull market. When the black line crosses below the red line, we are heading into bear territory. Clearly in the beginning of 2016, the red line is above the black line, the bear is about to attack. So be careful when you plan to buy stocks in 2016 and 2017. Patience is the key to avoid long period of waiting.

At the beginning of 2016, again the index has drifted below the 200day MA telling us that a bear market may be just the beginning. Savvy investors are cautious now in 2016 and expect the bear to attack any time now. Two glaring cases happened in 2000 and 2007 when the black MACO line crosses below the red line, the bear started to attack. The same thing is happening in 2016, what will be the consequence? Most likely the bear will be active again. It's a warning for us to run to escape the bear.

Jeff Clark's interesting story about two hunters meeting a bear in the bush serves as a reminder for investors. The first hunter got ready, putting his running shoes and was ready to run. The second hunter laughed and said: "What the heck you are doing? You will never outrun the bear!"

The first hunter replied: "I don't need to outrun the bear. I only need to outrun you." Do you want to be smart like the first hunter?

Let us examine Roger's second quote, that markets often fall lower than you can possibly imagine. This part is the most difficult for me to get it right. When it's the exact bottom? My assumption is always wrong and it offers great risk of losing money. A good example is the energy sector. Huge supply of fuel and the poor economic situations have caused the prices to fall during the period 2014 to 2015. Energy related stocks have also fallen. In USA from summer 2014 to mid-December 2014, crude-oil prices fell 48 per cent. The S&P 500 Energy Sector index - a diversified group of energy stocks - fell 27 per cent. During this short period, the stocks appeared to stop falling, many seasoned investors piled in and started to buy energy stocks. But history tells us that the price trading side way for months and the Energy Sector index fell another 20 per cent from the previous low at September 2015. The price of oil continues to fall until the beginning of 2016. The price reached $28 dollars per barrel before it rebounded into the $30s, remains flat until March and begins to pick up to $50 in June 2016. Any chart will tell a better story regarding the prices of oil falling in two stages during 2014 to 2016. Roger's second quote seems to be reinforced as it unfolds accordingly.

The expensive problem for average investors is that they are wrong at the extremes: too bullish at the market tops and too bearish at the market bottoms. If you risk the most, you lose the most. For example, when gold has gone from $300 to $1700, you assume gold will go to $5000. Another example was when oil trading at $110 a barrel, it must be the buy of the decade at $50. What happens in 2016, oil is at about $30. Be careful in your interpretation. You may lose your shirt. Next round before you jump in, remember Roger's two quotes.

The price of oil is at the peak in July 2014. From 2014 to January 2015, oil price fell 37 per cent and from January 2015 to September 2015, oil price fell another 20 per cent. Those investors who put in a lot of money into energy stocks at the end of 2014 will have to live with paper lost or wait for a long period for energy stocks to recover. What do you think the market will play out? I made the same mistake. The only difference is that I bought only small number of shares of energy stocks to 'dip my toe' in the market when the price fell almost 50 per cent. The experience is not so painful. The loss is small compared with those who bought a lot. Now I will wait for the uptrend to begin. What is an uptrend? It's a series of prices experiencing higher highs and higher lows. The disadvantage of waiting for the uptrend is that we won't catch the bottom. It's compensated by less risk. An uptrend is when the prices agree with my views. Once I know the uptrend is in progress, I will add more energy related shares to my stocks. I also remember how the market will surprise people. Just when the market's next move will be, this can easily fool you. We need to give our imagination a workout when it comes to both the upside and downside potential with any investment.

The year 2015 is a bad year for commodities. In the year 2015, commodities' prices continue to fall. The commodity index is down for 23.7 per cent from January to December 2015 and 27.2 per cent from the high to low for the year. Oil was down 31.1 per cent for the year and 45.7 per cent from high to low. Gold was down 10.5 per cent for the year and 19.7 per cent from high to low. Emerging market stocks performed poorly too because most of them followed commodity prices. In Australia, value stocks like Rio Tinto, BHP Billiton and many mining stocks are suffering because of falling commodity prices especially iron, copper, uranium and oil. Gold price drops 40 per cent from the peak in 2011. The prices are still falling and soon they will stabilise. The uncertainty in 2016 gives gold a push upwards. How high can the price of gold go up? Harry Dent is not optimistic about the price of gold. He predicted that the price of gold will fall further. In the beginning of 2016, he is wrong, but for how long? The natural resource market goes through huge cycles of boom and bust. It is in the bust mood for a long time. I will wait for a few more months or years for the uptrend to begin when the commodity prices start to pick up. When the time comes, I will scoop up these value stocks in quantities. I will also start buying gold and energy stocks when the uptrend begins. Just like what most of the billionaires do, I too may one day be one of them. Warren Buffett is starting to buy energy stocks at the end of 2015 and in 2016. I will follow soon. What are the reasons to do so? First thing to note is that the sale of cars in USA in 2015 is at record high at 17.5 million cars, the peak in last fifteen years. Second, oil is falling not because of demand but of massive oversupply. Third, there is a self-correcting problem. Highly leveraged and undercapitalised oil producers will go bankrupt. Their assets will be taken over and production stops. Soon the market will recognise the supply and demand situation and the oil price will stabilise. Once this happens, oil and related stocks will stop to fall and begin to pick up.

Oil price fell from $105 per barrel in mid-2014 to $30 in February 2016 that is 70 per cent fall in about twenty months. According to the U.S. Information Administration (EIA), the world's oil supply rose from 91 million barrels per day in 2013 to 96.3 million barrels per day in October 2015 that is 6 per cent increase in supply in just two years. But demand is not increasing as fast as supply. World oil demand was 91.2 million barrels per day in 2013 and the EIA estimated of the demand in 2015 is only 92.8 million barrels per day. This is an increase of about 2 per cent. That means the surplus oil went from 200 000 barrels to 3.5 million barrels per day. This explains partly why the oil prices collapse. Even if Russia agrees with Saudi Arabia to freeze their rate of production now in 2016, the surplus will still persist. With the sanction of Iran lifted, the country is going to accelerate its oil production to boost its economy. This will add extra millions of barrels of oil per day to the market, aggravating the surplus equation. Getting Iran and Saudi Arabia to agree to cut production is a wild dream. The two countries never see eye to eye. The surplus will persist and oil prices will be suppressed for the time being until other geopolitical events emerge.

The present, lower fuel prices at a level of $30 to $45 per barrel will begin to work magic for some countries but not oil producing countries. Can this turn out to be a stimulus to the economy? However, no doubt consumers are winners. That's the benefit lower fuel price brings. Lower fuel price implies cheaper transport cost and lower prices of consumer goods. The monster, inflation, is temporarily tame as long as interest and mortgage rates are low. Another benefit is cheaper airfare because fuel is the single biggest cost of airlines.

Cheap oil is the 'new normal' for some time because of increasing supply and a slow growth in China. The emergence of alternative energy sources also has some effects now. In the longer term, the role of solar energy and new technique of storage will create havoc to the oil industries. Will you invest in energy stocks in 2016? It's still too early to say that the energy sector has bottom. Many emerging markets are affected by the low oil prices. The implication is clear, we need to stay clear of stocks especially energy stocks for the time being even in emerging countries. Until and unless I see at least a few higher lows to be sure the uptrend has begun. Patience is the virtue for my new philosophy of investing in energy stocks. Patience is important when you are investing in the right stocks. It can make a difference between losing 30 to 50 per cent and gaining 80 per cent of your money. But patience alone will not make you rich. It is only part of the puzzle in investing especially energy stocks. In order to truly build wealth, you have to pick the right stocks and you have to pick them at the right price. You need both half of the equation. You need to choose the right companies. Picking wrong companies, especially energy companies, you may wait for the reward that may never come in the next few years. The picture for the oil market is not attractive at the beginning of 2016. Most of the OPEC countries are producing at maximum capacity. Even if they agree to cut production, the countries involved will not stick to the agreement. Self-interest is paramount. Sanction on Iran is lifted and she is planning to ramp up extra production from 500 000 barrels now to 1 million barrels per day by the end of the year. Iran is not thinking of cutting production. At present, she is producing 2.8 million barrels per day. Saudi Arabia is producing 10 million barrels per day. America is now the biggest producer of crude oil and the surplus will linger for sometimes. Unless the MiddleEast war turns into big scale fighting and production of oil disrupted, oil will remain suppressed for the time being. Unless a geopolitical event takes place like what happened in 2002 when America invaded Iraq. Crude oil price was $19.69 per barrel in January 2002 and by February 2003, crude oil per barrel was nearly $40. Investors who got in early had made a tidy profit. Within the two years, the major oil stocks went up more than 100 percent cent as indicated: BP (77%), ConocoPhillips (141%), Chevron (103%), Total SA (355%) and Woodside Petroleum (98%).

Geopolitical tension is building up in Syria in 2016. The possibility of Turkey, Saudi Arabia and other Sunni Muslim countries attempting to invade Syria to dethrone the Assad government is there. But Syria is backed by Russia, Iran and other Shi'ite Muslim countries. A war breaking up will boost the price of crude oil. Can this be the beginning of third world war? Can history repeat? Savvy investors are getting ready to benefit from another geopolitical event looming around. The same global geopolitical tension that caused oil to spike thirteen years ago may repeat. If it happens, get ready to benefit from the oil stocks. There is also a strong correlation between global conflicts and the prices of oil. History reveals that when war breaks up, supply is disrupted and demand goes on. No wonder Warren Buffet started to increase his shares in energy stock Philip at the end of 2015. I am getting ready to buy oil stocks in Australia and USA if such a geopolitical event takes place.

Gold, Silver and Platinum Investments

The decline of stock prices at the end of 2015 boosts the price of gold as insurance or safe heaven. Relatively the prices of platinum and silver are quite constant. In February 2016, platinum was at a discount of more than $250 to gold. Silver was at about $15 per ounce; gold was at about $1200 per ounce and platinum was at $925 per ounce. How is this happening? Platinum is supposed to be worth more than gold. Platinum is harder to get out from the ground and it is more exclusive in the Jewry Stores. Normally the price of platinum is usually above that of gold. In 2016 it is not. Platinum is traded at a big discount to gold.

If you look at any chart showing the price of gold plotted against the price of platinum, you will notice that most of the time, the price of platinum is above the price of gold. The price of platinum is always higher than gold most of the time from 1989 to 2011. But everything changed after 2011, the price of gold has overtaken that of platinum and the gap is getting bigger in the beginning of 2015. Logically, buying platinum has a better chance of making good profit than gold. The price of platinum will eventually catch up with that of gold. At the present, the declining of the stock markets is giving gold a good run. The price of gold has gone up more than 20 per cent at the beginning of 2016 and is moving upwards when stock prices are declining. This gap is confirmed if you look at gold to-platinum ratio. The ratio is about 1.2 to 1.5 in 2016, telling us that gold is expensive relative to platinum. So opportunity of making money is there if you start investing in platinum.

For the last thirty six years, the average gold-to-platinum ratio is 0.83 ounce of platinum to one ounce of gold. Today 2016, one ounce of gold is equivalent to 1.27 ounces of platinum or more. So gold is extremely expensive relative to platinum. By this measure gold is expensive. This reveals that the price of gold to platinum is clearly above 1.35 in the beginning of 2016. The discount creates a big opportunity for us to buy platinum and make good profit. A few times in the past that the prices of platinum traded at a discount to the price of gold, platinum prices outperformed going forward. During this type of situation, the price of platinum outperformed that of gold in the next twelve months by about eight or more percentage on average. Another situation is that when the price of platinum dipped to a discount of gold, platinum prices never underperformed that of gold in the eighteen months later. Today discount is massive at about 21 per cent and the possibility is that platinum may soar more than the average of 8 per cent in the near future. Are you preparing to bet on this increase? So today 2016, platinum has the components under the CHU strategy. It is cheap, hated and I am waiting for the uptrend to emerge.

The ratio of gold to silver tells us how many ounces of silver it 'costs' to buy one ounce of gold over the last forty five years. The average is fifty six ounces of silver to one ounce of gold. Today 2016, it takes seventy eight ounces of silver to buy one ounce of gold. Instead of buying gold now, it is more logical to buy silver. So if you are focusing on buying gold, a better alternative is to buy silver and platinum instead. This is a better bargain in the precious metals world.

In January to March of 2016, the price of gold has risen about 20 per cent and any technical chart will show that the price still has room to move higher. Frank Holmes, CEO of US Global Investors pointed out the 'Golden Cross' for gold. At the end of February, gold experiences a 'Golden Cross', a technical indicator that occurs when gold's 50-day moving average (MA) crosses its 200- day MA. This is the first movement within twenty four months and Frank takes it as a sign that gold price might move higher up. Do you believe in technical analysis? Only time will tell that such forecasting is reliable. Many investors including those from the banks seem to concur with him that you should buy some gold as insurance when interest is going negative. Buying silver and platinum may bring in better profit as insurance in 2017 onwards. Historically the prices of these metals usually did well when interest rate turned negative. It is happening now in 2016. Gold price bottomed at $1050 in December 2015. In the first three months of 2016, gold rallies to $1270 per ounce, a 20 per cent rise in just three months.

As an investor, knowing that gold price is on its way up, I will not only buy gold now but I will start to accumulate silver and platinum for longer term investments. Another factor is that when interest is low, buying gold is the preference to real rate of interest. If you were to compare interest rate to the price of gold, you will notice the opposite of the trends. The contrast is dramatic when interest rate is negative. Take a close look at negative interest rate from 2011 to the beginning of 2014, the price of gold increases exponentially. This awareness is important if you are interested to invest in precious metals like gold, silver and platinum.

A clear trend shows that when real interest is low or negative from 1973 to 1981, gold price moved up and from 1982 to 2000, real rate of interest rose, gold price was flat. From 2008 to 2016, the real rate of interest was low or negative, the price of gold soared. This indicates that the price of gold is going to move further up in 2016. Remember that when cash and gold pay no interest, people will choose gold.

Another metal in my investment radar is aluminium, which is the main metal not iron used by Tesla to make electric cars. Iron and steel are no longer the preference for cars because of its weight. The number of lithium battery electric cars is growing exponentially; the metals aluminium, lithium and related companies are the best places for us to invest. With the metal oil revolution taking place now and the new solar 2 megatrend in progress, people who know where to put their money will be the next batch of millionaires.

Performance of Stocks in 2015 and 2016

Any S&P 500 chart gives an indication that the USA market goes up for six straight years from 2009 to August 2015 and finally stalls, it's likely the market is at the peak or almost peak. I would take this as a precaution to avoid buying new stocks in USA or in emerging countries during 2016. As the list of stocks hitting new lows grows by the day in 2016, the smell of fear in investors' behaviour is getting stronger day by day. And panic behaviour might be just around the comer. I would preserve cash waiting for a big correction. What do you think? Will the debt bubble in USA burst? I will wait for opportunity for a 25 to 50 per cent correction to pick my value stocks. This happened during August 2015 and the beginning of 2016. But market recovered by the middle of 2016 and continues to climb upward with minor corrections.

If I were to buy stocks in 2016, my preference will be tankers or airline-related companies booming with low fuel prices. Another sector I will pick now is the plastic package industry and biotech stocks. Plastic compound polypropylene and polyethylene used for plastic packages come from oil products. These compounds become cheap and will boost the profit of the plastic manufacturing industries. As long as the price of oil is kept low, these industries will boom and become profitable. Investing into value stocks related to these industries will give you reasonable profit in 2016.

The health and biotech sectors are doing well. The baby boomers generation is retiring by batches and their demands for medical treatment will be on the rise. Remember the baby boomers hold a lion share of the world's wealth. New discoveries of drugs to keep the baby boomers healthy are always in big demand. New vaccine known as 'Alpha Cell' therapy is about to be approved by FDA in 2016. The ability to spot the company responsible for this discovery will make you rich. Many biotech companies were doing well in 2015. Their fundamentals are still intact. This awareness and information are important when oil price is kept low. This type of opportunity is only medium term. We experienced the cycle of oil prices and we saw how it affects the plastic package industries before. Health and biotech sectors are always in demand as the boomers population age. Past experiences are valuable to help investors make money in the volatile market in 2016.

At present, the sentiment of the stock markets everywhere is driven by fear and stock prices are falling significantly in the beginning of 2016. Many of the countries are already in the bear market. Soon US market will be expected to join the crowd. To be prepared for a long period of bear market, we should keep cash ready whenever the market rebounds. Will the low prices of oil affect American's economy significantly like the housing bubble in 2008? Many analysts do not think so. Housing is significantly related to the health of the economy contributing more than 10 per cent of the American GDP whereas the oil market only accounts for 2 per cent and is not significant. They think that low price of oil will put more money on consumers' hands and the consumers' sentiment will be boasted. People have more money from transport's saving and they have more money for other products which may serve the economy better. Patience is the key word in this falling market in 2016. Many value stocks are on sale soon and when it is the right time to scoop them up and enjoy the rebound to their true values. Investors who have the gut to pick up value stocks during the fall of August 2015 and the beginning of 2016, have been well rewarded.

CAPE Introduced by Benjamin Graham

Benjamin Graham takes into consideration the moving average of ten years instead of one year. His method gives us the true value of how cheap the market is now. Instead of PE, many value investors are in favour of cyclical-adjusted price/earnings ratio (CAPE) which is independent of the economic cycle we are in. The CAPE ratio gives a long-term picture of the market. The concept of CAPE will be discussed further under the language of stocks. The average P/E for ten years is 16.7 and in the beginning of 2016, the S&P 500 is traded at a CAPE of 23.9 which is slightly cheaper than 2008 (CAPE 24.2). What does this number tell us? This is a first red flag. A big correction is imminent in 2016. It happened at the beginning of 2016. You can check the truth for the projection in 2016! The Dow's index is down in the beginning of 2016. The oil price is at record low favouring airline and tankers related stocks. But for the general markets for stocks in the S&P 500, the returns will be disappointing in 2016. A recovery of the S&P 500 is in progress in the second half of 2016. Will this recovery hold in 2017?

Another red flag is revealed when we compare net total debt and total earnings. In the period 1999 to 2005, the net debt was above the earnings. From 2005 to 2014, net debt and earnings are moving closely. During this period, the stock market was doing well. After 2014, the relative debt is diverting away from the earnings. This big divergence is telling us that the stock market will not be good in 2016 onwards. How long can the situation last? Debt is diverting above a broader measure of earning from 2014 to 2016. The last time debt exceeded earning was in 2001 due to weakening earning. Even in 2008-2009 recessions, the difference is not so glaring. According to Harry Dent, this divergence is heading into a recession or deflation in USA in 2016. According to him, the rippling effect will be felt worldwide soon. The economic winter season for the USA economy had just begun in 2016. Do you believe the prediction? You see, individual investors tend to mimic the actions of others around them. Many of the actions are not rational. The 'herding' phenomenon may quicken the process of sending the market into bubble territory. Another factor called 'scatter fear' is gaining momentum. It is just human nature. We are wired to stick close to the group since our cave ancestors did. You need to be aware of this. We are not living in caves now and we need to think differently from the herd. During this environment, there are always some sectors performing very strongly and others perform poorly. I have taken precaution and I have sold most of my stocks except those stocks related to airline, biotech and tankers. I also kept some of the stocks related to health and internet businesses. You should also take precaution if you are interested to keep your wealth. The risk of a big market correction is on the way in 2017 or 2018.

A Glimpse of Light at the End of the Tunnel for the Oil Sector

The energy oil sector is tremendously cyclical. Back then, oil prices had fallen from $145 per barrel in mid-2008 to $34 per barrel in early 2009. Many oil-producing companies reduced their production resulting in less drilling equipment and services. Oil services stocks plunged more than 71 per cent during this period. What we saw eventually is oil prices recovered and oil production picked up. Oil services stocks followed and soared. The oil service index rose 133 per cent from the low of 2009 to its high at 2011. Today, it appears history is about to repeat. About fifteen months ago, there were about 2000 drilling rigs operating in the oil field of USA, but in 2016 there are about 698 rigs left. A big percentage drops in drilling activities. This sounds bad news but it is actually a good sign for investors. All these signs indicate that we are close to the bottom of the oil sector. The prices of oil will fall further before the bottom is reached. The beginning of the year 2016 gives a glimpse of the fall to $28 per barrel. Is this the bottom? The 'sandpaper phase' may be long and you need patience before buying oil stocks. How long will this flattening of oil prices last? If the price-to-book ratio of a group of oil stocks is an indication, then a look at the oil services price-to-book (P/B) ratio can give us a glimpse of the future of oil stocks. The ratio is still healthy indicating that oil price will move up. Harry Dent disagrees with this and he predicts that oil will eventually drop to $10 or less per barrel after 2016. This conflicting interpretation is food for thought if you are waiting to invest in oil stocks. But the price of oil never reaches $10 per barrel. Harry Dent's prediction is way out.

According to Stansberry Resource Report Newsletter to monitor a group of oil service stocks is the price-to-book ratio (P/B). It is simply a ratio of a company market's cap divided by its assets, minus liabilities. The ratio of most oil stocks tells us that we are very close to the bottom in the sector. The P/B ratio of a company simply represents the value of the company's iron equipment (tools). When in full operation, the market value for them is four or five times book value. When equipment or tools are left idle, their values are back to the buying prices. The averages of this group of oil service stocks give a good indication.

For the past thirty five years, the average ratio which tracks the major service of oil service companies has been 2.6. It means the values of machineries (tools) are worth 2.6 times the book values. There were five incidents where the P/B index plunged to its extreme low value. The last time this happened is in 2009 when the P/B ratio is 1.2. The lowest price for oil was $34 per barrel in early 2009. Will history repeat? Your guess is as good as mine. Right now the trend of the oil sector is still down. Patience is the keyword. At the beginning of 2016, oil price per barrel dropped to $28 and is hovering around $30s and $40s. Soon the price of oil recovers to almost $50 per barrel in June 2016. The price is hovering around from $46 to $50 in July. I think for the year 2016, the price of oil will be in the range from $40 to $50 per barrel. I am getting ready to pounce when the scenario repeats. The supply and demand equation will repeat. At present, there is a big surplus in oil and gas. The prices may drop and many companies abandon ship because it's no longer profitable. Soon, the supply will diminish and the demand will pick up and prices of oil will climb. Are you ready for the repeat of history as happened before? I will start buying energy stocks when the uptrend is in place. The waiting period may be long or may be not too long. What we need is patience and cash ready when the opportunity arises.

It looks like we need the patience of Warren Buffett who waited thirty years to buy GEICO. We may have to wait few years or not too long to buy oil stocks. Remember how your failure to imagine possible outcomes may have tripped you in the past. Keep your cash ready and keep in touch with the latest development and when situation improves, you must be ready to act.

The prediction of Harry Dent will become invalid as soon as geopolitical event takes place in the Middle - East. The possibility of escalated tension and invasion of Syria can be happening soon. There is going to be a big scale military exercise involving 350 000 soldiers, 20 000 tanks, 2 450 airplanes and 460 helicopters from various countries like Turkey, Qatar, Egypt, Jordan, Bahrain, Malaysia and the host country, Saudi Arabia. Will this military exercise in 2016 turned out to be an invasion of Syria? If this geopolitical tension turns out to be a full scale war in Syria, the prices of oil will definitely not stay low for long. No full scale war is declared but only tension and uncertainty.

I believe that the right price for oil is hard to find especially that we are near a market turning point or a market bottom. No one knew the right price to pay for stocks in early 2009. No one knew the right price for real estate in 2011. What we saw after that was the massive price swings and high volatility. My observation is that the same thing is happening in the oil market today, early 2016. We experience a daily swing of 11 per cent and daily loss of 7 per cent. It does not mean that oil price is at the bottom. It indicates that we are near the turning point for oil prices. Based on volatility alone, we sense that prices of oil will soon go higher. This is contrary to the doom theory of oil from Harry Dent.

According to Harry Dent, the end of the tunnel for oil is still a distant away. So 2016 will not be a turning point for oil prices. The price of oil is predicted by Harry to reach $20 per barrel and eventually $10 or less per barrel before recovering. This scenario does not paint a good picture for the future of oil industries. If Harry Dent's prediction is right, the USA tracking industry will most likely to be killed, together with the economy of Russia, Saudi Arabia and many other oil producing countries. We will wait and see whether Harry Dent's prediction will come to pass in 2016! So far he is wrong. We saw the effect of subprime cries of 2008 which triggered the global crisis and meltdown. Will the oil bubble bursting create drastic effects on the world economy? The trigger has been struck and we are waiting for the result. A word of reminder, according to billionaire Ken Fisher, the share market is 'The Great Humiliator'. We can't imagine how the market can surprise people. The winter season of the market is just beginning in 2016. According to Harry dent, it may last a few years until 2022 before the spring economic season begins. Then the price of oil will recover. The waiting will be long and painful for oil producing countries. It appears that his prediction does not hold water. But there is certain amount of truth in his worry. You should not totally overlook his warning.

The Commitment of Traders (COT) report just confirms that in January 2016, future oil traders are getting negative about oil. Negative sentiment is at 150 but the present is about 220. It is not extreme yet, telling us that oil price will fall further. Sentiment can still fall further before hitting the negative extreme. This appears to confirm what Harry Dent has predicted that fall of oil price is not over yet. A possible oil rally may be on the way, but at this moment, the indication is still on the downtrend. By the middle of 2016, oil recovers to $50 per barrel and fall again to $45 per barrel. The price may fall further. Temporarily Harry Dent is off target.

The natural gas prices remain low in sympathy with oil prices. The last three years prices of gas are trending downward. The downtrend does not speak well for the gas industries. Are we seeing the bottom now? Your guess is as good as mine. It appears that the price of natural gas has reached the bottom just before 2016 and it's on the way up temporary. With the extended winter cold in February and March, the price may touch $3.00 per thousand cubic feet (Mcf). The gluts of natural gas will eventually supress the price of natural gas when the cold winter is over. The declining prices of gas in USA in 2015 are obvious. The price per thousand cubic feet (Mcf) of gas declined from its peak at $6.00 in February 2014 to $2.20 in January 2016. The future for gas does not look attractive. As the price of oil recovers in July 2016, the price of gas follows. The future for gas and oil is still doubtful because of over-supply.

Shifting of Energy Landscape

The future of oil and gas as a source of energy for the future is in doubt. This is mainly due to the idea of a single person who discovered the source of free energy from the sun. According to Albert Einstein in 1905, the source of energy particles from the sun reaching the earth is a rich source of abundant free energy. The problem is to convert and store the energy particles for our daily energy need. Today, a breakthrough is at sight. Now scientists are able to harvest this source of cheap and plentiful supply of solar energy and stored up for our energy requirements. Big investments are pouring into this source of cheap energy. Soon this new form of solar energy will be so cheap that will make other sources of energy from fossil, oil and gas redundant.

A small company has patented this new technology harvesting and storing this plentiful supply of solar energy into fuel of the future. This source of free energy will be so cheap that other energy industries will be made absolute. As investors, this information is worth pursuing.

The truth is; the world needs energy more than anything else. The sun provides infinite amount of energy we need. The only problem is harvesting and storage. We have found an efficient method of storing energy with lithium. We are making a transition from oil to metal oil, the oil of the twenty-first century. The lithium demand from 2011 to 2016 conveys a clear message that the transition shift in the energy sector is beginning. As investors, getting into companies pioneering the usages and services of metal oil will make us very rich. Paying attention to the media circus and the American politics, most of us fail to see that billions of dollars are being poured into the lithium and solar energy market. When everything becomes clear, the early investors into the lithium and solar energy market will be the most successful. From 2005 to 2015, global consumption of lithium has doubled. It is expected to continue. Global demand is expected to double again by 2022. Elon Musk, CEO of Tesla, is building his gig-factory to produce lithium battery for electric cars and his Solar City. Many more such gig-factories are in the planning stage. The revolution in stored energy with lithium will make many new millionaires. At the present moment, Tesla is in a development stage and the company is not making money yet. I believe in the genius behind this man driving to revolutionise the transport industry. The implication of his discovery will have far reaching effect in the energy sector. A new and effective use of solar energy through this storage system is just emerging. Soon the whole energy sector will undergo revolutionary transformation because of the clean, cheap and infinite source of energy from the sun. Investors who are savvy and proactive will be the next batch of millionaires.

Biotech Companies for the Future

During the slump of the oil sector, there are some other sectors of the market experiencing growth. The transport sector involving airlines, tankers, plastic industry and the pharmaceutical sector are growing. The health sector is the next attractive field for investment. For example, a new vaccine called Alpha Cells therapy is waiting for approval in 2016. A tiny company or related companies holding the patent of manufacturing this vaccine will sky rocket in price soon. Take your research seriously to locate this company or a giant company preparing to merge or joint venture with this small company. You can easily become another millionaire.

The year 2015, many small biotech companies in USA were doing very well. Most of their biotech companies experienced superior growth. Companies like Trovagene (TROV) and Affirmed N.V. (AFMD) shot up 130 and 290 per cent respectively in the year. I believe these companies together with others like Celdax Therapeutics (CLDH), Synergy

Pharmaceuticals (SGYP) and others will do well in 2016 and 2017. Another trend to take note for biotech companies is the phenomenon of the big fish swallows the small ones. Large pharmaceutical companies like Merck (MRK) and Pfizer (PFE) need to expand and develop new drugs for growth. The problem is that research and development for new drug takes a long time to succeed. So it appears easier to buy up companies which are already in the later stages of development in a new drug or develop a partnership with these small companies. We can anticipate that many small biotech companies will be taken over by the giant companies. For investment purpose, such anticipation can bring in great premium for the small companies. Your guess is as good as mine. This is the investment game I usually get excited. Small companies like Pacific Biosciences (PACB), Celgene (CELG) and others are likely candidates for the giant pharmaceutical companies. The year 2016 and 2017 will be good years for biotech companies. Many of the small caps with good profits and with discoveries of new drugs will see their prices move upwards. They are likely candidates for takeover by the big brothers. Valuations and expectations in the sector are high. There will be some companies which enjoy high valuations and cannot live up to expectations and will see their prices drop drastically.

However, the biotech sector still offers good investment prospect in 2016 onwards if you pick the right stocks. For example, a new discovery of a new vaccine known as 'Alpha Cells' therapy is about to be produced. FDA approval is about to happen in 2016. Thanks to the effort of Nobel Prize winner, Dr Ralph Steinman who himself suffered from cancer. He was given a few months to live but he managed to live on for more than four years. He died three days before the award ceremony and the Nobel Prize was given to him posthumously.

Alpha cells therapy not only destroys cancer cells but also makes sure they never return. This is equivalent to reprogramming the immune system for a full proof adaptive response to future cancer threats. Alpha cells vaccine and therapy are acting like the general directing the army of cells to destroy cancer cells and get ready to mobilise our immune system to destroy any other cancer cells from regrouping. Clinical trial is almost over and is waiting for FDA approval. If you can spot the tiny company or companies having the patent to produce this type of vaccine curing all types of cancer, you can be very rich. You have to keep looking and researching into medicine helping people to live longer and healthier. Get ready to position yourself to help others and help yourself to become a millionaire if you move fast to buy this small company which hold the patent of this therapy. Remember the price of the company Amgen which increased thousands of percent in a matter of six years. History will repeat if Alpha cells vaccine therapy gains FDA approval sometime at the end of 2016. The early bird investors will become the Alpha cells millionaires.

Dividend as Residual Income

Strictly buying a stock for dividend can be risky during turbulent time. You may get your dividend at a reduced rate and lose your investment capital. A more logical thinking is to wait until the turbulence is over and the market is beginning to recover. There are many ways of creating residual income through investment in assets and stocks. Dividend from any growing stock is a good investment. Residual income like rental or dividend is recurring each year. You need to be aware of timing and the cyclical nature of each sector. In Australia there are many companies giving good dividends. They are paid on a yearly or half-yearly basis out of the companies' profits and provide investors with a steady stream of income. Some investors like retirees live off the proceeds, while others reinvest them to enjoy the full benefit of compounding in the long run. Investors also enjoy the tax benefits in the form of franking credits. Capital gain is another good source of income. But buying stock can also result in losing capital. So before you start investing in stocks, arm yourself with good strategies to give you an edge. For most of us we will start our career as an employee. It does not matter which profession or job you are involved. The important thing for us is to be aware that we will never have financial freedom if we live from paycheque to paycheque. We need a little bit of financial planning and never get into unnecessary debt especially credit card debt. Start your life with some saving for the purpose of investment. If your salary is not adequate for you to have much saving, start look around to do some part time jobs to enhance your saving. The first few years of your working life is critical if you start your financial planning on the right footing. After working for a few years, most of us would have at least some saving to start our long journey in investments. Investment in stocks and getting dividends is a good start. I have a word of encouragement for you. Stock investment is still one of the best ways of wealth creation. Look around, most of the rich people are good investors in stocks. During this period of low interest rate in Australia and USA, keeping your money in good dividend value stocks is still better than having your cash in the bank and earning 1 or 2 per cent interest. Many of the dividends are fully franked meaning tax paid. In USA and Australia, from 2010 to 2015, dividends from double A stocks are far superior compared to interest from the banks.

Investment in AArated dividend stocks in USA and Australia outperform not only interest from the banks but also much better than the percentage gain of S&P 500 from 2005 until now 2016. Investing in AArated dividend stocks generally gives better return than interest from the banks. Picking the right AArated stocks can make you rich with dividends and capital gains.

The banks are paying very low interest in 2015 and 2016. People with cash seem to choose stocks or gold instead of interest. If you need the cash to do business or other project in a year or two, you need to think carefully. Even value stocks will be affected by the present economic cycle and sentiment. A friend of mine has some money which he plans to buy his property in a year later. He is getting very low interest rate from the bank. He looks at a telco stock like AT&T which is giving about 6 per cent dividend. He told me that he intends to put his money in the stock to collect the interest in a year. I do not discourage him but I ask him to check what happened to AT&T during the last recession 2008- 2009. Using his iPhone, he checked the chart of its price. He was shocked to find that the price of the stock dropped from $40 to $24 during the recession. So what is the use of 6 per cent dividend in a year later? But if investing in a value stock for a long term, then it's different. Eventually AT&T went back to higher prices. So we need to be careful if you intend to invest just for a short term especially during turbulent time. Timing holds the key to short - term investment. When the market plunges, it's good news for long-term investors for they can buy stocks on sale. The economic cycle will repeat.

Overcome the Belief that Investing in Stocks is Unfair

We always believe that life is unfair and investing in stocks is also unfair. It's true that there is no absolute fairness in any field. In the investment pond, the big fish are eating the small fish. In investment, information is king; knowledge and experience are weapons to make big profit. Investment fund managers and other big organisations seem to have a big advantage over ordinary investors like us. They have teams of researchers on hand to sift through information to find hidden signals that give them a big advantage in investing. They are well equipped with high-speed computers and databases to analyse whatever information available. They have the time and resources to access information ordinary investors like us can only dream of. It sounds like a losing game for us as ordinary investors. But nowadays with high speed computer at home and the viability of information readily; the investment playing field is more level now. To be a successful investor, we have to rely on our own research and due diligence. We have to learn and able to detect higher signals the pros are looking for with their fancy computers. We need to detect what fund managers and others are doing. For example what makes these big fish jump into a social media company's stock or technological stock before the earnings report are out, sending its price rocketing. How do they know what to buy in before the announcement of the actual result? Actually as ordinary investors, we can also make such anticipation if we have studied the company's activities and its performances from quarter to quarter. We need to study the company's revenue, profit, cash flow patterns, and business activities. An indication is clear if a company's profit has been increasing exponentially during its cycle, our anticipation is equally reliable for us to take appropriate action. This consciousness and awareness of such a skill must be practised again and again until we can intuitively execute the skill automatically.

Information is king in investment. For example, if we have detected that directors and insiders of a biotech company or technological company start buying their own stock ahead of regulatory approval of a potential blockbuster new drug or invention, it's time to follow. The big fish know such development through research and contact. We can also access such information if our due diligence is focused on such development in a targeted company. Our research must be up to date and we allow information to flow freely to us. It is not possible to trace every company for such situations, but with modern information available, we can focus on cutting edge companies which are under our research radar. We have to be well read and keep informed regarding new researches and developments. We have to respect such information once it becomes available. The following strategies adopted by fund managers and other pros can be replicated to help us to become successful investors.

First, learn to buy before the earnings surprise. We can also make big money by anticipating good earnings of companies before the results are announced. Buy the stocks before the fabulous earnings results and enjoy the ride of their increasing prices. 'Playing' the earnings surprises can also become our strategy to make money. But it is easier said than done. It's time consuming and to be a good player, we need the secret of repetition to be successful. We will focus on a few companies under our radar and know their activities under our finger tips. The secret of success is repetition and mastery of such a technique. There is no fixed strategy to follow.

Second, learn to follow the smart money. Many investors use to follow their masters like Warren Buffett, Jim Rodger, George Soros and other well-known investors. Whenever these big investors buy certain stocks, many investors follow. Even the pros like to mimic each other. There are many successful investors around. I like to follow investors like Bill Spetrino, James Altucher, Sean Hymen and others. When institution players buy, many pros follow. If we can sift through the recent reports regularly and find some of the big institutions' moves, we can also benefit from their intensive research.

Third, learn to buy when insiders are buying their own stocks. This is a good strategy to follow when corporate leaders are buying their own stocks. Heavy buying of their own stocks is a good signal that something good is happening in their companies. How do you know? This information is usually reported under SEC regulations. It is difficult to track down most of the companies under this type of situation. But keeping in touch with companies in your portfolio may be sufficient for us to make good money.

Another strategy to invest is to follow the trend of each stock. We can make use of the 200-day moving average to help us in detecting the big trend. Generally for a big uptrend, the 200-day moving average is below the price index of a stock. It's time to add the particular stock during the period when the moving average is below the index line. On the contrary when the moving average moves above the stock's index, a correction is on the way. It's not the time to buy the stock. This technical indicator serves as guide for us to buy or sell a particular stock.

If we can focus on investing value stocks with plenty of cash flow, increasing revenue, good profits and potential of growth, and using the above guiding strategies, our chance of making money is much brighter.

Human Behaviours in Stock Investments

Behavioural science reveals that we are all fallible, we cling to our own prejudices and we are resistant to new points of view. Good decision-making is about weighing information and putting the appropriate weight to each piece of information. This is easier said than done even for a seasoned investor. Research in the field of behavioural finance found that investors' trading behaviour is easily predictable. They sell their winning stocks early and they hold on to their losing ones. They always believe that the price they pay is reasonable and the price will recover soon. They forget the right price for a stock is what someone else is prepared to pay. But over time, the value of a good stock will shine through. But it's difficult to decide at any time whether the price of a stock is above or below its intrinsic value or true value. You need to be an independent thinker! You need to know the business involved. Is the business of the company rock solid? What about its profit, dividend, growth, and cash flow? Is it the right time to buy? The key to right timing is a willingness to take a contrary view to market herd. Remember what Warren Buffett said:

> "When everything is certain, you need to ask questions. Be fearful when everybody is certain and be greedy when everybody is fearful."

Many a time I had found a stock I wanted to invest in. I had done my research and was ready to pull the trigger. But I finally talked myself out at the last minute. And a few weeks later, I found the stock had shot up. I started kicking myself for my inaction. This happened to me many times, and I regretted each time. I was determined not to let this habit of talking myself out of a good investment another time. Again I found a stock for investment and I was feeling the same unease again. Anyhow I was determined to buy it. But this time after my purchase, the stock went down. I was caught unprepared and regretting my action. Now I promise myself to do more due diligent. So I managed to talk myself out of my next investment and found that it went up. I was not in it again. All these feeling and confusion seem to create doubt and confidence in my stock investment. This self-doubt comes from my lack in confidence in my strategy. I am determined to overcome this self doubt once and for all. How do I do it? I become aware that this self-doubt is deep down in my subconscious mind. I learn that most successful investors have something in common. They continuously learn from their mistakes and their successes and refine their approaches. They believe in individual understanding that comes from experience. My own experiences teach me that nothing teaches me better about risk than losing money. I am lucky that I experienced it early in my investment journey and it leaves me plenty of time to grow rich slowly. I really make an effort to eliminate this set of self-doubt by replacing it with a set of established strategies I learned from successful investors. Self doubt is an emotion I need to control in my investment decision. I keep using these strategies until they become autopilot cutting off emotion in my decision making.

How do I eliminate emotion and guessing from my investment decisions? I search for strategies where I can cut off emotion from my investment equation. I read and follow some of the strategies used by successful investors to eliminate emotion from the investment decision. Here is a good example for us to consider. According to Peter Lynch, 60 per cent of the stocks are overvalued and only 40 per cent of them are undervalued. To separate the undervalued 'gold stocks' from the overvalued 'fool's gold' is a problem. Peter develops a new system to uncover some of these value stocks without using his emotion. He makes it simple by rating each identified stock from 1 to 10. His formula is simple.

He assigns a number for each of these metrics: dividend, cash flow, and growth potential to a stock. He converts a stock score to its 'ideal price' by comparing its stock price with its peer group. This gives an indication of the price the stock should be trading. By comparing the actual stock price traded in the market with it's ideal price, Peter obtains the score difference. The greater the difference between the actual price and the 'ideal price', he assigns a higher rating to a stock. At the extreme, the most undervalued stock will have a score of 10 indicating a strong buy. The most overvalued stock will have a score of 0 telling you to avoid. In short a stock that has a score of 7, 8, or 9 has more profit upside. And a stock's score of 3 or below has more downside, offers little, except future losses and grief. Remember that there is never a perfect system. By doing this due diligence, you put the odd in your favour. Keeping safety investment in mind, Peter will only buy a stock he knows at least 20 per cent cheaper than its ideal value. He will take profit when a stock is traded at 20 per cent over its ideal value. Peter claims that the beauty of his system is that it takes every iota of guesswork and emotion out of his investment decisions. Sticking to this rigid system, Peter is able to make profit most of the time. I like his system mathematically. It removes my self-doubt; guesswork and emotion form my investment decisions. I may need to modify the system a little bit to suit my personality and my style of investment. A burst of insight tells me that I need to follow this type of system to be successful in investment. First I need to know what work and second I need to make it work. A scientifically and mathematically validated system is always better than my own guesswork when investment decisions are to be made. You have a choice. I have my mine. I would like to embrace a higher dimension of consciousness into my investment.

These behavioural problems also apply to selling a stock. I have this problem in my investment experience. When I hold a stock, I just can't bring myself to let go of it, even if the logic screams to sell it. I think many people share from the same experience. Investors holding energy or oil stocks in 2014 have lost at least 50 per cent. Now I realise that this is a normal investor's behaviour. But it costs me money. This awareness teaches me a new strategy not to place too much attachment to any stock which defies sound financial decision making. I need a system to protect my limited capital. I have to follow my golden rule not to lose more than

15 or 20 per cent in any of my stock, either from my purchase price or from its peak.

I have another problem. I suffer from three kinds of reaction when a stock I bought went on a substantial gain. First is my belief that I will never go broke taking profit. Many of friends believe that they should lock in their profit. The problem is that my early entry to a stock almost always missed out the best part of the gain. The experience is very terrible. My friend bought Blackmores at $30 and was very happy to sell at $45. He felt that he was very clever because he got 50 per cent profit. The stock went on to $60. If he sold at that price, he would have made 100 per cent. Later on, the price of Blackmores went on to $90 and today it is at $130. If he has adopted my first golden rule in investment, he would have got a holidays home. Another friend bought TPM at 38 cents, and he thought he was very clever when he sold all of his stock at $2.80. After a few months, the stock was at $4.00, then $7.00 and today it is at $12.00. Most of investors suffer from this kind of pain involving missed gain and it often hurts more than a loss. Because of this experience, many greedy investors suffer from 'Missed the boat reaction'. They rush in to buy when the price of a stock keeps going up. Little do they realise that the value and its price is inversely proportional. Every stock like Apple, IBM, Microsoft, and others has its own cycle in terms of price. What goes up has to come down! Now I use to take note of this phenomenon before I join the crowd. It is always true that you are not going to sell precisely at the top, and you are not going to buy precisely at the bottom. For me, I will handle my portfolio like an engineer who handles a train. When stocks go up, my portfolio should be mostly long. I will add more to my portfolio as long as the price of each stock is reasonable and its growth is intact. From time to time, stocks go down. Sometimes they go down a lot. So a trailing stop is handy. What is the percentage from the peak my trailing stop should be? I usually fix at about 15 per cent. It's good to stop the train. Sometimes, it may be good to reverse the train. This is selling a put in option on the particular stock which you think will fall drastically. This is another alternative to benefit from falling trends. But it's not sensible to start and stop your train at will. In an uptrend, do not stop your train. Only slow down or stop your train based on your predetermined trailing stop. Even in a down-trend or recession, there are companies that thrive. For example, during recession, many pharmaceutical and consumption companies are doing very well. We can still invest in certain stocks during recession. So if we stop the train totally, we would have missed many opportunities. If I am nervous about certain stocks, I will reduce my holding or sell them off using my trailing stop. Following this principle with discipline can make you rich because the downside is capped but there is no limit to your upside.

Another belief is that investors sold their stock for a good profit and wait for the price to fall before they buy again. In the case of Blackmores, a friend bought at $30 and sold at $60 and he waits for the price to fall back before they buy. Again he misses the chance to gain more than double their money when Blackmores is at $130.

Of course it's easy to know what we should do from hindsight. If I knew a year ago what I know now, I would have put all I have into Blackmores at $30 and held on until it reached $130. I would have laughed all the way to the bank. What should I do to benefit fully from my stock investment? I have a new resolution! I will put in daily practices in the form of meditation that can help me to remove these negative charges and outdated mind-sets from my investment system and replace them with more logical thinking including patience. I will start implementing the new system regularly until I achieve autopilot status. I will welcome calmness and the limitless power of my new consciousness to control my decisions. I will allow this consciousness and awareness to accelerate and become my guiding force in my investment mission.

We are caught in what we see in terms of the price of a stock. But in actual fact, we need to consider the quality and potential of the underlying business like Blackmores in USA and TPM in Australia. In this context, what reasonable price for Blackmores or TPM should we pay? If each of these companies is able to grow above its average rate, the current price is still cheap. If earning does not grow or in fact is dropping, than each of these companies is ridiculously overpriced. We need to consider what factors are driving sales and can they continue. What are the risks the company faces? Is there a margin for safety for the price now? We never know the answers to such questions with certainty. It may be time consuming and difficult. Unless we have a reasonable idea of the company's performance, we have nothing other than the madness of price fluctuation. Following the guidelines of the golden rules can bring some certainty and confidence in our investments. If the price of company like Blackmores or TPM is still sensible, the market is volatile, I will be patient waiting for the right price to buy in. I think there are many other stocks exhibiting these types of characteristics. And the best driver of share price growth is solid business performance. Buy into a company at a reasonable price when it shows sign of growth. Opportunity for buying good stocks comes once in a while. We have to be vigilant and keep looking out for them. A market decline is always a great time to look out for companies that held up. They are usually tried and true businesses. They are considered the strongest of the strong and are usually well-managed companies. They have the ability to weather the market storms. What do these companies normally do? They do not do anything fancy or speculative. They provide basic services and consumption businesses. You can be sure that when the market recovers, these companies will be the front runners or will explosively take off. We have to do our due diligence and search for them in order to be successful and become rich. I waited until the market settled and started picking stocks in this category. I have benefited from this type of situation and I am optimistic that this approach will always work even during downturn. Other types of companies to look out are start-up companies in media, biotech, finance, and technology companies. These are the venture enterprising companies that can take off explosively. Great investor like James Altucher makes full use of this type of investment to make his fortune. He claims that his network is his most valuable asset. He tapes on his vast network of friends for information. I follow his style of investment and I increase my wealth regularly. This power of thought based on concrete ideas can make any one rich. Research into it and believe in it. Anyone can be rich.

I used to fall in love with some of my investments. They are like my friends and I used to stick with them for a long period. Now I know it is a silly thing to do. I need a rational strategy as a basis of my financial decision making. I am determined to avoid holding on to falling stocks and selling rising stocks. Observing market momentum reveals that falling stocks continue to fall and vice versa. It dawns on me that I should do the opposite of what I had been doing. This disposition effect is a regular behaviour of most investors. I have to set my goal instead of making decisions based on the value of the individual losses and gains. I also need to avoid the endowment effect which describes how people will assign more value to things purely because they own them. I used to think that the stocks I hold are more valuable than those I do not have. I am wrong. I must be suffering from the familiarity effect where I value stocks simply because I own them or they are household names. In Australia, we have companies like Westfarmers, Telstra, TPM and Commonwealth bank. Investors are biased towards companies in their own countries or states. In many parts of the world, people have been observed to buy companies from their own states or country. Many concentrate on familiar blue stocks that are perpetuated by coverage they receive. Their news and their performances are usually highlighted. They are familiar with banks and telco companies which they use every day. They know the companies and think that they understand them. The buy-and hold strategy has worked. There is also a sense that if you do not hold these stocks, you are missing out.

All these beliefs regarding stocks are in our subconscious mind. Not all beliefs are bad. Some of the beliefs help us to make profit. Only those beliefs which cause us to lose money should be erased and replaced by better ones. So we need certain amount of discrimination separating the good ones from the bad ones. If nothing has been done, you are most likely to repeat some of the bad beliefs without even knowing what you are doing. First you need to erase those beliefs identified as bad because they hinder you from proceeding and progressing. These limiting beliefs may be stifling away your potential of making money. Erasing these beliefs is like dissolving them from telling you not to try new ideas and implementing new habits. The clearer you are regarding these limiting beliefs, the faster you get results in your investment life. It's all about replacing these negative beliefs with positive ones. Make a commitment to change beliefs repeatedly until you are filled with positive ones. The difference between investors who struggle and those who achieve seemingly impossible feats lies in the changes of outdated beliefs in their subconscious mind. For example when an investor drops and dissolves the belief of buying a stock and holds for life even when the company is not growing, there is nothing standing in the way for him to maximise his profit. A change in attitude makes all the difference. There is nothing to hold him back from achieving good profit in his investment. Now I am going to share with you an important process of replacing these outdated beliefs with a new set of strategies so that you can benefit from your stock investments. A set of new beliefs as part of the consciousness engineering is going to be planted into your mind. I will suggest that you learn meditation or mindfulness and use the power of your infinite mind to visualise these new beliefs so that they become your new realities in stock investments. These set of golden rules in stock investment are simple to use and if use effectively with discipline, you can easily increase your profit many times. You have to use these golden rules consistently, patiently, and with great discipline. Soon these strategies in investing will be your realities.

Investment Golden Rules

There is no such thing as a perfect system of investing in stocks. Most successful investors like Warren Buffett, Peter Lynch, Jim Rogers, James Altucher, Bill Spetrino and others have their own system of investing. Each one of them has trust and confidence in his own system developed through the process. They do not jump from one strategy to another. They follow their own system. Each one of them has discovered a system that works for them and they keep repeating it over and over again. They adhere to their own rules and guidelines. I do my own research through reading and through my own experiences as an investor. I look for guidelines and come out with the following golden rules to maximise my profits. I want plenty of money to live the life I want and be able to bless others.

First, I expect to lose when I buy any stock but I define the limit I am willing to lose. I have decided to adopt a trailing stop strategy to cut loss if a stock I pick falls about 20 per cent. I will immediately instruct my broker selling the stock. I have strictly adhered to this trailing strategy. There is no ifs and buts business. This strategy will ensure that a big loss is avoided and a big gain is preserved.

What does 20 per cent trailing stop mean? Take for example, if I pick a stock at $10.00 and if the stock's price rises to $40, my trailing stop will now move to $32.00, 20 per cent below the peak price or slightly less. By following this strategy, I still keep a big profit. To make this strategy effective, I must not hold too many stocks in my portfolio. On the other hand, if the stock falls from $10.00 to $8.00, I will sell immediately to avoid a big loss. This trailing stop strategy has become my first golden rule. I have just adopted a computer program to help execute the trailing stop strategy.

Second, if I pick the right stock that keeps on rising, I will let the winner run until it reaches its peak and starts to fall. I will keep the big picture of the trend, allowing minor corrections along the way. A trend is a good friend. Once a trend is identified, I will be patient to allow it to progress until it wears itself out. What is a trend? It's simply a series of price movements in one general direction. Some trends go up and some go down. When a stock is in a big, multiyear uptrend, I should keep my investment on the 'long side' the bullish side. Any big correction occurs; a trailing stop strategy of 20 per cent applies. This predetermined price at which I will exit a stock holding helps to stop literally from a good profit. The beauty of this strategy is that it allows me to stay long during an uptrend. The strategy allows minor corrections all along the uptrend. I have a few good experiences using this strategy to benefit a few thousands percent profits. In any recession, when the downtrend starts, this strategy allows me to keep a big slice of the profit without sacrificing much. This teaches me a great lesson about patience to allow a rising stock to flow without being too eager to take profit. During my initial stage of investing, I looked too closely at taking profit, resulting in selling all the good flower stocks. I kept most of my losing stocks too long resulting in big losses without knowing the philosophy of risk management. I was an amateur then. An amateur looks at immediate profit first while a professional looks at risk.

Third, I learn to ignore the exciting stories created by analysts, traders, brokers, friends and the general public. This consciousness has been planted into my unconscious brain. I will not construct an investment portfolio out of public opinion.

Information from these people is not solid. They are just combinations of theory, interpretation, guesswork, spin, hunch, and imaginary fears. It's more important to understand the business you are investing. I will not invest in business that I do not understand. I will look into the numbers in the business quarterly report. The following metrics like revenue, profit, dividend, cash flow and potential growth are important. I will establish my own rating system by assigning numbers 1 to 5 to each metric. The stock with the highest score in each sector is my top priority. Such a system will eliminate guesswork and emotion out of the investment equation.

Fourth, I will follow a simple strategy to pick my stocks. I follow Mr Graham's simple strategy to minimise risk by picking stocks with PE below ten and a debt-to-equity ratio below fifty. I do not strictly adhere to the single metric called PE. I also look at the growth potential of the business. For long-term investment, I look for companies with potential revenue growth, cash flow, profit, dividend, and management. Once I have identified a company, I will be patient for the right time to buy the stock. Simple is better than smart in investing. Being cautious and not overestimating the limits of my knowledge become my investment practice. Reminding myself about many things which I do not know is important. Knowing what I do not know is much more useful in stock investment than being brilliant. Past failures and experiences in investments teach me a great lesson. Now I know if I want to be a successful investor, I need a combination of gumption and patience and get ready to pounce when opportunity presents itself. It is waiting that helps me as an investor. Most people just can't wait for the right time. When is the right time? If you look at the successful investors and the time they pour in their money to buy cheap value stocks, it is the right time. Most of us will join the herd when the market is at the peak. We do not want to miss the action. We have exhausted all our funds chasing after many of the overvalued stocks. When a big correction comes, opportunity for making money presents itself. Unfortunately, these impatient investors like us are now on the side-line. If you suffer from this lack of deferred-gratification gene, you need to work extra hard to start downloading this valuable metric called patience of waiting for the right time to buy into your subconscious mind. Start implementing such patience repeatedly until it becomes your style of investment. Until and unless you do that consistently, you never become rich through investment.

Patience holds the key to investment success. Most investors know what companies they want to invest in. To be successful in investing, they know that they will make plenty of money if they can develop the ability to wait until they get the rarest opportunities to buy the businesses at the right price. The waiting is long and they need to have the patience. In his younger days, Warren Buffett wanted to buy the business GEICO, an insurance company where his mentor made a fortune. He waited and waited for almost thirty four years until he got the right opportunity to buy the company at a very cheap price. After one or two decades, he made 400 times the amount he invested. This is an excellent example of one of the great wonders of patience.

Fifth, it's never a good way to buy a stock based on its price. It's never a good way but a lousy approach. A smarter, safer and frankly more profitable way to evaluate a stock is based on its business. I will start to look for a good deal and the right time to buy the stock. Is the price overvalued, undervalued or just at an ideal one? Knowledge of the true value of a stock is important. I will make sure that I do not overpay for a stock. How do you know if the value of the company is worth more than the currently reflected in the stock price? The real value of the stock price should be based on its business, its balance sheet, its revenue, its earning and the factors responsible for its growth. The current and future PE ratios are determined factors of its growth and its worth. Finally, I will decide the highest price I am willing to pay for the stock and still receive my 6 to 8 per cent annual return. I do not require complicated technical analysis to help me picking a stock because it is based on logic and number rather than historical prices and momentum. I will avoid stocks priced cheaply by historical measures. It is worthless if there is no way to assess its true value.

Sixth, a good time to pick a stock is when inside trading is carried out legally. During open period, directors and executive staff are allowed to buy their own stock. The first clear indicator is when the company lawyers, who are usually non investors start buying the company's shares. They must have seen something great about the company's performance. This is enough strong signals for us to follow. Another strong indicator is that when a cluster of senior executives buying the stock at the same time. Something good is happening to the company. The difficulty of this approach is usually not easy to detect this type of scenario. It's worth keep looking, the right button is always there and fortune may smile at you.

Last but not least, there is another strategy to pick stocks when certain commodity price begins to drop. Take for example in 2014 to 2016, the price of oil drops drastically, there are companies like airlines and shipping transportation companies prospering because of the cheap fuel they enjoy. Oil price slump drives surge in tanker rates. Crude oil price peaked at June

2014 ($110 per barrel) and dropped drastically to $30 per barrel in January 2016. The rates of tankers are surging from its low of $35 per day in June 2014 to its height $110 per day in January 2016.

The most destructive oil crash during this period 2014 to early 2016 will create great prosperity for ship owners and airline stocks. The world's largest ship broker noted that while oil fell 35 per cent in 2015, the average earning of ship carriers jumped $67 366 per day, the most since 2009. So for 2016, you should be looking for companies benefiting from the bearish oil price to invest. Since the cost of fuel is a big part of expenditures, companies involving tankers and airplanes will prosper in a period where the price of oil is suppressed by glut. The awareness of the economic implication is important for investors. Similarly oil-producing and servicing companies will benefit from booming oil price. There are always companies moving inversely proportional to any particular commodity prices. In 2016, we expect the price of oil and gas to stay low and flat. I do not know what others will think. For me 2016 will be a good year to invest in profitable companies involving transportation using airplanes, ships and motor vehicles. The cost of fuel consumption will give these sectors great profit. Profitable companies with logistics and transportation as their source of income will be my choice for investment.

One other factor related to oil rout is that it will drive fuel prices further down, boosting tanker and airline profits. As investors, we need to be aware that the very thing which is negative for oil markets is positive for tanker and airline markets. It is also positive for many types of transportation companies depending on oil and gas fuels. In 2016, you will see a supply-driven boost to the transportation markets which come at the cost of the oil market. In 2016, I am ready to pick profitable companies related to transportation: tankers, airlines, and logistics companies. In 2016, many of the airline stocks in Europe, Australia, USA, and Asia will definitely take off enjoying cheap fuel cost. If Harry Dent is right in his prediction that oil price will be low for a long period; then these stocks will enjoy low fuel cost and make good profit.

On the other hands if OPEC and Russia agree to cut supply, the price of oil will not stay low for long. You need to be alert of any new development coming up. Do not depend only from one source of information. The oil price bottoms in January 2016 and then recovers to about $50 per barrel in

June and July. The price will range from $46 per barrel to $50 per barrel during the last few months of 2016.

A Glimpse of Light for Mining Stocks

The world mining index shows that metal prices have been falling from 2011 until now 2016. In the last thirty five to forty years, there are three occasions where the mining index dropped drastically through eighteen months. They happened in September 1974, June 1982 and January 2009 and the falls were 58, 59 and 62 per cent respectively. Within eighteen months in these three occasions, mining stocks crashed drastically and then they rebounded. Investors who bought into value mining stocks after each of the drastic dips made an average profit of 102 per cent in a short period of two years. In the last eighteen months beginning June 2014, mining stocks are down 64 per cent. Will history of rebound repeat in 2016 or 2018? Your guess is as good as mine. I am waiting patiently for the metal prices to pick up. There are many value mining companies in Australia like Rio Tinto, BHP Billiton, Santos and others. The prices of these value stocks are extremely low now. The prices are expected to be falling slightly and 'sand papering' for a certain period of time. The waiting can run into months or years. These resource companies are under my investment radar. Since China is the biggest trading partner for Australia, and China is experiencing a downturn now, the waiting can be long. Any uptrend starts for metal prices, I am ready to scoop up some of these value stocks into my investment portfolio. If you want to be rich, you should take advantage of the situation. Get ready to invest in resource companies as soon as the sector shows sign of recovery.

The General Market Situation from 2016 Onwards

If we examine the general USA stock market represented by the S&P 500, Large Cap Index, the 2015 performance reveals by its index that it may represent the top of the bull market since 2009. It represents the first down year since 2009 March bottom. What do you notice in the chart of S&P 500 Cap Index? A big drop of its index in August 2015 is a bad sign.

The index rebounded in October 2015 but it did not reach the height of July 2015. In December 2015, the index started to fall again and continued until February 2016 before the index rebounded and kept moving up.

The glaring point to note is the August 2015 sell off. Throughout the year the market struggled. This clearly indicates the worst is yet to come. Early 2016, the decline continued before the market recovered. Many believe that the American economy is back in recession in spite of the official data. There is no more money easily available after the Fed stopped QE. The bond markets, the Credit markets, the ISM manufacturing index are all pricing in recession. Even the US inventories hit levels are associated with recession.

The year 2016 will not be good for stocks worldwide especially China. We have seen the Dow Industrial Index fell almost 1000 points from its height in the first five days of its 2016 trading. A fall of 6 per cent and most likely the fall may continue. A sudden rebound took place after June 2016 and the market started to recover.

Another glaring factor is the corporate profits relative to GDP. It is at their record high in 2015 and rolling over. As most of us know, corporate growth depends on three factors: economic growth, financial engineering (including buy-back) and increased productivity. With the US backs in recession and the end of QE, the first two factors are removed. And while the growth initially in the first half was marginal, there was no growth in the second half of 2015. All these factors indicate that growth is practically nil for the coming year 2016. My guess is that a big correction in the stock market is on the way. It is not a question of if but when! It may not happen in 2016 but later. I have already sold most of my stocks and keep my cash. Not all sectors will be affected by the slowdown. I will only keep stocks on tankers, airplanes, internet companies, plastic package companies and biotech companies. For any sector, we use to project the trend to be a straight line but actually it is cyclical. The fundamentals, profit and dividend of a company are still the deciding factors for me to buy a stock. Buying a value stock at the right price will be advantage in terms of profit. Patience is the key. Learn to be defensive and you can invest another day. When a big dip occurs in 2016, it's time to pick up value stocks for the future.

Beginning 2016, the broad Stock Market in USA was already in a bear market mood. Be aware that the S&P 500 index is heavily skewed by giant stocks like Amazon and Goggle. Take note that Amazon is traded at PE 870 and in 2015, it went up 120 per cent. I think this stock is overvalued. In 2016, it's time to sell the stock including super stocks like Apple, Coca Cola, Facebook and others which are also overvalued in 2015. A big correction is on the way in 2016 onwards. During the first five days of trading in 2016, the Shanghai Composite Index fell 15 per cent; London is down 6 per cent and Paris is down 7 per cent.

The actual turmoil of Dow's Index for 2015 including the first few months of 2016 signals the beginning of bear market. The overall market is down starting August 2015. It recovers slightly and is down again in the first few months of 2016. In the first few months of 2016, Frankfurt is down 8.5 per cent and New York is down 6 per cent. All indications point to a big coming correction. The S&P 500 index shows that by February 2016, the Dow's is back to that of August 2015. The fall is expected to continue in 2016. But the market recovered after that. The year 2017 will be challenging for the US market. I am waiting patiently for big correction to happen and I will apply my CHU strategy to scoop up value stocks when the time is right. According to Harry Dent's prediction, the Dow index will drop to 6000 by the middle of 2017. I think such big drop is unlikely unless Third World War begins. Let's wait and see whether such a prediction comes true. Get your cash ready and buy when such phenomenon happens.

An Alternative View of the Market after 2016

From 1968 to 2015 the consumer index is related to the S&P 500 index. There is a strong correlation between sentiments and stock market peaks at 1968 and 2000. During recessionary times like the years 1974, 1980, 1982, 1991 and 2009, the consumer indices were all very low. During these times the stock markets were also experiencing their lows. The present consumption confidence index in 2016 is about 100 which is considered reasonably high. My interpretation is that the stock market should hold on temporary until such confidence is affected.

What is the implication of consumer confidence index on the stock market? You will notice that when both consumer sentiment peaks during the years 1968 and 2000, stock market also peaks about the same time. Consumer sentiments bottomed about five times in 1974, 1980, 1982, 1991 and 2009. During these times the market was at their very lows. They all coincided with recessions. These historical incidents clearly show that sentiments are important. Consumer sentiments bottomed during recessions and peaks during the tops of bull markets. According to Dr Sjuggerud, we are neither at recession nor stock market peak. So the stock market still has space to move higher. The February 2016 dip had rebound. By July 2016, the S&P 500 index and Dow's Index recovered, indicating that the stock market in USA still has space to move upwards. We will wait and see how the market will play out in the last quarter of 2016 and 2017. This interpretation appears to be opposite to what Harry Dent predicted. Who is right? We will wait and see.

In 2016, most of the world markets are already in bear territory that is the markets have fallen of more than 20 per cent from the peak. In early 2016, the roll call of world markets in bear territory is as follow: Japan (- 23.2%), England (- 21%), France (- 24.3%), Germany (- 28.3%), China (- 46.7%), Hongkong (- 32.5%), and Australia (- 21%).

The USA market seems to be healthier and the S&P 500 is down 13.2 per cent from the peak. The fall was just beginning in 2016. Actually the American stock indices are already in bear territory: Dow Jones Transportation (- 24.1%), Russel 200 (- 25.6%) and KWB Nasdaq Bank Index (- 26.1%). All these indications show that from now onwards, the markets will not be good for sometimes. Management of portfolio and cash management will be the keys to benefit from the rebound. Hedging into precious metals like silver and platinum will be preferred to gold. But gold is still the preferred metal for country like China to hedge against stocks big decline. For small investors like us, we may think of the logic of hedging using platinum and silver. These two metals are cheaper relative to gold and their demands are picking up. In the near future, these two metals may be more profitable than hedging using gold. Many value stocks will be on sale soon if you have the cash ready to benefit in the future. Investors with vision will be the future beneficiaries. With Brexit happening in 2016, these precious metals will certainly be activated. This period of uncertainties do not help the stock market. And with interest rate almost at negative territories in most countries, the sentiment will be affected. The investment in gold, silver and platinum appears to be the alternatives.

Alternative Investments during Uncertainties of Stocks After 2016

Whenever stocks are making investors nervous like what we experience at the beginning of 2016, metals like gold, silver and platinum have tended to hold their values well. The S&P 500 index stocks have slumped more than 10 per cent in January this year and rebounded in February, gold is shining bright at 20 per cent up in the first three months of 2016. Most of the companies are trimming or suspending their dividends especially oil companies.

Dividends cut in 2015 surpassed that of 2008. All these happenings are forcing many investors to turn to precious metals like gold, silver and platinum. Beginning 2015 and 2016, the global demand for gold is scorching hot. In China alone, physical delivery of gold in 2015 from the Shanghai Gold Exchange reached a record of 2596 tonnes, representing more than 90 per cent of the total global output of gold for the year. China central bank is also buying gold adding 16.44 tonnes to its reserves in January 2016, in its attempt to support its currency, the renminbi.

In 2015 and the beginning of 2016, sales of gold coins in USA and Europe are picking up. Sales of American eagle gold-bullion coins reached 124000 ounces in January 2016, up 53 per cent from a year ago. Last year 2015, prominent investors in Europe bought 1.65 million coins, four times more than that was bought during the 2008 financial crisis. I will follow the money and I will bet on precious metals during this period of uncertainties.

Another worry regarding interest rate is emerging. In some countries like Japan, Sweden, Switzerland and Demark, interest rates have dropped below zero into negative territory. Will USA follow the trend? The possibility is always there as the economy begins to create havoc in the country. In a world where we are charged interest to put our cash in government bonds, holding gold and other precious metals as a store of value suddenly becomes more attractive. As investors, we need to be aware that in the past, the metal share has an inverse proportional relationship with real interest rates. From March 2009 to October 2015, this inverse relationship is clearly exhibited. As investors, this awareness is critical for shifting investments from stocks or bonds to precious metal especially gold.

Will the negative nominal rates spread to USA and other countries? It seems like a far-fetched idea but such monetary policy is always possible as happening in the countries mentioned. As prudent investors, it may be wise to follow the money and invest part of your cash in precious metals to hedge against economic crises. The uncertainties of stocks from 2016 onwards can be devastating and if we just sit and wait for its recovery, we may have lost our shirt.

Understand the Subconscious Mind

A little secret I discovered some time ago reveals the role of the subconscious mind regarding critical things not only in investment but also in the games I enjoy. The amazing discovery of the thing that stands between me and my abundant life is the insidious abundance blocks lodged in my subconscious mind. Clearing these blocks becomes possible using the simple tools called meditation and visualisation. Replacing these mental blocks in the subconscious mind with the practices and habits of great investors is a choice. When I started to use these new strategies and practices regularly, and consistently, my investment result improves. Eventually, I enjoy success. I applied the same analogous approaches to my games. At first I did it for my basketball game and later golf. I enjoy playing golf and I play quite well. After years of experiences and through the process, I have downloaded a few critical habits into my subconscious mind. I keep practising them and they become automated as my playing style. These few critical habits are simple. First I train myself not to swing too hard. Second I keep my eyes on the ball. Third I keep my head still while I swing. Fourth I do not take big risk. I keep these few critical things in mind and I discipline myself to follow them whenever I play. I eventually become a good golfer. The practices of my stock investment are analogous to the critical habits of playing golf. I have a few golden rules and I have downloaded these rules into my subconscious mind and I keep practising them until they become my style of investment. I am not bogged down by the market noises and people's advices and I know most of them are not useful. I usually rely on my strategies and follow my golden rules. With this discipline, I always come out ahead. The pursuit of profit by following the golden rules is analogous to following the critical things of my golf swing to play well in the game.

During my initial stage of stock investment, I made big mistakes by selling my winners too soon and kept my losers too long. I am wondering why many of the investors are making the same mistake I made again and again. Is there anything to do with our conscious mind or subconscious mind? Logically we should be motivated to prune the losers and let the winners run. But in the battle of these two contrary motivations; we let the irrational one influence us more. Is there a psychological reason why we do the irrational things? It's natural that we focus on our winners because winning generates the feel-good chemical dopamine deep in our brain. Paying attention on our winners makes us feel good, and so our winners become our darlings and our losers are usually neglected. We may not look at losers so as not to feel bad. The chemical dopamine provides us the sense of motivation and we are motivated to do things that tend to boost it. It is a powerful drug. Selling a winner creates a flow of dopamine and we feel good. This is addictive and we keep selling winners without letting them run. It becomes a habit. This is deeply planted in our subconscious mind and we keep enjoying the good feeling. But we miss the chance of making our fortune. Why we keep our losers without pruning them? Another factor in our subconscious mind we have no control. Maybe we keep our losers hoping that they may turn around. The hope that one day the losers can recover and generate another delayed feeling good experience. Perhaps the anticipation of a positive result generates more dopamine than the actual winning. It keeps us hopeful of a turnaround in our portfolio slackers. Another possible reason is that we enjoy the joy of denial because we do not want to face any loss. The focus on loss causes dopamine to plummet, making us feel bleak and hopeless. So we prefer to shift our attention away from our loss as long as possible. Many of us have learned that the consequence can be devastating. What should we do? A little bit of understanding of the function of our subconscious mind will help.

First, eliminate the outdated beliefs and feelings in our mind. A new space is now created in the mind. And it is time to download this trailing stop strategy into your subconscious mind and start practising it to cut loss as soon as possible. Learn not to get trapped by keeping your losers too long. Prune them as soon as possible and let your winners run to help you in full maximum benefit throughout your investments.

When you pick a winner, let it run. Remember the trailing stop strategy when any stock slips about 15 per cent from its peak. This will ensure you always enjoy your handsome profit from any good run. This approach, once it becomes your investment principle, will make you very rich in stock investments.

The Language of Stock

Every industry has its own language. The stock market is no difference. To understand investment in stocks, you need to understand many terms and its language. Here are some of the basic terms to understand. The revenue of a company is the amount of money the company receives. Its net profit is what the company gets after minus all the expenses. The earning per share (EPS) is the net profit divide by the number of shares of the company. What is price earning (PE) ratio? It is simply the ratio between current price of the stock divide by its annual earnings per share (EPS) for the past year. If the PE of a company exceeds the average of the sector, the price of the stock is considered high. A simple indication is that if the PE is low, it means the price is cheap and if its PE is high, it means the price is expensive. Remember that the factor PE is not the sole determinant for you to buy the stock. If the PE is low and the potential of such a company is not there, it is not advisable to buy and hold the stock. There is another concept known as the PE Gap which gives us a simple number to help our decision making. The PE Gap is the difference between a company forward price to earnings ratio and it's forward earning growth rate. When the gap is positive, that means the company is overvalued relative to its future earnings growth. The stock is now overvalued and if you buy now, you are overpaying for future growth. This tells us to avoid such buying. But if the gap is negative, that means the company is undervalued relative to its future growth. You will buy because you are getting the growth of the stock at a discount. Such a technical concept can be helpful to us as investors. Applying the PE Gap methodology to small caps can provide the highest probability of creating a positive return on most of our investments. With understanding and due diligence, this strategy can be developed further to create many winners.

Terms we need to understand like Enterprise Value (EV) and Free Cash Flow (FCF) can help us in decision making. Enterprise Value or EV is the amount of money it would cost to buy a company's outstanding shares and repay all its debts. Free Cash Flow (FCF) is the amount of money left after a company pays its bills and makes the necessary investments in infrastructure and equipment. The ratio when EV is divided by FCF gives a good indication of the strength of a company. A low EV ratio (below 20) gives a strong indication to buy the stock of the company. The strategy of using this ratio may turn out to be extremely profitable in the long haul when we buy a stock at the dip to the valuation level. The quality called patience is required for any investor to enjoy this strategy of investment. This is one of the most valuable qualities most of the successful investors have. They wait for the right time to buy a stock and hold it for a reasonable period to benefit from each of their investment. Let us take note of what Fulton J. Sheen said:

> Patience is power. Patience is not an absence of action; rather it is 'timing', it waits on the right time to act, for the right principles and the right way.

Another ratio is known as Cyclically Adjusted Price Earnings (CAPE). This ratio, a cousin of PE, is introduced by economic professor Robert Shiller from Yale University. It is simply the ratio between the price of the stock to its earnings ratio with one adjustment. Instead of one year's earning, it includes earnings from the past ten years. The advantage is that it smoothens out booms and recessions. It gives a useful long-term view of the stock or market. The average CAPE from 1881 to 2015 is 17. The ratios at Black Tuesday (1929), Black Monday (1989) and Peak Tech

Bubble (1999) were 24, 19, and 45, respectively. Each time disaster struck, the market corrected drastically. Now July 2015, the CAPE ratio of S&P 500 index is 27. What do you expect? This is an indication that the market is 48 per cent more expensive than the average. A drastic correction in the stock market is due now. A possible plunge of 34 per cent from the current price is possible! But CAPE is just a ratio and is not perfect. It's useful to spot a long term trend but it cannot time the market. A high CAPE gives us a warning that the USA market is high and we have to be cautious in investing in the market. The duration of the current bull-run has exceeded the average period of all bull runs. This is a strong indication that the prices of stocks in USA are overvalued. No one can tell when the next crisis will hit. It's imminent! We need to be careful now. The financial market isn't healthy in 2015 and 2016. The August 2015 dip is an indication. A big correction is due. Going into 2016, we need to be careful. There are different views regarding the stock market after 2016. Most of the views are not favourable. From the consumer sentiment index, there is still little room for the market to rise. But Harry Dent predicts that the Dow Industrial Index will slip to 6000. It's interesting to see how the market will go after 2016.

Understand another Term: The Trend

Many billionaires just buy and hold to follow the trend of a stock. Warren Buffett bought CocaCola and just let the big trend flows. Following trend has created more profit than all the other methods of investing in the stock market. Do you believe in this statement? If you download this belief into your subconscious mind and implement it consistently, you can join the group of rich investors. Mr Banny Backus claims that this strategy is one of the most successful strategies ever used in the financial market. Investors using this strategy have made more billions than any other single strategy in investing. Most successful investors make full use of this strategy to dominate their investing landscape. This is the super simple strategy for anyone to create wealth. Investopedia gives the following definition of trend:

"Trends followers try to find a great up-trending stock; buy it and ride it until the trend changes. After all, if a stock keeps going up, wouldn't it be great just to buy it and let it double, triple, do what it does? Because up-trending stocks go through stages of higher highs and higher lows, these traders should have loose stop and should not be worried about the outside factors such as heir stock being overextended, as long as the stock is still going up. Trend-following trading is reactive in nature. It does not forecast or predict market or price levels. Prediction is impossible. Trend trading demands self-discipline to follow precise rules (no guessing or wild emotions). It involves a risk management system that uses current market price, the equity level in the trader's account and current market volatility. Trend traders use an initial risk rule that determines position size at time of entry. This means they know exactly how much to buy or sell based on how much money they have. Changes in price may lead to a gradual reduction or increase of their initial trade. On the other hand, adverse price movement may lead to an exit of the entire trade. Historically a trend trader's average profit per trade is much significant higher than the loss per trade."

There is no such thing as a perfect system to enter into an uptrend for any stock. Some analysts suggest that for trend following, simply buy on new highs or new lows to enter the market. Another approach is to buy on pullbacks on shorter time frames within the overall long term uptrend. So price is the only thing that matters when a stock is on the long term uptrend. Fundamental is no longer important in an uptrend. Trend followers believe that all information is inherent in the price itself. It is the price that makes news, not the other way. The following steps may help in determining a long term uptrend.

First, we look at price chart of a stock for several years to determine whether it is on the uptrend or downtrend.

Second, once a long-term uptrend is spotted, we need to choose an entry point to start buying the stock. Traditional trend traders will buy when a new high is reached. I will wait for a pullback in a shorter time frame chart and buy the stock.

Third, we need to be patient for the trend to carry our position into profits. This is the most difficult part for most of us. It is a slow and grinding process. Self-discipline is in big demand.

Fourth, we need to have a clear picture when to exist the trade. I use a trailing stop strategy of 15 per cent from the peak of any new high. It is difficult to know that an actual change in trend is happening. We need to follow a very strict rule for exist if we want to lock in our profits. In fact, exist is more important than the exact time of entry in a long term uptrend for any stock. Trailing stops are designed for us to lock in our profits as we allow a long term uptrend to run its course. Remember every stock has its own cycle. Even stocks like Apple and Microsoft have their uptrends and eventually their downtrends. Trailing stops are sell orders which follow a predetermined price in a profitable direction. Modern technology allows us to set it via our trading platform. It is executed automatically after the trailing stops have been put in place.

When a stock embraces a long - term downtrend, every low is lower. When such a long - term downtrend is spotted, it is critical we take action immediately. Do not allow a small loss to become a big one. When a stock or currency is on the downtrend, we have to respect it. I have always adhered to my trailing stop of 15 or 20 per cent from the peak or buying price. This golden rule is critical from saving me a big loss. Market can always rise higher than you think and it can also fall lower than you can imagine. Experience tells me that I have to respect any trend and don't try to outsmart it. The period of downtrend can be an irrational one. The long period of time can make you insolvent. You have to be aware before you lose your shirt. When the price of a financial asset is on the downtrend, it can continue, losing you more money. Just be aware when you hold such a stock when it is on a downtrend, you could easily be crushed. A good example is the Chinese stock market. Harvest China A-shares Fund was at $26 during September 2014 and during June 2015; it was at $54. The stock was on an uptrend rising 145 per cent. From June 2015 to September 2015, the market is on the downtrend falling 44 per cent to $32. If I follow my trailing stop strategy, I would have gotten out once the market falls 15 per cent from its peak. I would have retained a big profit following the uptrend and do not suffer the devastating impact of the downtrend.

Let us look at oil. During June 2014, the price of oil was $110 and at September 2015, price was at $48. A downtrend is almost 58 per cent. If this is a long term downtrend, the period may last a year or two. We have to give due respect.

Even currency, when on a downtrend, we have to give due respect. The Australian dollars during September 2014 was worth USA $0.94 and at September 2015, it was at $0.70. It falls almost 26 per cent. Is the Australian dollar cheap now? It may stay there a certain period. A little bit of patience is needed here. As soon as the commodities prices start to pick up, it's a good time to favour the Australian dollar.

The Emotional Stock Market

In sports, we tend to be emotional when we support a particular team or a particular player. In games like basketball or tennis, any outstanding player like Michael Jordan or Roger Federer is worth millions of dollars. If you look at their track records, they are worth their salts. They deserve their billings because they are great players in their fields. I always gave my support to these two players whenever they played and I became emotional for their victories. I supported and always wanted them to win the game.

In investments too, we are emotional with our stocks. We all expect that when all the information of a stock is made public, the stock price will trade in line with the company's value. It does not work this way. The stock market is also highly emotional. In the short term traders and investors are just like us; they become enamoured with celebrities and the stocks they support without looking at the track records. This creates volatility, pushing some stocks down in spite of good records or otherwise. Being aware of this disconnect will provide investors like us to make some good profit. The trick is being able to pick the Michael Jordan or Roger Federer of the market, stocks that have a strong and consistent track record. Those stocks have an edge to continue to propel them higher. I will look at stocks as if they are sportsmen. Looking at their past performance and their current ranking in the sector are my first task. The question I need to answer is that whether there is another company that can unseat it as top dog in its business. The brand product is important. Human habits are difficult to change. Brand is important because the human brain works by using patterns and recognitions. These patterns or recognitions help us in making our everyday decisions. That's brand value and a company has the brand value, it's harder for a competitor to steal market share from the business. For example, Altria (MO) spun off its Kraft division many years ago, and Kraft was a brand leader in a certain segment of the food market. It establishes a brand for a long-term advantage. Companies like Apple (AAPL), Qualcomm (QCOM), eBay (EBAY), Microsoft, and IBM all have an advantage in the market to be a leader over the long term. We have to look for short term and long-term advantage of a company. For example, IBM had a huge advantage in the mainframe business, but that advantage was wiped out when new technology replaced that business. Similarly Blockbuster was wiped out by on-demand video streaming. Why is IBM still a market leader whereas Blockbuster sank? IBM survives and prospers because it innovates and it evolves with the technology. IBM makes employee timekeeping machines, automatic meat slicers, and coffee grinders. It has a wide customer base business: 490 out of Fortune 500 companies as its customers. Blockbuster did not recognise the technological changes while Netflix recognises the coming changes by switching from DVD delivery to online streaming. So it's important that if you invest in a technological company, you need to look at the short term advantage as well as the long term whether such a company can pivot and innovate whenever technological changes take place. If you cannot answer these types of questions, it is best that you do not take action to buy such a stock. The business advantage of Netflix has pushed its price to a new height. Whenever you recognise such an advantage in any stock, it's always a good to buy when the price is right. Why? Because the stock market is emotional in the short term; over the long term, value wins. Understanding this little bit extra will help to make you a better and more successful investor. This will give you the confidence whenever a value stock is dropping. Once you recognise a company which has a leading position in the market that cannot be stolen, you will want the stock price to drop and buy it cheaper to benefit in the long term.

Don't Follow the Language of the Herd

Most of us are living in a level focusing on two worlds: physical and cognitive. The physical things we see and touch are the absolute truth. We give each thing a name and everybody agrees on it. The cognitive world is full of ideas: culture, religions, and social practices. All of these are manmade. All these cognitive variables are constructed with the development of languages. Our modem world is built on such ideas. We are in the process of a cognitive revolution. The words of the language of the herd we use frequently such as career, passion, meditation, entrepreneur and others are just cognitive constructs in our mind. Most of us see things like culture, religion, and other social practices as real. We are suffering from the indoctrination of these constructs. Many of them have passed their expiration dates. Many of these cognitive concepts that bind us to our existing life are based on nothing more than an absolute model of reality. These bullshit rules like hard work equals success; fats are bad and carbs are good; cholesterol causes heart disease; we need a college degree to succeed in life; and many others. Many of us are not aware of them. We forget to reason. We do not think well. We tend to follow the herd. We imitate for convenience. We have the herd mentality.

Even in stock investment, we are hardwired to follow the herd. A part of our brain called amygdala drives this response. It consists of two tiny structures deep in the brain that connect emotions and fear. In common language, it is known as 'fight or flight' system. When individuals do not follow the crowd, the amygdala starts firing. They become frightened and nervous. This instinct was useful in prehistoric days when there was safety in numbers when trying to avoid predators. This instinct works against many investors causing them to buy at the top when everyone is buying and sell at the bottom when the herd abandons their stocks. An important lesson to learn and profit from this situation is to sell when everyone wants to buy and buy when everyone wants to sell. When the market experiences big correction like in 2008, it is time to add shares of your value stocks. Many investors who had done that enjoy great profit.

All the fears and herd mentality are with us. All these are inherited and passed to us without using our rational choice. Many absolute ideas are passed on from generation to generation. We never question their validity and reliability. If you cannot think well and avoid the herd mentality, you are going to continue losing money in the market. Most of us are living at this cognitive level. We never live to our full potential mentally, spiritually and physically.

As we evolve further, we will begin to move up to another level mentally. We will begin to question the world around us. We begin to wonder if there is more things to life than just believe what have been handed down. Why do we need a degree? Why do we believe in a certain god? We become more conscious and we are beginning to ask questions about everything. We are on the path to learn, to grow and expand our abilities in every aspect of our life. We want to live an extraordinary life focusing on things that make sense to us. We avoid things that do not make sense. We begin to question things like love, relationship, abundance and others so that we can develop our own rules that can empower us and help us to reach our full potential in all aspects of life. In investment especially stocks, we need our own golden rules and strategies instead of following the herd.

An Analogy of Herd Mentality

One day a farmer visited his daughter's school. She is attending Year Three. The farmer was standing beside his daughter. The school mathematics teacher asked the class a mathematics question.

> If you have two dozen of sheep in an area surrounded by a fence, and two of them jumped over the fence, how many sheep were left in the area at the end of the day?

The farmer told the daughter that there is none left at the end of the day. She shouted the answer 'none left' to the teacher. Well, said the teacher:

"You sure do not know your subtraction!" The farmer answered for the daughter. "May be not. But I am sure of my sheep."

Based on the story of the sheep, we can derive the same analogy of the share market. Like sheep, most investors like us inherently follow the crowd. It's the popular herd mentality most of us are wired to behave in the market. We tend to watch what others are doing and react accordingly. We always think that others in the market might know something that we do not know. We need to understand that this reaction is not logical if we have done enough research and due diligence on a certain stock. If we bought a stock and are happy with its performance, we are in fact in a better position to assess the situation than many others. Also the controlling body of stocks require all companies listed to disclose material information to the market so that investors can access the information at the same time. In spite of the situation, most of us seem happy to buy when others are doing so even the stock price is overvalued. Any imaginary bad news seems to spread like wild fire. People panic to sell and everyone follows. We behave like the sheep in the herd. When two sheep jumped across the fence, all the others would just follow. Most investors behave like these sheep. When they see others selling in panic, they just follow. They follow and share their imaginary fear. This mass exit sometimes causes certain good stocks to plunge in price. This awareness is important if we want to benefit from this type of mass exit. Picking up good stocks at bargaining price can make us rich.

A Bigger Picture of Investing in Stocks

We seem to forget that when we buy a stock, we become an owner of the business. They actually represent a tiny portion of the business we thought was a good purchase when we hit the 'buy' button. But, by and large, it appears that most investors are responding to the general market optimism or pessimism of the day, without keeping the bigger picture of their investment in mind. This explains that most of us are not doing better than the general market situation. If we can replace this outdated belief in our mind with up-to-date information and develop the contrarian mindset, this volatility can be exploited to our benefit. The best time to buy share is when the price of a value stock drops drastically, bottom up and in the process of recovering. This reminds me to use the CHU strategy to benefit from a stock. Using this strategy correctly can make you very rich. Just a recollection of language: C stands for cheap; H stands for hated and U represents uptrend. Buy when a stock begins its uptrend after falling from the cliff and moving side way for a period.

Knowing where we are in the grand cycle of stocks is crucial. If we know that we are at the bottom, that's where the best deals are. Albert Einstein gave us the equation $E = mc^2$ connecting mass and energy. His genius gave us the source of the sun's power, explaining radioactivity, making space travel possible, explaining time itself and leading to the big bang theory. It links three distinct parts of nature: energy, mass and speed of light into one universal law. Another genius by the name of Philip J. Anderson came up with an equation $18 = 14 + 4$ known as the Grand Market Cycle. The Grand Equation originated from the understanding of historical cycles of land in America. The 18 in the equation refers to American land prices that move in an 18 year cycle. Just like Einstein's equation, this Grand Equation is applicable to economic crashes, stock market high and low, and commodity cycles. Anderson is able to place the American land data back 200 years since 1784 and he discovers an 18year cycle of land prices. The cycle keeps repeating itself every 18 years. The estate peaks around 1818, 1836, 1854, 1869, 1888, 1908 and so on. Average out the distance between every peak in American land sales since 1800 and 1910 is about 18 years. Each peak is followed by four years of decline or recession and so on. This thinking is different from the mainstream thinking that recession is caused by bubble. Here, recessions are linked to land cycles. Anderson discovers that stocks and commodities are related to land prices. Bank credit blows up and deflates in synch with land prices. He was able to use this Grand Equation to predict housing prices and also stock prices rising for fourteen years followed by four years of downturns. The real estates and also the stock markets follow the $14 + 4$ pattern with slight adjustments in different countries. The stock markets always recover first and the property market follows. The new cycle begins anew fourteen years up and four years down. If you believe this Grand Equation, the last recession was 2008 2009 for stock market in USA, the next bubble will only burst in 2023 or 2024 that is about fourteen years later. American recession will only begin in 2024 to 2027. The stock market in America still has a few more years to go. This is contrary to Harry Dent's prediction. This extra information serves as food for thought.

Can we apply this strategy to buy value stocks related to oil and energy in 2018? Only Warren Buffett is wired differently from others. He has started to increase his investment in oil - related stocks in late 2015 onwards. Everyone is selling their oil - related stocks because of glut and over supply; oil prices have fallen terribly, but our greatest investor is picking value stocks related to energy. I am getting ready to increase my share in oil related stocks later. Any sign of oil price recovery, I will start scooping up value oil stocks. The waiting period may be months or years. Patience is always the key to investment success.

Invest in Tiny Growth Stocks

Many investors in USA try to build wealth mimicking Warren Buffett's every move. Most of them do not know that Buffett did not start out buying the stocks he likes such as Coca Cola, IBM, American-Express and others. On the contrary, Buffett started on his road to become wealthy buying stocks from certain segments of the market people never heard off. He thinks differently from the herd. Now he is too rich to be involved in these tiny growth stocks which he used to kick start his wealth. This type of value roadrunner stocks had made him millions. They enable him to start investing in his favourite stocks like Coca Cola, IBM and others. These types of tiny value stocks that made him his first fortune cannot absorb his big capital anymore. Buffett portfolio is too big for him to buy these kinds of tiny value stocks that made him rich initially. But for ordinary investors like us, we can still make good money to secure financial freedom for our retirement. Learn to use strategies such as CHU or others to take advantage of the market fluctuations and economic cycles. Understand the economic cycles of each sector and be patient to benefit from these cycles. Perhaps the Grand Equation can offer valuable information where your station is before you invest in stocks or properties.

Are you at the end of the grand cycle or just the beginning? Avoid investing during the peak of any of the cycle. Information is power and knowledge used appropriately can make you rich.

There are still many tiny value roadrunner stocks out there and if you can identify them during any big dips, you can still make tons of money. The initial strategies Warren Buffett used can bring wealth and financial freedom for anyone who has the patience and aptitude to locate these stocks. Tiny value companies with potential have great prospect. These small companies are usually run by their founders who are hungry for success. They are usually innovative and make use of modern technologies. They are the future blue chips. So keep looking and develop your own strategies to spot them. Where do we look?

First, look for companies that reside in high growth industries and have the potential for disruption.

Second, look for companies which have something meaningful to offer.

Third, look for companies with strong balance sheets, plenty of cash, ideally no debt.

Fourth, look for companies with good competitive edge over their peers.

Fifth, look for innovative companies which have technological advantage for future growth like manufacturing cars using metallic oil or electrical cars. Companies producing or marketing metallic oil or lithium can be good investments.

History over the last ten years gives us a good glimpse of many of these stocks like Priceline.com (up 6060%), Astronic Corporation (up 2070%) and Intuitive Surgical (up 2280%). There are many other small roadrunner stocks enjoying dramatic run in their profits over the last decade. These are the small caps which investors like Peter Lynch, Warren Buffett, George Soros, and others exploited to kick start their wealth. Just look at the gains in just ten years of the following stocks in USA.

	Company	Ten year to total returns
1.	Monster Beverage (Nasdaq: MNST)	10530%
2.	Questcor Pharma (Nasdaq: QCOR)	8390%
3.	Priceline.com (Nasdaq: PCLN) Green Mountain Coffee	6060%
4	Roaster(Nasdaq)	5340%
5.	Apple (Nasdaq: AAPL)	4730%
6.	lllumina (Nasdaq: ILMN)	5040%
7.	Terra Nitrogen (NYSE: TNH)	3950%
8.	Alexion Pharma (Nasdaq: ALXN)	3110%)
9.	Core Labs NV (NYSE:CLB)	2280%
10.	Intuitive Surgical (Nasdaq: ISRG)	2280%

Source: Bloomberg from 2001 to 2011

The total gain for each of the above companies is dramatic. If you have put $1000 into Apple in 2001, you would have $40000 in 2011 and $1000 in Monster Beverage, you would have $105300. If anyone picks the right stock and holds it for ten years, his return is unimaginable. Now you will understand why the top investors like Warren Buffett and many others are billionaires. All of these companies started their epic run as tiny companies. If you start developing your strategies to locate value tiny stocks now and eventually you will join the rich. There are many of these types of value stocks out there. According to Bloomberg, 177 of these tiny stocks were recently up more than 100 per cent. There are many of these under value stocks in every market in the world. You can join thousands of people who become millionaires if you are determined to find these value stocks.

Investors use various algorithms or strategies using various criteria to pick stocks. Through back testing, they are able to see how their methods would have worked out in the past so they will have a better idea as to what their probability of success now and the future. Although past results are no guarantee of future results, the experiences provide something to guide them. Just ponder about this. If your stock picking strategy did nothing but lose money, year after year, stock after stock, over and over again, you will be sure not to repeat the strategy. The reason is obvious. Such strategy does not work. On the other hand, if you had a strategy that made you plenty of money, year after year, stock after stock and time after time, you will stick to such a strategy. Of course you are not going to have a strategy that is perfect. As long as your strategy works more than 60 per cent of the time, you are going to make money in the long run. You must have a mechanism in your trailing stop to cap any of your losses. As long as your strategy picks more winners and losses, you can feel confident that the next stock you pick will have a high probability of making money.

Speak the Language of Investment Confidently

A confident investor knows his strategy ins and outs; he never has a second guess himself. If he had an outstanding strategy that performs well in both the bull markets and bear markets, he feels confident that the best research has been done to put those stocks in his buy list. My own experiences tell me that once I put in long hours of research in creating that strategy through best thinking and the data available, I will not be swelled by any story I read or looking at another possible chart of buying a particular stock. This gives me confidence about the pick. And that what a truly tested strategy can provide, a time-tested analysis applied to any stock that is included in my buying list. This eliminates the emotion and human bias out of my investment equation. I will wait for any correction and buy the stocks in my list. This will give me peace of mind after investing.

We use to hear that in stock investment, the key is patience. I learn from my experience that patience alone won't make you rich or wealthy. A more important skill is to pick the right companies, buy them at the right price, then be patient while you wait for the market to recognise the value of these stocks. You need to understand that every stock has its true value or a range of true values. If the price of the stock is traded above this range of true values, the stock is overvalued. On the other hand if the stock's price is traded below its true value during a recession or when sentiment is poor, the stock is undervalued. Understanding its language will help and encourage you to buy the stock when it's under-valued.

How to pick right stocks? The simple thing to follow is to buy companies that are on the top of the list in their business. These dominant players tend to set the bar for the industry. They tend to do well even in tough times. Buy them during recession or when sentiments are poor. They tend to be the first to benefit when industries go through consolidation or when sentiments improve. These companies have reputation based on brand value and their solid track record. In USA, the strategy of focussing on the dominant players usually paid off consistently for many investors. These dominant players like Coca Cola, McDonald, Johnson & Johnson, Apple and others provide growth as well as good dividends and buy-backs. Understanding the language of stocks is critical. Dividends are part of the profit of the companies given out half yearly or yearly. Profitable companies enjoy healthy cash flow generated from day-to-day business. They are able to service their debts, give out dividends, and even buy back their own shares.

You need to understand the language of stock buy-backs. Some analysts claim that stock buy-back is simply a way to artificially inflate earning per share for a stock. It is true for some cases but not always. But for companies like Apple, Michael Kors and others, it is absolutely false. For example, Bill Spetrino explains that when Michael Kors bought back its stock, the company was using its revenue in the best way possible to generate more income. It's an investment choice for the company. If a company can buy back its own stock at a cheap price, it can get an outsized return. It may be better than buy other shares of other companies as investment for the company. In this case, Michael Kors knows what its return is going to be. According to Bill Spetrino, the company is expected to earn $4.32 per share in 2015. That means that every share of stock the company buys at $42, it is getting a 10 per cent return. But the company has a $4.20 per share in net cash. If you analyse in more detail, the current stock price of Michael Kors is $42 - $4.20 = $37.80. So if you divide the earnings of $4.32 by the net stock price of $37.80, you get a return of 11 to 12 per cent. So it is logical for the company to buy back its own stock to get a return of 10 - 12 per cent on every dollar it invests to buy back its own shares. It is obvious that it's an excellent idea for the company to buy back its own stock. On top of that, the company has no debt. I have no doubt about the analysis and I will start buying Michael Kors in 2016 at $42 or less. Understanding the language of any stock will be a great advantage to help you to become wealthy.

Understanding the fundamentals of a company is important before we make any decision to buy the stock. I will only buy companies which enjoy profitability. Whatever potential you can think of, profitability is a critical element for a company to grow and prosper. The best way to determine profitability is profitability ratios. These ratios give a clear picture of the financial performance of a company. Comparing these ratios of a company with those of its peers in the same sector gives a clear picture whether the company is undervalued or overvalued. Tracking the profitability ratios over a period of time tells us whether the company is performing well or on the decline. All the information helps us to decide whether to invest in such company. What are these profitability ratios?

The most popular profitability ratio is Return on Equity (ROE). The term ROE measures the amount of profit that a company generates through the use of shareholders' equity. It is easy to calculate this ratio. ROE is just a ratio of the net income of the company divides by its average common shareholders' equity. The number of shares fluctuates through buy-back or other means throughout the year and we take the average number. Shareholder equity is the total company assets minus its total liabilities. Equity is share capital plus retained profits minus treasury shares. Shareholders' equity represents the amount by which a company is financed through common preferred shares. So a company with a higher ROE is better because it can generate cash. But this is not very accurate. Some sectors require little capital whereas others like mining and oil sectors require heavy capital. Comparing ROE for similar sector is more valid than across sectors.

To understand the health of a company, we need to know the four fundamental statements: balance sheet, income statement, cash flow statement, and statement of shareholders equity. The following will give you a concise picture of balance sheet with an easy example. Next is income statement. The cash flow statement with an example is shown next followed by statement of shareholder equity.

Balance Sheet

A balance sheet shows a balance of a company's assets, liabilities and shareholder equity. In simple terms, assets are everything of value that the company has including the intangibles like trademarks and patent. The table on the next page gives you a clear picture what are a company's assets. A comparison with the corresponding quarter a year ago is also included. Assets include physical property, inventory, equipment, vehicles and others. Cash is also considered as asset. Liabilities are all the debts, all obligations and promises of providing goods and services to customers in the future. The table in the next page reveals all liabilities of a company. A picture tells a better story than all the descriptions regarding assets and liabilities. A comparison of assets and liabilities of two periods of the year is usually given. The first column on the left hand side states the assets of the company and the right hand column give the figures of each asset for the two periods. The second left hand column shows the liabilities and stockholders' equities and the right hand column gives all the figures. The figures have to be balanced for the period. The data given in the next table are just about a fictitious company created to show the example of a balance sheet.

Dr Sin Mong Wong

Consolidated Balance Sheet of XYZ Corporatio

Consolidated Balance Sheets
Dollars in millions except per share amounts

	December 31, 2005	2004
Assets		
Current Assets		
Cash and cash equivalents	$ 1,224	$ 760
Accounts receivable - net of allowances for uncollectibles of $1,176 and $1,001	9,351	6,901
Prepaid expenses	1,029	746
Deferred income taxes	2,011	566
Other current assets	1,039	989
Total current assets	14,654	9,962
Property, Plant and Equipment - Net	58,727	50,046
Goodwill	14,055	1,625
Intangible Assets - Net	8,503	429
Investments in Equity Affiliates	2,031	1,798
Investments in and Advances to Cingular Wireless	31,404	33,687
Other Assets	16,258	12,718
Total Assets	**$145,632**	**$110,265**
Liabilities and Stockholders' Equity		
Current Liabilities		
Debt maturing within one year	$ 4,455	$ 5,734
Accounts payable and accrued liabilities	17,088	11,459
Accrued taxes	2,586	1,787
Dividends payable	1,289	1,065
Liabilities of discontinued operations	-	310
Total current liabilities	25,418	20,355
Long-Term Debt	26,115	21,231
Deferred Credits and Other Noncurrent Liabilities		
Deferred income taxes	15,713	15,621
Postemployment benefit obligation	18,133	9,076
Unamortized investment tax credits	209	188
Other noncurrent liabilities	5,354	3,290
Total deferred credits and other noncurrent liabilities	39,409	28,175
Stockholders' Equity		
Common shares	4,065	3,433
Capital in excess of par value	27,499	13,350
Retained earnings	29,106	28,806
Treasury shares (188,209,761 at December 31, 2005 and 132,212,645 at December 31, 2004, at cost)	(5,406)	(4,535)
Additional minimum pension liability adjustment	(218)	(190)
Accumulated other comprehensive income	(356)	(360)
Total stockholders' equity	54,690	40,504
Total Liabilities and Stockholders' Equity	**$145,632**	**$110,265**

Income Statement

Income statement reveals the amount the company earned over a specific time period. In most cases, a quarterly or yearly income statement is usually reported. In addition, the statement includes costs and expenses to earn the revenue.

The bottom line of the income statement is the company's actual earnings or losses over the period. For investors like us, we are interested in companies with strong fundamentals which increase over time. The significant thing included in the income statement is the earning per share (EPS). This is the total amount shareholders will receive if all the earnings are distributed to shareholders. Most companies only give up dividends less than 30 per cent of the total EPS. The EPS is calculated by the total net income divided by the number of outstanding shares of the company. If you open up any company listed in the stock exchange, you can easily see the presentation of its income statement in its quarterly or half-yearly report. This income statement report is common and in big volume. It is not included here because of its size.

Cash Flow Statement

Cash flow statements give the account of the movement of the company's cash; the life blood of the company; the cash generated by the company and how the cash is spent. Cash flow statement indicates changes over time rather than total amount of cash at certain point. It reveals the net increase or decrease over the period. Usually, cash flow statements are divided into three primary sections. Each section reviews the cash flow from operating activities, investing activities and financing. A better way to explain cash flow statement is through a table shown in the next page. The table reveals a comparison of two corresponding periods of operating activities, investing activities and financial activities. The upper section shows its operating activities, the second section reveals its investing activities, and the last section is the financial activities. You may not be familiar with income statement. The income statement of a fictitious company XYZ Corporation is shown here to familiarise you with income statement.

OPERATING ACTIVITIES			
Cash received			
Goods and services		24,337	25,925
Appropriations		1,348,424	1,294,468
Net GST received		73,217	70,105
Other cash received		22,073	25,668
Total cash received		1,468,051	1,416,166
Cash used			
Employees		527,752	492,744
Suppliers		775,223	758,300
Borrowing costs		4,299	685
Cash transferred to the Official Public Account		113,076	119,865
Other cash used		122	44
Total cash used		1,420,472	1,371,638
Net cash flows from or (used by) operating activities	11	47,579	44,528
INVESTING ACTIVITIES			
Cash received			
Proceeds from sales of property, plant and equipment		671	57
Total cash received		671	57
Cash used			
Purchase of property, plant and equipment		33,577	49,372
Purchase of intangibles		116,392	108,327
Total cash used		149,969	157,699
Net cash flows from or (used by) investing activities		(149,298)	(157,642)
FINANCING ACTIVITIES			
Cash received			
Appropriations - contributed equity		116,227	123,197
Total cash received		116,227	123,197
Cash used			
Repayment of borrowings		16,446	15,166
Total cash used		16,446	15,166
Net cash flows from or (used by) financing activities		99,781	108,031
Net increase or (decrease) in cash held		(1,938)	(5,083)
Cash and cash equivalents at the beginning of the reporting period		7,116	12,199
Cash and cash equivalents at the end of the reporting period	5A	5,178	7,116

Statement of Shareholders' Equity

The statement of shareholders' equity shows all equity accounts that shape the equity balance of the year and it includes common stocks, net income, paid capital and dividend. It is a basic statement of how the ending equity is calculated. The statement provides the answer of the equity balance on the first January to thirty-first December of the year.

The way the statement of shareholders' equity is simple and is shown in the following page.

First, the starting equity is reported followed by any new statements of net income for shareholders and new investments for the year. All losses and dividends are subtracted from the equity balance revealing the ending equity balance for the accounting year. Obviously the net income is needed to calculate the ending equity balance of the year. It includes current assets, fixed assets, shareholders equity, total shareholders' equity and liability. That is why the statement of changes must be prepared after the income statement.

Statement of Shareholders' Equity

XYZ Corporation
As at June 30, 2005
(In thousands of US dollars)

Current Assets		Liability	
Cash & cash equivalent	5,000	Accounts Payable	25,000
Marketable securities	25,000	Accrued liability	10,000
Accounts receivable	40,000	Notes Payable	5,000
Notes receivable	25,000	Unearned Revenue	6,000
Inventory	45,000	Current portion of long-term debt	1,500
Prepaid expenses	2,500	Current portion of capital lease obligation	600
Total Current Assets	**142,500**	**Total current liability**	**48,100**
Fixed Assets		Long-term debt	18,750
Investments	7,500	Deferred income tax liability	500
Machinery & Equipment	60,000	Long-term capital lease obligations	7,500
Buildings & Land	200,000		
Intangible assets	75,000	Total long term Liabilities	26,750
Total Fixed assets	**342,500**		
		Shareholders' Equity	
		Preferred stock	20,000
Total Assets	485,000	Common stock	90,150
		Retained earnings	300,000
		Total Shareholders Equity	410,150
		Total Shareholders equity & liability	485,000

The above table is an example of how a statement of Shareholders' Equity looks like. It shows the basic statement of how the ending equity is calculated. This picture speaks better than all my description. Understanding the simple language of stocks and business will help us understand the fundamentals of a company and help us to choose stocks wisely for profit. We do not need a business degree to understand the health of a company.

Advantages of Investing in Tiny Value Stocks

There are many advantages of buying tiny value stocks in our current market. Most big investors and analysts normally ignore these tiny stocks which have difficulty getting financial help from big banks. Most of these tiny value stocks have very low debts. They are seldom noticed unless we start looking into their performance and their businesses. Why do you need to buy tiny value stocks?

First, investing in tiny value stocks provides higher returns. Picking the right stocks can easily make you very rich. History tells us that the average rate of growth of small value caps out pace that of the big brothers with a significant percentage. The law of averages tells us that for small investors like us, we will enjoy a bigger return in investing in small value stocks.

Second, most small value stocks are local home growth companies. They are primary domestic. They are usually the innovative and drivers of growth for the country's economy. In USA, companies like Wal-Mart, Microsoft, Apple, Starbucks and others all started as home grown companies before becoming international companies. All these stocks are reflecting American entrepreneurism. So if you succeed to locate any new innovative companies now, you will not only enjoy the next breakthrough success story but also make yourself very rich.

Third, most tiny value companies are frugal and investor friendly. Small companies manage their money tightly because it's difficult for them to assess big bank loans. They rarely borrow and do not have big debts. So they focus on their stock price that is actually favouring investors. They are normally selling products or services based on intellectual properties which are usually provided by the founders and employees. They are not capital intensive companies. It's less risky in terms of cash flow and less risk for investors in terms of bad debts.

Fourth, tiny companies are usually run by their founders and are usually undervalued and underfollowed. They are full of fresh ideas and the management is hungry for profit and growth. The top managements are usually the majority shareholders. It's a powerful incentive for them to succeed. Investors know that the interest of the management is aligned with theirs.

Fifth, tiny value stocks have the power of 'creative disruption' for being innovative and exploiting Internet marketing. For example, Priceline practically obliterated the traditional travel agency business by making it easier and cheaper to book airline tickets, hotels and others. Unlike big companies which have difficulty of innovation because they enjoy tradition and other benefits. For example, in 1975 Kodak passed on the first digital camera because of fear of disrupting its profitable film production business. Others launched their digital technology and benefited from their digital photography. Once a thriving company, Kodak went bankrupt in 2012. There are many tiny-value companies out there and they will be the blue chips of the future.

Last but not least, tiny-value companies provide opportunity for investors because of less competition. The big fish ignore them and so are the analysts. Investors have the bargaining power to buy cheap but value companies. Small tiny value stocks are usually domestic and they are less affected by any major events like recession or inflation and world events. The returns from investing in tiny value stocks will be attractive for the long run.

Mistakes Can Be Your Blessing

In investing, everyone makes mistakes. The ability to learn from any mistake is critical. In his last newsletter, Warren Buffett admitted that he made an early mistake that cost him millions. He is now worth almost $70 billion. What separates him from all of us is that he is not crippled by his mistakes but he sees them as valuable learning experiences. My own experience tells me that when I lose money, I always remember it. The more it hurts, the more you remember and the more you learn. I used to hold on to my losing stocks resulting in big losses. Now I behave and act differently. I only allow any wrong pick of stock to lose at most 20 per cent of my buying price or its peak price. Following this trailing stop consistently; I manage to contain and capped my loss or retain my profit. I used to sell my winning stocks too early. I did not benefit fully from any good run. Now I follow a new approach. As long as the stock price is moving according to its trend upwards, I will wait patiently until it runs out of steam. Any dip of about 15 per cent from the peak, suggesting that the trend cycle has changed; I will exit and take my profit. This new strategy gives me a solid approach to lock in my profit. It gives me a solid approach to avoid turning a big profit into a loss. I follow this approach consistently and it makes me rich.

When I started investing in stocks, I usually bought on the strength of friends' recommendations without doing my own research. Some stocks went up and I made some money. Many stocks went down and I lost a lot of money. Now I am aware of my own mistake. And at the age when market data and information are freely available on line, there will no longer be any excuse for me not to do my own research. Advice is still necessary. It does not mean that you do not have to do your own due diligence before you invest in a company. I am aware that no system is perfect. I will still make mistakes because my interpretations and understanding may not be right. I learn to modify my behaviours after each mistake, but sometimes circumstances can provide different interpretations. Now I learn not to depend too much on generalisation but on my own understanding based on my own experiences. My experience of loss is the greatest lesson I ever learned. I do not want to repeat such failure again.

Even in property investment, timing and location are critical. I remember when I bought my first property, my first home for the family. I bought it in a hurry without looking at the location. The price of the house was reasonable, but the location is not nice. The terrace house I bought is facing a road. My wife was never comfortable with the position of the house. She felt that the house is not peaceful. I worried that one day a careless motorist will drive his car right into my house. After staying there for a few years; we decided to upgrade our house to a better location. So I repainted the house and sold it for a good profit. The person who bought my property did not stay there. It's his investment property. So the location does not bother him. This experience has taught me a valuable lesson to look for a right property in the right location. My second property is in a nice location facing a green field. We enjoyed staying there for twenty three years while I was working there. We bought it for about seventy one thousand Malaysian dollars and when we left for Australia, we sold it for about 350 thousand Malaysian dollars. We made a good profit in terms of percentage. If we have hold on to it, the property is worth over a million now. But in our mind, our home is not an asset when we stayed there for many years. It was a liability during the period. We had to pay mortgage, assessment, quit rents, water bill, electricity bill and maintenance bills. It took money out of our pocket. There was no income from the property. Anyhow it was a necessity. Our family needed a roof over our heads. We are lucky to enjoy such a capital gain when we sold it. Our liability turned into a final asset.

Strategy for Change

Research into the networking of our brain reveals that our neuron connection can easily be intentionally modified. Our subconscious mind can be loaded with self-doubt, insecurity, fear, embarrassment, shame, procrastination and lacking of confidence. These are the factors affecting our quest for financial freedom. Our inner world shapes our outer manifestation. Without self-belief, we will not be motivated to visualisation and take appropriate action. All these unnecessary elements will tend to sabotage our plan. No matter how much reading, research and action we take, our financial situation will not change much. Each one of us has a financial ceiling created by our experiences, perceptions, our brain patterns and our environment situations. These are the accumulations of our beliefs, perceptions and habits accumulated during our life time. We are not aware that they are in our subconscious mind. Do you have a choice? You can only choose if you are aware of them. Hopefully after reading this part of the book, your consciousness will drive you into action. What action should you take? A better choice is to replace these financial killers with a set of new successful belief patterns, practices and neural circuits to break your financial ceiling.

Our brain has two parts: the conscious or the rational logical part and the unconscious or emotional brain. Financial success can only be achieved if your subconscious beliefs and perceptions agree with your conscious mind. The emotional brain has a bigger say. Before we put in any more effort to change our financial situation, we need to let go of these unwanted beliefs in the subconscious mind. They do not serve your financial goal. Once this is done, it is time to download characteristics of the rich and successful people into our mind. Once this is done, your consciousness evolution is about to take off. You would have effortlessly integrated some of the most useful beliefs, habits and practices of the successful and rich into your mind. What are some of these characteristics? A whole section of these characteristics will be available and will be discussed fully for your digestion. Some of these new beliefs are as listed above. They should be allowed to be implemented intentionally and regularly. A lot of practices are required for the neuron connection in our brain to form permanently just like physical training building up our muscle. The more practice the better. More characteristics can be added as we gain confidence. These collective actions become our habits and eventually become our autopilot thinking and action. This repeated style of investing will become our tool of wealth creation. Your financial ceiling will be shattered and a higher financial income begins to take shape. Once the unloading of the old beliefs and loading of new ones become successful, you will discover that the process is as easy as changing the temperature of you room by adjusting the thermostat.

I follow Burt Goldman's meditation strategy called Quantum Jumping. After a few practices I discovered the most beautiful life changing experience I ever had. The door to abundance is opened to me and everything I visualise becomes possible.

The human imagination knows no boundary. I have a new Quantum Library in another parallel universe. Everything I can imagine becomes a possibility. In our universe, we have Google to provide any information we require for growth. We can get valuable knowledge from any successful person to give us his or her deep insight in the topic we need. The imagination of a Quantum Library in the next parallel universe is conceived and there is no limit for us to embrace a new system of belief that will enhance our health, wealth, spirituality and fulfilment of life in any new reality. Life is a choice. You can choose where you want to be. I choose to be rich, healthy, and happy. Living a life of excitement is my goal. I choose to replace my outdated beliefs and load my mind with a new set of habits, beliefs and practices of successful people. I choose to make these characteristics my own by implementing them daily until I reach an autopilot stage. I can imagine the day when abundance begins to smile at me. I can imagine the day will come when everything becomes effortless; when things just flow and I know which direction I am moving. I enjoy being rewarded abundantly for making things happen in my world. I believe that it is possible. I set the intention and I take positive action for my dreams to become reality.

Make a Fortune in Stock Market If You Are Right 60 Per cent of the Time

When I started my investment in stocks, I did not concentrate on making money. I am a more defensive player than an offensive one. I wanted to make sure that I do not lose money. The first thing I decide to do is to develop a system telling me what stocks I should not buy. I make an assumption that 60 per cent of the stocks are overvalued. By removing this 60 per cent of the stocks, I am left with only 40 per cent of the remaining stocks to choose. The chance that I will pick a winner is much increased. At a glance mathematically, 60 per cent is not far from 50 - 50. But it turns out to be a tremendous advantage if I can consistently win 60 per cent of my stock picks. I can easily be a happy and profitable investor. These are the words of the famous investor, Peter Lynch:

> In this business, if you're good, you're right six times out of ten. You're never going to be right nine times out of ten.

If 60 per cent is good for a great investor, it must be good for any others like me to develop a system that I can pick six or more winners out of ten. It's not easy to pick more than six winners out of ten. A strategy I adopted is focusing on value stocks. Many growth stocks are also value stocks. Knowing value stocks based their earning, dividends and profits, the chance of error is less.

This eliminates the guessing part out of the investment equation. Many years ago, a friend of mine bought Priceline and Amazon because he thought that these are value and growth companies. He made good profits because these stocks went for a big run. In every industry, there are value stocks experiencing tremendous growth. The difficulty is spotting them. Once spotted, these value growth stocks can bring in big profits exceeding 100 per cent or more. Using a trailing stop strategy, any error in picking a stock is capped at a maximum of 20 per cent loss. So a 60 per cent of big winners will outperform 40 per cent of losers at 20 per cent capped loss. This is a long - term investment strategy to ensure profit.

I agree with Jim Pearce, chief strategist, personal finance. He made a comparison of investing in stocks to the performance of professional tennis players. Professional tennis players winning about 55 per cent of the points they played; they are already making a name and money in the circuit. Players like Roger Federer won about 60 per cent of the points he played and he had already amassed a fortune and won many grand slams. Similarly winning about 60 per cent of your picks investment in stocks can make you a wealthy man.

Investments for the Future

History of the share market gives us a strong indication that if we are visionary enough by picking a right growth stock; we can easily enjoy financial freedom before our retirement. For example, in Australia, if we had bought one thousand shares of CSL at $6.50 in 2004 and keep the stock until now, we would have made a fortune when the price is at $100 per share. Similarly if we had bought 1000 shares of Domino's Pizza at $3.60 in 2008, we would be enjoying a big profit when the stock price rises to $50. A more dramatic one will be TPM. In 2008, if you had bought 10 000 shares at $0.28 and hold on to it until now, the share is now at almost $12.00, you will be laughing all the way to the bank. These are just a few of the stocks in Australia that enjoy tremendous growth. In USA, there are more of the stocks enjoying huge growth. Think of it, investment in the share market is still a good way to enjoy financial freedom when we retire. There are still many growth companies out there. Can we spot them early?

Do not assume that you have missed the opportunity. There are still many sectors undergoing revolutionary changes. The world is changing very fast in adapting many forms of renewable energy. We are looking for anything cutting edge in technology affecting transportation. Many people in northern Europe have already embraced the use of renewable energy including using electric cars. About 20 per cent of the population in the archipelago of Orkney in northern Scotland are using electric cars. Consider the introduction of electric cars only happened in 2010. This appears significant and it is going to be better in the future. In countries like Norway, the Netherlands and USA, the number of electric cars used is growing fast. Soon the whole world will be moving in the same direction. Instead of using gasoline, we will be using renewable source of metal oil in the form of lithium (Li). On a global scale, five years after the introduction, more than one million electric cars have been sold. In less than four or five years, this will be the annual sales number. Compare the number of electrical cars to the number of cars using ordinary internal combustion engines; it is only monumental. In 2015, it is estimated that 80 million cars will be sold and only 1.25 per cent of the cars are electrical cars. This is barely an accounting error. But if we are looking for growth story, there are few as exciting as this one.

For investors like us, it is not the small percentage of electric cars sold today, it is about the number going to be sold tomorrow. Today only the rich can afford electric cars because the lithium battery cost is still too high. Technology is fast catching up and our genius Elon Musk is thinking hard and acting fast. Soon the cost will be half or less and electric cars will be within reach to everybody. If you look around today, you will notice that most of our electricity is generated by coal than solar or other sources. But all of us know that coal is on the way out and solar energy and metal oil using lithium are beginning to boom. Which sector will you be investing? Similarly, the conventional cars still dominate the automobile industry today, but the combustion engine is no longer the superior technology. In the future, the conventional vehicles will be neither cheap nor efficient to operate compared to electric cars. Tesla's Giga-factory for lithium battery will soon be in production in 2016. Other players are also moving to cut down the cost of lithium battery. The metal oil revolution is triggered. The combustion engines will soon be an absolute technology with no further improvement. The renewable technology using lithium or metal oil is still in its early stages and getting better and better day by day. The solar revolution is taking place now with new technologies. So as investors, what should we do if we want financial freedom? Will you invest in this growing industry or stick to the old ones. Your guess is as good as mine.

This early stage of transformation is similar to the introduction of model T machines vehicles last century. Many naysayers commented that the vehicles will never be able to compete with the tried true horse and buggy. We saw what had happened! The company that manufactures electric cars, Tesla, went public in a few years ago. Now GM is also manufacturing electric cars. Apple Corporation is joining the race. Electric cars with an electric range of 300 miles are almost here. What should we do as investors? I will suggest you try test drive a VOLT, LEAF, or a Tesla Model S, to acquaint yourself with technology of the future. I believe that electric cars are the future. Be aware of the development and investing in the right companies will ensure your financial freedom. One thing is clear. We have to start investing in companies involving both electric cars and lithium production. While the rest of the investment herd is milling about and still sitting on their hands on the volatile market; we should look well into this new solar technology. Soon homes, businesses and factories will be powered by solar energy. Early investors into electric cars and solar companies will be the coming new millionaires. A new way of life can also bring wealth and prosperity if you start investing into new solar technologies before others join the fray.

A strategy known as 'follow the money' strategy can help you to make big money. Follow the money strategy is simply follow where the smart money is investing especially newly listed companies with great potential. This smart money institutions managed by people like Warren Buffett, Soros and Bill Gates know something about a company which ordinary people like us never have the chance to find out. We sail with the smart money buying into companies they are buying. People like Bill Gates, Mark Zuckerberg, Richard Branson, Jeff Bezos, Vinod Khosla and Elon Musk are pouring billions of dollars into solar energy and metal oil companies. This is a good strategy and our probability of going wrong is reduced. This strategy can also be applied to other inside trading involving top executives of certain companies buying their own stock. They know something which we do not know. Something good must be happening to the company. If you buy option, it would be good to buy a call option for such companies where the money is going. The profit will be multiplied many times. Another form of information is always available from the U.S. Securities and Exchange Commission (SEC). Fund managers managing 100 million or above are required to file forms (called '13Fs') every three months. These forms detail their transactions of shares: shares they sold and stocks they bought. These elite money managers have valuable research knowledge which can help small investors like us to gain advantage of their million dollars of research for free. Even during this turbulent period 2016, reading through the forms of '13Fs', a surprising finding reveals that many top investors like Carl Icahn had 16 per cent of his $29 billion portfolio in the stock Apple (AAPL) and David Einhorn had 12 per cent of his $5 billion portfolio in Apple. Many other top investors had substantial holdings in Apple too. Why do all these elite investors hold Apple shares? The reason is that Apple is a fantastic company trading at a fantastic price. It is the most profitable company. During the last 12 months, it generates 234 billion in sales and a 23 per cent profit of $53.5 billion. The two ratios: EV/EBITDA and EV/FCF used to measure whether a company is cheap or expensive are respectively 5 and 6.5; telling us that Apple stock is cheap during the dip in 2016. Apple stock had been cheap during 2008 and early 2003. I am ready to put my money into Apple when it dips now. Any chart available gives a better picture of the value of Apple stock. Apple was cheap during early 2013 when the two ratios were very low and the price of Apple went for a run of almost 750 per cent upwards. Will history repeat itself in 2016? I think the chance is good for the stock in 2016 onwards. Most investors are concerned with its growth. But Apple, such a huge company, is growing more than double in four years. The concern is that it can't keep growing at the same rate. Another concern is that 66 per cent of the company's revenue comes from its' iPhone. This makes the company susceptible to competition. Apple is working its way into lithium electric cars. This gives a little hope for diversification and growth. My faith in Apple is strong and I will keep buying its share as long as the two ratios tell me that the price is cheap. The chance of being wrong is small. My 20 per cent trailing stop will help me to navigate my risk. If history repeats, which happen most of the time, I will have a good harvest.

Understanding Inside Trading

Although we know that inside trading is illegal; there is an exception when inside trading is perfectly legal. During open period, CEOs, directors and company executives are allowed to buy their own company's shares. As investors, we face the difficulty of detecting this type of scenarios. There is always a time lapse before we can detect this type of cluster buying. We wonder why these top executives spend so much money to buy their own stock when they have already own tons of shares. As usual humans are greedy and they want more wealth. Undoubtedly some good news or good profit is on the card. There are additional signals to help us benefit from insiders trading.

The first signal is that when the company's lawyers who are usually non investors, start buy the company's shares. This indicates that there must be something really great regarding the company's quarterly performance and its growth. Investors like us can seldom be wrong if we follow and buy.

The second signal is when a cluster of senior executives including directors are buying their own stock. Something good is happening and we can seldom be wrong to follow.

The third signal is when members of the management staff start buying the company's shares. When this type of scenarios happens, it's raining bargain, I will use buckets, not thimbles, to scoop up the stock for my portfolio.

The difficulty to detect inside trading can now be minimised because of information availability. Every company is duty bound to report top executives holding positions in the company. Even majority shareholders have to report regularly their holding position in the company.

Ways of Investing Your Money

There are generally four simple ways of investing our hard - earned money. The first is an unsuccessful way. Many of us suffer from this unwelcoming way. The second way is using long - term investment. This is a proven way. Experiencing varying degrees of success along the way and still make plenty of money. This is a preferred way for retirement. The third way is for the short term, making money out of luck. The fourth way is for the short term, making money out of fraud. In the long run, the third and fourth ways converge to the first and investors lose their capitals. I believe that there is only one consistent way to invest successfully that is long term. I invested in stocks and properties for long term. I bought two investment properties for an initial payment of about 16 thousand Malaysian dollars each and held them for over forty years. I collected rentals from them for the first fifteen years and had a surplus as cash flow while I paid mortgage. After the period, the properties generated full cash flow for my family for more than twenty five years. I collected millions of dollars of rentals for the two different periods. I sold them after more than forty years each at a price of more than a million. The percentage of profit over the long period comes to thousands and thousands of percent. Similarly for some stocks which I held for many years, the profits are measured in terms of thousands of percent. These examples simply reinforce the power of long - term investments. My advice to individual investor is that when you invest, take a longer-term view and measure your success in terms of years. You would have an advantage over the short - term investors. The average investor is trading and speculating but not investing resulting in small gains or sometimes losing money.

A Simple Strategy for Option Trading

There is a simple way of making money in option trading. What is option trading? Option trading is the most misunderstood financial instrument. I must admit that I was scarce of option trading initially. I did not understand how such an instrument could be used to grow my wealth. I went into Google and read that almost 80 per cent of optional traders lost money. I got frightened. I researched further and found that option trading is better than insurance - you win either way! Do you like to go into insurance business and collect premiums for insuring people against catastrophes? You can be a seller of puts because there is a big demand for them. In fact Warren Buffett made use of this instrument and raked in $4.9 billion dollar by trading option. So I think that you too can also make money instantly and never worry about the direction of the market.

But you need to know what it means to sell a put. Many investors consider options as simple way of increasing your money power. If you buy a 'call option', it gives the right, not the obligation, to buy the stock at an agreed upon price before a certain date. Similarly if you buy a 'put option', it also gives you the right to buy the stock at an agreed upon price before a certain date. Usually a call option is involved if the price of the stock is rising. A put option is the opposite when you expect the price of a stock falling. Simple call options are a bet the price of the asset will go up. Put options are a bet the price of the stock will go down.

Make Money When the Market Goes Up or Down

For example, on the fourth of October 2015 if you have bought Facebook's November 6t h 109 call option for $3.49, this will give you an option to sell Facebook before the sixth of November for $109.00. On the sixth of October, the price of Facebook went up 6 per cent. You would have make 90 per cent overnight. The great potential of making big money quickly is there if you do it correctly.

This simple strategy is well known to everyone trading options in Wall Street. Just like playing mini-baccarat in the casino, you can win if you just follow the trends. If more 'banker' occurs, buy 'banker' or otherwise 'player'. Many beginners in this game seem to win because of their ignorance of the game and they just follow the trends. If you intend to make some money playing options, you simply follow the trend; you are unlikely to lose money. The trick is that you do not have to know anything about options and just follow the trend. If the graph of a stock or asset is going upwards, you buy a call option; you assume that the price will continue to go up. If it is trending down, you buy a put option; assuming it will continue to fall. If you can stick to this simple way of trading option, you will definitely make money over a long period of time. You only have to spend a few minutes a day to buy a put option or a call option. You also need to be aware that a prevailing trend upwards or downwards will not last for-ever. And because a trend changes constantly, you need to be adaptable constantly. The ability to sense a changing trend comes through experience and awareness of economic situations. So before you register and use 'BinaryTilt' platform to trade options, do your own research and due diligence first. There are some companies like 'R-4 Trigger' and others claiming that they can help you make great money in options trading. You may want to put aside a certain sum you can afford and follow their techniques. Be open-minded and give your money a chance to grow.

I suggest that for a beginner; always start with a conservative number of contracts. Some knowledge of risk management is necessary. For me, if I buy a put option of a certain company, I must always be sure that I am comfortable to own the stock at the price I specified in my put option. Occasionally I may have to buy the stock if it falls below the target price. Since I have done my due diligence, there is profit to be made with the stock. I must have spare money to buy the stock. But I have pocketed cash from the Option Money Machine. It makes sense because I am buying the stock I want at a discount. I will never buy an option for a company unless I am comfortable owning the stock. Most investors are worried about selling a put option because they may get stuck with the stock. My advice is that when you sell a put option, you must be comfortable to own the stock outright.

Using Credit - Spread Strategy

What is a credit - spread strategy? It is a conservative strategy designed to earn income while simultaneously limiting your losses. And if you have chosen using weekly options, your term is only seven days. Immediately when you sell a 'credit-spread' contract, you receive the cash as part of the deal. If the stock goes up (in a week) or does not fall to the target price, you pocket the upfront money as pure profit. This is how you can make money if the market goes up.

For example, I really like a stock XXX and the market is riding on price momentum. On October 5, I sold five credit spread for a credit-spread of 0.43 credit. On October 8, I sold them, meaning I pocketed 0.43 of the five contracts amounting to $256 instantly. You can keep repeating if the market is still rising and keep pocketing whatever amount you specified.

Repetition is the secret of success by following the trend. If you have to take up the stock, you must be comfortable with the target price.

The market will crash or a big correction is inevitable. All of us are aware of the economic cycles. The difference of option trading and buying a stock to hold is that option sellers have better control. The beauty of option trading is that you are not locked in for a long periods of time. The average option trading for most people is thirty to sixty days. Using the credit spread technique for just seven days; you have the advantage to do what you want. The goal of such a technique is to find stocks which can help you to profit from the volatility of the market. Plenty of research and due diligence are required to help make informed decisions. Based on the principle any option trade chosen is assumed to generate profit or you are comfortable of owning the stock. So guessing is no longer the issue. The goal is to find the low-risk, high - reward trades that not only protect your capital but also generate good profit from the volatility of the market. You can also enjoy the flexibility of buying a put, a call or a credit-spread option. All these explanations sound confusing. These trades are just like riding a bike, once you do it yourself and learn how to ride a bike, it's easily repeatable. Do not let fear hold you back!

An Interesting Story

There is an interesting story I read from *Wall Street Time*. Andy Abraham was an employee in the gardening products section of a retail business for eight years. Business was bad and Andy was fired in October 2013. He went through a tough period with his wife Lorena and a daughter Jenny. Seeing no future in him, his wife wanted to leave him and he contemplated suicide because he was so depressed. He met an old friend from the same hometown and they had a beer together. His friend, John Green, introduced Andy to use binary options trading by depositing $500 into his trading account to start with. John Green taught him a simple 'follow the trend strategy'. Andy followed this strategy rigidly because he had no knowledge of binary options trading experience. He is open minded and willing to try. This adaptation is his key to surviving change. Within a few months, his life was totally different. On the first evening, he used the 'BinaryTilt' strategy, Andy made $60, more than 10 per cent of his initial deposit. He kept repeating the process, and after months of options trading he accumulated tens of thousands of dollars in his account. Within a year after he was forced to leave the company, he is now in position to do something great. I remember the quote of Charles Darwin:

> "It's neither the strongest specie that survives nor the most intelligent. It's the one most adaptable to change."

Andy makes the change. He wants to work and helps others. He went back to his old company when he heard that it was about to close the branch all together. He negotiated with the owner for two weeks and finally decided to buy the company for $1.67 million. This is the amount he made just within a year from his options trading. He is able to hire all his old friends to continue the retail business. He renames the retail company 'Jenny's Place'. He still continues to trade options a few hours a week while managing his business. He is now contemplating expanding his business elsewhere into a chain of stores known as 'Jenny's Chains'. Doing option trading correctly can easily provide us with empowerment to serve others.

How Warren Buffett Use Option to Make Millions

Warren Buffett famously started buying Coke in 1988 and today his company holds the big share in the stock. As of December 2014, his company holds a stake of $16.9 billion in Coke. It is interesting that Buffett used option to build Coca-Cola fortune. He uses a conservative and safe strategy called option that most investors are not aware off. In 1993, when Coke was traded at $39, a price level Buffett considered as overpriced. What did he do? He did not sit on his hands and waited for the price to drop to a more reasonable level. He used a simple option strategy to buy a put option at $35 ($4 below the price at the time) and he harvested $7.5 million before he bought a single share of the stock. He collected the money upfront. What does it mean when he bought a put option to buy the stock at $35? He had promised to buy the stock at $35 if the stock fell to the price that far. If the stock price fell to $35, he is obligated to buy at that price. Guess what, that was what he intended to buy Coke at the price. If the price never drops to $35, he will keep the $7.5 million. It is pretty cool. Either way he wins. As it turned out the price never reached $35 and kept the amount $7.5 million. He kept repeating to buy his put option as long as the price level is high. He kept earning his millions without buying any extra share. It is possible to multiply your income without buying any extra share of a stock. You can do the same thing without selling your value stocks.

The best part is that we can use option to profit from any kind of market: up, down, flat and choppy. Recently option-trading volume has exploded about 40 per cent annually and more investors have discovered its power to enhance and protect their wealth.

Earning Steady Income Selling Option

Before anyone embarks on the journey to sell option, it is critical to understand that along with consistent income comes higher risk. This method of investing is not suitable for risk - shunning conservative investors. Such a strategy is suitable only for investors who understand the risk and willing to accept it, in return for consistent income. There is no 100 per cent sure of profit in the stock market. Every productive strategy has a corresponding risk attached. Investors who understand the risk and able to manage such risk have the key to long - term success. Understanding option theory and various strategies of option trading is just the first step towards success. The ability to locate the right options to trade is more important than all the knowledge you have. Most investors struggle to find the right options to sell. Applying the best strategies of selling options of a wrong company will not produce result. The following five essential rules will help you to locate the right options to sell.

First, locate only stocks undergoing high volatility. Try locating stocks that are trading at a high volatility with reference to themselves. Pick those stocks in the top 5 per cent of their historical volatility. When option premiums are expensive, it is more attractive to sell options than to purchase them. Remember that there is good profit to sell high - volatility options; the risk is also higher.

Second, only sell option strikes which are unlikely to be hit. What does it mean? For selling an option of a stock, find the strike price that is unlikely to be hit prior to expiratory date. An easy way is to check for major technical resistance and support levels. Only sell options that are solidly above (or below) the technical resistance levels.

Third, always try to sell close to the money to maximise the profit. Here 'the money' means the 'strike price' in option lingo. So the closer to the money, the higher premium you collect.

Fourth, sell your option far from the expiratory date. There is less risk in collecting premium than in selling close to the money. The further from expiration, the greater the time premium and more profit to the seller. Investors know that it is time premium that makes all the money. The longer the time-frame, you will have the better chance of success. It's less likely that the option will go against you. Managing this risk can bring reward.

Fifth, always sell on opposite side of the news. Take advantage of following the pattern of buy on rumours and sell on the news. This is the proven strategy to follow.

In today's environment, when dividends are no longer attractive but the risk of losing capital is high, selling options can be an alternative source of consistent income. All these strategies are not easy to follow if your subconscious mind is not programmed for option selling. The only sure way to success for option selling is to download all the necessary theories and strategies related to option trading. Understanding them clearly is the first step. Download every strategy you come across into your mind. The second step is to start practising and applying them to selected stocks you have identified according to the volatility scale you have. You have to keep repeating until you are comfortable with those strategies which create profits for you. Once you achieve that, you need to keep repeating them to increase your profits. You will be on the way to financial freedom.

The 2016 - 2017 Bear Market Survival Program

Beginning 2016, the world markets are entering a bear phase. By definition, a drop of 20 per cent from the peak is considered a bear market. The oil sector is suffering and the financial sector is not doing well. The Australian financial sector especially the banking industry is doing well until 2015. The global financial problem is beginning to be felt in Australia in 2016 onwards. The financial sector in USA and Europe is not healthy. In February 2016, investment bank Deutsche Bank announced a $7.3 billion annual loss, its first since the financial crisis. Investment Credit Suisse announced a loss of $6 billion for the last quarter of 2015. Shares of these companies fell to the lowest levels since 1991. Many of the European financial giants are facing problems.

Since July 2015, the Financial Selector Sector SPDR Fund (XLF) has consistently and dramatically underperformed the benchmark S&P500 index. In USA, stocks in bank sector are struggling. Banks like Wells Fargo (WFC), JPMorgan Chase (JPM) and Bank of America (BAC) are down on an average of 15 per cent through 2016 (February). A loss of about $360 billion in market cap so far in January 2016 has been estimated, the second biggest single month since 1990. What do all these information convey? The financial sector serves as the most important indicator for the American economy. The prices of financial companies rise and fall according to people's ability to make and save; launch new businesses, and repay debts. Demand for bank loan falls, borrowers struggle to pay back, people are spending less and banks are not performing. These are clear indications that the economy is not doing well. The energy and the banking sectors are leading the way to a struggling economy. Things could get much worse.

As investors, what must we do in this situation? I think we must be ready for the worst-case scenario. Brexit adds further problem. Time to practise prudent portfolio management action is necessary in 2016 onwards to protect our portfolio and conserve cash. The first thing I would do is to raise cash now and hedge it with precious metals like silver and platinum instead of gold. I think the return of the hedge with silver and platinum will outperform that of gold in the future. Some investors will use distressed corporate bonds to generate current income and future capital gains especially now 2016 to 2017. When all dusts settled, it's time to pick value stocks which are going on sale now. These value stocks will eventually give you thousands of percent profit in the future.

Dividends versus Interest in Australia

If you live in Australia, where would you put your money in share or fixed interest rate in the bank? Many of the Australian companies like Woolworths Ltd (ASX, WOW) have fallen more than 30 per cent since 2015. You need patience to pick up this stock which is on sale now. There are many other stocks on sale now. Do your due diligence and wait for the prices to fall further. The Australian share market is in the bear territory beginning 2016. This is natural and a bear market comes along after every few years. To be logical, bear markets are indeed the reason why the share market has done well over time. In Australia, it is not an exception. Perhaps, volatility is the reason why a risk premium is created, encouraging investors to abandon or buy stocks. It is in fact the very reason why the stock markets are the greatest wealth creation vehicles on earth. Remember the CHU strategy. Apply the strategy when the time is right. Patience is the keyword.

A thousand stories regarding dividend yield compared to fixed interest rates have been told. The growth of each individual stock is not even considered. In Australia, the difference is greater in the end of 2015 when interest rate is low.

In 2016, most of the stocks in Australia have fallen and share prices are considerably cheaper. The fear is still lingering that the stock market will fall further. There is a possibility that RBA will soon cut interest rate to as low as 1.5 per cent. This ultra - low interest rate in Australia, USA and across the world does not motivate us to put money in fixed deposit. I will still prefer to put money in high - yielding value stocks for the long term. What type of stocks to buy during this volatile situation? In 2016, keep an eye on Telstra, one of Australian biggest and best companies, whose price has fallen significantly. At this moment February 2016, it yields a fully franked dividend of 5.7 per cent which is great in a low interest environment.

In the medium term, when oil prices are depressed, I will buy airline stock like Qantas and tankers-related companies. I will also buy Telco companies during the dips. I will wait patiently to buy mining companies whenever there are signs that commodities prices begin to pick up. Rio Tinto, BHP Billiton and other resource stocks are in my radar list. I will wait patiently for oil stocks to recover. At this moment, the beginning of 2016, the sentiment is bad. Everywhere, the share markets are falling because everyone is living in fear of the market collapse. As Ben Graham pointed out, the day-to-day market isn't a fundamental analyst, but a barometer of investors' sentiment. Do you take it seriously and think like one of the herd. Do you agree that the recent market drops representing the market's knowledge that tough time is ahead? The market price for each stock is just a reflection the average insight of the market participants. The herd mentality of most investors is pushing the price of most stocks further down. Do we follow the crowd and abandon our stocks?

Harry Dent Prediction

The picture painted by Harry Dent gives us more worry. According to him, new bubbles take up new height and then burst; they ultimately crash and fall lower than the last crash. The first major sign, according to him, is in August 2015 when stocks broke below the upward channel. Each previous bubble started to burst after similar uptrend lines were finally broken. Then stocks rallied in the last quarter of 2015 but did not achieve a new high, and now in 2016, the stock market starts with the worst scenario. It's the worst start for the year 2016 in the history of Dow. This adds to the worry for stocks this year onwards. Harry asserts that bubbles do not correct but burst. He predicts that the next low for Dow is going to be 5 500 to 6 000 by mid-2017. We will wait and see whether his prediction comes true.

In the beginning of 2016, everywhere the market is on the downtrend. The stock market of Brazil was down 77 per cent since 2011; Russia is down 70 per cent and China is down 44 per cent since 2015. Will the Dow follow as predicted by Harry Dent? Harry Dent predicts that stocks will fall 70 per cent by 2017. The Dow index will fall to 5 500 to 6 000 by 2018. Do you believe his red flag?

Another sign to watch is that the small caps in the market fell by almost 26 per cent in January 2016 and more typical stocks moved into a bear market. Consistent poor performance of small caps occurred during the bursts of 2000 and 2007. Harry points out that this is another sign that the stock bubble is about to burst. Another worry is that the S&P 500 fell below 1812 indicating a lower result. Whether Harry's prediction is just another guessing work, we will wait and see. As investors we need to be careful when we start to buy during this dip in 2016. I will prefer to be patient and wait until the storm is over before buying stocks. The waiting may be long but when the recovery starts, don't let the boat leave without you.

Now we know that we can't depend on the prediction of any analyst. Harry Dents' prediction is way out. In the last 20 years, the market suffers from three major corrections. The last one is due mainly to the Covid-19 pandemic in 2020 and the USA market fell dramatically. The herd mentality of investors caused the market to fall in spite of the robust economy.

Interest rate is low and the government is printing trillions of dollars to provide fund for the pandemic.

If you have courage in investing while the market corrects and pick up value stocks, you would have made tons of money when the market recovers. The rich investors do that and they become richer.

Ordinary investors like us are paralysed with fear and sit still. We miss the opportunities in the last three major corrections. The Dow Jones Industrial Index after each correction keeps rising and now it has exceeded 35 000. It appears that history always repeats itself. Be aware of history. Do your own research and due diligence. You too can be rich when you retire.

S& P 500 Index

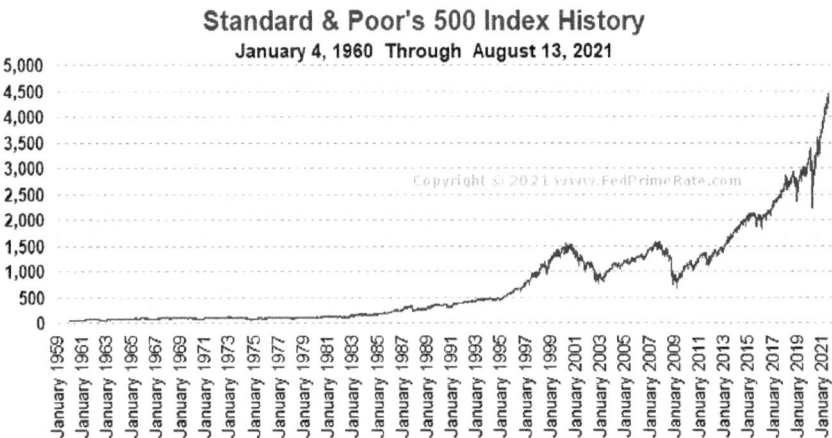

The S&P 500 Index from 1996 to the Beginning of 2016

Harry Dent's pessimistic view of the stock market after 2016 is shared partly by another well-known analyst, Dr Steve Sjuggerud, from True Wealth. In 2016, the downtrend is just about to begin. What is the implication? In the last 20 years, we are mostly in the uptrend mode telling us to own shares. But unfortunately, we are now in downtrend line right now. For me I would avoid owning stocks now until the storm is over. Now is the time to avoid buying stocks. I will follow my trailing stops closely and play better defence than offense. I will choose to play safe. I am hoping that the prediction of Harry Dent is wrong. But I am not going to bet against him because of his past successes in forecasting. Precaution is better than cure. The possibility of being right all the time in economic forecasting is not absolute. A downtrend is on the way and precaution is the keyword. The chance of Harry Dent prediction being wrong is very high.

Relationship between the Price of Gold and US Dollars

The US dollars are at all time high relative to a basket of foreign currencies at the end of 2015. The five-year US Dollar index which measures the value of the dollar against that of euro, Japanese yen, British pound, Canadian dollars and Swedish krona (in order of weighting) is all time high. By this measure, the US dollar is worth 22 per cent more than five years ago. Folks who own US dollars can now buy 22 per cent more foreign goods, services and real estate. Gold is an international asset. The relationship between gold and the US dollars reveals that they are inversely proportional. When the dollars get stronger internationally, it can buy more gold. It looks like the value of gold goes down. When the dollars get weaker internationally, it can buy less gold. It looks like the price of gold goes up.

The relationship between the value of the US dollars and the price of gold for the year 2015 is in agreement. The dollars is gaining international strength while the price of gold is slowly creeping up without being detected.

Gold has been on the uptrend for two years. A better understanding of what is happening to the gold market is an advantage. Understanding what is happening to gold relative to the US dollars and gold relative to other currencies is needed. Gold is actually rising faster relative to other currencies. This understanding will help us to make right decision to buy gold or other precious metal stocks like platinum and silver.

When silver booms, it really booms as shown in the years 1976 to 1980 (1 206%), and 2002 to 2012 (413%). In 2016, indication is that silver is about to move upwards. Will history repeat in 2016 onwards? I think it is worth the risk to bet on silver from now onwards. What do you think?

Stock Investment for Long Term

One of the quickest ways to financial freedom is still investment in stocks. Investing correctly into growth stocks provides not only consistent dividends but also capital growth. Just as an example, if you had invested $5000 into Westfarmers Ltd in Australia during the eighties, you will be very comfortable to retire now. In Malaysia, if your father had invested 1000 shares of Public Bank or Genting Highland in the sixties for you, you are now a millionaire. Similarly,
in USA, if you had put down $1000 into Apple shares in the nineties; you are comfortable in your retirement now. Looking at these super examples, the right approach to retire comfortably in the future is to put your money into growth stocks as early as possible. Timing is important as the economic cycles repeat themselves.

What is our first goal of investing? We want to buy low. We want to buy stocks whose prices underestimate the values of the underlying assets or earnings. We want to buy value assets with future potential. We need to keep looking for instances when the market is wrong when prices dip. The prices of stocks are determined by the consensus of the participants. We need to believe in ourselves instead of following the herd. We must not think that majority is always right. So we need not take instruction of the big group who knows less than us. The market is just the group of participants who are selling and buying. The group seldom maintains objective, rational, neutral and stable positions. The market is not a clinical and fundamental analyst. It is merely a barometer of their sentiment. Warren Buffett used to act in contrarian to the market sentiment and made his fortune. Every investor knows of his famous quote but they seldom follow. He knew that the market does not have an above average insight; but it often is above average in emotionality. The prices of stocks only reflect the average insight of the participants. As we follow the market, it becomes obvious that when a big number of participants panic, the emotion seems to snowball. Participants influence each other, and their emotions compound, so that the overall panic in the market can be higher than that of the individual. The fundamental and potential of most companies are on the side lines. Remember Warren Buffett waited for over thirty years for the extreme low value of the stock GEICO to scoop up its shares. He made a fortune on the stock his mentor invested heavily during his tenure. Thus we, as better investors, should not be dictated by the market. In fact, contrarianism is built on the premise that we should generally do the opposite of what the crowd is doing, especially at the extreme. In 2016, the price of oil is moving in the direction of the extreme, and the oil-related stocks are at rock bottom. What are you thinking? I am waiting to use the theory of contrarianism and scoop up oil-related value stocks when the uptrend begins. This also applies to commodity stocks. How low do stocks like Rio Tinto, BHP Billiton and many other value mining stocks will go? We need to exercise patience and opportunities to buy these value stocks will soon present themselves. I will wait until it is absolutely sure that the worst is over before I start buying into the market. This type of market pull back can be used to increase my portfolio values higher.

As insurance for your portfolio of stocks, you can make use of options to maximise your profit. You can make use of 'credit spread' as a low risk strategy for generating monthly income in a volatile market. This strategy provides an alternative way to enhance profit for your portfolio without having to continuously monitor your brokerage account. By now you should be familiar with something called 'put', which is an option contract giving the buyer the right, but not the obligation, to sell a specified amount of an underlying stock at a set price within a specific time. The buyer of a put option estimates that the underlying asset will drop below the exercise price before the expiration date. A put is a bet that the price of the underlying stock will depreciate relative to the strike price. This is the opposite to a call option, which gives the buyer or holder the option to buy share at a specific price. Instead of selling a put option, we use a credit - spread strategy which allows you to actually receive cash (net credit) for executing them, while protecting you in an ironclad way. With a credit spread, you sell one put contract, and you buy one at a lower price (the price you intend to hold the stock). You pocket the difference between the two contracts. This is a good insurance and the money is deposited into your account immediately. This is a repeatable trade that comes with practice and experience. Learn this credit spread strategy as an additional way of profiting from your investment in the stock market.

Summary and Generalisation

Besides investment in assets or properties, investment in stocks wisely is one of the possible vehicles to become rich and wealthy. Many of the value stocks provide good dividends and growth.

Many new millionaires are created every year and others are downgraded. It is believed that every stock has its true value. The ability to buy a stock below its true value will ensure profit. The problem is in the determination of the true value of a stock. Every investor has his own ways of determining this value before buying the stock. Generally we make our decisions based on its revenue, profit, dividend and growth. Many successful investors have found their own strategies in determining the true value of a stock and make a fortune from their investments.

Understanding the economic cycles for each sector of the economy will be a big advantage in stock investments. The last seven or eight years are the great years for stocks after the 2008 - 2009 bubble burst. This bull market is brought by the commodity led boom created by the central banks, nurtured by China's huge investments in fixed assets. In USA the run is also propelled by students' loan and car loans. All these are coming to a halt. Beginning 2016, this epic boom is over. Commodity prices are on the decline especially the energy sector. The second half of

2015 witnesses the decline of oil and gas prices and the decline continues. It seems that we are witnessing the beginning of an epic bust. The last 120 days beginning August 2015, we saw the decline in most of the major sectors like oil producers, transportations, emerging markets, junk bonds and commodity prices. In early 2016, the oil prices bottom and recover due to rumours that Russia and Saudi Arabia will cooperate to cut production. This may turn out to be a smoke screen for oil. The real fact is that USA oil production in 2015 is higher than that of 2014 and the production of US on shore oil and gas firms continue to soar. In spite of oil at around $30 per barrel in February 2016 and about $50 in June, there are many drilling in Texas fields where the production cost is only $12 per barrel. In 2015, the production of oil in USA increased by about 10 per cent. It's hard to imagine that the prices of oil will escalate when USA's production continues to grow in 2016. With the sanction on Iran lifted, the country is accelerating its production of oil to grow its economy. The surplus will be there. Moreover, lower energy prices are good for the economy of most countries except those too dependent of oil production. What are the implication to many industries with low prices of oil and gas?

First, the obvious impact of cheap oil is on companies that have higher cost of production. The destruction of off shore oil industries will happen because they become uneconomical to function. Resort giants at the Gulf of Mexico and Brazil are the first victims of cheap oil prices. Stocks like Freeport-McMoran (FCX) and Petrobrass (PBR) are both down 91 per cent and the stock price. Transocean (RIG) is down 87 per cent.

Second, those service industries for off shore companies are the next victims. The service industries like companies providing air transportation, insurance, maintaining and powering them are going to be affected. Companies like Era Group (ERA) providing helicopter service to rigs off Mexico is hit badly.

Third, many transportation companies for energy are now affected. Their boom has ended when off shore transportation slows down. Companies like Tenaris (TS), Union Pacific (UNP) and Cheniere Energy (LNG) experience a terrible downgrade. These companies become part of the domino along with other chain suffering from cheap oil. Oil energy transportation average becomes a good indicator for a bear market.

The next victims are the firms that sell into the broader supply chain of the oil and gas industry and those that provide services to its employees. Banks that finance oil and gas development like Cullen/Frost (CFR) and others are downgraded. Retailers like Cabela's (CAB) providing outdoor outfitters for the employees suddenly lost most of its business. Finance companies providing credit to oil and gas employees in terms of loan on cars and others are now suffering big losses. Makers of trucks like General Motors (GM) are also affected. Even the investment arm of Warren Buffett into energy companies will be greatly affected. But his holding power may be the saviour for the future. This may last for a few months only and by June 2016, the oil price recovers to about $50 per barrel. The prediction of Harry Dent is on hold. Will the price of oil maintain throughout the year 2016 and 2017? Your guess is as good as mine.

The good side of cheap oil may be time for us to pick up world best and most important companies at super cheap prices. We may be able to buy some of the value stocks in commodities at a 90 per cent discount. The present destruction of offshore oil fields may present future opportunities for making big money when the same technologies that lowered production cost on shore fields will eventually put to use on offshore fields. Investors with foresight may reap big profit in the near future. Solar energy is going to replace fossil energy soon. So be prepared into metal oil and solar energy storage system for future energy source. The change is inevitable and investors should follow the clue and change accordingly.

USA is not yet in the bear market but soon. During a bear market, cash is the king. Perhaps hedging our cash with precious metals like silver and platinum is more logical than buying gold. How long will this bear market last? Nobody knows. We need to understand the difference between a bear market driven by fear and the one driven from deteriorating fundamentals. In Australia, experts know that this bear market is driven mainly by fear. We need to see some of the facts on the table.

But one thing is certain, if you buy a stock at a price which it is worth at the time, you can sleep soundly. When the economy recovers, the true value of the stock will adjust. Buying a value stock at clearance sale price now will guarantee you a big profit when the economy picks up.

CHAPTER EIGHT

DIRECT SELLING TO PRODUCE RESIDUAL INCOME

Introduction

Many people believe that life happens to them and they settle for a life that is less satisfying. Do not just sit there, paralysed by inertia and worst fear. This consciousness is important. This is the beginning for you to realise that the subconscious mind has an important role to play. Little do we realise that living a life of our dreams and working towards financial abundance; all start with our mind sets. We need to adopt the belief and practice of a millionaire and think like one. Millionaires enjoy cash flow, capital gains and streams of residual income. There are many ways of creating residual income and cash flow. I have discussed some of them in the last few chapters. Besides writing, property investments, business profits, dividends from stocks and portfolio growth, CD recording, franchising, there are others ways of creating residual income. Directing selling for well-established networking companies like Amway and 4Life can be a good way of creating residual income. All of us want financial freedom. However, today many of us are finding it harder and harder to keep our head above water financially. Many of us are giving up hope and feeling that winning the lottery or inheriting is the way to become rich. But we do not have to give in to negative thinking. There are always many ways of getting ahead financially. We must have a clear mind to think effectively and constructively. Start to think well, speak well and write well now. If you do not have such a tool; it's time you learn to meditate; begin the process of visualisation and gain life vision of your dreams.

Network Marketing and Franchising

Read about the successful stories about people involved in network marketing. Retrain and rewire your brain by downloading the strategies of these successful people in the business. Make use of the four elements of the Mastery Strategy and apply the principle to network marketing. The strategies used successfully for network marketing leaders can be replicated and mastered. The role of the centre part of your brain or your subconscious mind can be activated by downloading the approaches of successful people in network marketing. Besides high impact learning and good support, you must have good reason to be a contractor of network marketing. Practise intentionally and persistently until you achieve your dreams of financial freedom. You do not have to change your career immediately. You can have part-time business at home. Most importantly, you must have a meaningful goal to work for. Of course financial freedom is one of them. There must be other meaningful things like helping, providing service and value for others you have in mind. I cannot speak for you. I work for financial freedom because I have an ambition bigger than myself that is I want to contribute and help others especially those I love. Creating values for others and financial freedom for my family are major drives.

Do you know the difference between financial security and financial freedom? Holding on to your job provides you financial security. Once you lose your job, you lose your financial security. We all want our boss who cares about our well-being, who can provide a vacation in some tropical islands and gives relief from our monthly bills, expenses and overflowing debts. We work longer hours and work harder; hoping that our companies will take notice and we will get a raise. And everything will work out, right? It may not be always right. The truth is, most of these dreams are not going to come through unless we make a change. A change in the way we approach our jobs and, more importantly, the way we create other forms of residual income. This reminds me regarding the first fundamental thing we need to do well. That is thinking well. Think about taking control of your life. Do not allow your thoughts to repel money. Think well and use your imaginations. If you have the brain of a poor person, you need reprogramming. You need to eliminate those beliefs and habits and download the characteristics of a rich brain. As soon as this is done, your brain will be a new machine driving you into the valley of wealth. You will see risks as opportunities. All your self-doubts, fears, uncertainties and procrastination will vanish. Unless we do it early, we are destined to live by someone else's rules, conditions and limitations. If you have no aptitude for writing, singing, sports, investment in properties and stocks, what other kind of change do you have? What kind of financial priorities can you adopt without starting over completely? May be you need a shift into a different field like network marketing for established companies. Direct selling for Amway or 4Life could help increase your earning potential. May be we need a Plan B! Many of us have never owned any business. Do not worry. You do not need experience or extra qualification. What you need is courage. You must be willing to go where few have ventured before and never let a lack of experience stand in the way of your dreams. Your dream of financial freedom is common. All of us share the same dream. It's time we join these self-made millionaires and start your own businesses. All of them have meaningful goals why they want to make millions. So do not let fear or inertia paralyse you from taking your first step.

Creating financial freedom requires taking some risks. Most of us are conditioned to fear of change. We stay at jobs for their security, no matter how many dead ends we run into. We buy into the myth that we will be successful if we get a degree, get a job, work hard and invest wisely. It's safe, it's easy and you will enjoy financial freedom. It's a lie. Business ownership may not come cheap. Franchising is also expensive. For those who can afford and have a passion for franchising, it's a good strategy to create wealth through established businesses like McDonald's, 7Eleven and others. Many entrepreneurs have succeeded in this type of franchising business. One good thing about franchising is that these organisations provide valuable training and support to help you succeed. If you have the means and aptitude for such venture, you should never hold back. If you have financial problems and you are an employee, then you have other alternatives. Many franchise fees can be costly and is not for the average person. And we have not added insurance, employees, marketing, office space, and others. On top of all these, you will be tied to your franchise for hours each day. You cannot hold on to your job. You will lose your time freedom. If you do not have such big capital to start a franchising business, think of alternatives.

Join the latest trend of business, based on one simple-to-learn component: word-of-mouth. Some people call it direct selling, network marketing or relationship marketing. Companies like Amway, 4Life and others realise that it is the single most cost effective way of bringing products to market. Opportunities abound to market the products and services of these existing companies through word-of-mouth for people like us who want to turn our lives around. It's a model that has been around for more than half a century. These are not the only companies available for you to be involved in direct marketing. Turn to Google, you will find many other successful network marketing companies.

Many entrepreneurs who dare to take up such a challenge like network marketing for established companies are now self-made millionaires. You can be one of them if your temperament suits such a business. The advantage is that you can work your business around your existing job and still qualify for the incredible tax advantages of owning your home-based business. Many people have made it their full-time career. The choice is yours. I will choose a business that's right for what I want to accomplish. Start investigating various companies especially those with good track record like 4Life, Amway and others. What types of products you are interested and are marketable? You must believe in the products before you can pass on its remarkable qualities to others. Many of the successful entrepreneurs are users themselves. They know the quality of the products. My choice is to look for successful companies like 4Life or Amway which are going to be around forever. Once you are decided, start look for proven system for success that you can use immediately to get your business off the ground. There is without the often-prohibitive start-up costs.

Financial Security and Financial Freedom

I must admit that I had both financial security and financial freedom when I was working. I was a qualified teacher with a bachelor of science degree with honours. My job provided me with a little financial security. I was struggling to make ends meet with my meagre salary. I had an extended family of nine people under my care. My financial security is under attack every month. I have no alternatives but to strive for financial freedom instead. So there is a difference between financial security and financial freedom. Initially I did not dare to venture into something else. I was frightened of losing my job because I had so many bills to pay and so many people to support. I meditated and my visualisation told me different things. My life vision emerged. My creativity tells a different story. I realise that I can have both financial security and financial freedom. I needed a different mind-set, a different attitude and a different skill set. I needed to be honest to myself and also I needed to be a good teacher. I must use my spare time effectively to create both linear and residual streams of income. I did both successfully. Providing extra tuition classes during the weekends and lecturing part-time in institutions of higher learning for extra linear income is my first strategy. Writing textbooks and investing became my alternative strategies. With some saving from my extra income I started investing in properties, stocks and business joint ventures. I managed to create streams of residual income. If I am allowed to relive my working life, I might have chosen direct selling for established network companies like Amway or 4Life as another alternative way of getting residual income and cash flow. I was able to retire at the age of 51 because I have achieved financial freedom. Although there is a difference between financial security and financial freedom, I prefer to embrace both during my working days. To some people, financial security is just the opposite of financial freedom. To them, the more security you have the less freedom you inherited. Clinging on to your job or paycheque creates less freedom for you. Thinking over this issue, if I were given a choice between the two, I would choose financial freedom instead of a paycheque for financial security. In fact during my working days, I was lucky to have both financial security and financial freedom. My financial freedom far outweighs my financial security. My financial freedom removes fear from my life equation. I became more confident and acted more courageously even when I was serving as principal of my school. I did not worry about my paycheque any longer because I have financial freedom. My recurring income keeps growing exponentially and I feel very secure financially. I was able to retire at the age of 51. After almost two decades of struggle I had managed to remove money from my life's equation. So I have the confidence to pursue the important things in my life. What are these things? I realise that life is about new experiences, growth and contributions. These three important metrics in my life have been discussed earlier.

People's Fear

There are many types of fear. Some of them are fear for failure, fear of losing our job, fear of disappointment and many others. A survey around the world shows that older people fear losing their job than anything else. Their fear is legitimate because a lot of people are running out of money during retirement. This is a real concern especially in developing countries. Most people have financial security in the form of their monthly paycheque but they do not have financial freedom. To remove the fear from your life equation, you need to start thinking how to create streams of residual income and cash flow. By working hard in your job, you are unlikely to have financial freedom. You need to change your mindset and attitude towards life. While you are young and working, start something of your own like having a direct-sale business for network companies like Amway or 4Life. The advantage of a direct-sale business is that you do not need big capital to begin with. Investing in stocks, properties and business is fine. These investments need capital. You need to start saving to build your fund for investment. You have to do something because working life is short. Everyone has about thirty years of working life. You need to think well.

Direct Marketing through Established Network Companies

According to Robert T. Kiyosaki, there are four categories of people that make up the world business. The four categories are simplified into E, S, B and I. The abbreviation E stands for employee; S stands for self-employed; B stands for business owners and I stands for investors. Many of us are in the E category. We depend on our paycheque every month. If you have a small business and you are self-employed, you are in the S category. If you are in big business hiring others, you are in the B category. If your income springs from your businesses and investments, you belong to the I category. I was lucky when I was working, my income flowed from four sources: paycheque, rental, royalty, business and investments. So I was in both E and I categories. I enjoyed the best of many worlds. My observation of people in these four different categories reveals that each category of people have different values and they speak different languages. People in the E category usually look for secure job with benefits. I was one of them. I inherited this core value because I was looking for security and a long-term pension as a government servant. When I became aware of financial freedom, I moved away from the 'E' category to embrace the 'I' category. Many thanks to this magnificent move, I am able to enjoy my retirement with all the freedom I have now. People in the S category always want something done right and they do it themselves. They have small business owners because they value independence. They speak different language. They say, 'I am going to do it myself.' They get paid through commission or the amount of time they spend on the job. The smartest people like doctor and consultant get paid through its enterprise. Another good way to start a small business is direct sale through Amway or 4Life. People in this category want to be the best in their field by being at the top of the business. People in the B category usually start from nothing and build a great business. They are people with powerful life missions. They are different from people from the S category who aspire to be the best in their field. People in the B category are looking for the best people in their field to join them and strengthen their business. They can leave their business to others and still get paid. They are usually the rich owners. Those in the 'I' category are usually the people with much freedom and they enjoy financial freedom. They enjoy and love the idea that their money is working for them. They invest in real estates, business ventures, stocks, bonds and others.

Which category of the four mentioned suits you? Which category will bring you financial success? I cannot answer for you. I can only answer for myself. I knew by following the E category strictly, I would have retired with poverty. I moved away from E into I category helping me to achieve my financial freedom. Today, my investments and digital publishing provide the ongoing passive or residual income in millions without to go into my office. My observation reveals that many people fail to become successful financially because of fear. They fear to move from the E category to S or I category. They only move from one job to another. Nothing venture nothing gain. Pull up your sock, save some of your income and move into the S or I category. You will never regret when you retire.

Ways to Become Rich

Most of the world's new millionaires are not born rich. In fact many of them started their careers without any experience in business, without much money and without any technical skills. I have learned that there are many ways to become rich. I was a top class basketball player in my state, Penang. I could not become rich because such talent has no market value in Malaysia. But in USA if you have exceptional athletic talent like many of NBA players; you could strike it rich. If you are a top executive or CEO of a corporation in Australia or USA, you can earn a huge salary with stock options; you can become rich. Building a business such as direct sale business for Amway or 4Life, you can also become rich. Most of the rich are in business and they become richer. But starting a traditional business nowadays requires big capital and most of us do not have such amount of money. We also do not have the operational, selling and leadership skills to succeed. So how do you dream about starting a business when so many of the avenues are closed? So a direct selling business can be a good business to start with. You do not require big capital. This is another way for any person who is willing to work for it. What you need is your positive attitude to help people and you want to teach. Direct selling 4Life is a revolutionary way to achieve wealth. It's an opportunity. It does not require prior qualification.

The direct sale industries like 4Life or Amway do not care what college you went to, how much money you make today, what race or sex you are or how good looking you are. What you need is a positive attitude and a willingness to work with people and serve them. It is one of the businesses in which every one of us can attain financial freedom. But starting a direct selling business involves minimum risk. Taking that initial step by starting direct selling for Amway or 4Life; you are buying a ticket to your financial freedom. This is an easy way to become a business owner. Once you fall in love with any of such companies, the sky becomes your limit, literally. The industry pays for productivity that is the more you put in, the more you get out. It's not about working hard but it is about working smart. The ability of teaching others to spread the same philosophy will make you much richer. So thinking and speaking well are critical. Here is a sound advice from a self-made billionaire, J. Paul Getty. He said:

> I would rather have 1 percent of the efforts of 100 men, than 100 percent of my own efforts.

Imagine that you are a landscaper. What do you do? You will start to look for houses and offices that need your services. If you do it yourself you can charge $500 each job. You can only do one job at a time. If you have ten or twenty groups of others to do the job and you pay each group $450 for each job, you would make $50 per job. If each month you can get fifty jobs, you would have put $2500 in your pocket. Does it sound better for you? In direct selling business like 4Life, the business thrives on word-of-mouth marketing. The more persons you have under you, the more you get. That's the benefit of relationship marketing. You get paid for such recommendations. As an independent contractor, you're encouraged to find others to join the same type of business. Are you willing to try and make the change? Change your perspective and you change your finance. It's about exposure and spreading the message. Introduce the products that you already know and services that you already use and like. This strategy based on 'word-of-mouth' becomes your business. Unfortunately the school does not teach you financial education regarding direct marketing. Direct selling teaches you values not taught in the school curriculum. It teaches you to become a business owner. More importantly it teaches you to take charge of your own destiny. It becomes a business school for you. It teaches you real-life training in sale and building networking. It teaches clarity in communication skill of how to successfully duplicate your efforts to reach out to like-minded people to become financially free. Initially it can be challenging and tough. You will begin to build a network of salespeople and start duplicating your effort. Once you can build a support system, the process begins. Being focused and committed, your chance of success is there. Most people will encounter initial problems. They stumble and find difficulty of getting started. By being aware of these challenges, you will be better prepared to stomach these initial encounters. One good thing is that you will not be fired. Direct sale companies understand and know that your success is also their success. The companies care primarily for your willingness to change your attitude, to learn and to grow with them. They appreciate your gut to stick to your mission of owning a business. Slow and steady wins the race. Many direct selling companies like Amway, 4Life, and others have fantastic products which all of us need. Once people use the products they will keep coming back for more. Once you achieve this level of contact and networking, your passive income or 'freedom money' will start to flow into your account. This money will keep flowing into your account whether you work or not. Once this freedom money starts to flow freely, it is time for you to devote wholly your effort to build your direct sale business. You do not need your job and monthly paycheque anymore. Residual income is recurring and you do not have to work for it any more. But it's fantastic if you can keep expanding your business that makes you rich. You will join the group of successful businessmen getting others to work for them. They will help to produce income for you. This is one of the ways for you to become rich. You are not only becoming rich; you are also helping others to become wealthy. This is the simple philosophy that when you create value for others, you create value for yourself. Which do you choose, job security or financial freedom? But it's direct business perfect for you? It all depends on you and your attitude. I cannot answer for you.

Dr Sin Mong Wong

Successful People in Network Marketing Business

I must admit that I was never involved in network marketing or direct sale business. My son and his wife are involved. They are quite successful but not to the level of being rich. They manage to create a stream of residual income of a few thousands a month. They have three children and this passive income is just enough to take care of the three kids' education. They are still building up their direct sale business with 4Life. Hopefully they will succeed.

I read about Dr Rob Robertson, an emergency medicine specialist. He is an extraordinary person who has successfully combined his profession with that of a successful entrepreneur. He and his son were co-owners of the nutritional company. They got to know about the network marketing company 4Life, everything changed. They learned about this new company, they were intrigued about the potential of this company. They sold their own nutritional company and became the first distributor in 4Life research. He is passionate about the practice of using nutritional supplements and lifestyle changes as preventive and proactive forces in health. Soon he learned the power of residual income. His two sons also became 4Life distributors. They were equally successful. They form a powerful group of distributors leading the company in sales. Today 4Life nutrition products are distributed in more than forty countries and Dr Robertson's organisation is involved. With his regular residual income, he does not have to be there all the time. This gives him plenty of time to spend with his wife, children and grandchildren. His lifestyle is transformed by being a network marketing business owner. He is able to do what he wants; he has time to pursue his interest, he travels and he writes. This is what he says:

> I get up each morning without facing the pressure of an unchanging, day-to-day environment.

He and his wife, Dawne, are living their dreams and have travelled all over the world. Do you want such an advantage? Do you want financial freedom? Everyone should give a thought about this type of business. If I am not a successful writer and investor, I would have started to be a distributor for 4Life. I believe I can easily create another stream of residual income.

The freedom created by having a direct sale business like 4Life or Amway is that you do not have to engage in a particular daily routine. Just like Dr Robertson, his day just evolves and never duplicates itself. Although he keeps himself busy because he loves what he does: he attends e-mails from distributors; answers phone calls and sets time to write each day. He has the advantage because of his medical background. He feels strongly that the emphasis on treating illness and diseases should be replaced by prevention using nutrition supplements and lifestyle changes as preventive and proactive forces in health. He is a happy man because happiness is being busy. Happy people are usually more productive. According to him, most unfulfilled people are those who are looking for things to do. I share this experience. Most fulfilled persons always have something meaningful to do. He is a leader. We can look forward to emulate his examples which inspire us. His example of growing his business that covers the world provides an important message for us. By taking up the challenge of direct networking, we too can be prosperous and happy.

Adopt a Visionary Approach

I have my dreams of financial freedom. I believe you have yours too. We want to spend more time with our friends, family members and pursue our own interest. We want new experiences, growth and contribution. The truth is, things are not going our way unless we are prepared to make drastic changes. Do you think that your job alone can bring financial freedom? Unless you take control of your job and start to build your own business of any kind, you are destined to live by someone else's rules, conditions and limitations. Are you feeling helpless? You are not alone! Most people share this dilemma. All of us are looking for alternatives to the roads their lives have taken them. I share these experiences. My salary as a teacher did not take me anywhere. I found alternatives: providing tuition services, part-time lecturing, publishing, properties, stocks and business-joint venture to gain financial freedom. I did not include network marketing business because of my ignorance.

Network marketing business like 4Life and others have generated billions worldwide. If you start to look for business, starting a network marketing business like 4Life can be rewarding. A big percentage of rich people own a business. Many start from scratch. They are willing to go where only few have ventured. They never let a lack of experience stand in the way of their dreams. Their dreams, just like yours, included financial freedom and also freedom from the constant threat of unemployment. There is fear of pension plans and other benefits being reduced or even eliminated when their job security is threatened. So why aren't you following the lead of millionaires who start their own businesses? Are you one of those who fear change? Many people stay in their jobs for security, no matter how many dead ends they run into. Many follow career paths that others recommend. They never ponder over the recommendations which may be ill-advised. We are easily deceived by thinking that if we study hard, get a degree, work hard and invest wisely, we will become rich. The lack of financial education does not offer much help. It's safe and it's easy to become rich. You will quickly find out that this is a lie. But starting a business is not easy and it's not cheap. Franchise fees can be a huge sum which most of us do not have. The average franchise is not for the average person like us. And if we include insurance, employees, marketing, and office space, the sum is beyond most of us.

Starting a franchise business involves working more than five days a week, opening the store in the morning and locking its doors at night. You would have less freedom in terms of time. Remember, the franchisor earns up-front fees and gets paid royalties based on gross revenues, not your profit. The franchisor benefits whether you do or not. Instead of thinking of starting a franchise business, you can have alternative businesses which are started by individuals like you. Companies like Amazon.com, 4Life, Amway, Sprint and others provide good models. This way provides anyone interested in starting his or her own business. We call it direct selling, network marketing or relationship marketing. This is the new trend of business. And it comes down to a simple method known as word-of-mouth. This is the single most cost-effective way of bringing products to market. Opportunities abound for marketing nutrition products from 4Life through the word-of-mouth for anyone who wants to turn his or her life around. While you build your network through this process, you are helping the company save millions in advertising, millions in storefronts and millions in distribution. All these expenses can be distributed to the direct agents making most of the successful distributors very rich. You do not have to start from scratch. The products are ready made and the training will be provided cheaply to whoever has the attitude and courage to start. The 4Life business has been around for more than fifty years. It's something you can do in your spare time. It's a home-based business. It can be a part-time or full-time business. It all depends on you. All that matters is your willingness to make a change. You can change your perspective. You can change your finances and you can change your life towards financial freedom. If the company meets your requirements, the sky is your limit, literally.

Some Successful Stories

There are many successful stories for people who are involved in network marketing business such as 4Life and Amway. Dr Rob Robertson's quest for the best in healthy nutrition took him to 4Life. He went to the top and became a self-made millionaire. He feels passionately about the practice of using nutritional supplements and lifestyle changes as preventive and proactive forces in health. I like his personal philosophy:

> Always have one more thing to do each day than you have time for it. That way, you awaken each day with work to be accomplished.

Another successful person in this relationship marketing caught my eyes. Herminia Nevarez is just an ordinary veterinarian. His salary did not provide him the financial freedom he aspired. He worked long hours and he was motivated to do what he could to have more time with his family. He got a phone call from a friend who later became his sponsor. After receiving all the detailed information regarding network marketing techniques; he decided to take advantage of the 4Life opportunity. He dreams of financial freedom so that he could take frequent vacations with his wife and have more time to spend with his kids. According to him, the goals he set when starting 4Life business were financial freedom and the ability to do good for others outside his family. He met his goals and found much more with 4Life. He has more time with his family and does things that he truly enjoys. He travels around the world and shares the 4Life opportunity with thousands of people. That is the vision he had when he signed up with 4Life. Now his entire family is involved in the business. He reiterated that his wife and children are part of his success. Even though his business has its beginning at Puerto Rico, his birthplace, now his business is multinational. He is still expanding his network and expansion. I believe that within the next few years he would have built one of the largest organisations in the history of relationship marketing.

Here is how Herminia describes his lifestyle working together with his wife:

> Now I decide which days and hours I am going to work! It's up to me to decide how much time I should devote to my business, according to my priorities. Every minute I dedicate to my business brings me great satisfaction. And now we can work from home together, it's easy to continually share the fruits of our success. We both gain much from knowing that we have helped many others in our organisation gain greater freedom, reach their goals and make their dreams a reality.

Nothing in life is impossible. Everything you propose to do like finding financial freedom for your family can be done by conquering the fears and obstacles along the way. To be a good marketing agent for 4Life or Amway, one of the obstacles to overcome is to learn to be an entrepreneur and a business manager. It's a good option if your vision is to gain financial freedom and help others.

Another successful story is Juan Rosado, who worked as a security guard before he became involved with 4Life. He believes in the dreams he describes in his book, *The Guard Who Paid the Price for His Dreams*. When he joined 4Life, he had four simple goals to fulfil. Even these simple goals seemed like dreams to him because he never had the means to make them into realities. His four simple goals are: to retire from his job as security guard, buy his home, trade in his old car for a new one and become debt free. A friend by the name of Dr Herminia Nevarez called him about a new business opportunity. So in April 2000, Juan started his journey as a contractor for 4Life. Soon his dreams became reality. He and his wife, Damaris Zapata, have seen some of their highest aspirations come true. They are able to make radical and positive changes in their lives. These are Juan words:

> Our lives have changed for the better and also have become examples for other people. You can't put a price on the deep sense of satisfaction you feel when you achieve one of your dreams or meet one of your goals. Now my family enjoys a greater degree of freedom. It's been very gratifying to give them a better lifestyle and great vacations. I have more time to share with my wife and daughters. I even have time to pick up my older daughter from school. These are all things I could not do before, because I had neither the time nor the money to make it possible.

Juan has touched the lives of many people through his network marketing business 4Life. He has a network of 40000 people in various countries working with him as a team. This is what he likes best. He has achieved the highest rank in 4Life - Platinum International Diamond. He is helping thousands to realise their potential and dreams of financial freedom. He encourages others who are thinking to start their own business to fully analyse the benefits and potential 4Life offers as a network marketing company. This inspirational story can serve to motivate anyone who dares to dream of financial freedom while working. What about you? Living from paycheque to paycheque will never bring you financial freedom.

Further Examples of 4Life Network Marketing Success

Ray and Barbara Meurer were struggling until they learned about network marketing 4Life in 1988. Ray began to educate himself in dietary supplements and was intrigued by the products of the company. Because of his past failures in network marketing, he was not interested initially. A friend encouraged him to meet 4Life leaders and he reluctantly agreed. He was touched by the friendliness and humility of two of the founders: David and Bianca Lisonbee. Ray felt welcome and sensed a team environment, rather than the cut-throat atmosphere he experienced before with other direct - selling companies. He joined the network marketing company 4Life even when he was in and out of hospital for several years. He tried and persevered in his new business. Finally he found success. His incomes increased exponentially and by 2004, they were honoured at a 4Life convention for being one of the recipients to achieve the status of Platinum International Diamond.

Now, Ray is beyond excited about the future of 4Life. He believes that the business is on the verge of exploding. He encourages young people like you to take a good look at the opportunities provided by the company 4Life. This is another possible path for many of us who dream of a better life. This business is not complicated; it's about applying yourself. 4Life opportunity crosses international borders and translates into every culture. People around the world are getting interested in the prosperity and wellness that this company offers.

Another success story involves Jeff Altgilbers who was a house painter. He was new to 4Life, and it took him only ninety days to be awarded what was the highest pin at that time, the International Diamond. He achieved his goal of $5 000 within three months. He became aware of network marketing 4Life through friends. At first he was sceptical, thinking that it might be another 'miracle-product hype company'. He became curious when people started to tell him about the product (Transfer Factor 11, 4Life flagship) and its effects. A friend Dave Daughtrey provided Jeff tipping point by getting him interested in the 4Life opportunity. It took some time for him to make a full commitment before letting go his house painting career. He was involved in another network organisation before. He was familiar with building a business organisation. He became self-employed and his last eight years was with 4Life. When he signed up with 4Life, he did his homework well. He left North America to build his business that he had never seen. He met some of the top leaders and was impressed with 4Life corporate management. His life was totally transformed after joining the network marketing company 4Life. He made his money and he helped others. He became a more compassionate person. He travelled through nine countries in Asia and married a Taiwanese wife while selling 4llfe there. People in Asia want a better life and they are prepared to work hard to get there. He is interested in music and plays in bands as he travels around Asia. He has written more than twenty songs in the past two years, a dream made possible by promoting and recruiting members for his network marketing company 4Life as a way of living. His income keeps increasing. He shares his philosophy of life.

> I don't define success by money, cars or houses. I had all that before 4Life. I just cherish my life and being able to spend time travelling, seeing the world and experiencing new cultures. I have a house in Guam where I love to retreat to. It's on a mountain overlooking the Pacific Ocean.

He is successful because he leads by example. He is able to develop leaders within his international team. He leads by examples. He shares his view:

> Leadership is a lifetime subject we study, but for which we never get a degree. We never graduate from life's leadership school. The more we perfect our thinking and training, the greater our thinking and training, the greater our organisation will grow. First show the way: teach your leaders simple basic truths about how to build this business. Go the way: never ask your leaders to do anything that you don't or wouldn't do yourself. Always live the leadership messages that you preach.

The Bible has a good example. Do not do unto others what you do not want others do unto you. Always help people to get what they want and you will have what you want. Always try to create value in others and value will search for you. My experiences tell the same story. Providing services and values to others, you are creating financial values for yourself.

Inter Personal Skills for Success in Network Marketing

Not everybody has this special interpersonal skills to be an entrepreneur as a network marketing agent or network marketer. Can personal skills be taught? I think so if a person has mastered the first two basics: thinking and speaking. To be a network marketer for 4Life or Amway, one must have the passion and must believe in the value of the products. Most of the agents are users themselves. The attitude of the person is equally important. If your intention is to bless and help others, you can be for sure you will be blessed. You must also believe that if your mission is to create values for others; you will receive value for yourself. I can think of some of the characteristics that can help you to become an entrepreneur in direct sale.

First, you must not be afraid of failure. In direct sale business or network marketing, rejections are common features. You must be sensitive of rejections and take them graciously. Treat every rejection as a challenge and use it as a tool to sharpen your intuition in your next approach. If you keep sensitise your intuitive instinct, you will soon develop the skill of detecting potential customers. You will also learn to retreat graciously when you sense that the person you approach and speak to is not the right target. You can detect his or her interest from the conversation. Such an inter-personal skill can be developed and taught if you have the passion for sale and you have good thinking skill and you speak well.

Second, when you approach any potential customer, avoid introducing your products immediately. Learn to treat every potential customer as a social friend. Find out his interest first and start a conversation based on his interest not yours. Only from your conversation you can detect whether his family needs the supplements you are going to introduce. Once you detect that the person is not interested, learn to retreat graciously without wasting your valuable time. Only when the person shows interest in the values of the products, you will begin to explain how the products can help. Always exercise patience and do not pressure any one to buy your products or be an agent. Always leave room for him or her to contact you if he or she requires the product or interest as a business agent. Always leave the deal open.

Third, once the guy shows interest in your products or to be a network marketer, you must be able to explain to him what the products will do to the other guy and his family. This part of the interpersonal skills can be taught and trained to almost perfection. In addition, you need sale and recruiting tools to demonstrate the effectiveness of your products. This can help in turning a retail customer into a networker in your down line.

Fourth, you should try not to talk about yourself, your wants and your needs at all. You should focus on things that are of interest to the guy on the other side of the table. Remember the guy on the other side in not interested in you and your business. He is only interested about the benefits for himself and his family. Like everyone, the guy on the other side of the table is selfish. He does not care what is for you. You have to develop the skill of convincing him the benefits of the products to his family. This is what most guys want for his family. You need to be down-to-earth, telling inspiring stories, providing compelling testimonials, listing all positive aspects of your products and company.

Fifth, in your conversation with others, learn to praise their achievements and say kind words about their well-being. Learn to be friendly all the time. Do not make any judgement about the guy's opinions and ideas. Most people do not like to be judged. Learn to complement and build on his ideas. Encourage the guy to reveal more about his interests and needs especially about his family. Humility is the key to conquer his fear. Know the supplementary needs of the family first before you introduce and try to create value for the other guy's family during your encounter with him. Timing is important when you can satisfy his needs by creating value for the family. Indirectly you are creating value for yourself.

Sixth, sale of the products is only one aspect of the network marketing business 4Life. A more important aspect is to create a team of network people to enlarge your business. Scouting for potential agents under your team is most important to be a successful entrepreneur for network marketing business like 4Life. Being friendly and supportive is the beginning to attract potential agents to join your group. The ability to convince them that you can create value in the enterprise and the joint venture with them will help them to take the initiative. The skill of scouting for talents and get suitable people to join your grouping will help to grow your entrepreneurship. The set of skills required and the correct mind set take time and repetition to develop. The right attitude is required for success. To help you to succeed, you need a variety of tools including audio tapes, videos, a website or at least a brochure for the potential client to take away. Always leave something for the customers to contact you if they ever change their mind. Make these tools available to anyone who wants to join your networking and become a networker.

Last and most importantly, it is not only money. Money is just one scoreboard of the success in direct sale business or network marketing. A lot of it is about fun, meeting people and about coming up with business idea and seeing it work. It's about meeting new friends and partners. It's about helping others to live healthily. It's about travelling and visiting new places and meeting strangers. The financial benefit that comes with the enthusiasm and excitement is financial freedom.

As parents, this is another possible business for our children if they have the passion for sales and meeting people. Many millionaires are created by this well-proven network marketing business like 4Life or Amway. If our children can develop the set interpersonal skills, they can be successful in this type of direct sale business. They do not require a degree or other academic skills. What they need is the ability to think and speak well. Many of these interpersonal skills can be taught if our children have the passion for marketing and sales. This provides another alternative for them to create residual income and financial freedom. Many of the interpersonal skills can be taught and learned if our children have the passion for marketing. The procedure is easily done in three simple steps if our children are willing to make the commitment to allow their passion for network marketing to bear fruits.

The first step is to learn all the necessary skills of successful network marketers. Learn to accept guidance from those who are successful in network marketing. Make use of the tools they have developed. Do not think of shortcuts for an easy way. By following their footsteps in handling the right tools to large numbers of people, your chance to succeed is enhanced. You need to define your meaning goal for wanting to earn big money. Mostsuccessful marketers, once they achieve their financial goals, they have another value they truly treasure that is to help others. They want to create better training system and a better environment for others. They provide the basic training for their downline marketers. They know that by providing service and creating value for others, they are creating value for themselves.

The second step is to eliminate all the outdated beliefs about sales and marketing from the subconscious mind and unload these new set of interpersonal skills to replace them. All of us need to do something meaningful where material wealth cannot. You need to look beyond your material needs. You need to learn to serve and help others.

Third is to consistently practise these skills regularly to master them until you are successful. The challenge will be there but the result is financial freedom and enjoying abundance. If you cannot conceptualise having big money, you probably will never earn that much money. You have to develop the affluent attitude. You become your own boss.

To earn big money in direct network marketing, direct selling to customers is only a small part of the enterprise. Bigger money is made from recruiting marketers to join your team. You have to learn from your up line partner strategies how to effectively recruit distributors. Direct any interested prospects to your tools available and contact them a couple days later to learn if they are still interested. If so, arrange for a three-way call between you, your prospect, and up line partner. Once they join the team, you need to train your distributors to follow this system and approach. Most people are interested in big money and more free time by involving themselves in network marketing. The Internet is an easy way to keep in touch and provide information. All in all, straightforward selling is still an effective way to approach prospects and get them to purchase your products or become network marketers. So the more people your approach, the better chance you will succeed. Wealth grows on its own momentum but you must plant the seeds. In direct network marketing, you must start planting the seeds. If you just sit, paralysed by inertia and fear, you will likely never and ever succeed.

Forget about your past and do not worry about your future. The moment you sign up as a network marketer, you build your own future. Remember all the steps and practice them consistently. Prepare to work hard as well as smart. It's not that easy otherwise every network marketer is a millionaire. You need to be passionate and have the right mindset. Know the company and its products well. Be honest to yourself. If you are not enthusiastic to follow procedures and discipline, the business may not be right for you. You must learn to enjoy the journey of network marketing to become wealthy.

CHAPTER NINE

INTERNET MARKETING AND DIGITAL PUBLISHING

Introduction

I f you want to market your own products or start your own business and make your dream come true, opening a physical store is no longer a wise move. The impact the Internet on publishing, newspapers, bookshops, travel agencies, banks, and a host of other industries is obvious. Can we join the crowd to benefit from the unstoppable progress of the Internet? Many people have made use of the Internet to profit from the online trading. The digital publishing model is one of the best strategies you can adopt. What is digital publishing? It is a strategy of marketing information products including books. Just look at Amazon, its digital book sales (e-books) far exceeded its physical books. This gives a strong indication of the future of digital publishing. Many traditional bookstores are facing extinction. But digital publishing is growing at about $1 billion every year since 2008. Forrester Research predicted that digital e-books sales will exceed $9.6 billion by 2016. What will happen by 2020? Most likely self publishing books will outstrip traditional books by then.

These are hard facts for us to respect and take advantage of. We are at the threshold of digital publishing explosion right now. Any one aspires to be entrepreneur, it's time to develop your own products and take full control of your financial freedom. We focus too much on the financial aspect as an employee. We work too hard and too long for a good salary. In the process we lost our freedom. We do not have the time to do what we are passionate about. To enjoy financial freedom, we need to take care of our time freedom too. So we need to look at alternate ways to earn money. The high salary as an employee is not the answer. With the digital marketing explosion now, an opportunity is available. There are hundreds of ways to start an online business. One of the most lucrative ways is to start an online digital publishing or inter-net marketing. You can easily turn your hobby or passion into a lucrative product in digital publishing or marketing. Everyone has some form of special talent or knowledge which others want to acquire. You have something special where you can share and at the same time earn some money. You can easily become rich. I have no doubt about your ability. You must have the guts to start and produce something others are looking for. The most critical thing for our children is to make sure that they think, speak and write well when they are in schools.

History reveals that from Amazon to Apple, some of the greatest companies of the world started their life from the garage. REA group is perhaps the best Australian contribution to the league. The company is capital light in nature, with great benefit from a powerful network. Its website is popular and expanding. The company has formed a partnership with a mortgage broking group AFG to make property investment simple and less stress from our comfortable room. It provides potential buyers the convenience of various loan options in the same website. Potential buyers usually look out for website with the greatest number of sellers. Many companies are starting to build their own websites to do business. There are many other possibilities to start a website to do business. Learn from the pioneers and follow their procedures. Let the infinite power of your imaginary mind do the rest.

The Advantage of Online Publishing

You do not need to rent an office. You can function in your home or garage. Are you ready to take the first step toward your greatest possible life? Each of us has an entrepreneur within us. It is bursting to manifest itself if you give yourself a chance. Your dream of creating something new is now. I was a mathematics textbook writer. My avocation of humanising the teaching of mathematics is now on display. I can reach out to more students everywhere. I can also apply the passion of writing to create digital products that can make a difference to people's life. Now that I have done it, I must think of something else. I am thinking of online marketing in terms of e-books and physical books. So the concept of online publishing and marketing becomes important. I can do all these stuffs while staying at home. If you have the passion in writing or marketing, you can do the same.

It is estimated that by 2016, half of the retail sales will be influenced by the Internet. An estimated sum of almost $962 billion will be transacted through digital business in USA alone without mentioning the rest of the world. Follow the advertisements online, you will realise that online business is just the beginning. The opportunities are limitless. The most attracting online business is digital publishing. You only need to have your own information products and do your own Internet marketing. What is Internet marketing? Start your own website and invite people to come to your site. Your goal is to get them to become your customers. You sell them your digital products. You will direct your customers to an affiliate site where they pay for your products. You can also use your website to recommend digital products of some affiliate sites and you get a commission. It is better that you have your own digital information products. The products can be in the form of written scripts, books, video and audio. This system can be a multiplier for your business. Your customers are introduced to other products instead of one. You can also have affiliate digital products from other websites for sale and you get a commission. The important thing to achieve is to increase the traffic of visitors. Messaging is critical. Why do visitors to your website need your products? Once you can convince them about the service you provide them and the products you have, your business has begun. First you need to be passionate of your products. Second you need to believe in your products. What type of products do you have? It's better to look at products which are currently popular.

Research into current popular products available in the Internet and you will notice that articles such as love, relationship, happiness, financial freedom and successful life are selling well. Everyone wants to live a happy, healthy and abundant life. You need to be dedicated and write well. How to help others to get abundance? You need to do your research. You need to be transparent. When a visitor is convinced of your products, the sale is done. They only need their credit cards or bank prepaid cards. Once the traffic increases, your customers' base also increases. Your website will do all the work for you automatically. You do not need a store room. So there is no inventory to keep. You are marketing digital products. You can spend more money on advertising. More values can be achieved by helping others and you can scale your business tremendously faster. Your business will grow. You will never believe it. This is a simple philosophy to adopt by creating values for others and you create values for yourself.

Online Business

When I started writing and publishing mathematics textbooks and guidebooks, I had no idea what an online business was about. I went through the normal publication procedure and got my 10 per cent royalty on the marked price of each textbook I wrote. Searching for information through Google, I came across something called 'Internet marketing'. These are real people who make tons of money using their computers (Internet) in their own homes. How is it possible? They make money by marketing information online. This is the modern digital goldmine. In the yesteryears there were not many computer engineers who can help. But nowadays, information is everywhere. Anyone who aspires to become rich can use this channel. I want to be one of them. I only need to know one breakthrough idea to get started. Once started, the money train will keep moving and I will have the freedom to become rich working on my passion at home. When I started writing *The Journey Through Four Seasons of Life*, I had the concept of self-publishing as my vehicle for publishing.

The book is marketed in two forms: physical and e-book. I wanted to make a difference to others' life and leave a legacy of myself behind. This is one pretty big task. My dream came true not through luck or coincidence. It is sheer bold perseverance, relentless dedication and hard work. Now I sit back and enjoy the money that keeps flowing into my account. If anyone told me that I was going to make such big money through digital information, I would have laughed. I did not know the meaning of digital information. I have just discovered a modern gold mine. It's a digital publishing gold mine. Formerly I wrote school mathematics textbooks for secondary schools for Malaysia. The market is limited to secondary schools but the reward is big. But now the world is the market through digital publishing. There is no limit. I have just completed my second motivation book, *Consciousness towards Abundance*. Hopefully this new book will provide different strategies helping people to gain financial freedom. Remember the self-published book, *Rich Dad, Poor Dad* written by Robert T. Kiyosaki had so far sold more than 30 million copies by 2015. Each book is about $20 and the writer shares about 50 per cent of the profit. The sale quoted is only on physical books. What about e books? You can imagine! How much has the writer pocketed? Such a success must have totally transformed the writer's life. He had been laughing all the way to the bank for the last decade. By now he must have many books (about 18 books) to his credit. I had about two dozens of mathematics textbooks and guidebooks to my credit. I have published my first motivation book and the second is ready. The third "Enjoy Eighty Five Years of Abundant and Productive Life" is almost ready. I am enjoying the same success with a smaller quantum. I hope I can catch up one day and make more contribution to humanity.

Do not be crippled by fear. The fear that you are not good or smart enough is not logical. The fear that you do not have enough experience is self-inflicted. And the fear of being judged by others is imaginary. The fear of creating inferior products remains untested. A fear of success, wealth and happiness will eventually sabotage you from taking action. Remember if you harbour these fears, you are not alone. The truth is, if you are only conscious of these fears and if you do not prioritise your effort to eliminate them in your mind, you are not going to succeed in anything you do. Taking massive actions will not help. You have to be aware that all fears are only imaginary. These beliefs and fears are deep down in your subconscious mind and they have to be got rid of. How do you do it? A tool called meditation together with visualisation is readily available. You can easily learn and adopt such a simple system to help eliminate these fears from your mind. Some people seek help in the form of guided hypnotherapy to eliminate such fears. Practising mindfulness can also help. Once this process is used, you can easily download habits and practices of successful people in the digital world into your mind. These practices can easily be replicated and used successful. Knowing your passion helps to create something you are good at. All types of information are available through the Internet. Many of the successful entrepreneurs in digital publishing are offering free courses for you to emulate. Make an effort to learn new thing such as Internet marketing and self-publishing. Thinking, speaking and writing well can give you an advantage in self-publishing. Soon you will be on the way to financial freedom. A new road map to financial freedom is now available. The digital publishing and online marketing explosion is just at the beginning. The market has no limit. The digital revolution is just at the initial stage. The world population has exceeded seven billion people. The number of Internet users exceeds two billion and is growing. Everyone has his or her own talents that others require. Create something for others can be a good business. Jump into the new bullet train of digital publishing and enjoy your journey to prosperity, abundance, and success.

Digital Publishing

Digital publishing embraces every aspect of publication. It caters for self-publishing and other products which are sold online. It is now a multimillion-dollar business. Digital publishing is now the new way people read, learn and grow. It is also a new way for many to start and grow their business. It is my new passion as I spend each day doing what I love. I love writing, reading and research. Everything is a click away from my fingers. Everything I want is instantly available now. I make my money and I enjoy my freedom. I am my own boss and I can spend whole day at home with my family. There is no limit to my financial growth now. Anyone who wants to be extraordinary can begin now. It's simple. Find something you are good at. Put up an information product you have on the website and you can collect your money. That is what I do. I write something that can change people's life if they adopt. This digital publishing is in the form of e-book and also advertised for real physical book if you require one. When I wrote my mathematics textbooks and guidebooks, I tried very hard to humanise each concept to create connection between mathematics concepts and real life situation. I became popular and my books sold well in Malaysia. I was invited by the Curriculum Development Centre to lecture teachers on my discovery. I also advocated that teachers should be curriculum makers and that drew plenty of attention. I loved doing all that and felt that I now easily spread my ideas through the Internet. Eureka, I got it. I was rewarded plentifully. I knew I am going to be millionaire. I put my humanising strategy to teach mathematics in the Internet. I will reach more teachers and students all over the world. Internet marketing has the sky as its limit.

It is a simple process. First you built your website and market your digital products you have created.

Your advantage is your EPH that is your expertise, product and hobby. Choose your niche that is going to benefit others. For example, my niche in my mathematics publication is the process I use to humanise a mathematics concept. Once the niche is identified, you create a digital product. The website becomes a multiplier for you. It becomes your delivery system to market your products. The sale begins and you will soon realise your goal by growing your business. People assess your website and buy your products: advertisements, affiliate products, information, e-books, videos and others. Your business depends on the traffic. More traffic in terms of people assessing your website, more customers are likely and they will pay for your digital products. You do not have to deal with physical products requiring store room and initial payment to acquire them. Once you have produced your digital products, they are stored in the website and the transaction is done digitally without your presence. You can scale your business by getting affiliates to bring in visitors. You will share revenue generated with them. With their help and mutual benefits, you can reach customers throughout the world. What each of your customer needs is a computer and a prepaid bank card to make the purchase. The process is repeated again and again. Digital products are now the cheapest and the best.

The sale of each digital product has no limit as long as the traffic keeps increasing. Once a good network is organised, the sale will be unlimited. More products can be added as the popularity grows. The possibility of diversifications is unlimited. If you are serious that you want financial freedom, you must be committed and convicted to start this journey of digital publishing. The sky is the limit.

Dedication and Perseverance

Every journey begins with the first step. As described in my first motivation book, *The Journey Through Four Seasons of Life,* my journey in my life was tough. I had to work the butt out of me. When I started working as a mathematics teacher, I was already 30 years old. I borrowed $4 000 Malaysian dollars from my second brother-in-law to finish my science degree. It took me twenty months at $200 per month to pay back my loan without interest. I am very thankful to my brother-in-law for his help. I was a graduate teacher on a Honda motorbike for two years because I could not afford a car. When I got married at the age of 32, I inherited an extended family of nine persons. Life was tough and I had difficulty putting food on the table. If only I have digital information like now, I would not have taken more than a decade to have my financial freedom. My salary as teacher was not adequate. My wife's salary as a nurse is worse. I had to depend on a lot of side-lines to make ends meet. Necessity is the mother of invention. I started giving tuition classes during the weekends, lecturing part time at various institutions of higher learning and teaching further education classes. I also started writing textbooks to earn extra income. All the extra earnings from these extra activities help to set me free from my financial burden. I have found something I love doing. I have a new passion in writing and I enjoy it. Once I managed to get money out of life equation, I have time to think of new experiences, growth and contribution. These dedications and perseverance stand the test of time. I am ready to exploit the Internet market trend.

From normal publication I have moved towards digital publishing. Now the sky is the limit. This online publication has totally revolutionised the distribution of information, knowledge and marketing. This is the age of digital information. A new gold mine has been discovered. I am going to exploit this new avenue and benefit from it working at home. This shows that dedication and perseverance to your passion and doing the things you love will finally pay off.

Why the World Needs Digital Information

A new avenue has been created for us to share experiences and information. Every one of us is special. Every one of us is unique. Everyone has experiences and skills that others want to learn. Our passion, our special knowledge or hobby may be our speciality or gift developed through years of experience. It can be just a better way of doing something. An avenue is available for all of us to share what we know best. Everyone has something special that others want to learn. Thank God that when I became successful, I loved writing all those mathematics textbooks and guidebooks. The purpose is to help students learn mathematics.

Another passion emerges. I loved writing. *The Journey Through Four Seasons of Life* is my first motivational book. I couldn't believe the joy I got in writing the book. Now I begin to enjoy penning down my next book, *Consciousness towards Abundance.* It is almost like warm water and energy that flow through me. I have found another passion. Before that I had always encountered a hard time finding my directions in life. I have found it. The passion comes from the decision of how I am going to help others in their life. With the digital publishing revolution in progress, the process of sharing my ideas to help others becomes easier.

A new digital publishing business is born. The new business does not need an office space. It is done at home. This is the value I am going to give others and they have to pay for it. Through digital publishing, they can easily assess the materials cheaply. The business created is the problems I am helping them to solve. The business is the pain I help others to alleviate. I teach others to become successful. That is part of the purpose of my life. I had many problems before that and I managed to overcome these problems because of an important awareness. I had a hard time through the journey of my life. I was having those crappy feelings and issues that are so challenging to my life. I could not find the direction until I overcome the limiting beliefs in my mind. Once I overcome those challenges and issues, I felt that I have a responsibility to help others. I have found a formula and an answer to life's direction. The discovery is simple. We only need to unload positive values into our subconscious mind and start implementing them. After many practices such habits become autopilot in our life. I found my passion to help others and discovered my gift of writing. This gift shows the way in a new digital publishing business. I have a website now. You can access my works by going to www.sinmongwong.com.

Another Strategy to Create Passive Income

How to build a niche profit website memberships? This is similar to starting a website for digital publishing. There is a slight difference because website memberships allow members to participate in the enterprise. In this world, there are 3.1 billion people using the Internet and all of them are potential members if the contents of the website memberships are attractive, useful and appealing to them. This is a wonderful way of creating reliable recurring income if your website can attract many active members who can benefit from the contents of your website. If your website can add one member or more a day, soon you are in the business. Just like a song earning recurring income when the song is played. The writer keeps getting recurring income. Similarly the website membership site serves as a private club for sharing information and interest by similar interest community. People of the same interest and appeal want a sense of belonging sharing special information appealing to them and helping them to grow and their preference. There are plenty of people who are prepared to pay for research and information making ready for them. They join as members paying a small sum monthly and saving their valuable time to search themselves. They exchange money for time! To them, time is money and they have a shortcut to obtain available information such as fixing your computer which slows down after unloading a video; where to buy a window mechanism for your old car; how to lose weight without much exercise; where to live cheaply in certain parts of the world, and many interesting things about lifestyle. Membership of the community of like-minded people can make contribution to the common platform for forum, stories, songs, sports, relationship, cooking lessons, catering business, ways to avoid allergy, discussion and common contents of interest. The contents must be of interest to a big segment of the Internet using population. Once the website is established and attracted enough members, you are already in the business. The reliable recurring income is created. The starting cost is low to launch your Internet membership site.

Choose a topic with a niche like tennis in sports. How to improve your backhand? By showing some of the best backhand hitters like Roger Federer, Djokovic and others executing their shots for you to imitate. A step-by-step process of their backhand execution can be shown. A series of video for other skills is also included for you to learn and imitate. Repeated practice is necessary for mastery of any skill. After many training and practices, these essential tennis skills will be downloaded into their subconscious minds. Further repeated practices of these skills are necessary before these skills are automated. Let them know that repetition with discipline, consistency and persistency is the sure path to become a good tennis player. This new belief is necessary for members to succeed as a good tennis player.

There are many interesting topics you can include into your membership website. Any topic of interest such as how to improve your writing skills or how to be fit and healthy can be included. You must be passionate about it to get paid for it. Choose a platform, a specialist website to enrol members. The cost is not big. To begin with, you need friends or experts to help. The Internet business is not complicated.

Add contents as you continue to expand your membership website. Not all contents are necessarily self-made. You can buy contents which are expensive. You can also get free contents from the public. Many of the contents which are declared free from organisations like YouTube. Everybody can access videos from YouTube and use them. You can add your comments like you may not agree with the idea, add forum comments for members to discuss and contribute, give constructive ideas and encourage members to participate and contribute.

How to attract members? All Internet users are potential members. Pick contents appealing to them. Articles about marketing linked to other websites can be added. Members' referring system can also use to increase the number of memberships. Just imagine if you can get a member to your website a day, your success is guaranteed.

CHAPTER TEN

THE LANGUAGE OF ABUNDANCE

Introduction

To me, success in life includes financial freedom, well-being, healthy and happy. We need to learn to speak the language of abundance fluently to achieve success. Where to begin? To begin with, I make a commitment to like as many people as possible. I also make another commitment to help as many people as possible. I understand all these natural laws of attraction when I taught Newton's laws in applied mathematics. I know by doing so I will eventually get what I want in life. It is not easy to like and help everyone we happen to meet. The world is full of all types of people. I have to make sure that I mix with people of the same interest and people who speak the same language of abundance. I choose people who have positive attitude, always optimistic and considerate. These people will certainly influence my thinking and my behaviour. I want to laugh as often as possible. So it's important that I mix with cheerful people. I believe that laughter is contagious. I want to be one of those people who can laugh at anything they do and enjoy. My simple philosophy of life is that if I like a thing, I will enjoy doing it. If I do not like it, I will change it or avoid it. If there is a thing I have to do regularly and I cannot change or avoid it, then I will change my attitude to like it and eventually enjoy doing it. Be careful that if you do not change your attitude, then you would have planted the seed of unhappiness in your life. This awareness will be my guiding principle to live a happy life. Happiness is only one aspect of my pursuit of abundance. Mixing with people who speak the language of abundance fluently can be influential. The choice of friends is important if we want to learn and speak the same language. Immersing ourselves in the pool where the language of abundance is spoken every day can be contagious and motivating. The choice for me is crystal clear.

Experience, Growth and Contribution

Life is about new experiences, growth and contribution. So it's important I live at the present. This moment is always important. Experience whatever is for your growth. Keep learning and experience new things. That's the way to grow. The process is critical before you can make any contribution. What is contribution? It is what you give back to society. Contribution can come in many forms. Providing your service in any form such as helping a friend, giving something to the poor, making something for your group of friends, giving aids financially to the needy and many others are all your contributions. Contribution in the form of written materials and recorded advices is equally important for the advancement of mankind. There is no limit for our contribution. By your examples you may have unconsciously encouraged others to contribute too. Many such habits and practices are usually contagious. I always believe it is better to give than to receive from others. Society will be better served if we have more givers than takers. The entitlement mentality will be questioned and discouraged if everyone is encouraged to contribute.

Human beings are gregarious animals. So it's important that we stay connected to others. Collective efforts are usually more powerful in any project. Give support generously and you will find great support for your own project. Every one dreams of living an abundant life. To be successful and productive in your life, the important thing is to like your work and form the habit of working happily. My observation reveals that happy people are usually productive people. Our attitude and self-discipline are two important ingredients to help us to achieve success.

First lesson I learned to be happy and successful in whatever I do is to make friend with myself. If you have a friend who keeps putting you down as your mind does; a friend who keeps looking for your faults; a friend who keeps hurrying you to do something; a friend who demands your attention; a friend who keeps criticise you; you do not want such a friend. The worst is that the friend is you yourself. You start to reject yourself. So it's important to think well, treat yourself well and be a friend to yourself. This situation is not right. We need to know how to make friend with ourselves. We need unconditional friendship. Stop beating or criticising yourself. Drop all types of expectations about yourself. Show compassion and be kind to yourself. So if you want to be happy, you need to love yourself. You need to be a good friend to yourself. Try to lower your bar of happiness for yourself. Just be happy by telling yourself that I will be happy after my morning bath. I will be happy after my morning coffee. It's important that I will be happy now. See all the good things are happening to me. I remember the names of people who have helped me. I am grateful to all of them. I am grateful to the universe providing the light and air for my convenience. I will start smiling and the world will reciprocate.

The second lesson I learned is that if I want to be successful, I need to smell like success. This does not mean I need to be perfect. I need not be very rich right now. It simply means that I am all right now; I am good at the moment. Life is good for me. I appreciate it. I am grateful for it. I will focus on the good parts of my life and not the bad ones. It may take some time to achieve that I am my best friend. This will empower me to bring in all the energy of happiness working for my success. New ideas, friends and opportunities will soon make their appearances. Embrace this thought and be my own cheer leader. Enjoy and cheer all the way while you try to accomplish your goals. I will start to learn the strategy necessary for me to accomplish this feat. This book will help you to achieve just that.

Third, to be successful to achieve abundance in your life, the support of your spouse or partner is another critical component. Without your spouse's support, you won't get anywhere. Not everyone enjoys the support of his spouse. Many entrepreneurs in Network Marketing and Digital Publishing face unsupportive spouses because of many initial failures.

When I wrote my first motivating book, *The Journey Through Four Seasons of Life*, I faced the same problem. The book involves some parts of my spouse's life with me. It is a self-published book and it involves a little investment. Many people who are not in the field of publishing use to make all types of assumptions which are imaginary fear.

One of them is that you will be cheated. It is true that over 90 per cent of published books do not make much sale. People will harm you and your family because you reveal your success. Un supporting spouses reject success because of the fear of failure. Ignorance of wrong assumptions is happening everywhere. We need to forgive our spouses for their ignorance of their faulty thoughts and imaginary fears. Love them unconditionally. Writing is my passion. Nobody can stop me. Not even my spouse. My confidence in writing is solid and I had written more than two dozens of mathematics textbooks and guidebooks in the last thirty years. My financial freedom comes from my writing and publications. I have just completed writing my second book, *Consciousness towards Abundance*. Another book is in the pipeline, *Enjoy Eighty Five Years of Abundant and Productive Life*. People seldom think well when their thinking is blurred. They overgeneralise, speculate, fortune telling and conceive many other faulty thoughts mentioned in chapter One. For those involved in network marketing and digit publishing make sure you are well informed about the networking opportunity you are considering. Make your love unconditional and approach your spouse with patience and honesty. You need to acknowledge your past failures but point out the advantage of failure as a learning experience. Allow your spouse to ask any questions related to your network marketing or digital publishing and ask your spouse for support. If your spouse still withhold support on a solid business, you should think of an alternative. If your life partner is always against your business, others will also follow. Who can be there for you? I remember a saying in Missouri, USA:

"You brought her, now you dance with her!"

Some people believe that it is far better to leave a horrible marriage with half your assets than remain and lose your whole mind. I choose to forgive. The decision is yours.

A smart and kind woman or man is hard to find. Let's face the facts. A smart woman is needed in our life to organise and strategies how to live our lives. A smart woman is needed to give support to enable the man to optimise his efforts to make a prosperous future. If you feel empty when the person is not around you, please don't let her or him go. It is not hard to find a man loving a woman beyond imagination and you do not have to find a reason to. It's just love. Too often most people do not realise what the other person means to them until they lose them. Men and women think differently. Many of us do not think well and speak well. Many people are not aware of faulty thoughts. We make many wrong assumptions; we make judgements too often; we generalise too loosely; we label others without knowing what we say; we badmouth others without reasons and all these do not make us a smart or kind person. There is a deep gap in communication that very few men or women understand. If you keep putting your partner down, the gap is widened and communication is not possible. This consciousness and awareness is just the beginning. Learn to accommodate and speak kind words for your spouse. Your spouse is not perfect and so are you. Life is what the couple makes it. Finding faults every now and then is to be avoided at all cost. Remember to keep half of our eyes closed for we are not perfect ourselves. Live, share and love the ways we are.

The Language of Affluent Consciousness

One of important components of abundance is financial freedom. To achieve this aspect of abundance is to learn to speak the language of affluence consciousness. The first step of learning this new language is to activate the rhythm of your affluent consciousness. Open your eyes and alert your ears; you will notice the attitude, habits and the language spoken by successful and wealthy people. They speak a different language from people of middle class and the poor. This self-awareness strategy will help you to speak the affluent language as soon as possible. What is this self-awareness strategy? This self-awareness strategy is simple to implement. You need to start now or immediately. Each evening, you are required to re-examine the things you have done and the words you have spoken. Are you happy with the things you have done? Are you happy with the words you have spoken? If not, what are the things you want to do differently and what are the words spoken you want to change if you have the chance again? This conscious awareness if practised every day, you will be more aware of the things you do and the words you speak. You want to do things properly and correctly. You need to add values and support to others. You want to speak words of encouragement instead of putting people down. Be aware of faulty thoughts mentioned in Chapter One, is a good beginning. You will think before you speak. If this awareness is practised daily, you will find that the things and words you want them change will become less and less. Initially you may not notice many of the things you have done and words used have affected your thinking and behaviour. As you practise this strategy of re-examination, you will notice that some of the things you have done each day, you can do them better in different ways. You become aware of the wrong approaches of doing things especially financial matters. You will have less regret of the words you said. You learn to think and speak well. Keep using this strategy every evening, you will find that the number of things you want to do differently begin to diminish because of your awareness and thinking well. You become aware of your self-limitation and beliefs controlling your thinking of what you deserved. You become aware of things you do and you will avoid self-sabotaging in whatever thing you do. As soon as you realise that you have to overcome these silly thinking and doing things, your thinking is activated by the awareness, you are ready to transform your life. It's easy to say than actually practising the awareness strategy consistently daily. I went through this whole process and I am ready to share my experiences. When financial matter is concerned, we need to be aware of things like the value of money when we make a purchase. I notice that most working people usually have a list of items to buy and they just pick them up in the supermarket. They do not look at the prices of the items sold in the market. My wife and I are aware of alternative places to buy the same items at a much reduced cost from alternative places. The cost savings can easily be in the range of 30 to even 50 per cent of the supermarket purchase. This has given us an advantage of saving and budgeting. Self-awareness is absolutely necessary when a decision to buy or to improvise is made. Many a time, we buy something on impulse because it's cheap. But the trouble is that we never use it. So it's a waste of resources because we do not need it. This awareness teaches us to think of alternative before we buy an item. The ability to source is also necessary for any business to prosper. By practising alternative sourcing we are able to save for other purpose like investment or providing other facilities for the home. By practising the awareness strategy every evening, we are able to slim down our budgeting and have better saving for raining seasons. We begin to accumulate some good money over the years for investments and make money work for us. We learn to speak the language of affluent consciousness and soon wealth creation becomes part of our lifestyle.

Many people disagree with our approach of being prudent. They believe that they should enjoy what they earn because life is short and they believe they do not know what will happen tomorrow. I respect their view. But deep in my heart, I know that they are not going to join the wealthy class. They are speaking the language of poverty consciousness. Living from paycheque to paycheque or debt without any investment is a sure path to poverty when you retire. You will develop the dependent mentality and the government will have to care of you when you retire. In developing countries, the governments are not there to take care of you. This partly explains many old people sleeping on the five-foot way in big cities.

As parents, it's our responsibility to teach our children to speak the language of affluent consciousness as early as possible. This awareness strategy will not only influence our children's wealth creation but many other aspects of their lives. First, it activates them to think well if they have made mistakes during the day. For example, if a child is rude to his friend during playing time, he can re-examine his action in the evening and think over his language used. He will learn not to be rude next time in the same environment. He has to keep reminding himself to say good things and be kind to others. A habit he has to cultivate every day. Children will learn to create values for their friends and at the end of the day they will be creating values for themselves. They will learn to give help and support and they will be rewarded the same way.

Once we learn to speak the language of affluent consciousness, our imagination and visualisation of wealth creation can be achieved with awareness and discipline. Depending on our salary alone may not be enough to help us to become wealthy. We need to be aware of possible streams of multiple residual incomes. We need to speak the affluent language in order to expand our means of creating wealth. Many of potential strategies of creating residual income are discussed in this book and there are many more sources available.

Some Changing Lessons towards Abundance

In order to find happiness in my life, I have to make some drastic changes. First, I learn to love people as they are. So my habit is not trying to change them. This habit enables me to make friends easily. They are different from me and I learn to accept them as they are. They have their self-worth as I have mine. I do not require outside verification and validation of my self-worth. It comes from within. We are all different. We do not have the same perception about things. I do not have to please everyone around me. My reputation is not under my own control. So it's important I learn to please myself. The same principle applies to others. I choose to be happy myself. The person who matters most to me is myself and the chance is that if I am not happy, people will not be happy with me.

I realise that I do not attract what I want in life but I attract who I am. Believing that if I perceive and focus long enough on what I want in life, I will get it. Now I realise that such perception is incorrect. But if I purify my heart and mind to serve others, to create values for others, I will attract many beautiful things and plenty of abundance. I will concentrate on giving and serving others. I do not have to chase after abundance, for I know by serving others, abundance will chase after me. In other words, if I create values for others; I am creating values for myself. This is plain and simple. On the contrary, if I am full of negativity in my heart and mind, negativity in all forms will show up in my life. The result is unhappiness and abundance will shun me.

I have a choice in life. I choose the earth as my heaven. So I do not have to seek for another heaven in my life. This realisation is critical for me because I focus on doing 'good things' and everything I attract is good and beautiful. This is my new spiritual beginning. On the other hand if you concentrate on bad things, what you get in your life is hell. So It's better to live in heaven first before thinking of hell.

Life is a journey of three stages. Every stage is important to me. I want to enjoy this journey. I embrace my simple philosophy of life. I do what I love and love what I do. I want to embrace compassion and kindness. I will let kindness be my act of my compassion. I learn not to stress over everything. Stress in the form of negative feelings and the awareness of stress can be a positive thing. It can serve as GPS working for me. I learn not to be stressed out by negative feelings and emotions. It becomes a guidance system working very well for me and showing me where I am heading. I am aware that I am heading towards what I want. This system tells me where I stand in relation with my alignment between my inner state and reality of who I am. Any deviation causes stress giving rise to negative feelings and emotions. Perhaps a negative feeling is a good guidance telling me that I am moving in the opposite or wrong direction of the desired destination. So when I feel good, I know I am focusing on what I want and when I feel negatively I am focusing on the lack of what I want and I have deviated from my natural state. Being aware of stress makes me change direction and it always allows positive energy to flow again.

Empowering Beliefs

The universe is made up of energy. Matter is energy. I believe that there is an invisible force which created this universe. You can call it God as long as you are not thinking that God is a person. This invisible force becomes available to me when I stop trying to do it all by myself. I learn to connect with the energy of the universe. There is a purpose why I am here in this world. I believe I am here to experience, grow and contribute. I am part of the universe. I have a role in this universe. I learn to enjoy whatever I do. I want to share my experiences through this book. I enjoy the 'flow' of the moment; I allow each event to take its natural course. So I open myself to flow. When my inner state is in alignment with my reality; I am inspired with the right ideas and actions allowing my full potential to blossom. All of us seek abundance and we will keep trying. I will allow the Divine to act freely through me and create miracles for me. Creating values for people through my books became my mission. People are attracted to me wondering what a magnificent person I am. I enjoy inspiration and momentum in action in my life. This is an internal transformation which only I can do from within. This belief of the natural forces is deeply planted in my subconscious mind. I have the responsibility to nurture it well and let its splendour bloom.

I embrace relaxation. Feeling good has an incredible effect on my well-being and health. Realising that my inner-state influences my external reality begins. I begin to thrive. Thinking, speaking and writing well early are the stepping stone. Once I learn to control my thoughts, feelings and stress levels my life begins to transform. I abandon my anxiousness as I move towards my goal. My goal towards abundance thrives as my desire is inspired from my heart. I know immediately I have the power to fulfil this desire otherwise I would not have it.

Another realisation hits me. I embrace positive thinking. Being positive, there is no limit of what I can do. I am a no limit person. By embracing that I allow my full potential to blossom. My belief, my confidence and what is going on within me, my inner state, influence my experience. What draws people towards me is what I emanate and radiate from the state I am in. So I need to ensure that the message that comes from my inner state must not contradict my words. This reflects the importance to my thinking and speaking. Otherwise I am sending a double message.

I learn to take life as it unfolds. Life is never smooth. Any obstacle is a challenge. My experience of rejection makes me stronger. I always trust my heart and intuition and I always know what to do and where to go. No matter how many doors are closed to me, I will not give up and rejection will make me stronger and more determined. I have to take care of my mind set and my inner state which embrace my inner beliefs, my habitual thoughts I keep thinking, my expectations and my perception about the world.

These qualities of thinking, saying and focusing become my main attraction. A few rejections make no difference to my inner state and my mind set. The quality of my inner state influences my actions, the quality of my behaviour, the quality of my results and the quality of my life.

The world is no longer the same from the primitive one. We still live in a competitive world. We use to think that only the fittest one survives. But in this modern world, it is no longer true. I believe that cooperation is healthier than competition. I work to improve myself and keep busy so that I have no time to compete with others. I do not allow someone's performance to motivate me otherwise I am under his control. Especially in teaching and writing, we are all working together for a common good for humanity and any separation will only weaken us, creating pain and suffering.

We live in a complex world. We cannot be expected to know everything. I do not allow ignorance to control me. Every day I make up my mind to do a bit better at everything I do not know. I do not say 'no' to new ideas. I want to try new things. To succeed in my life, I only need to master the things I do well. I will keep repeating doing things that I do well. Success is the only way we get. I make a commitment to think, speak and write better today than yesterday. I will keep doing that daily. By doing that I know I can never fail to do well.

All of us experience failure before. We do not have to believe we are the victims of the world. Do not allow negative statements to influence you. Do not play the victim game. And do not allow outside forces to influence your life. I speak for myself. I take responsibility of my own thoughts, feelings and actions. If any negative thought or statement arises, I will not react but pause before responding. I will not behave as if I am a victim but show my inner strength and power. In reality, I believe I am complete; I am full and I am enough. There is nothing that is needed to change me. I believe I am good now. I am full of energy. All the negative thoughts, playing victims have no ground in my spiritual DNA. I am the seed that contains everything enough for me to grow into a full tree. I only need a right environment favourable to the unfolding of my full potential.

There is no end to my personal growth. My personal growth does not end when I graduated from the university. Growth is a life-long process for me. I realise that growth only cease when I stop breathing. Even in my retirement, I am still trying new experiences, growth and I am still motivated to contribute. This book is intended to be another contribution to human abundance.

Do what you love. Embrace your passion. I am delighted to share my experiences. During my playing days, I kept practicing my basic basketball skills and I kept enjoying doing them. I kept performing well during the games. Following my passion and heart led to my success in both basketball and academic. Practising my skills in writing helps me be a better writer. Aligning my passion with the power of the universe energy adds more abundance to my life. I believe everyone can share the same belief and prosper.

Contentment is my secret to happiness. I embrace self-love. I realise that what I need is already within me. Welcoming all the characteristics of happy people in my life makes me happier. There is nothing lacking in my life. My daily meditation and visualisation provides the peace, solitude, quietness, abundance and happiness I seek in my life. Now I add a new life vision to my visualisation. I live a realistic life but many miracles happen on the way.

Last but not least, I am an extension of the source of universal energy. I believe I am an amazing infinite soul and I have infinite potential. I know I am unique and I am beautiful. My nature is full of pure energy. My natural state is full of joy, love, satisfaction, appreciation and abundance beyond anything I can imagine. I know I am aligning with my reality, my source and I have everything I ever wanted. I always think that I am magnificent. I allow a constant flow of well-being and inspiration through me and I do not allow negative beliefs to take root in my subconscious mind. This choice makes me a positive person. I learn to relax for everything is well. I am on the right path and I am guided. All things I want are manifesting in front of me. When I face anything negative, I have a new tool. Negativity helps me to make my choices, preferences and set my clear goals. It activates my desire and sets the course for my dreams. It serves to expand and unfold my potential.

Simple Steps towards Abundance

The purpose of sharing my experiences is to help people so that they can help themselves to reach their potential in achieving abundance in life. The first step is desire then there is decision and choice. The second step is awareness, information and knowledge. The third step is to take action implementing whatever knowledge you know. Before taking massive action, you need to be aware that the transformation must come from within. All negative beliefs and habits in your subconscious mind have to be eliminated first before you download these new beliefs in the form of new knowledge before implementing them. All these recommendations and strategies do not mean much to me when I started meditation. Meditation is just a contemporary way of living with awareness and mindfulness. They only make sense to me after I have successfully implemented them and finally achieve my abundance. Once I have started seeing abundance in my life, poverty and lack seem to disappear. I start to look at life with joy; sadness starts disappearing. My happiness seems to welcome heaven on earth. I have added another dimension and another quality to my life. I have a new environment where I can be whole; I can have my feet firmly on the ground and yet can touch the sky. It helps me to connect with the universe. It puts my life on the fast track to abundance, happiness and release the power of imagination over all things.

CHAPTER ELEVEN

THE LANGUAGE OF SPIRITUALITY

Introduction

After learning the language of the basics, the language of abundance, the language of money, the language of finance, the language of stocks, the language of the mind and the language of happiness, now it's time to learn the language of spirituality. The ability to speak the language of spirituality will enable us to connect with the universe. We will think differently. A new life vision and a better relationship with others are just the beginning. How to discover the soul greatest vision of my life? Before I started meditation, I thought that I could only acquire spirituality if I were religious. Partly it can be true because religious people use prayers to enhance their spirituality. Nowadays things seem to be different. People think differently. Many people claim that they are spiritual but not religious. What does it mean to be spiritual? The consciousness evolution leading to spirituality no longer travels through the path of religion. People now accept that a religion is a relative truth catering for those who believe in the religion. Others who do not believe in any religion can still find their way to spiritual growth through consciousness of doing good things that can contribute to the advancement mankind. Human beings are creative and many ways towards spiritual truths are being created like meditation, yoga, mindfulness, institutions of spirituality and others.

Spirituality

What is spirituality? Spirituality is the awareness that the universe is friendly and is ever ready to be conscious of our well being. The realisation that the universe is on our side is the beginning. We need to listen to the voice of the universe. Will the world be different if you take over the world? There is an invisible force outside us that determines our consciousness and the universal spiritual laws that govern our experiences. These spiritual laws are analogous to the physical laws like the gravitational force, Newton's laws of motion and other physical laws. If we allow these universal laws to be implanted in our subconscious minds, our spiritual walk will begin. This leads us to imagination, visualisation, life-visioning and forming our life manifestations. We need a process to facilitate such imagination and visualisation to take root. You can choose religious practices and prayers to enhance your spirituality. I choose meditation and mindfulness to awaken my spirituality. The universe begins to welcome me to the world and there is a purpose for me to be here. I always think that I am here for a purpose and that purpose is to make the world a better place by serving others. This belief is the beginning of my spirituality. The laws of the mind are made known to me. My thoughts will influence my perceptions and my perceptions determine my reality. The importance of thinking well is critical. The imagination of the life I want to live begins as I describe it. The way I describe each aspect of my life will ultimately help me to live the type of life I visualised. If I describe my abundance well, I will live with the abundance. The life vision is conceived and I work towards that vision. The vision must be connected to the universe. If we keep working for the common good of mankind such as being kind to others, love others, serve others and make all the necessary contributions to make life better for others, we are beginning to experience spirituality. In addition, to be spiritual means eternal and our soul never dies. You can think of God as eternal as long as God is not a person in the sky or in heaven. The universe or God is always friendly and is serving us to grow to our full potential. We become spiritual when we come to know and are aware of ourselves, our intelligence, our abundance, our understanding, our connectedness with others, our uniqueness as an individual, our relationship with others, our sharing of talents and gifts, our purpose as spiritual beings and finally the transformation of our spirit and soul. Once we start to create values for others, we are actually creating values for ourselves. Spirituality becomes a mutual force.

My observation about people leads me to believe that practically all people are good and spiritual. They care for their families, their wellbeing, their education, shelter and their security. We are hijacked by a few unscrupulous few who practised violence, robberies, murder and all types of troubles to others. They believe that the universe is against them. They are not spiritual. The actions of these few uncivilised human beings are causing us pain, doubt, worry, fear, uncertainty and worry about our families' security. Their actions cause us to be suspicious about our neighbours and our relationship with others. We become frighten of strangers. All these perceptions are actually contrary to the nature of the universe which is friendly and ever willing to provide everything we seek. The universe has plenty to offer us and it is our own duty to live to our full potential. This awakening call strikes me. For any spiritual growth to begin in my life, I need first to master the language of the basics: thinking, speaking and writing. You see and you describe. You see good things and describe them vividly; you will eventually live a fulfilled life. On the contrary, you keep seeing bad things happening and keep describing them until you live such type of life. Thinking well is necessary to calm and activate our consciousness to availabilities and possibilities. It's only when you can imagine and visualise your life vision, then can you work towards that vision. Then you will be able to ask empowering questions and I believe that the universe is obliged to response. To every problem, there is a question waiting to ask. To every question we ask, the universe has an answer ready. We need to find the answer. To every answer, the universe is asking us to take action. We need to repeat the action to master it. To every action, the universe has a way of life for us. We need to live a life with purpose as an awakened human being and to live our full potential. We live to serve and to make the world a better place for all. This is spirituality at work when we become awakened human beings. Our awakening consciousness has a role to play in our service to others. This will be our expression of life and our contribution to others. Whatever career we have, our calling is clear. We are here for the purpose to make the world a better place.

Strategies to Enhance Spirituality

Every one of us is created with a purpose and we have to know our calling. We are here in the universe to make a difference, no matter how small is our contribution. We need to learn to be generous in giving. This consciousness is triggered through different processes. Many people seek religion to awaken their consciousness to spirituality. You can also achieve this consciousness of harmony between the mind and soul through meditation, mindfulness, yoga and prayers through your religion.

I choose meditation to enhance my spirituality. I need to find a way of living where my full potential will blossom. My soul will be calm and at peace to enable me to grow and experience the goodness of the friendly universe. This awakening is necessary for my full consciousness to function leading me all the way to serve and contribute to the well-being of others. This consciousness is the seed of love and kindness to grow and spread like branches of a tree. Whenever I meditate, my brain waves slow down to an alpha stage enabling me to imagine, visualise and see the life vision of the area I intend to build. The moment of enlightenment helps to build the consciousness of serving and contributing to humanity in an area intended. This is spirituality at its best when we are conscious of others and their well-being.

I am a Born-Again Christian. I believe in Jesus and I appreciate his wisdom and teachings. I must admit that I believe and appreciate the teachings of Jesus but I am not religious. I embrace the common belief that I can be spiritual without being religious. I can enhance my spirituality through meditations or prayers. I learn to say kind words and always have words of affirmation leading to self-healing and being thankful for the wonderful things I receive. This consciousness is critical for my spiritual growth. Uttering words of praise and affirmation is always in alignment with my subconscious beliefs to give and serve others. The power of the subconscious mind is always the driving force to motivation and action. The secret of spiritual grow is through repetition of prayers or meditations until actions taken become auto-piloted. We are here for a purpose. We are here to serve, contribute and support others. We are here to add values to others. This is the way of life embracing spirituality. Once the tree of spirituality is planted firmly, my duty is to nurture it daily so that it is allowed to grow into a full grown tree providing shades for others.

The Benefits of Being Spiritual

First I need to find methods of becoming a spiritual being. I choose meditation, mindfulness and prayers as my immediate tools to achieve my goals. These tools help me to awaken my spiritual awareness. In addition to meditation, I have added another practice called Quantum Jumping to add flavours to my imagination. My imagination and visualisation lead me to a life vision enriching every aspect of life under the term abundance.

What are the benefits of speaking the language of spirituality? Nowadays we hear many people saying that they are spiritual but not religious. I agree with them. Being spiritual is an awakening consciousness of our well-being and that of others. There are many benefits of being spiritual. I speak for myself and the benefits I enjoy.

First, living a spiritual life of serving and supporting others brings happiness to my life. Happiness is essential for my productivity, leading to abundance.

Second, living a spiritual life allows me to love my work and enjoy doing what I do in writing, teaching and investing. I find a purpose of what I am doing. I accumulate wealth with the intention to bless others. In return I am blessed with more. The more I give and contribute the more I am getting in return.

Third, being spiritual, I become aware of many things such as the needs of the poor, the needs of the weak, the needs of my family and my relatives. I am grateful of all the blessing I receive and I grow to become generous by providing them with what I have. By giving I become happier and I begin to work harder to get more so that I can give more.

Fourth, being an awakened spiritual human being; I begin to lose my own selfishness. I want to give more to society. I begin to work tirelessly to pen down guidelines and advices for others to live a happy, productive and healthy life.

Fifth, being a spiritual being, I find it easier to learn the language of many fields of interest like the language of basics, the language of money, the language of abundance, the language of the mind, the language of investments and the language of spirituality. I begin to enjoy the sharing of what I know about abundance.

Sixth, being spiritual gives me the awareness of creating value for myself by creating value for others. In most of charity works, I adopted this philosophy in many faces. I offer many services to people I serve without asking for anything in return. Given support to organisations by creating value for them without any intention of getting something back becomes my habit. The better service I bring to people through my services, the greater value I get from them. I have unconsciously created more value for myself. The response of people to my books reflects that value I have created.

Seven, being spiritual being, I have been continuously creating the principle of success for others through my teaching and administration as a school principal, unconsciously I have created value for myself and my own success. I didn't know this secret of success until I have unloaded and practised those beliefs and habits of wealthy people in my subconscious mind. If you want to increase the success, both financially and personally, start looking for ways to create value for others. It's similar to what the Bible teaches. You reap what you sow. Create values to others and you will reap more values in return. This act increases your spirituality.

Last but not least, being spiritual, I become aware of my responsibility. Giving back to society part of my fortune is my obligation to share with others. This is spiritual awareness that not all people are as fortunate as me.

Spirituality through Meditation

Many people enjoy spirituality through mindfulness, yoga, prayer and meditation. I did not know that when I was a student. I used to daydream when I was young. I used to close my eyes; imagining things I want. This process soon becomes my meditation. I started practising it when I was a student in Penang. I thought I was involved in daydreaming. I used to close my eyes while I was sitting comfortably on my chair before I started studying. My intention was to slow down my heartbeat and allow my imagination to function well. My journey of visualisation began. What is meditation? According to Osho:

> Meditation is a state of no-mind. Meditation is a state of pure consciousness with no content. Meditation is the awareness that I am not the mind.' When the awareness goes deeper and deeper in you, slowly, slowly, a few arrive-moments of silence, moments of pure space, moments of transparency, moments often nothing stirs in you and everything is still. In those still moments you will know who you are. This is meditation. When mind knows, we call knowledge. When heart knows, we call it love. And when being knows, we call it meditation.

When I started my secondary schooling in Penang, I was terribly affected by my past memories during early childhood. I believed I was the victim of my circumstances. I felt that life was unfair to me. The situations at home and all the negative headlines in the media left me helpless. I had a terrible childhood until 15 years old. After standard six in a Chinese primary school, I was dropped out from government secondary school. I was 12 years old and I had to work as a rubber tapper. I had to attend afternoon missionary school in the afternoon and every night I had to work keeping the inventory for my father's sundry shop during the emergency. Everything was out of control. All the negative energy seemed to work in bringing me down. I did not enjoy my childhood. The change came when I started my secondary schooling in Penang, boarding in my eldest sister's house, when I was already 16 years old.

My new environment provided me a new freedom in terms of time and space. I had all the time of the world to pursue my game basketball and my study. I did not have to work in the morning and at night any more. I attended a missionary secondary school in Penang in the afternoon because

I was an averaged student. I was already 16 years old attending Form Two or Year Eight. My standard of English was weak and I had to catch up to understand most of my lessons. I had to struggle very hard and in desperation, I started daydreaming or meditation every day before I started preparing my lessons for the day. I was facing all the external roadblocks that seemed to be getting in the ways of my goals. After a few practices of my newly discovered meditation, I began to imagine and visualise what I wanted in my life. I began to change direction and think differently. I began to think well. My regular visualisation triggered my sense that there was no reason for me to hold on to those toxic memories that did not serve my situation then. I had all the time and freedom in my new environment. I did not understand how my subconscious mind worked then. I was ignorant. Anyhow I managed to get rid of the negative energy that had worked to bring me down. During each meditation, before I started my study; I was able to bring myself into a calm and steady state that I enjoyed clarity of thought and seemed to lead me in the right direction. Managing my emotion and fear became critical for me to succeed. Getting rid of them from my mind was my choice. I began to see my future clearly. Setting my immediate goals for my sport and study came naturally. In my lesson preparation, my meditation seemed to bring in new focus. I discovered a self-study strategy prepared lessons before attending classes every day. I had benefited from my regular meditation every day before studying. I managed to derive a stress-free mind, a deeper contentment and an emotional balance. Meditation together with regular exercise may be responsible for me to avoid high blood pressure until now. I was thinking well at the time and my self study strategy helped me to understand most of my lessons in school. I began to do well in my study and it gave me hope to become a teacher. My regular meditation also helped me to intensify my drill strategy in skills development. Meditation helped me to visualise many of my fake strategies in my offensive approach of my game. My skills in dribbling, shooting and various lay ups were almost perfected due to regular drill practices every morning. All these activities helped me to excel in the game and eventually I became a star player in my school, my hometown team, my senior league team in Penang, college, university and the states (Penang, Kedah and country) I represented.

Now I learn that there are many methods of meditation. Initially I had adopted a simple method of meditation which I thought I was daydreaming. Now I learn a new way of meditation known as Quantum Jumping introduced by Burt Goldman. During my school days, my simple method of meditation had really complemented both my sport and study. In sports, meditation has an important role to play in mental training riding all types of emotion through deep meditation. I came across many players who were very skilful and outstanding during practice sessions. But when these players were put into a competitive environment, they could not replicate their skills and performances due to mental strength or mental toughness. Perhaps they lack visualisation and repeated drill training under competitive situations. My advantage of performing well in competition could be due to visualisation and repeated skills practices every day until most of the skills became auto-piloted. I realised that there was no thinking required when I executed those skills during competitions. Most sportsmen required mental training and repeated drilling plus physical development to perform at their peak. My meditation provided me a mental rehearsal, creating mental images of the exact movements I wanted to emulate in my game. Active visualisation during meditation could provide the necessary ingredients such as inner calmness, patience for the right moment to execute a shot or to provide my teammate with a deceptive pass. All these automated processes had helped me to perform optimally during a match. My visualisation strengthened my mental strength or toughness and it complemented my dribbling and shooting skills in most of my competitive matches. These practices involving visualisation and drilling seemed to have an important impact on my style of playing. On many occasions, the opponents used two players to stop me from penetrating under the basket because of my superior dribbling skill. This move by the opponents was usually suicidal; creating a glaring hole for my teammate to receive the ball from me and shoot. This created confusion for the opponents' defence and before they realised it, the match was lost. The wonder of visualisation and superior skills in ball handling and shooting helped in creativity of play and helped my team's performance. This partly explained why my team won the Penang senior league basketball tournament in five consecutive years while I was a student there.

During my secondary school days in Penang, my practice of meditation every morning enabled me to discover my self-study strategy and the discipline to carry it out consistently, persistently and playfully to enjoy the process. This self-study strategy became my weapon conquering my quest for academic excellence. My self-study strategy involving pre-preparation of lessons before attending class became my routine every day. Regular meditation provided me a positive thought pattern helping me to become more discipline in adhering to my self-study strategy. My learning productivity soared and my academic results were excellent. My approach towards my study was right whispering to me that I was on the right track. I had caught the bull by the hone. Ambitions and goals stayed in my focus without distractions. Worries of performance did not affect me academically. I kept using the same strategy from Form Two to Form Five. The consequence is that I ended my Cambridge School Certificate with a string of distinctions.

There are other benefits because of my regular practice in meditation. My attitude towards study, playing and social interaction seem to improve. I become less critical of myself, friends and family members. My confidence of my future is enhanced. My self-assurance, positive attitude and warm heartedness make their appearances. It prevents shyness and I become more outgoing. It is a proven method for stress reduction and it improves the quality of my life. Whenever I mediate, it always slows down my mind to a deep state relaxation or alpha state. It enables me to focus on 'now' rather than dwell on what happened in the past or having fear for the future. It has tremendous health benefits to me. It provides me with not only clarity of thought but also a sense of peace and a direction of life. I feel great after each meditation. It sharpens everything including my concentration and my appreciation of my surroundings. It keeps my life fresh. During my students' days, these combinations created dramatic improvement in my health; boosted my energy level; helped me in manifesting creative ideas and problem solving related to my studies. I had optimal performance each day. It does more than just make me feel good; it heightens my sense, explodes my creativity, boosts my productivity and develops a scary accurate sense of intuition. It helps to increase my focus, solve problems faster and enjoy deep relaxation. It not only lowers stress but also reduces anxiety and quiets my mind. It also helps to accelerate healing both emotional and physical. Listen to what Buddha said:

The secret of health for both mind and body is not to mourn for the past, not to worry about the future, or to anticipate troubles, but to live in the present moment wisely and earnestly.

Little do I realise that by practising meditation, I have embarked on a journey to spirituality. This is the new awareness helping me to boosts my creativity in my life. When I was a student, it helped in improving my game and it enabled me to discipline myself to stick to my self-study strategy.

CHAPTER TWELVE

REFLECTIONS AND SUMMARY

Most of us are living a life far below our full potential. According to the insight of Plato, you live your whole life chained in a cave, facing the inner wall of the cave, where you see only flickering shadows that you mistake as reality. But the moment you are unchained and allowed to face the cave's entrance; you suddenly see the light and the world as what it really is; your perception of reality is forever changed. This story is analogous to your life story before and after you have learned the language of abundance. To have a clear vision of your potential and to achieve your dreams, you have to master the various languages leading to abundance. What are the languages to master? First is the language of the basics: think well, speak well and write well. Second is the language of money. Third is the language of health and happiness. Fourth is the language of investments: property asset, equities, bonds, option, digital publishing and others. Fifth is the language of abundance. Last but not least, learn the language of spirituality and let the universe serve through you. Most of us are not aware that we are programmed by an old and limited belief system that holds us back from reaching our fullest potential. .. until now. The story you have been told about your life and the way your life is being played out - is based on the assumption of how reality unfolds. You are not aware that these assumptions are not true. You have not discovered that you are truly part of a bigger story. Being unaware of the creative powers of the universe, you are unable to sustain the energy to live your life with full potential. You become the victim of your past. You need not worry too much. You can easily overcome this obstacle with the awakening of your consciousness. Once your subconscious mind is clear of these outdated beliefs, you can easily replace them with a new set of energised characteristics of successful people. Once you start to implement them daily and master them, the whole new world is dawned on you. You have a plan for action. The process will stop you from being the victim of your past. This key to unlock my subconscious mind was given to me during my meditation. Reprogramming my subconscious mind requires me to eliminate my past beliefs first. The next logical step is to unload new beliefs and practices of successful people. With the plan and enough practices, I became the master of the various languages which are fundamental to a life of abundance. With consistent practice, each field of interest begins to manifest itself. We do not need much motivation but action. Repetition of action holds the key to success. Being aware of it, I start to learn and keep practising them. Repeating these routines and practicing these new beliefs daily, they become my habits. My new experiences of the world become profoundly vivid, exciting and fulfilling in every way. Many interesting things happen to me. I do not just write down my goals but also write down my action plan for achieving them. A goal without a plan is just a dream so I need to go on track. I have a road map to speak the various languages of abundance. I want to speak each of the languages fluently to help me to succeed in life. You can have the same achievements. Learn to speak each of the languages well and you are on the way to success. You can have more clarity about exactly what to do and which direction to go to reach your goals. You will find that you can accomplish more in less time. You will begin to attract the right people and resources to help you to accomplish your dreams. You can tap into better resources of energy to accomplish what you do. You will feel supported and can easily make a difference in the lives of the people around you. You are like an electromagnet newly charged and you will be attracting all the abundance you dream off.

Every one of us has dreams. Every one of us has the habit of setting goals. We have learned from successful people that they have concrete dreams, visions or goals of what they wish to achieve. My observations tell me that most of these people adopt four qualities to help them manifest the end result.

First, they have the burning desire to achieve their goal.

Second, they have strong belief that their goal is achievable. Third, they have confidence and they expect to see their results. Fourth, they have a plan of action and carry out consistently.

They do not just dream but put their shoulders to the wheels that move towards their goals of abundance. They repeat and replicate their efforts until they become successful. They do not stop but keep growing their businesses or their passions. Their subconscious minds are reloaded with such beliefs and practices of the wealthy and happy people. Keep practising them until they become automatic. They do not have to put in much effort. They become their routines and their daily rituals. The power of their subconscious minds is driving all the activities without much physical efforts on their parts.

Even in the medical world, doctors are using the power of the subconscious mind to accelerate healing by telling the patients that they are given the most powerful drug which is only sugar pills. Even cancer patients can cure themselves by visualising themselves healthy. A new vaccine known as Alpha Cells therapy is able to mobilise our cells to combat cancer cells and eliminate them. This indicates clearly the power of our subconscious minds. Our thoughts control the cells of our body. Our thoughts are controlled by the subconscious mind. Similarly the same psychological factor is applicable to us in goal setting to help us to become more successful in our life. This helps to activate our desire, belief and expectancy in our subconscious minds.

The Necessity of Thinking Big through Thinking Well

The first basic thing our children need to learn is thinking. Thinking well is necessary for them to achieve whatever goals they set. This positive mental attitude is the prerequisite for them to think big. There is nothing wrong when your children are ambitious and aspire to make a difference to humanity and the world. The skill of thinking well can be taught. So as parents it's our duty to provide every opportunity and facilitate to help them to think well. I believe that once your children have succeeded to download the necessary characteristics of thinking well into their subconscious minds and start practising them regularly, their natural instinct of thinking big will emerge. Knowing faulty thinking can help in the process of learning to think well. This conscious awareness can be implanted into our children's mind to help them from falling into these faulty thinking traps. This awareness has to be practised and sensitised so that they know how to avoid such traps in their thinking process. The secret of avoiding faulty thinking habit is constant reminder and consistently avoiding. The habits of creative thinking and critical thinking are skills that can be learned. Parents are in best teachers in this respect. If any parent feels that he or she is not well prepared to do the job, the book is a good source of reference.

The Advantage of Speaking Well

Speaking well is an art to be learned as early as possible. All of us know the things we must learn and master before we can speak well. Our children need to be taught to speak only worthy things in their daily encounter with friends and others. There is certain amount of honesty involved to teach them to say things that they mean. The advantages of the ability to speak well are too many to mention. First, when your children speak well, they look taller, more attractive, look bigger and people soon learn to respect them. If they are trained to be assertive, they even look more handsome and always stand out in the group. People who speak well have a head start in life.

The Reward of Writing Well

If your children think well and speak well, they will eventually write well. Writing is a skill that can be trained. The earlier we train our children to think well, speak well, we can easily encourage them to write well. They can exercise their idea muscles and their creative mind will easily be developed with parental encouragement. Just like me, I discover my writing skill when I was working as a teacher and it became my passion. Until today, that passion is still burning. Even in my retirement, I still have plenty of things to write. I am always busy writing and feeling happy. I always have something to do. I become productive. Time does not stand still. The opportunity of writing well is a skill our children can cultivate and master. It may become their passion and even become wealthy and fulfilled.

If your children are thinking well and speaking well but they are not writing well; then there is a problem. The problem is simple; they cannot sit still for a long period. They are too active moving around. A good way is to start them on a meditation course. They soon will learn to sit still and start visualising. They will learn to sit quietly and enjoy silence. That is the time to start them writing down their imaginations and thoughts into words. The journey begins with the recording of their ideas into words and soon they will be writing more than we expected.

The Strategies to Help You Achieve Wealth

Depending on your salary, you will never become wealthy. You only have linear income. The moment you stop work, your linear income ceases. Most rich people do not depend on linear income. This book explores some of the strategies of creating streams of residual income and cash flow to create wealth. Not all strategies will suit your talents, your educational levels and your personality. Let your imaginations and your exposures lead you to many other strategies available. Some of the common strategies discussed in this book are just the tip of the iceberg.

The most common investment for most salary working people is acquiring a rental property to create residual income. The rental property can be a residential property or a shop lot. Here the tool you use is debt, a good debt. As long as the rental covers the monthly instalment and other expenses, you have created a good debt that helps your cash flow. Planning and initial sum of money are required. Management and cash flow are critical.

Another investment involves stocks. Investing correctly, you enjoy residual income in the form of dividends and also enjoy capital growth. Most of the world billionaires are great investors. They know how to make their money work for them. Every one of them has their own strategy of investing and their strategies are all different. They stick to their successful strategies and they keep repeating them to make their fortune. The only extra technique most of them adopt together with their unique strategies is flexibility. They are very flexible whenever they find that their strategies are not working; they are prepared to change course. They always have plan A, plan B or even plan C. They are also involved in stocks options. Stocks option is simple. There are only two kinds: a call or a put. Many of them make use of selling option as insurance for their stocks. Another quality of these great investors is that they are terribly patient. When opportunity presents itself; they are there to harvest their catch. If you want to join the rich; you need to develop your own strategy of investing, be flexible and be patient and do not follow the herd.

This book also touches other strategies of creating residual income or passive income through property investment. This type of investment uses debt and the leverage system. Some initial savings are necessary to start the train moving in asset investments. Other strategies of creating passive income include direct selling, digital publishing, creating websites to attract members with common interest and publications.

The Necessary Steps towards Fulfilment

All of us want to live a life of abundance and fulfilment. All of us want our children to be successful in life. Successful in life includes financial freedom, position of influence, happy, wise and fulfilled. They need experiences, growth and contributions. The first thing children must do is to master the three basics: thinking, speaking, and writing.

To most people, life is a long journey through three critical stages: learning, working and retiring. After achieving financial freedom and living healthily, the next thing we aspire is fulfilment to accompany our happiness. Fulfilment is a feeling we long to have each day in our life. We will not achieve that if we are not aware of mindfulness. I want to share my experiences how I manage to have fulfilment in my life. I learn to love and accept myself a little more today than yesterday. I sit back to enjoy and watch my own transformation.

First, I make an effort to integrate all my achievements and excitements in both my games and works into my identity. As I write my autobiography, I stack them together by listing them in order of importance. I feel good and recognise them as parts of my life. They are all connected to my life and I want to feel them again. They leave a lasting memory for me to cherish and appreciate. I also remember the obstacles I had encountered and how I managed to overcome them. All the happenings and actions I have taken seem to enrich my life. I can feel the sense of fulfilments.

Second, I am very thankful for all the helps and assistances I received while I moved through the three stages of my life. I am grateful to my eldest sister and her husband for providing me accommodation for me to finish secondary school in Penang. I am indebted to my second sister and her husband who provided assistance to help me finish my university education. I am grateful to my third sister and her husband who provided the initial sum of money for my investment property. I love my wife and thank her for her home management to allow my extended family to survive during our initial working careers. I am filled with emotion as I recollect these aids and helps I got. I am thankful to all the small things that had happened to me. The practice of gratitude begins. I am happy and proud that I was able to reciprocate by providing helps both financially and provisionally to my younger sister and brother including my relatives for their university education. I feel proud and fulfilled. There are many small things that happened to me throughout my life. There are too many to list for me to feel good and happy. There is no shortage of things to help me feeling fulfilled.

Third, I learn to say 'no' to many things that are detrimental to my health and well-being. When I was working as a rubber tapper after my primary school years, I learned to say 'no' to smoking. This big 'no' has done tremendous good to my lung health. I am very thankful for such a big 'no'. 'No' is sometimes the hardest word to say when it involves your emotion. In relationship, I need the courage to say 'no' to a relationship when the other partner did not show respect for who I am. A well-placed 'no' had saved not only my valuable time but emotional trouble. I do not want to be hurt and humiliated. Nowadays I do not entertain people who are rude and hurting me. I have the right to say 'no' to anything that is hurting me and any standard that no longer serving me. I am not going to entertain people who drain my creativity and expression. I need to be assertive and be true to my real self. I am confident I have the power to create new, positive beliefs about myself.

Fourth, I will say 'yes' to do things I am passionate about. I want to have a great enthusiasm for tomorrow. I will say 'yes' to build deeper relationship with people I love. My passion is writing, investing and playing the game I love. I need plenty of time to be involved in my passions. I am not confused between 'no' and 'yes'. When it comes to life and my passions, I always say 'yes'. I want life's greatest experiences. I am aware that in life 'yes' opens doors to many things. As I practise saying 'yes' to life, good things happen. Even opportunities I have shut out before coming back to me. Even people I kept at arm's length show up to assist me. My relationship with others improves when I adopt an aura of acceptance. Unconsciously by saying 'yes' to life, I open a space for universal good to fill. So when coming to gain new experiences, I prefer to leave 'no' out of my vocabulary for the day. By building strong connection, we not only enhance our relationship with others but also live every day to the full. The satisfaction and the enthusiasm will further energise us and we enjoy more of life. Loving people and rendering services will encourage more enthusiasm for tomorrow. We will harvest more fulfilment. Now I believe that my body is healthy, my mind is brilliant and my soul is tranquil. There is no force that can prevent me from manifesting my abundance because my subconscious mind is solidly planted with the desired beliefs and habits. I have practised them repeatedly that they are now on autopilot. I believe that I am reaping what I have consistently and intentionally sowed.

A True Abundance Mind-Set

All of us want our children to acquire a true abundance mind set. What is an abundance mind-Set? They are happy, at peace, having self-belief, having good relationship, having the power to choose the life they want and full of positive energy to attract whatever they desire. And as a result abundance, joy and success follow them. They are aware of what they want in life and most importantly, they have the belief and determination and fire in their bellies to get it. They know what they want and they avoid fears and doubts on their path from stopping them. There is a simple technique called 'destiny tuning' where all your outdated beliefs and practices are eliminated first before the set of new beliefs and habits of successful people are downloaded into your subconscious mind. What are the habits and practices of successful people? A summary is given here.

Habits and Practices of Successful People

Most of us are ordinary people who can become wealthy through our years of working by following the habits and practices of the self-made rich. Studies have shown that ordinary people become rich because they follow the following things. They form good financial habits very early in their working lives. They learn how to balance their needs to become wealthy and economically productive with their needs to enjoy life. They know that they cannot enjoy life if they are addicted to consumption and the use of credit. They neither borrow nor earn just to consume. They arenot credit dependent and they lead a simple life. They have control over their money. They understand the meaning of frugality. They save as much as they can and they understand the power of compounding through investments. The instruments they use to become wealthy are usually assets, properties, stocks and business. The following characteristics of rich people should be made known to our children.

First, they learn to manage their debt and do not allow debt to manage them.

Second, they spend their money wisely, getting maximum value for every dollar.

Third, they continuously work to increase their linear and residual income.

Fourth, they are aggressive savers far outpacing their peers.

Fifth, they are disciplined investors. When they find a good strategy, they stick to it.

Sixth, they know how to expand their means. They dare to take risk and learn to manage it. They seldom let their limiting beliefs stop them from growing. They are creative and they think well to expand their means. They live a life without limits.

Last but not least, they learn the languages of abundance, including health, happiness, spirituality and the language of the basics: think, speak and write well very early.

All these characteristics can be downloaded into our subconscious minds when you start working. The earlier we start practising them; the earlier our savings will grow. As soon as our fund accumulates; the time for investment begins. Remember that if we depend on our income alone, we will never become rich. We have to learn to let our savings work for us to become rich.

We also want our children to be happy, healthy, wealthy and fulfilled. Once these habits and practices of the rich and successful people are installed in their minds, it's time to teach our children to consistently and persistently practise them until they become their own habits and practices. With the new positive energy level and a higher rate of vibrations; the forces of the law of attraction will force the universe to provide us and our children the manifestation we desire. This 'destiny tuning' does not need hard work and more extra effort. This tuning, once auto piloted, will force the universe to give us what we want. A little bit of efforts, regular practices will be enough. This magical transformation will attract the abundance we desire. This is the secret behind the secret to abundance. We have the choice. We have to make the change so that our children will learn the hard lesson to become rich and enjoy abundance.

Some Secrets of Abundance

What you dream off and expect, you will get them. I am happy because I expected it. I am rich because I expected it too. I expect to be fit and healthy; I expect it too. I am blessed because I expect it. I have downloaded all the strategies necessary to be happy, rich, fit and healthy into my subconscious mind to replace the outdated beliefs and habits I acquired during childhood. I did not stop there; I put into practice those strategies until I achieve abundance. I do not allow any failure to hold me back. Happiness comes after financial freedom. I am able to have financial freedom because I allow the wealth building power of compound interest and streams of residual income to run its course in my life. Once I invested correctly; I literally become a millionaire without doing much. I found my passion in writing and I enjoyed it. Enjoying spirituality helps me to provide service for others and also create values for others. Indirectly I create values for myself and enjoy financial freedom. I still enjoy writing and I keep writing to keep my mind active. I keep on enjoying what I do and continue to do it even now. I play my games not only to enjoy them but ensure that I am always fit and healthy. I played basketball seriously for many years and I enjoyed the excitement of competition. The discovery of the drill strategy to excel in my game became my living principle. The endurance principle overflows into another self-study strategy which ensured my academic success. I recorded all these strategies into my first motivation book: *The Journey Through Four Seasons of Life*. My aim and intention are simple. I will read them and use them to succeed not only in games but also in life. The key to master any skill, game or music or life specialisation is repetition.

Words of Reflections

I need to rise above my thinking patterns; the ways I see myself and everything around me, then I begin to see progress in my life. I need a new perspective to solve any of my problems quickly and a new way of approaching new challenge. I need a deeper understanding of my subconscious mind and embrace the reality that I am a limitless human being. I want the universe to come alive through me. Jesus allowed God to work through Him. He is God. If you allow God to use you, you can also be a mini god.

The first thing I need to adopt is to think well. What am I thinking? I need to be aware of it. This is the prerequisite of transforming my thoughts. Am I the victim of my past memories? Am I affected by these limited toxic beliefs and habits I grow up with? I do not want to be discouraged, overwhelmed and disconnected with the universe. My first step to take is to eliminate all these toxic beliefs. I do not want them to be part of my life. I need to refocus and replenish my mind with positive beliefs. I need a plan to act and ignite my passion to move towards the direction of abundance. I want to shift my attention towards things that bring me joy, feed my heart and inspire me. I need good experiences and feelings. I need to connect myself with things that matter and to ignite my passion. To do such thing I need to sit comfortably with my feet on the floor to begin my meditation. I become aware of everything around me. I become my own witness watching my thinking. I will take my easy breath and feel the rhythmic beats of my heart. I can feel the space within my chest that my physical heart occupies and the space my spiritual heart occupies that is all around me. I am thankful to my heart doing all the wonderful work it does every moment to keep me alive. My heart holds all the memories and images of my thinking. I think of my favourite sport, basketball, I played when I was young. I enjoyed all the excitement and I can still hear the cheers of my supporters. Such are the memories I still cherish. I value my self-study strategy which helps to carry me to my present position. Without such a well-tested strategy, I might not be where I am now. I remember all the discoveries I made during my working days. I remember all the helps I received from relatives and friends. Many of them are no longer with me. I am unable to repay the gratitude due to them. I cherish and treasure their helps. I can only help those who are in need now. I now learn to fill my heart with images from nature that I particularly love. My garden is full of fruit trees that provide me with delicious fruits. I thank them for blessing me. I think of the birds, lizards and small animals that frequent my garden. I picture them happy and healthy, romping, flying and playing in my garden. I fill my heart with images of these beloved beautiful little creatures that are blessing me. I imagine the wonderful path leading from my home to the summit of Mt-Cootha. I enjoy walking and dancing all the way up the hill. My fitness gives thanks to such a beautiful path. Whenever I reach the summit, I enjoy a bird's-eye view of the beautiful city of Brisbane I call home. Now I expand my heart to all human beings past and present, who came into contact with me all the years. I bless and thank each and every one of them from my heart. I can imagine the blessing and gratitude lifting them up and filling their hearts. The universe provides for the creatures with air, water, shelter, food and its beauty. I thank the universe for all her love, abundance and life-sustaining generosity. What a wonderful world we have.

New Resolutions

From now onwards, I will learn to love myself, be sure to put aside a little time for myself to relax, spend time with friends, members of family and to reconnect. I will take time to love myself and will allow me to focus on what is really important. I will learn to shift my mind from all worries. I will learn to live this moment and not to worry about things that had already happened or will never happen. If necessary I will set aside say thirty minutes to think about the challenges and how I can overcome them. Once outside this time, I will not allow unnecessary worry to emerge. And I will move to another topic or subject which I like to do and focus. I will use the time set for thinking of challenges creatively to find solutions to my challenges. I will accept some things that are out of my control. If I find that I there is nothing I can do about it and then I will just let them go. I will begin to cultivate appreciation of things I have and be grateful of many things happened to me. This will help to shift my energy to a more positive space. I will begin to experience joy instead of stress. I will practice mindfulness and focus my attention on the here and now.

www.ingramcontent.com/pod-product-compliance
Lightning Source LLC
LaVergne TN
LVHW021650060526
838200LV00050B/2290